CW00793775

EMPATH:

2 Books in **1**:

The Emotional Survival Guide to Narcissists, Codependency, and Narcissistic Abuse. An Intense and Unconventional Journey into Your Emotions for Regaining Control of Your Own Life

MELODY ANNESLEY

Empath

Table Of Contents

Narcissistic Abuse – Codependency – How To Analyze People

EMPATH:

How To Understand Narcissistic Abuse Syndrome And Heal From A Codependent Relationship With Your Parents Or Ex-Partner. No More Narcissists or Emotional Codependency.
It's Time To Be Happy

MELODY ANNESLEY

PART I

NARCISSISTIC ABUSE

Introduction PART I – NARCISSISTIC ABUSE

So many people often don't stop and wonder whether they are narcissists or what narcissism is. Well, the word narcissism derived from a Greek myth that refers to a youth that cannot pull away from their reflection. In Greece Narcissus was beautiful. However, narcissists, on the other hand, do not have to be attractive for them to believe that they are. Mainly because they think that they are superior to anyone else, even though that might not be the reality. 'I am living with a narcissist and do not know how to disentangle myself from them.' Well, this is one of the situations that so many people ask me about during our self-help sessions. Others do not seem as though they have entirely given up on their partners and would like to know whether there are possible ways in which they can deal with their narcissistic partners so that the relationship is as good as possible.

Well, others already know that the only option is for them to leave, but they do not have any idea where to start. In other words, they have not made up their minds what to do. They are probably so much in love that they do not realize what harm the relationship is causing them. Others choose to stay for the sake of the children, or religious beliefs about 'for better or for worse, till death do us apart!' The reason why I am writing this is that I have been where you are.

I have been in an abusive relationship and could not get through the denial stage that you are in right now. It was not until I decided to 'choose me' that anything changed. You may be thinking 'I will try everything possible to make things good between us again.' No disrespect, but you have to get up from that dream before you get hurt badly. Narcissists are not people who are keen at seeking professional help. It may be because being defensive is their hallmark.

However, it is also true that there is no proven treatment, but we often recommend talk therapy to understand the nature of their behaviors better.

If you are in a relationship with these kinds of people, you have to know these things about them

Most of the ways narcissists cope are abusive; hence the word 'narcissistic abuse.' The truth is someone can be abusive, but that does not mean that they are narcissistic. Most addicts and people with mental issues like Bipolar disorder can portray an abusive behavior. The point is it's abuse, no matter the abuser's diagnosis. If you are a victim of abuse, your primary challenge is identifying it, establishing a robust support system and learning the best way to strengthen and protect yourself.

You have to realize that narcissistic abuse can be emotional, mental, financial, sexual, spiritual and even physical. The severity of narcissism and abuse exists on a continuum. It may range from sweeping those feelings under the carpet or channeling them through violent aggression. Typically, what you do not expect is for a narcissist to take responsibility for their actions. For most of them, shifting blames to others is the order of the day while some of them try to self-reflect and are capable of being remorseful.

There is a difference between malignant narcissism and sociopathy. A person that has more narcissistic behaviors and acts maliciously is often said to be a malignant narcissist. They are just not bothered by guilt. They often can be sadistic and take pleasure in seeing others suffer. Because of paranoia, they can get defensive as a means of protecting themselves.

Inasmuch as malignant narcissism may resemble sociopathy, sociopaths suffer from a malformation of the brain. Inasmuch as they may portray some narcissistic traits, one thing that you have to bear in mind is that not all narcissists are sociopathic, mainly because their motivators often are different. While a narcissist props up an ideal persona for people to admire them, sociopaths tend to change who they are so that they can achieve their self-serving goals. In other words, a sociopath will want to win at all costs even if it means breaking social norms and laws.

The thing with a sociopath is, they do not want to get attached to people. A narcissist, on the other hand, does not want people abandoning them. They depend on others' approval, and while in some cases they might plot to make their agenda successful, they are often more reactive as compared to sociopaths, who are cold and calculated.

Being a narcissist is mainly focusing on enhancing your self-esteem because they are often perpetually insecure about their personality and how people perceive them. They tend to hide this insecurity by appearing so overly confident when the truth of the matter is that deep inside them is lurking doubt about their self-worth. However, when their self-esteem dips, they end up making one of the two choices:

Becoming depressed and ending up hating themselves and feeling ashamed

Becoming grandiose and trying to convince people that they are nothing but perfect, unique and all-powerful, while in the process devaluing other people and seeing them as inferior or 'less than'

Naturally, they tend to choose the latter. Reminds me of a wise saying that my mother always told me: "When they feel fat, they start complaining about your weight" and guess what; she was correct!

Chapter 1. What is Narcissistic Abuse?

Narcissistic abuse violence is a form of violence where the victim is exposed to Narcissistic abuse trauma. One of the challenges with Narcissistic abuse violence is that unlike physical violence, there might not be physical scars as evidence. Narcissistic abuse violence happens each time the victim is subjected to emotional distress. In many cases, Narcissistic abuse violence is accompanied by verbal or physical violence.

Many people are victims of Narcissistic abuse violence at some point in time, but they are never aware of it. Without proper understanding of yourself, and what your life is about, you might never know when you are under attack. It also becomes difficult to come up with effective strategies you can use to cope with the trauma from such abuse.

While anyone is susceptible to this kind of abuse, women and children are the most affected by Narcissistic abuse abuse. The attacks target perceptions, feelings and thoughts. Narcissistic abuse abuse might not be physical, but the effect on the victim's persona is just as bad.

In a relationship with a narcissistic partner, there are several symptoms, reactions and conditions that the victim might experience which are a sign of abuse. The narcissist conditions the victim by creating experiences in relationships which have a negative impact on the victim. Here are some of the signs you might be suffering Narcissistic abuse abuse in your relationship:

- Intense insecurities – your abuser identifies your personal insecurities and over time, uses them to put you down. Your insecurities grow stronger and you cannot trust anyone.
- Disbelief in yourself – many victims' lives change for the worse because they no longer believe in themselves. Your confidence is eroded to a point where you can no longer trust your judgement.

- Incapability – victims of abuse who were once assured and competent in everything they do suddenly become incapable and uncertain about everything.
- Anxiety – you live a life of uncertainty and fear. You are constantly afraid something bad will happen. You don't trust good things because you believe the happiness is short-lived and will turn for the worst soon after. You also feel emotionally drained and incapable of enjoying true happiness.
- Indecision – victims who were once grounded become indecisive, confused and unable to trust anyone, not even themselves.
- Esteem issues – Narcissistic abuse abuse erodes your confidence. You cannot see yourself as anything better than what your abuser says you are. You shy away from the public, afraid that everyone sees the weaknesses in you.

These are the effects of Narcissistic abuse abuse. They manifest in different ways, but one thing is certain about them – they erode the very core of your being, your personality. If you cannot recognize yourself, how can someone else?

Narcissistic abuse violence by narcissists is meted out to victims in different categories. We will address five of the spheres of life where healthy relationships are important, and how narcissists take everything away from you.

Children And Families

- Trust issues

Life is one big frightening place for a child raised by narcissists. Strings are attached to everything, especially love. Children need unconditional love, however, children of narcissistic parents grow up learning that there is always something attached to it. Such children grow up suspicious of affection. It becomes difficult for them to trust anyone, especially those who are getting too close to them (Keene & Epps, 2016).

Interestingly enough, while such children struggle to embrace genuine affection, they are drawn to toxic relationships and affection. This happens because the feelings shared in such relationships are those that are too familiar, they can relate. Toxic relationships become a comfortable place for such children.

It is easier for a child brought up in a narcissistic environment to trust a bad person disguised as their savior than it is for them to trust someone who is genuine and offers emotional stability.

Toxic people are an embodiment of the same challenges the children endured when growing up. Because their minds have been conditioned to embrace such instances, they are not afraid to interact with toxic people. They learn not to trust, or not to trust too much – this is easier because they have done it all their life.

- Inability to commit

Children raised in a narcissistic environment struggle with commitment issues. When you meet them, at first glance they seem like they are looking to establish commitment with someone. However, deep down they fear commitment. These kids grow up alienated by the people closest to them, so it is difficult to commit to someone or something. Commitment for such children is often on the basis of what feels right at the moment, not because they really want to commit.

Long-term relationships are not easy to get into because the feeling of being tied down to something is odd. When they encounter someone who loves them truly, it is unsettling because they have to open up about their vulnerabilities to this person, and they are not sure whether this person will stay or walk away. When you grow up alienated by family, stability and forever relationships become a fallacy to you.

Commitment to someone for such a child means that they are giving up control of their lives. Someone else is in charge of their emotions. Naturally, such children will go into defense mode to protect themselves from being hurt. They know the feeling, they have lived through it, and cannot risk it again. When facing the prospect of an intense relationship, it is easier to withdraw, even without a reason.

They find it easier to give up on someone who loves them and push them away, than be with them and experience unconditional love.

- Hyperactive attunement

Hyperactivity is one of the symptoms victims of abuse learn to help them cope with their abuser. It helps them know when things are about to get messy. They are keen to subtle changes in the way the abuser responds to them. This makes them realize changes in facial expression, tone and so forth. They can also identify contradiction between gestures and spoken words.

It is so exhausting to learn all this as a child. However, it is also important for them because it is the only survival technique they are aware of, which can help them avoid unnecessary pain. They grew up on the lookout for verbal, physical and emotional cues from narcissistic parents and caregivers.

This defense mechanism helps them get through a lot, and protects them from the unknown. However, it also breeds a sense of prediction, which can be very unsettling for someone who is genuine, but does not know how to align their words and gestures. For the child, it might be impossible to control how people react, but they can use this technique to choose the relationships they can cultivate or end.

- Afraid of intimacy

Intimacy is an emotional minefield for children raised by narcissists. When they try to open up, it is easier to share too much about their struggles in the hope that someone might feel their pain and genuinely ease their pain. The challenge here is that they often end up with toxic narcissists whose only desire is to prey on their weaknesses and exploit them for everything they have.

This is one of the reasons why such children are afraid of intimacy on in life. Intimacy requires that you open up to your partner. You have to be vulnerable around one another. You must allow your partner to see you for who you are, with all your weaknesses, embrace you and love you endlessly.

Exposure to so much hurt while growing up destroys the concept of intimacy for these children. Instead of allowing someone the chance to hurt them, it is easier to cut them off, close all avenues leading to their emotions (Yates, 2010). They crave intimacy like everyone else, but it is so huge a risk. At times the prospect of opening up to intimacy brings back nasty memories, and it is easier to forget about intimacy altogether.

- Affinity for toxic relationships

Toxic relationships are normal for children raised by narcissists. They have a lot of experience in this, and it is easier to embrace these relationships because they almost always know what to expect. They embrace abuse as a normal thing, and that is why they find it easier to entertain people who belittle or envy them.

In early adulthood or on in life when they take stock of their friendships and relationships, they realize they have so many toxic people in their lives that they are comfortable around. This happens because they share a bond. The struggle is all too familiar, it is the only thing they know.

- Emotional sabotage

Narcissistic parents create an unhealthy relationship with their children. Children grow up afraid. They know one thing leads to another, and are pessimistic about some situations. Respect and true love are foreign to them. If they come across someone who loves them unconditionally, it can be unsettling.

What does it even mean to be loved without expecting something back? How does someone even do that? This crisis sets the stage for emotional sabotage. Unconsciously, the child finds a way to sabotage that relationship because it is too good to be real. The defense mechanism for these kids is usually that anything that cannot come too close to them cannot harm them.

It is okay to protect yourself, but at times it comes at a price. Many opportunities are lost, opportunities for learning, growth, careers, and personal intimate relationships.

Relationships

A narcissist is a living example of a myth. They are no more than make-believers. They have a concept of themselves that they hope you can trust and believe. It is all lies. Narcissism has a damaging effect on relationships. Relationships require effort from both partners. As a victim, your relationship is anything but a joint effort. A narcissist partner will turn your life upside down and by the time they are done with you, you might not have the slightest idea who or what you are.

One of the difficult things in a relationship is telling whether you have a narcissistic partner, or if they are overconfident. A narcissist will abuse you emotionally, leave you feeling worthless (Lee, 2018). The following are some of the signs of emotional abuse that you need to be aware of in a relationship with a narcissist:

- Rationalizing the abuse

Abuse in a relationship hurts on so many levels. Victims of narcissists usually end up normalizing the abuse to the point where they deny it happening in the first place. You minimize and rationalize the problem. This is a survival mechanism that helps the victim dissociate from the pain of abuse. You get to a point where you feel your abuser is not a bad person. They had to react the way they did because you probably did something terrible to provoke them.

This kind of abuse happens after the victim is conditioned to believe that they are helpless without the abuser. A narcissist will do all they can to ensure you rely on them for survival, and by this point, the relationship is one-sided, with the victim doing all they can to appease the abuser and meet their needs.

There are instances where the victim goes as far as shielding their narcissistic abuser from the law, instead of facing the consequences of their actions. To convince everyone else but themselves that they are doing okay, some victims are conditioned as far as posting happy photos and videos of their relationship on social media, while the real story is different.

- Fear of success

Narcissists do not just take away your happiness, they take away your life. At some point, you stop doing the things you used to love. Success becomes a myth for you, because it makes you happy, yet your partner hates it when you derive happiness from anything other than themselves. Talent, happiness, joy and everything else that interests you becomes a source of darkness, reprimand and reprisal.

As this continues, you become depressed, lose confidence, anxiety sets in and you learn to hide away from the spotlight, allowing your partner to shine instead. What your abuser is doing is not keeping you away from your wins because they feel you are not good enough; they do it because they are afraid your success will weaken their hold on you.

- Self-destruction and sabotage

A victim of narcissistic abuse will replay the words and actions in their mind all the time until it becomes second nature. You learn to associate certain actions in the relationship with violence and reprimand. You almost expect a negative reaction from your partner each time you do something. This amplification of negativity will grow into self-sabotage, and if your partner is a malignant narcissist, suicide might not be so far off.

Narcissists condition you to expect punishment for basically, anything. Their constant accusations, criticism and verbal abuse pushes you to a life of guilt and toxic shame, to a point where you give up on your goals, dreams, and feel worthless. You convince yourself that you are not worthy, and you don't deserve anything good.

- Unhealthy comparisons

Triangulation is one of the tactics narcissists use to manipulate their victims into submission. In a relationship, it gets worse because you end up comparing yourself to someone else all the time. When your partner keeps making you feel you are not good enough and goes as far as introducing a third party into your relationship, this is emotional terrorism. You have to fight for their approval and attention with someone else.

Comparisons are quite unhealthy. You see yourself in a different light. You wonder what they see in other people that they cannot see in you. You remember the days when your relationship was still new, and wonder how you let yourself go and became worthless. It is demeaning.

- Survival through dissociation

Detachment is a survival technique that many victims of narcissistic abuse embrace. Other than detaching from their partner emotionally, they end up detaching from the environment around them. You go through life like a zombie, unable to feel anything. Your life is a mess, and you are unable to connect your emotions to physical sensations. They each exist independent of one another.

When facing a situation of emotional distress, dissociation becomes your way of life. This is the brain's way of filtering out the emotional impact of distress and pain, protecting you from having to experience the full wave of terror (Torres, Vincelette, White, & Roberts, 2013)

- Fear of the unknown

People who have experienced trauma tend to shy away from anything that might relate to it, or symptoms of the traumatic event. It might be a person, a town, a building and so forth. As long as something reminds you of the traumatic experience, you are conditioned to avoid it altogether. The same applies to victims of narcissistic abuse.

Over time you learn to be careful about what you do and the things you say around your partner. You are happy when they are gone, but the moment they come back home, your life turns into one endless pit of darkness. Living a life where you are constantly walking on eggshells around your partner is so demoralizing.

You find yourself anxious all the time, worried that you might provoke your partner into a fit of rage. You worry about setting boundaries because your partner never seems to recognize them anyway. You want to avoid confronting your partner, and you do your best not to, but for some reason, they provoke you to get them worked up.

- Unhealthy compromises

In order to meet your narcissistic partner's needs, you have to compromise on your needs, emotional or otherwise. Everything about you comes second after your partner. Your physical safety also becomes less of a priority to your partner or yourself.

An individual who once lived a very happy and satisfying life ends up living purposely to satisfy the needs of their narcissistic partner. Many partners in such relationships give up their friendships, goals, hobbies and lives to satisfy their abusive partner. Sadly, the more you give up, the more you realize your partner will never truly be happy or satisfied with your sacrifices. It gets to a point where you have nothing left to give.

- Health problems

Many victims of narcissistic abuse develop health issues along the way. A victim who has maintained a healthy lifestyle will start gaining weight suddenly, while some will lose weight. It is also possible to develop serious health problems as a result of stress, because most of the time your body works too hard to balance your cortisol levels. Your immune system also suffers from the trauma.

Sleep becomes a challenge for such people in a relationship, because you don't feel safe sleeping even in your own house. You experience frequent nightmares, and are dazed most of the time when you recall the trauma you have been through.

- Self-isolation

In order to make themselves the center of your world, narcissists will try to isolate you from everyone else in your circles. Some victims are made to quit their jobs and stay at home. The problem with this kind of isolation is that it persists to a point where the victim embraces it. The abuse you experience is shameful to you, and because you don't want people to know about it, you self-isolate.

Chapter 2. Codependency

Codependency is a part of the reality of an unhealthy bond or relationship that can manifest in a variety of ways, not only in the narcissistic relationship, and will always show up with a narcissistic partner. So, what is codependency anyway, and who is to blame for it?

No one is to blame, and accusing one partner of being more at fault than the other, is just a product of unhealthy relationship dynamics, both with the self and others. By definition, codependency is essentially a condition of behaviors in a relationship in which one partner will facilitate or enable the other partner's irresponsibility, addictive tendencies, mental health issues, immaturity, and even their under-achievement.

Typically, if you are in a codependent partnership with someone, you are likely in need of something from it as well. Oftentimes, the narcissist will need all of the affirmation, accolades, and praise, while the partner is need of someone to take care of and nurture, allowing them to have a sense of fulfillment by meeting someone else's needs. This can be just as problematic as being a narcissist because it requires that you are dependent upon another person to make you feel worthy of existence. The codependent partnership is just a loop of the same behaviors and patterns being repeated over and over again until someone breaks the pattern. A codependent partner works well with a narcissist because they exist to feel helpful to someone to feel loved for their efforts, and all the narcissist wants is someone to fulfill all of their needs without having to give anything in return.

So, if you are a codependent partner, you may be interested in asking what kinds of traits you might exhibit if you are in that type of personality spectrum. The helps to identify the characteristics of what a codependent might look like.

Characteristics Of Codependency

To understand the relationship dynamics prevalent in the narcissistic relationship, having a grasp of the other partner, who is not the narcissist, will be helpful. In the end, it takes two to tango, and if you are in a long-term or even short-term partnership with a narcissist, you might need to start asking the questions of why you might be drawn to that person in the first place.

So, a codependent person will often work to meet the needs of others in the sacrifice of their needs. This act is an assumption of responsibility that is not required but will offer the codependent a sense of purpose, as well as the narcissist someone to meet their every need.

An increase in self-esteem for the codependent comes from controlling their emotions, and by proxy, those of their partner, effectually keeping the peace and making sure that everyone feels satisfied; however, the state of control over emotions prevents the real feelings, issues, or personality disorders from being identified, leading to the behavior loop between the codependent and the narcissist.

Codependents will often feel anxious, worried, or have boundary confusion revolving around intimacy with their partner. This is realized in their attempts to have their needs met by their narcissistic partner who only offers intimacy when it will benefit them, and so the codependent will often have a distorted view of their attractiveness, desire, or right to feel intimacy with their significant other.

One of the greatest indicators of someone being a codependent partner is enmeshment. When you are unable to have authority or autonomy within your relationship, you may decide that you are not whole without the other person and will enmesh yourself in their reality, feelings, and circumstances, blending your realities.

Additionally, codependents will usually, unconsciously, choose partners with addictions, abusive tendencies, mental or emotional disorders or issues, and impulse disorders. These are not the only circumstances, of course, but they are common attributes of a codependent partnership. The reason is that there is a lack of definition of the self, for both the narcissist and the codependent. The codependent feels a sense of self when they are caregiving or controlling another person.

A codependent person will deny their feelings, or that there is anything amiss in the relationship, because of their patterns of thought or belief about what a good partner does for the other. A narcissist will easily convince a codependent that they need to continue to be self-sacrificing, and so, the two work well together to continue manipulating these realities.

Here is a list of some of the common characteristics of a codependent partner and if you or someone you know can check off three or more of these, then you are likely in a codependent state in your partnership:

□ Depression

□ Compulsive activities (i.e., food binges, shopping sprees, constant house cleaning).

□ Holding in emotions

□ Constricting feelings

□ Anxiety

□ In a regular or excessive state of denial

□ Overly diligent, of hypervigilant

□ Abuse of substances

□ Sickness or illness caused by stress or anxiety

□ Victim of physical, sexual, or emotional abuse (recurring)

□ In a relationship with a person for over two years who has an addiction, without ever asking for help, or seeking therapy

□ Can't handle being alone and will make extreme efforts to avoid being alone

□ Perfectionism

□ Extreme desire for affection and/or acceptance

 Low self-esteem or self-worth
 Feeling a lack of trust
 Dishonesty and/or manipulation
 Overly controlling behavior
 Severe feelings of emptiness and/or boredom
 Intense relationships that are often unstable
 Subordinating your needs for the acceptance of the person you are with

These are some of the hallmarks of a codependent partner, and there are certainly a few more characteristics that can manifest, but these are the core characteristics. You may need to sit down and make a list of some of these qualities and try to determine if these concepts are reflected in your relationship. If so, you will need to understand how a codependent partnership is an unhealthy way to experience love and that there will need to be some shifts and changes in your reality to help you identify your true feelings and desires with your relationship.

Signs of Narcissistic Abuse

When you become repeatedly exposed to these types of abuse, you eventually begin to develop telltale signs of an abuse victim. Of course, not every person will follow this exact pattern or exhibit every single symptom on the list, and an absence of any of these symptoms does not automatically mean that the person is not being abused. Familiarize yourself with this list so you can recognize abuse in either yourself or in others.

Detaching or Dissociating

Dissociation is a form of coping mechanism in which you detach from your emotions. Oftentimes, your emotions are so overwhelming for you that you feel the need to detach from them altogether just to survive. This is commonly seen in people who have survived traumas, such as rape or war, and can also frequently be seen in the victims of narcissistic abuse. When this occurs, your mind is attempting to isolate the abuse as the only way it knows how to cope with the abuse, and can cause some serious mental health problems if left unchecked.

It can lead to altered levels of consciousness and begin to affect your memory, as well as lead to serious health implications as well.

Distrusting Everyone

Due to encountering so much abuse by someone you once trusted and loved, you may become quite distrustful in response. You may constantly feel on edge, worried that you will be betrayed or hurt again, and your ability to make meaningful relationships may suffer. Instead, you remain hyper vigilant around other people, which only serves to heighten sensations of anxiety and drive wedges between yourself and other people. You likely suspect even those who you have never had a reason to distrust as being capable of harming you after your trauma.

Often or Always fearful

As a result of being so thoroughly betrayed, you may find yourself constantly fearing a repeat of the abuse. You may fear that your abuser will come back to you if you have escaped or you may worry that any happiness you find is a delusion. Because narcissists have a tendency to punish when someone around them is happy, you have likely repeatedly faced consequences to enjoying life, which as only served to make you worried whenever things go well. You constantly fear that the narcissist will be set off or that the other shoe will drop and your fragile moment of happiness will be shattered. You may develop a fear of enjoyment and because of this, you allow the narcissist to continue being the only one to enjoy anything. Of course, what the narcissist really enjoys is seeing his victims afraid of enjoying life.

Feeling of Walking on eggshells

Similar to being fearful, the feeling of walking on eggshells is that sensation you feel when you are desperately trying to tend to a delicate situation and you know that if you make the slightest mistake, no matter how harmless that mistake may seem, there will be a massive explosion. You live with that sensation constantly when with the narcissist; you feel as though she will explode on you at any given moment, even over things that are insignificant.

Martyring Yourself for others

Martyring yourself, in this case, refers to the act of making yourself suffer in order to benefit others. If you know that the narcissist wants muffins for breakfast but has not asked for them, for example, you might stay up late that night, making a batch from scratch to give to the narcissist, despite the fact that doing so means that you went to bed three hours late and are too exhausted to meet all of your responsibilities the day. You may find other ways to do this, such as canceling an appointment to get your hair done that you had been looking forward to in order to take care of the narcissist's laundry or canceling some other thing you have been looking forward to for something that the narcissist is relatively indifferent about.

Self-guilt and Blame

With self-guilt, you seek to blame yourself for what you have gone through. You know that you are in a bad relationship with a narcissist and that you could have better but you feel as though you deserve it. You guilt yourself into staying, saying that the narcissist needs you, and that you are to blame for your suffering. You must not have tried hard enough if the narcissist is not doing better yet, and you need to try harder if you want the abuse to stop.

You may even begin to blame yourself for the narcissist's abuse, telling yourself that you had annoyed your abuser into punching you and if you are more careful in the future it will not happen. You make yourself responsible for the narcissist's actions and that train of thought only convinces you that you deserved it and that the abuse was justified.

Self-sabotaging

When self-sabotaging, you find ways to prevent yourself from succeeding. Oftentimes, this is related to the narcissist destroying your self-esteem. You begin to believe what the narcissist is saying about your capabilities and act them out. If you are repeatedly told that you are unintelligent, you will begin to believe it, and you will make choices that reflect that. You may be quite bright, but your own choices will be made based off of your sense of self-worth. Self-sabotaging could also take forms such as making it impossible for yourself to leave the relationship when you want to by failing to take the steps necessary to grant yourself the independence you crave.

Chapter 3. Recognize The Problem And The Trauma Bond

When that mask is cracked, however, the vulnerable narcissist's true self is revealed. She is a person with no true sense of individuality, with no sense of self. She is self-conscious to a fault, perhaps due to trauma during childhood. Her narcissistic tendencies are little more than coping mechanisms to protect herself from the pain once felt as a child, whether trauma, neglect, or abuse. She may have been convinced so thoroughly during childhood that her suffering was due to her own deficits that she feels that she has to be perfect in order to be accepted, and that is exactly what she does pretend to be perfect.

Unlike the grandiose narcissist, who does not need validation from others, the vulnerable narcissist requires validation. She does not feel comfortable with herself and seeks others to help her feel better about herself. She thrives off of attention and care, and ultimately, playing the perfect victim, helpless to her circumstances and bad luck is the perfect disguise. She craves attention and nurturing from others, so she creates circumstances in which that is provided.

It then follows that of course, the vulnerable narcissist is quite concerned with how other people perceive her. She will make it a point to build relationships with other people, and she has no qualms when it comes to apologizing if doing so will help further her cause. She wants to be seen as the perfect friend, employee, citizen, mother, and any other role she slides herself into, and will often do things that appear to be good deeds, though that selflessness only happens when other people are there to see it.

An important thing to note is that because the vulnerable narcissist is so desperate for attention and nurturing, she is one of the only people who would actually threaten self-harm in order to get attention. The vast majority of people who threaten self-harm or that do self-harm are doing so for themselves, but the narcissist will threaten it to get those around her to rally around her and help her in what must be the most difficult time of her life, regardless of the fact that the hard situation she is in was self-inflicted. She is not likely to follow through with the threat, or if she does, she will not hurt herself badly enough to do serious damage. She simply wants to be the object of other people's sympathy.

The vulnerable narcissist is frequently quite passive-aggressive, especially when she feels as though her delicate mask that she spent so long crafting and perfecting is being threatened. She, like the grandiose, believes that she cannot be at fault and that at worst, she is a victim of happenstance, but that should not reflect poorly on her. Instead of overt threats or displays of power, she will instead make it a point to passive-aggressively instill guilt.

For example, if you have told your friend that you cannot change the date of your wedding to better fit her schedule, she may sigh sadly and say that she understands, and that since she obviously is not an important enough part of the wedding for her availability to be taken into consideration, then she will just not show up at all, and everyone will probably be happier for it. She says this in order to passive-aggressively instill guilt in you, knowing that most people will fall for it. However, the more threatened the vulnerable narcissist feels, the more overtly aggressive she will become. She is prone to temperamental explosions, and she will not tolerate any direct affronts to her already incredibly wounded, incredibly sensitive self-esteem. Even the slightest perceived attack on her self-esteem is enough to send her into a flurry known as a narcissistic rage, in which she will lash out at anyone and everyone around her with no regard to how they feel or react.

Malignant Narcissist

The vulnerable and grandiose narcissists, while oftentimes exhausting to be around, are typically not intentionally harmful in the sense that the malignant narcissist is. Their actions are largely due to personality flaws and an inability to perceive reality in an accurate manner, and while this does not excuse their behaviors, it does shed a certain light upon them. The malignant narcissist, on the other hand, loves to inflict pain. He is entirely aware of what his actions are doing and seems to revel in the suffering of others.

When you want to imagine the malignant narcissist, think of the stereotypical villain in a kid's television show: He wants to watch the world burn for no reason other than he thinks it will bring him joy. There is no extrinsic motivator, no tragic backstory that has caused him to think ill of others, and no real benefit to doing so. However, the malignant narcissist will get some enjoyment out of the act of impacting so many people so deeply, and that is enough. He thrives off of seeing people around him suffer, regardless of whether those people have wronged him.

The malignant narcissist, despite his ability to appear outwardly charming, has an incredibly fragile ego. The only way his ego really feels secure and he feels joy is in seeing other people suffer. He wants to be recognized so badly by others, yet feels an extreme sense of self-doubt and distrust about the world. He wants to be successful, though he rarely goes about obtaining it. Instead, he wallows in his self-pity and paranoia that people around him are seeking to expose his true, broken, and fragile self.

He typically presents himself with charisma, as all narcissists are prone to do, and may also rely heavily on promiscuity or seduction tactics, but that physical intimacy is meaningless to him. He does not see intimacy as anything other than a way to obtain power over another individual, and is only something he will bother with if he believes it will help him get his way.

The malignant narcissist has an inherent dislike toward generally accepted social conventions and frequently does things that violate them whenever he can get away with it. He has a tendency to lie to others when he has no reason to do so and steal just because he feels he can get away with it. The law has no power over him due to his own inherent infallibility as far as he is concerned. He will act sadistically or violently just because it allows for him to affirm his power. Because he is able to inflict harm, he feels as though he is more powerful. His lack of empathy means he never feels anything toward those he hurts, both physically and emotionally, and with his complete absence for empathy comes an absence of regret and remorse for actions.

Like all narcissists, the malignant has no problem manipulating others. He is willing to do whatever it takes to get the attention he desires. He is also more inclined to be more overt or forceful in his attempts to manipulate others, even if that means that his actions are more obvious to others. He does not care and fails to see how anyone can possibly blame him when he is so clearly infallible. Unlike how most other narcissists prefer their manipulation to be opportunistic, the malignant narcissist will go out of his way to manipulate just because he can, even if it serves no benefit to him in that particular moment.

The malignant narcissist is the most harmful of the varieties, toxic and violent, and should be avoided at all costs. His propensity for inflicting harm while enjoying every second of doing so makes him particularly dangerous. He does not care what happens to the people around him, and is not guided by a desire for love or admiration—negative attention is just as good to the malignant narcissist as positive—at the very least, it is still attention. He will not be bound by social norms or worrying about how other people may view him when acting on his sadistic impulses. He is dangerous and would not think twice about harming, maiming, or even killing his victim if he felt inclined to do so.

Chapter 4. Types of Narcissistic Relationships

One of the most difficult things for victims of narcissists is learning to let go. When someone is dear to you, it is normal to see the best in them. You try to get them help, try to understand them and hope that someday they will change. Unfortunately, this is not always the case.

Narcissists do not seek help. They believe they don't have a problem. If anything, in the mind of a narcissist, the person who thinks they need to change their ways is the one who needs to embrace change. It is so traumatizing, watching someone you love dive deeper into the abyss like that.

If you cannot change someone, at best you can learn how to cope with them. Remember that in as much as you might hold them dear, your first priority is your personal safety and peace of mind. In learning how to handle a narcissist, you can counter their manipulative motives and prevent yourself from becoming a puppet. The first step is to learn how to identify a narcissist, which we have done. You learn how to identify their manipulative traits, and what to do in order to counter their outbursts. In a relationship, it is very difficult when you realize you are living with a narcissist. The best solution is always to keep a healthy distance from a narcissist, especially if you know they can overpower your resolve.

Four-Point Framework For Dealing With A Narcissist

There are several ways of handling a narcissist. Before we look into them, the following are four of the most important things you should always keep in mind when dealing with a narcissist.

Positivity

Life throws many curve balls at you all the time. It never gets easier. To get through anything, you must embrace positivity and change your outlook about life. Narcissists will drain the life out of you, and by the time they are done with you, all that's left might be a shell of your former self.

People who maintain a positive approach to life generally live happier lives than most. Your happiness is one of the things a narcissist will go after. When you are happy, to them it means there is something else in your life responsible for your happiness, something other than them. Since your life must revolve around them, they will do everything they can to take away your happiness.

Narcissists will do random things to disturb your peace. They also monitor you to see the effect. It fills them with joy when you lose focus and are disturbed. They respond by pushing your limits further until you break.

Staying positive will help you learn how to handle a narcissist. They have an endless barrage of insults and ill behavior that they can hurl at you. Instead of bowing to the pressure, be positive and show them that you are not affected by the things they do or what they say. If you are persistent, they might soon realize that it is impossible to break you, and they have to make peace with it.

Positivity is not just about handling a narcissist, it is also about your mindset. You need to stay sharp because a narcissist will never give up on testing you. You can condition your mind to think positively, filter negative vibes and focus only on things that bring joy, meaning and satisfaction in your life. This will help you become aware of, and impervious to narcissistic manipulation.

Healthy boundaries

One of the top recommendations when dealing with a narcissist is to set boundaries. This helps, especially when you realize you are in an unhealthy relationship. The challenge with setting boundaries is that in most cases, people don't even know what their boundaries are. It is very difficult to change something you don't know you have.

Setting boundaries depends on your experiences and upbringing. It might be easier for some people to establish boundaries than others because of such predispositions. It might take some learning, but if you are persistent, you will get it right.

First, you need to learn what you are about. What are your boundaries? You must acknowledge your feelings. Boundaries are only effective when you know what you are protecting, hence what you are shielding yourself from (Newland, 2008). Does someone's comment make you feel terrible? Do you feel drained when you are in their presence? This is a good place to start.

Learning about yourself helps you evaluate your actions and choices, and recognize how you feel. Most people have leaky boundaries in their relationships, and at some point they give up altogether. In such a relationship, you become so engrossed in your partner's life that you substitute your life for theirs. Relationships are about two unique individuals coming together to form a healthy unit.

Take some time to rethink your life. Reflect and check in with yourself until you are aware of the difference between your partner or the other party to this interaction, and yourself.

Second, how do you know when your boundaries are crossed? Once you are aware of your feelings, you know when you are hurt. That is the point your boundaries are breached. Ask yourself how was your boundary breached? Here are some examples.

Scenario 1:

"Your partner always promises to take you out and meet their friends and family, but it never happens."

Scenario 2:

"Someone in your life is always asking for money, promising to pay back but they never do."

Scenario 3:

"A close friend or family member keeps calling you in the middle of the night or messaging about their problems, but they don't seem interested in solving the problems themselves. Each time they call, you cannot fall asleep after the call."

Each time these events happen, something breaks inside you. You feel disappointed, unloved, cheated, unappreciated and so forth. You already know what matters to you, and how you feel when those feelings are not appreciated. Now, you know how your boundaries are breached.

Third, you focus on how to reset boundaries. You are in charge of your life, and to borrow a common phrase in many establishments, *Management reserves the right of admission*!

Why should you put up with someone who has made it clear they don't respect anything you say? Having realized the things that hurt you and how, the step is to confront the problem. Address the person who keeps breaching your boundaries without a care.

Here are some examples on how to handle the scenarios above:

Scenario 1

Tell your partner why it bothers you that they haven't kept this promise. Tell them to stop making the promise altogether, and act on it once and get it out of the way.

Scenario 2

Remind them that since they have failed to honor their commitments, you will not lend them more money until they pay back what they owe.

Scenario 3

Tell your friend or family member that you understand their pain, but it is draining the life out of you. Ask them to seek professional help, and if possible, stop answering the calls.

By addressing these issues, you make the other person aware that they are hurting you, and they need to stop.

Fourth, you must learn how to ground your boundaries. Establishing boundaries is one thing, but maintaining them is not easy either. If you have weak boundaries, your partner will recognize this and can manipulate you into feeling guilty through backlash. However, the most important thing is that these boundaries are there for you.

You must respect your boundaries before you expect the same of someone else. Grounding your boundaries is more about awareness and strengthening your resolve. Meditation, deep breathing, chakra are some of the techniques you can use to enforce your boundaries.
While enforcing your boundaries, don't forget your emotions. They are valid. Trust in yourself. You are not wrong to set your boundaries. This is healthy, and everyone must respect each other's boundaries if you are to be happy together. You have individual boundaries and couple boundaries. Each of these boundaries are unique, and it is their independence that makes your relationship healthy.
Fifth, talk about your boundaries. Talk about it. Let your partner know you have boundaries and they have persistently crossed them, and you need them to stop. Fair warning, this might not always go well. If your partner retorts, argues back or lashes out at you for having boundaries, perhaps it is best you walk away and take care of yourself. It is clear that you are not a priority to them.
Backlash is usually one of the signs that someone does not acknowledge or respect your boundaries. Arguing with them about it is an acknowledgement of their disrespect, which opens room for unhealthy compromise. Boundaries are simple. If someone doesn't understand them, the best they can do is ask you to enlighten them about your boundaries and need thereof. This can help them understand you better, and why you need the boundaries.
Boundaries must come with consequences. People will always push your boundaries, at times just to see what happens. Decide on appropriate consequences and communicate them clearly. Setting consequences is the ultimate way of embracing your boundaries. Make this about you. After all, the purpose of boundaries is to honor your commitment to your inner peace, not to judge or satisfy another person's choices and actions.
Finally, take care of yourself. If the discussion about your boundaries did not go according to plan, don't spend your time worrying about it. Step outside, exercise, run along the beach, go for a walk or

something. Do anything that will prevent you from spending a lot of your energy worrying about what transpired.

Personal detachment

Narcissists will always project their flaws to you. They blame you for things that you have nothing to do with. They will undermine you and break your spirit. A good solution for this is to retreat and embrace a different approach so that you learn how to deal with their tirades.

Learn how to ignore their personal attacks. Don't take anything a narcissist says personally. When you do this, it is easier for you to handle the situation better. The last thing you want to do is pick up an argument with a narcissist because they will never listen to you. At best, let them know you don't agree with their position, and leave it at that.

Any encounter with a narcissist is most likely about them, and never about you. In order to identify and reject these attacks, you should understand your self-worth, believe in yourself, and shun any criticism that they might level against you.

Contextual evaluation

What is the situation at hand? Take time and learn the context before you respond to a narcissist. Some of their outbursts are not because they are narcissists but because of circumstances which eventually make them embrace the narcissistic personality.

A good example is when you are offered a promotion over your colleague who has a narcissistic personality, and was eyeing the position too. Working together might not be easy. Your colleague will easily resent you for no reason. They will highlight your mistakes and wonder how you got the job instead of them.

Even if your colleague is not usually a confronting person, they might develop a condescending attitude towards you. In any argument or disagreement, they will throw words like "*so you think you are better than everyone else,*" to vent and air out their frustration. It is always wise to assess the context of these tirades so that you know what you are dealing with and why.

Tips For Dealing With A Narcissist

A lot of things might run through your mind when you encounter a narcissist. It is normal that you might be engulfed by the desire to flee the situation. While self-preservation is important, you should also have it at the back of your mind that narcissistic personality disorder is a real mental problem, and if possible, encourage the individual to seek medical attention.

Besides those who have NPD, there are individuals who portray narcissistic characteristics. It is quite helpful if you know how to handle such people. This helps in managing your expectations, and creating a safe environment for you to interact with them without their narcissistic tendencies taking over. Below are useful ideas that will help you manage the situation better:

- Acceptance

One of the first things you have to do is realize that this person is who they are. Accept them. There is no version of themselves that you can create in your mind that will change their behavior. Many victims of narcissistic abuse suffer because deep down they hold onto a fallacy that someday, the abuser might change their ways. The only thing that might happen is your life changing for the worst.

- Deny them attention

Narcissists are attention hogs. Since they thrive on attention, why not shut them out? These are people who will do anything to be recognized. The attention might be positive or negative, but they will still thrive off of it. If you give them all the attention they need, the only thing that happens is that you end up sacrificing what is important to you, to satisfy them. Attention seekers like these will never respect you. They never see you in the same way you see them.

- Establish boundaries

The trick is not just establishing boundaries, but creating very clear boundaries. Communicate. Talk to the other person about what you feel when they do something that exceeds your boundaries. Set consequences and make sure they are aware of what it will cost them the time they cross your boundaries.

More importantly, hold them accountable for their actions. You have to be steadfast in your approach to dealing with narcissists. A narcissist will try to find the easiest way to get back control from you. While you set these boundaries, they might feel you are moving further away from them, which is infuriating. Instead, ensure you communicate the boundaries to them in a healthy way. Do it in a manner that does not feel like they are being attacked.

There are sacrifices you can make for people who are dear to you, like these ones. However, at the same time you must also be aware that some people might never change. If this is that kind of a person, then your personal safety and peace of mind comes first, and the best thing to do is to walk away. It does not matter if they are your parents, siblings or lovers; walking away might be the only way you stay alive.

- Retaliation

When you find out how to handle a narcissist, do not assume they will take it kindly. Expect retaliation. Some mind tricks might be coming your way, so brace yourself for impact. One of the common responses to your boundaries is that they will also give you a list of their boundaries or demands. Be careful because what might seem like a counter offer to your boundaries might be a manipulation tactic. It is common for a narcissist to state their terms in such a way that you feel guilty about your boundaries. They need you to go back to the drawing board and rethink your strategy. They can even make you feel like you are pushing them away. If you fall for this trick, you give up control of your life. Watch out for the sympathetic pleas, because in most cases, they are anything but sympathetic.

- Stand your ground

The last thing you can expect from a narcissist is that they will admit they made a mistake, or take responsibility for hurting you. Instead of owning up to it, it is easier for them to make you bear the responsibility for their actions. This is why you must always stand your ground. Be strong in your resolve because you know what is right. Do not give in to the manipulation. Theirs is an inflated ego that you can never truly please. Accepting the blame will only create more trouble for you in the future.

- No promises

You might have learned this about your partner already, their promises never materialize. You cannot keep up that unhealthy cycle. Instead of worrying about what happens, insist on immediate action. If they promise you something, make sure they do it right away. Hold them accountable for it and insist on action.

The reason why you need to do this is because most of the time, promises from narcissists are nothing but a means to an end. Whenever they make a promise, there is something they want from you. Once they have it, the promises become a distant memory.

Chapter 5. Addressing Self-Destructive Habits

Narcissists project a strong, over-confident, and selfish image that can easily get out of hand. This is malignant narcissism, the sort that leads to misery when the narcissist cannot get their way, or when challenged in a way the forces them to look at their own weaknesses. To prevent that, the malignant narcissist will go to great lengths and sometimes do some outrageous things.

They'll come off as know-it-alls who are above the rules. They'll project an image of great superiority and imply that everyone else is somehow beneath them. They win favor very easily at first, then that wears off once their lack of empathy is seen. That's what is about, some of the more common things you can expect from a malignant narcissist.

Nature or Nurture

During infancy, we have a totally devoted caregiver who treats us as the center of the world, making us feel as though we are all-powerful and can do anything we like. Under normal circumstances, as we mature, we begin to understand that we are separate from our caregiver, losing these notions and establishing trust as we learn that our caregivers are different people, establishing boundaries and eventually experiencing push-back to our demands and actions. By this process, we establish a healthy ego and begin to take steps toward realistic and mutually rewarding adult relationships.

Narcissists don't experience this maturation. This is usually when the caregiver cannot cope with the responsibility of completely caring for another person. They don't develop trust in their caregivers and never manage to learn that they are not all-powerful and that they cannot control others. Instead, they tend to remain stuck in their infantile belief that they are the center of everything and will manipulate the people around them to remain at the center.

Manipulation

When dealing with a narcissist, you have to expect at least some level of manipulation. They are attention addicts who are intent on protecting their vulnerable inner self, which translates into pushing or cajoling the people around them to pay the narcissist the attention they crave, to live up to their vision, and most of all, to refrain from doing anything that might force them to admit that their vainglorious image of themselves is wrong.

It really doesn't matter to them if the people they manipulate suffer from it. Their attitude is simply that you can't make an omelet without breaking some eggs. If the person they are manipulating pushes back, stands up to the manipulation, and makes the narcissist face their own ugly behavior, the reaction is usually violent, not necessarily physically, but intense and often vicious. They may slander the person, blame them for the narcissist's own actions, or demean them, whatever it takes to cow them into silence.

The manipulation tactics used by the narcissist are many and varied. Some can be quite pleasant, others are subtle, the rest awful. They may be used alone or in combination and will be changed as needed for the narcissist to achieve their goals. We've divided these techniques into three categories based on how the subject is made to feel: The Good, the Bad, and the Ugly.

The (not so) Good

 Love-bombing Their Partner. The victim has never felt so loved in their life. The narcissist will do this to hook their victim and reel them in quickly. The narcissist doesn't want to give them a chance to reflect, to look closely at what is happening, or to ask a lot of questions.

 Idealizing Their Partner. They build up a fantasy ideal of their victim and treat them as if they actually live up to that fantasy. Like love bombing, this can be quite pleasant for the victim until the narcissist turns on them, which will happen once the reality of a relationship sets in and they begin to see things about their partner that they want to change or eliminate.

□ Subtle Flattery. Like idealization, this early-stage tactic opens the door to other things by making the partner feel good about themselves and about the narcissist, good enough for them to allow the narcissist greater access into their life.

□ Mirroring Their Partner. The interest and attention usually die away once the narcissist attains the love of their love object, but in the beginning, they are avid in studying their partner's tastes, values, and beliefs in order to mirror those traits back at them with the goal of making them think they found their perfect match.

The Bad

□ The Victim Play. The narcissist deliberately plays the victim to arouse the sympathy of the person being manipulated, often throwing the pity party of the century in order to get them to do something.

□ The Obligation Game. The Narcissist's penchant for tit-for-tat and their ability to play upon our sense of fairness comes to the fore as they do something nice in order to obligate someone to do something for them, sometimes against the self-interest of the other person.

□ Making Excuses. Slightly different from the narcissist's victim play, here they are trying to excuse or justify their behavior by deflecting the blame and arousing the pity of the abused party. "If I had only received the money, I'm due," or "If you had just kept your promise not to…," the excuses always leave the narcissist as the victim.

□ Lowered Expectations. In any relationship, the last thing a narcissist wants is expectations from their partner. By lowering those expectations, a gradual process of diminishing returns in which the partner gets used to receiving less and less from the narcissist, they end up expecting little or nothing at all while the narcissist continues to extract what they want from the relationship.

The Ugly

□ Devaluation. The narcissist's word games can be used to undermine their partner's self-esteem. They do this by purposefully saying, or not

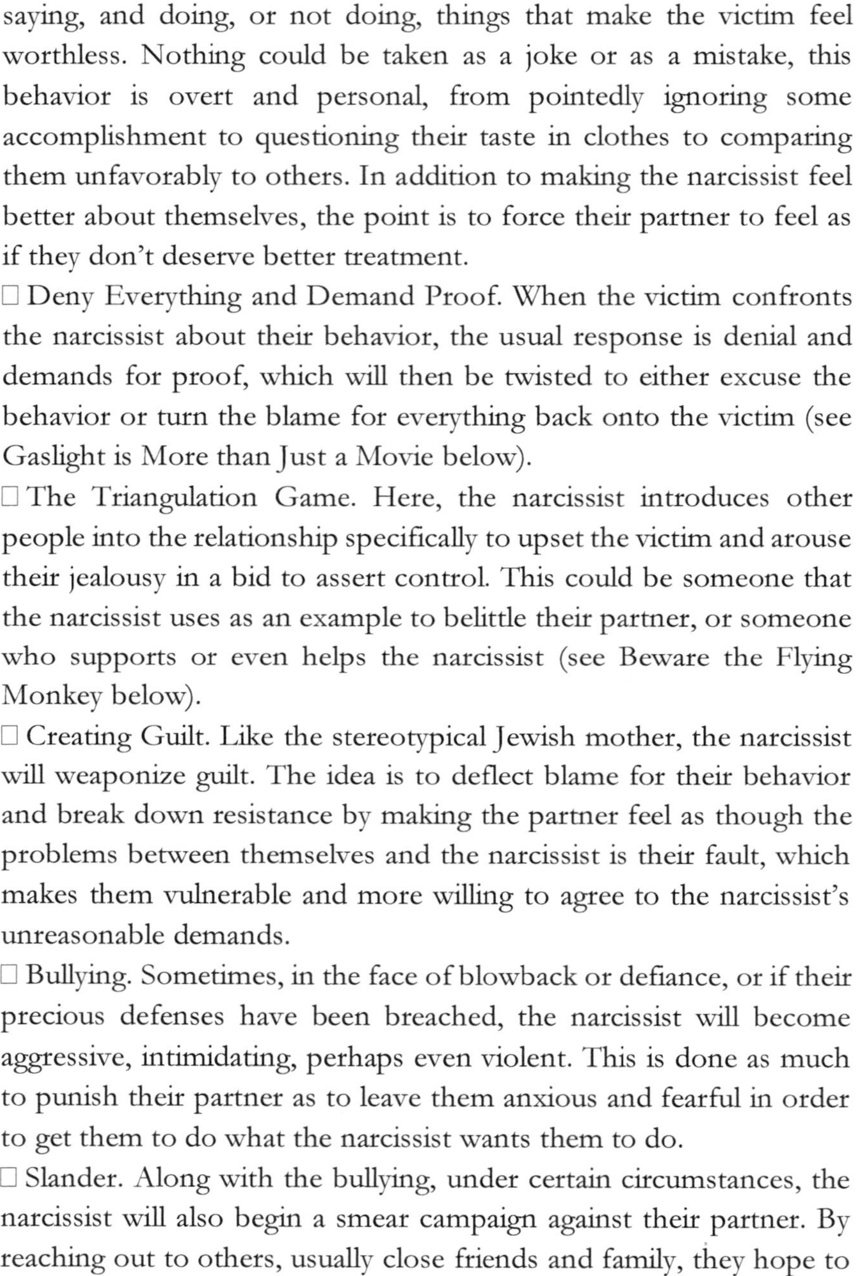

saying, and doing, or not doing, things that make the victim feel worthless. Nothing could be taken as a joke or as a mistake, this behavior is overt and personal, from pointedly ignoring some accomplishment to questioning their taste in clothes to comparing them unfavorably to others. In addition to making the narcissist feel better about themselves, the point is to force their partner to feel as if they don't deserve better treatment.

- Deny Everything and Demand Proof. When the victim confronts the narcissist about their behavior, the usual response is denial and demands for proof, which will then be twisted to either excuse the behavior or turn the blame for everything back onto the victim (see Gaslight is More than Just a Movie below).
- The Triangulation Game. Here, the narcissist introduces other people into the relationship specifically to upset the victim and arouse their jealousy in a bid to assert control. This could be someone that the narcissist uses as an example to belittle their partner, or someone who supports or even helps the narcissist (see Beware the Flying Monkey below).
- Creating Guilt. Like the stereotypical Jewish mother, the narcissist will weaponize guilt. The idea is to deflect blame for their behavior and break down resistance by making the partner feel as though the problems between themselves and the narcissist is their fault, which makes them vulnerable and more willing to agree to the narcissist's unreasonable demands.
- Bullying. Sometimes, in the face of blowback or defiance, or if their precious defenses have been breached, the narcissist will become aggressive, intimidating, perhaps even violent. This is done as much to punish their partner as to leave them anxious and fearful in order to get them to do what the narcissist wants them to do.
- Slander. Along with the bullying, under certain circumstances, the narcissist will also begin a smear campaign against their partner. By reaching out to others, usually close friends and family, they hope to

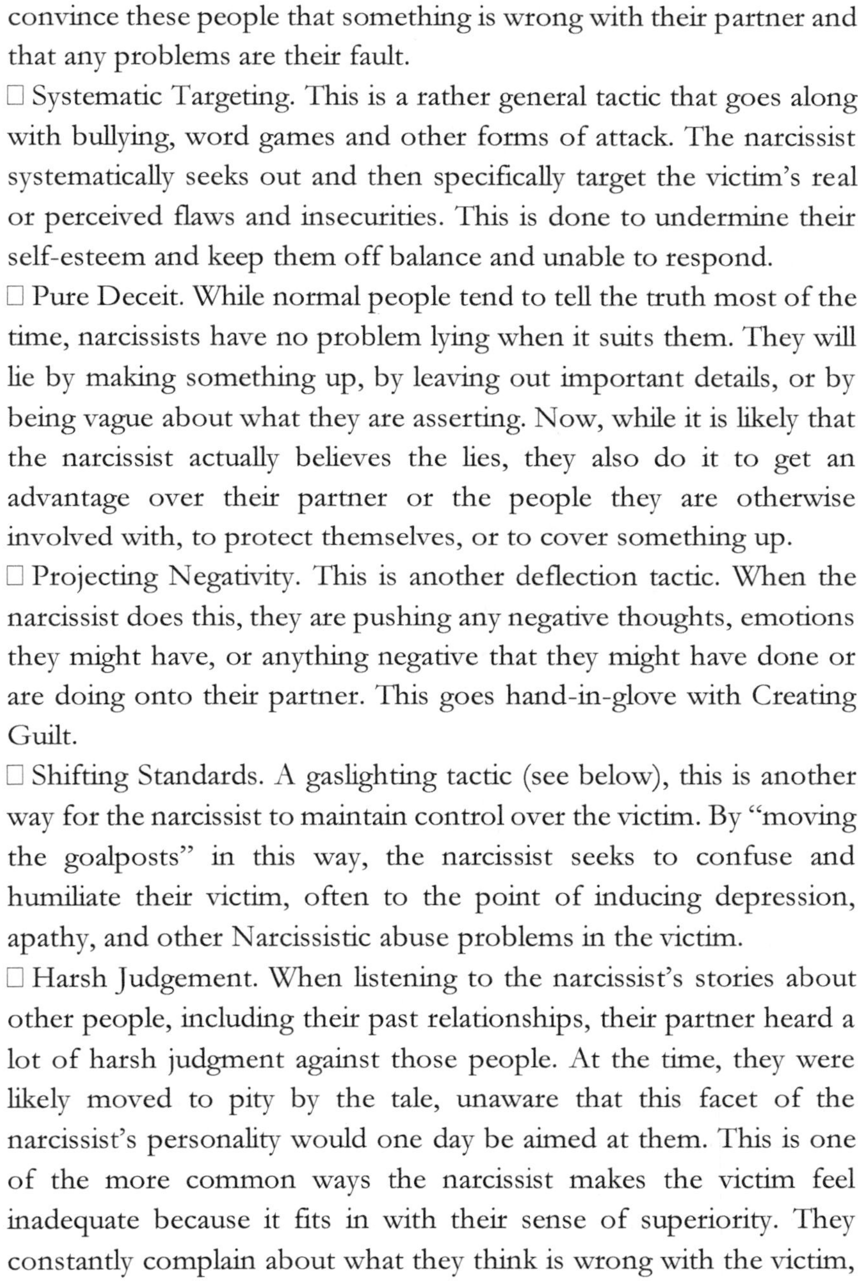

convince these people that something is wrong with their partner and that any problems are their fault.

□ Systematic Targeting. This is a rather general tactic that goes along with bullying, word games and other forms of attack. The narcissist systematically seeks out and then specifically target the victim's real or perceived flaws and insecurities. This is done to undermine their self-esteem and keep them off balance and unable to respond.

□ Pure Deceit. While normal people tend to tell the truth most of the time, narcissists have no problem lying when it suits them. They will lie by making something up, by leaving out important details, or by being vague about what they are asserting. Now, while it is likely that the narcissist actually believes the lies, they also do it to get an advantage over their partner or the people they are otherwise involved with, to protect themselves, or to cover something up.

□ Projecting Negativity. This is another deflection tactic. When the narcissist does this, they are pushing any negative thoughts, emotions they might have, or anything negative that they might have done or are doing onto their partner. This goes hand-in-glove with Creating Guilt.

□ Shifting Standards. A gaslighting tactic (see below), this is another way for the narcissist to maintain control over the victim. By "moving the goalposts" in this way, the narcissist seeks to confuse and humiliate their victim, often to the point of inducing depression, apathy, and other Narcissistic abuse problems in the victim.

□ Harsh Judgement. When listening to the narcissist's stories about other people, including their past relationships, their partner heard a lot of harsh judgment against those people. At the time, they were likely moved to pity by the tale, unaware that this facet of the narcissist's personality would one day be aimed at them. This is one of the more common ways the narcissist makes the victim feel inadequate because it fits in with their sense of superiority. They constantly complain about what they think is wrong with the victim, implying that they are sub-par and that they could be better if they only tried.

These are among the more common tactics that narcissists use to get under the skin of their victim, but two more deserve a little more explanation: Gaslighting and the Flying Monkey.

The question is, given the often-public floggings they risk by carrying out their narcissist's orders or covering up their actions, why do they do it? Because there is a pay-off for both parties, at least for a while. According to Hammond, these flying monkeys often have their own Narcissistic abuse disorder, and that allows for each to feed on their relationship in some way. The list includes:

 Narcissistic Personality Disorder. As long as they can garner power, influence, money, prestige, or some other benefit, the partnership works. Once those benefits are lost, or a greater benefit is offered, the narcissistic flying monkey flies away and could even turn on their former idol. Cohen is a good example of this in that he turned on Trump when it benefitted him more to do so.

 Generalized Anxiety Disorder. In this case, the constant anxiety of the flying monkey is attracted to the arrogance of the narcissist, but it lasts only until the anxiety eases.

 Co-dependents. The co-dependent feeds on the narcissist's need to be served and adored. The narcissist feeds on the co-dependent's quest for purpose and satisfaction by way of taking care of others. Of course, once the co-dependent recovers and turns from their people-pleasing ways, the disappointed narcissist will leave.

 Addicts. Just like a drug pusher on the street can make their addicted clientele do anything for the fix, if the narcissist is the one supporting the addiction, the addict will slavishly do or say whatever will keep them on good terms with their supplier. This relationship ends one of two ways: The addict gets clean and no longer needs what the narcissist provides, or the addiction worsens, and the narcissist cuts them off because they get too needy.

 Dependent Peronality Disorder. The narcissist loves this one because the depedent makes them feel so superior because in addition to obedince, they either include the narcissist in every decision they makor leave the decision entirely up to the narcissist. These relationshiprarely if ever end.
 Sociopaths. Herethe narcissist is useful to the Sociopath, who will use the outrageou behavior of the narcissist to veil their own nefarious deeds, orestrating everything while allowing the narcissist to think they are thone running the show. These relationships tend to end when circuntances change, and it benefits the sociopath to get rid of the narcisst.

The Uses)f Anger

Anger. It can manift naturally when the narcissist is disappointed, much like the tantruof a spoiled child; but it usually shows up when the victim claps ba at them and either threatens to expose the frightened little chilthat lays at their core or worse, actually do expose it. It can al be used as a carefully orchestrated way to intimidate their victi into compliance.
When it comes to an;, there are two types of narcissists we need to consider. The Grande narcissist, with their inflated ego and sense of entitlement, and thVulnerable narcissist, who is covering up their inadequacies.
You Can't Always GWhat You Want (But You Get What You Need)
Under normal circstances, when we are disappointed in something, we either kle the problem (Problem-focused Coping) or we deal with our erions (emotion-focused Coping). Either way, we cope with the disointment, put into some perspective, and move on. That, howeis not necessarily how narcissists react.
It would be easy to sayat the typical malignant narcissist's reaction is rage, especially at th they believe have managed to block their plans. It is an emotiorcused coping mechanism that might make the narcissist feel better a while, but it doesn't solve anything, and

it alienates the people who have to deal with thenarcissist and may, actually, be able to help the situation. That sal, it is a tad more complex than that. Studies have shown that graniose narcissists and vulnerable narcissists deal with disappointment ıfferently.

The grandiose variety, with their over-inflated gos and heightened self-esteem, cope with disappointment better, lapting to changing situations in ways that vulnerable narcissists, vh so much of their energy going to covering up their own sense inferiority and low self-esteem, simply cannot.

Chapter 6. Understanding Your Sense Of Self And Your Inner Strengths

Living in a narcissistic relationship is not without its challenges, as with any relationship in life. It requires that you are willing to understand all of the information that you have just read in this and apply that knowledge to find a solution. Not all of us who are in a narcissistic relationship feel like there is any reason to leave or any reason to accuse the other person of being at fault, perhaps, identifying the cause of their issue, or perhaps recognizing that there are options to living with a narcissist.

Sometimes, it is the best choice to evacuate as soon as possible, especially if there is a feeling or comprehension that some level of abuse might be involved. Narcissistic abuse is often very subtle and can be hard to identify. It builds up over time and feels like casual, off-hand insults at the moment, but as they accrue over time, you are looking at volumes of slights and awful words that destroy your self-esteem and self-worth to the point of denial about who you truly are as a person.

If you start summoning your inner strength so that you can quit, they suddenly change their tactics. They try all means to make sure that they suck you back in the same way a vacuum cleaner does: 'hoover.' They start doing something minor like buying you a small gift, commenting positively on your dressing, liking your social media posts among others. If that does not seem to work, they work harder by simply going back to the 'love bombing' In other words, the more you are resistant, the harder they try to win you back.

At this point, the sad thing is that many of us are vulnerable and we end up getting sucked up into the relationship again. Mostly it is because we start second-guessing whether there is change or if you will end up regretting this decision for the rest of your life and blah

blah blah. In other words, what you are doing is ignoring everything that you know about your abuser with the hope that they might have magically transformed into someone more loving, decent, stable and reliable!

Inner Strength

There are a lot of scenarios or realities that might not allow you to leave your relationship with a narcissist. You may be a person with a grown, adult child who is narcissistic, but you cannot afford to exclude them from your life because they are your child, and you love them. Another scenario might be that your parent is a narcissist, and you want to be able to have some kind of a relationship with them as you both grow older over the years.

In some situations, you may not be able to leave your narcissistic partner because you cannot financially afford it, or because you are truly in love with them and are willing to do whatever it takes to be with them. The possibilities are endless and unique to each relationship.

What can you possibly do to successfully live with a person, who is arrogant, egotistical, entitled, and emotionally abusive? Is it possible to be with someone for the long haul who is manipulative, willing to bully to keep you under control, withholds intimacy as a form of punishment, or has anger and emotionally exhausting outbursts? Surprisingly, the answer is yes. There are a few options for surviving from a narcissistic relationship, and if these don't work for you, then might be your best choice, at least for the romantic partnership.

1.Pay attention and study your partner.

This may seem like an odd tip, however, being open to stepping outside of your relationship to observe your partner and ascertain their level of narcissism might help you find what you need to be more present and accepting of their issue. It can help you to emotionally detach so that you are not emotionally abused, help you gain more information about their tactics for behaving in certain ways, and can help you reset the habits by taking a different approach to arguments and challenging situations. If you can be an outside observer of your partner so that you can analyze and organize their behavior, you might be able to regain your emotional balance and clarity about the situation.

2.Call out the problem.

This one might be difficult if your partner is in a state of total denial about their issue. In many cases, a narcissist might boast about their narcissism and cite it as being a healthy quality and positive attribute of their overall personality. Once you have shown your partner how you have identified their issue, which is not likely to go well, you may be able to help them understand more clearly the moments when they are portraying their narcissistic tendencies. You might carefully state, "please be mindful, your narcissism is showing up." Avoid sarcasm at all costs, and you might have an effective way of telling your partner when they are opening up the can of worms. This will likely only be effective if the narcissistic partner feels safe and that they can trust you.

3.Understand the cycle of abuse.

The abuse cycle goes something like this: feeling threatened, acting abusive as a reaction, and appointing themselves the victim, therefore, feeling more empowered. Once you understand the cycle, you can learn how to stop it from playing out.

4.Understand the Tactics of Abuse

Narcissists tend to be creatures of habit. Once they find a tactic that works, they will use it repeatedly until it doesn't work anymore. Here are the seven ways a person can be abused: verbally, mentally, physically, emotionally, spiritually, sexually, and financially. These types of abuse can be carried out in a variety of ways, some of them include the following: twisting the truth or lying, gaslighting, sexual persuasion, limiting financial access, two-way thinking, aggression, and intentionally confusing you. Try to observe these tactics without taking it personally.

5.Offer a little bit of "supply."

Remember what the narcissist wants the most? They want you to feed their ego, and the best way to do that is by giving them the attention they are craving in the form of affection, adoration, compliments, etc. Telling them how impressive they are or how good they are at something goes a long way. If you did this every day, you would be supplying the ego tank, which might alleviate other issues. It is not a manipulation tactic if you understand how NPD works.

6.Resetting expectations is helpful.

Since narcissists lack empathy, they won't reciprocate when you offer them yours. Allowing yourself to be present and loving without expecting that it will occur to the narcissist will help your reality within the partnership. Expect them to behave as they always do and adjust your expectation of what they will offer you in return for your love.

7.Establish healthy boundaries wherever possible.

A good example of creating boundaries is not to play the games of the narcissist. They may want to play a blame game or a name-calling game that will escalate and leave you feeling unhappy. The best way to handle a narcissist is to honor your boundaries. They may not like it at first, but you will be showing them that you don't need to act like they do to be in a partnership with them. Choose your battles and step away from an unnecessary argument by establishing your boundary.

8.Look for the good.

A narcissist is not an intentionally bad person. They are often just unlearned in certain mental and emotional skills that prevent them from fully understanding important life tools such as empathy, reciprocity, and unconditional love. Underneath their tactics and tools of manipulation and ego-drive, there lies a human being who wants and desires a life of love, just like everyone else. You might not want to make this your only survival tool, as it will only help you stay in cycles of forgiveness, when they need to be owning up to their actions, but you can notice the little things, like how they are good at grilling a steak or that they were always exceptional at bedtime stories for the kids.

Moving forward, let's look at some other information about the narcissist that might help you resolve some situations or issues if you want to work on fighting for your relationship, or at least, understanding your narcissistic partner to help you both function a little better in your partnership roles.

The Narcissist in Relationships

A narcissist is always looking for self-esteem enhancement. They may be considered "always insecure," and that is why they are always looking for someone to boost their ego. On the outside, they appear to be extremely confident, charming, and arrogant, but under the surface lurks a lot of doubt, issues of self-worth, and a low-grade shame that they will consistently deny.

Seeking out people who will effortlessly boost their ego and make them feel exactly how they are projecting their personality into the world is what they are after. When their need for self-esteem enhancement is not being met, they will do one of the following two things:

1.Get depressed. They can easily spiral downward into a shame-based, self-hatred that might not be easily remedied except with tons of compliments and accolades.

2.Over maximize their ego, citing their perfection, omnipotence, and amazing qualities in a grandiose and hubristic way. This can also lead to putting others down to inflate the self.

Typically, the narcissist will choose option two, not wanting to appear weak, flawed, or less than what they have boasted about themselves. If you are in a relationship with a narcissist, then you are likely to get the brunt of their need to put someone down. An example might be if they didn't get a promotion at work, causing them to feel incapable or unworthy, they might take it out on you by calling you "stupid" or incapable in whatever you are doing.

As you have read, narcissists lack empathy, and so, they don't feel bad if they hurt your feelings. It is possible they won't even see or notice whatever reaction you have to their hurtful slights, and if they happen to, it is unlikely they will care much about it. They might tell you that you are being too sensitive or blame you for having any feelings at all. To survive this reality, you will need to find a strong, emotional foothold for yourself so that you will not be easily hurt by your partner. Their goal is to hurt you to make themselves feel better. If you don't allow that to happen, then you resolve the pattern of abuse.

Key Facts About a Narcissist in a Relationship to Help You Survive

1.They do not accept blame, ever. They are unlikely to take responsibility for any wrong steps or misdeeds. If they did, it would wreck their self-esteem, and they never want to do such a thing as that.

2.They are unlikely to apologize. As much as it would be humiliating to accept any blame for something, it would be just as humiliating to apologize for it. Apologies suggest that they have done something wrong, and they are never wrong. The closest they get to an apology is the repetitious gift-giving or subtle threats like "you can pick where we eat tonight, honey."

3.They love to pick a fight. Drama and chaos are pleasurable to a narcissist, and so it will likely result in the drama that can incur from instigating little fights every day to keep themselves feeling alive and in a position of power and superiority. You won't win a fight with a narcissist so be willing to pick your battles.

4.They will not process feelings or discoveries that come from a past argument. One of the ways that people heal, grow, and evolve together is by communicating about their feelings and processing their emotions. This can usually occur after a big fight or an argument. In a healthy relationship, you can digest the cause of your fight together and learn what created the issue so that you can grow from it and not repeat it. A narcissist will not want or need to do this, and so you have to be prepared to let things go if it happens to come up again…and again…and again. Try using "we" language, instead of "I" language when you do try to talk about your feelings as a way to resolve issues at the moment. (Ex: I know we care a lot about each other and that we both want the same things in our relationship. We can find a way to be a little nicer to each other in the future, and we will work it out well.)

Boundaries for Survival

Narcissists don't have boundaries or notice when other people have them. In your relationship, it will be of significant value to you to be incredibly clear about what your boundaries are so that there is zero confusion for your partner. This might mean that you have to be clear about what kinds of narcissistic behavior you can tolerate and not let your partner cross those lines.

Some narcissist will have no boundaries about criticizing your appearance, taste in clothing, anyone's beliefs or values, the quality of someone else's relationship, and so on. Narcissists are good at hitting you where it hurts without much in the way of concern about the impact, as though they lack a filter. You may need to establish a boundary for several of these kinds of issues, like "say what you will about your parents, but leave mine out of your insults," or "I am not mad at you for suggesting my outfit is unflattering, but I will ask you to avoid comments of that kind in the future."

On another note, the drama queen or king inside of every narcissist might take unconscious pleasure in causing a scene in public, perhaps falling into a rage over the slow or terrible service at the restaurant you are eating at, or yelling at someone who accidentally bumped into them and caused their drink to spill on their clothes. Sometimes, they may take out the horrible service or the accidental cocktail spill on you, leaving you feeling humiliated and embarrassed.

However, many times, this needs to occur before you throw up a boundary is entirely up to you, but you might need to consider saying that you will not attend any more public outings with them until they are ready to accept that sometimes things can go awry and it isn't anyone's fault. If they are unwilling to see your side, you may need to accept that the relationship may not be worth the public humiliation. Another boundary that must exist is that you cannot allow excessive verbal abuse to occur. If you let someone consistently talk you down and make you feel worthless, they are emotionally abusive. These tactics are incredibly damaging to a person and are often the gateway for more harmful forms of abuse, like physical or sexual. It is important to have strong boundaries with your partner so that they know that you are unwilling to allow them to talk to you in such awful ways with such hurtful words. You may want to cut this off right at the moment that it begins to save yourself a deeper wound on.

If that isn't possible with your partner, it may be time to recognize that you are in an abusive situation and you need to remove yourself from as soon as possible. You will learn more about narcissistic abuse and how it can affect someone in a relationship with a narcissist.

Narcissistic Abuse: What Is It and How Will It Affect Me?

Emotional manipulation is one of the red flags, or hallmarks, of what narcissistic abuse can look like. A narcissist will utilize language in certain ways to shift the blame to their partner or someone else, cause you to question your feelings or reality, and give you the feeling that you are the one at fault and not the narcissist.

In a way, narcissistic abuse is a means of thought control because of the ways that they use language to foster guilt, regret, paranoia, self-doubt, and other mental/emotional states. Overall, the abuse is a form of mental and emotional manipulation that causes the victim of the abuse to question their desires, thoughts, personal autonomy, and more, all for the gain of the narcissist's priorities and intentions. Here are ways that it can appear in your life when you are a victim of narcissistic abuse:

 You might question your sanity.

 You could be convinced to mistrust supportive people in your life, like your family and friends.

- You may feel convinced that only the narcissist cares for you and loves you and that everyone else has abandoned you.

These situations are not always occurring all of the time and are the symptoms of being mentally and emotionally manipulated by the narcissist. It happens to manifest in these ways and can be very subtle and occur over a long time before you are even able to recognize that you are emotionally abused and manipulated.

Chapter 7. Self-Control And Emotional Balancing

You may have heard that you can't find love until you learn to love yourself. This is often true of most things. You can't learn to be patient with others until you learn to be patient with yourself. Sure, you might be more patient with others than you are yourself already. Yet, you'll find that when you control yourself at being patient with others, it is most likely a failure because you have absolutely no patience with yourself when it comes to that particular kind of mistake.

Often times, we request forgiveness because our intention was not aimed toward harm. You might say you're sorry but you did not mean to offend. What you mean is that it was not your intention to cause offense. In this case, you apologize and request forgiveness for that apology based upon the explanation that you did not mean to offend. When you make a mistake, ask yourself if you meant to make that mistake. If you did, you might have some further reckoning to do with yourself. If you didn't, you might approach yourself the way you would approach someone else who made an unintentional mistake. Or, you could approach yourself the way you would want someone else to approach your unintentional mistake—with forgiveness.

It's a strange thought, I realize. Being patient with others requires learning to be patient with yourself, and being patient with yourself requires treating yourself with the kind of patience you treat others. It seems paradoxical, I know. What it actually accomplishes, however, is the resolution of a paradox.

A paradox is something that seems contradictory but somehow is not. It seems contradictory that you'd need to learn to be patient with yourself to be patient with others because you're naturally more patient with others. It isn't actually a contradiction, though.

It means that if you take your more natural disposition to be patient and apply it to yourself, you'll be even more patient with others because you'll resolve those instances of complete inability to be patient with yourself. You'll resolve your failures in times of patience. Again, your failures when it comes to patience can usually be linked to those instances in which you afford yourself no patience. If you can afford yourself no patience for tardiness, you will be unable to afford others patience either. This isn't necessarily a bad thing. You could live a completely fulfilled life without patience for tardiness. The point is not about the matter.

The point is that the more patience you show yourself, the more patience you'll show others. Since you naturally show more patience to others than yourself, show yourself the kind of patience you show others. Once you've allowed yourself more patience, you will find you have more patience for others. It's that simple (or, that complicated). In either case, you can do it.

There are a multitude of activities you can do to improve upon your patience with yourself. Your patience with yourself is crucial for your ability to recover and develop new relationships.

It is important that you learn to guard yourself from entering into another relationship with a narcissist but it is also important that you do not become so impatient with anything that reminds you of the narcissist in your last relationship that you struggle to form new relationships.

The world is a more stimulating place than the narcissist you were with made it feel. You will need to come up with new activities to find yourself in the world again. The relationship you were in with a narcissist attacked your sense of identity, boundaries, reality, and control. You will need to actively participate in activities that put you back to a place where you can reclaim your sense of identity and control.

Your goal is to find activities to reestablish what was taken from you. You will want to reestablish your boundaries. You will want to reclaim your identity. You will want to find a relationship in which reciprocation is readily available and understood as important.

You have the tools in your home, neighborhood, and backyard to reestablish your boundaries. Actively pursue the reinstatement of your boundaries. You have the tools to reclaim your identity. Actively pursue your own sense of self. Recognize how it was stifled and how you can get it back.

Admitting that there has been a problem in your life that caused you to lose your sense of identity will be crucial for your recovery. You must get out into the world and find your place again. You must reclaim it without the narcissist you were in a relationship.

Yoga is a great way to stimulate a fruitful connection between mind, body, and one's surroundings in people who might not be ready to become active in institutionalized sports and other such strenuous activities. This is the perfect example of a theme you could take so far beyond the ten poses offered in this.

The ten poses offered were selected because they promote mindfulness which will help you reclaim your identity as you work toward mindfulness of yourself and your body's needs. The narcissist you were in a relationship with disrespected your body's boundaries and your mind's need for human connection and grounding in reality. It is time for you to find activities that tie you to the ground again and help you look inward.

Like yoga or anything else, mindfulness can be practiced and honed; it just takes a conscious effort. Conscientiousness is mindfulness, after all. You will hone mindfulness as soon as you start doing activities for yourself again. You simply have to do the work to articulate the experience and provide yourself with the understanding that you are doing things for yourself again.

These activities are meant to give you ideas to instigate theses experience and to inspire a reclamation of identity. Use them well but feel free to create your own experiences along the way. The point is simply to get started conscientiously.

You'll find that mindfulness/conscientiousness inspires self-reflection. If you have wondered how anyone can teach self-reflection, you've asked a great question. Some people seem to be turned inward. Others seem to be turned outward. We all seem to have the potential to change our gaze, though.

When you were with a narcissist, both of you gazed into them. Now it is time for you to start practicing gazing inward toward yourself and then outward toward other things than the narcissist that convinced you that your gaze was most worthwhile when it was on them.

Self-awareness is an important part of life. Children become self-conscious at a scary point in their life. We use the word self-conscious colloquially to mean something like bashful or socially anxious. Its literal meaning is essentially to be self-aware—to be aware of one's self as a self. Any child will become self-aware and self-conscious (both meanings now apply) without much warning. It is important that, when this happens, they know how to self-reflect and then speak to others about their self-reflections.

This is how we move between turning inward and turning outward. What you will be learning to do once again is honor your self-awareness and your ability to turn inward and outward. The reason for this is that you have had your gaze turned toward the narcissist for a long time. It is time to turn it toward yourself and others.

Some people get stuck in their inward lives. Struggles that result from this are numerous. This can make relationships challenging. It can make holding a job challenging. It is crucial to your recovery that you neither get stuck retreating totally back into yourself nor outward without reclaiming your sense of identity. The narcissist you were with was empty inside. He or she tried to empty you out too. Don't be like them. You have to find the substance within yourself without forgetting to do what the narcissist struggled to do—look outside of yourself too. You need to make these passages. You need to find yourself without getting stuck there.

The walks in nature will pull you outward. The daily tasks listed in the following will make you self-aware and test your ability to turn your sights toward something in the world. It will make you remember how to be more aware of your own body and your boundaries.

The point involved in all of the activities listed in the coming is to help you turn into yourself and out of yourself while reclaiming your identity and regaining your control. You need to recover actively. Your abuse was experienced passively. It is time to be active now.

Technology is precisely mediation, which makes it the opposite of immediacy. Technology is a go-between. Someone creates something for us. We do not have to engage in the world directly. We get to do it directly. We may not be able to speak with someone directly but with a social media app we can speak with them indirectly.

We can even spy on someone, making the experience overtly indirect. They don't have to know we are looking into their lives and interests because we can peek into their lives and interests indirectly.

Overall, this encourages more direct interaction between you and your world. One point these activities will continue to stress is that you actively consider yourself to be working toward your recovery every day that you are no longer in a relationship with a narcissist. So, of course, the first step is making sure this is right for you. Hopefully, the first couple of have helped you establish whether or not you were in fact in a relationship with a narcissist.

The last acknowledged why you might not have been certain about whether or not the narcissist you were in a relationship perfectly fit the textbook examples of a narcissist. You might have thought you were in a relationship with a narcissist but felt that the narcissist you were with knew how to hide being a narcissist at times.

The truth is that narcissists are good at hiding what they are ashamed of. They cannot handle shame so they do not want to feel it. They will avoid it. If they were ashamed of their parent who was a narcissist, they might be especially good at hiding. You must think of the surprise outbursts and the abuse you did experience. Otherwise, you won't ever feel like you're reading the right.

If you are sure by now that you were in a relationship with a narcissist, regardless of their ability to hide it from you occasionally, it is time for you to move towards acceptance of your abuse. Only once you accept the abuse you experienced can you move past it. It is time for you to acknowledge it and face reality in the way the narcissist could not.

You must undo the issues they caused due to the issues they had. First, you should realize that they may have passed on some of their tendencies to you. In other words, you might also now experience a difficulty to deal with shame, accept reality, put up boundaries, and have reciprocal relationships. You will need to get over these issues in order to recover.

Chapter 8. Re-Parenting The Inner Child

It is recognized in the world of psychology that narcissism often comes from a defect in the development of a healthy self. The widely accepted theory is that an individual's sense of self continues to develop throughout their childhood. Children grow, mature, and gain social skills through interactions with other people. Most children use their parents as a role model for gaining skills such as learning empathy, how to handle criticism and approval, and recognizing limitations in their own self. This is how they cultivate a realistic image of themselves and their parents. Problematic development may occur when parents lack empathy themselves, or fail to model healthy self-esteem to their children. Parents may be either excessively indulgent of the child, or overly critical. Either parenting style can have negative consequences on the child's growth and development.

Excessive Adoration

Parents who provide excessive adoration to their children do not balance praise with constructive criticism. They are overly permissive, show too much admiration towards the child, and do not share enough realistic feedback. The child grows up in environment that is lacking in parental control.

This type of parent often has narcissistic traits themselves. They see their child as an extension of themselves, and are therefore unlikely to see the child's faults. This causes them to become overly indulgent, praise too often, and to over-inflate their child's abilities, talents, looks and skills. In many cases, excessively adoring parents give their children all kinds of material goods to make them happy, but tend not to spend a lot of time with them. The children receive things and items from their parents, but not a lot of undivided attention.

An overly indulgent parenting style can lead children to develop a false sense of entitlement. These children grow up believing that nothing is ever their fault, and often maintain this belief as they mature into adulthood. Children in an environment such as this grow up privileged and spoiled, and expect that others will continue to do things for them as they wish. They never learn how to deal with feelings of disappointment as their parents never did anything to upset them when they were young.

Individuals surrounded by excessive adoration grow up without learning how to fail gracefully, and without the opportunity to build up a healthy, realistic level of confidence. Instead, they learn to associate their self-image with the amount of admiration that they receive from others. If the household has no siblings, these children are even more likely to develop narcissistic tendencies. Children without siblings are less inclined to have to share their parent's attention or defer to the needs of others. Some never get the opportunity to learn how to deal with conflict in an appropriate way.

Excessive Criticism

On the opposite end of the spectrum lies the parenting style of excessive criticism. Excessively critical parents are overly authoritative, harsh, and controlling. They never seem to be satisfied with anything the child says or does. They show too much parental control, set unrealistically high expectations of the child, and do not model enough understanding and empathy. Excessive criticism can lead children to grow up becoming Narcissistic abusely dependent on others.

Children growing up in this environment do not receive the love and attention that they need, and instead experience at least some level of parental neglect. These children learn quickly that they are not valued for who they are, nor are they loved unconditionally. Instead, it becomes clear to them that they mean the most to their parents only when they manage to meet unrealistically high expectations.

Children who experience an excessively critical upbringing are naturally at increased risk of developing fragile self-esteem. They grow up needing to draw attention and love from others, as they do not receive enough at home. These children learn to regulate their self-esteem according to the value that others assign to them. They feel they must conform to expectations in order to have a positive self-image, and grow up expecting others to do the same for them.

Narcissistic traits may develop as a defense to emotional abuse and unpredictable care from parents. Children can grow up to be emotionally needy in response to neglect and lack of empathy.

They may begin to over-focus on the part of themselves that brings admiration from others, and this can lead to an inflated sense of self. This causes them to become grandiose on the outside while remaining quite vulnerable and needy on the inside. These individuals develop manipulative behaviors and lack of empathy because this was what was modelled to them by their parents.

Chapter 9. Reprogramming And Rebuilding Self Trust

Find Your Self

Thanks to the chaotic nature of your emotions that we in the, your state of mind right now is not centered around your real self. You may even have forgotten who that person is, or was, before the abuse began.

That person is still in there, waiting for you to clear a path through the turmoil and the lies your abuser told you for them to come back. To find your self again, you need to step back and view yourself from afar. This means evaluating your current state in detail and then looking at that evaluation from an objective distance.

The best way to do this is to remove your thoughts and emotions from your own mind and put them somewhere else, where you can examine them more clearly. A great way to do this is to begin a daily journal, pouring all your emotions and the thoughts you've had onto paper. Make sure to concentrate on how you feel, not just on the events that made you feel that way.

Other alternatives include painting or drawing or writing your feelings in the form of poetry. Choose a medium that you feel suits you and will allow you to take what's happening on your head and put it on paper instead. It can take practice, especially if you're not used to giving voice to your emotions, but it's very important that you put every last piece of you onto that paper.

Take time every day for this activity. Close yourself into a private space where you won't be interrupted and where nobody else can see what you are creating. This is just for you – keep the results somewhere secure, so you don't have to worry that anyone else will ever see them.

And now read back your words or look at the picture you have created. View it as though it was made by somebody else than yourself. What does it tell you about the person who made it? What is going on in that person's mind, what flaws can you see in their thinking? Where, in other words, are they blaming themselves or torturing themselves for things that you, as the independent viewer, would not see them as at fault?

Sometimes you won't be able to see these things right away. It can help to come back to journal entries or drawings that you created several days before, now that there is some distance between the creator and your work.

Take time to your work regularly, not just focusing on today's entry but on all of it, right back to the start. As your healing progresses, you will see that reflected – and you will be able to look at the earliest entries and see the conflict your abuser imposed right there on the paper.

Creating a mirror of yourself in this way not only allows you to pour out all the damaging emotions in a safe way, it also allows you to see them outside yourself. It allows you to see the true you, and the progress you are making, and the progress you still need to make.

Reclaim Your Self

Many survivors discover in the aftermath of abuse that their abuser slowly yet surely changed them into a different person – one who focused on the activities, pastimes and ideas that their abuser wanted them to. Now, as you walk the road to recovery, is the time to rediscover what it was that you liked, loved and enjoyed.

This step is without a doubt the most fun and rewarding of all of them. Standing alone, in charge of your own life again, you finally get to ask yourself what YOU would like to eat for dinner. Where would YOU like to go this weekend? What clothes would YOU like to wear and what changes do YOU want to make to your life for it to make you more happy?

Right here and right now you have the chance to build your life exactly as you want it to be. This may not seem quite such a joyful idea as it would if you were not fighting the aftereffects of abuse, but it can be a valuable step towards recovery and the very experience of reclaiming your life can be an excellent therapy.

But while you do this, consider building up your own skill set. Consider choosing the kinds of activity that will make you more independent, more skillful and more capable than you were even before the abuse began.

This isn't necessarily to say that you weren't all of these things before. It's a way of proving to yourself that there is nothing you can't do if you choose to and that you have no need to rely on anyone else to help you through life. It's about empowerment and rebuilding the strength inside you.

Consider learning new skills, such as cookery or self defense or a language. Consider taking up a hobby such as travel or computer programming. Consider exploring your talents through a painting course or learning to play an instrument or take part in a sport.

Take this one step at a time – it can be terrifying to realize that the pillars supporting your self image have been torn away, even when those pillars were toxic and were shaping you into a person who suited your abuser's desires.

Listen to the little voice inside you that is saying, "I want". What does it want to do? Where does it want to go? Nourish this little voice, give it what it desires as far as you can.

It belongs to the real you, the one who was hidden in darkness. It's telling you how to become yourself once again – how to reclaim the joy of life in the way that will truly make you happy, how to take back control. With time, the very act of rediscovering yourself and giving yourself the gifts of choices that suit your real self will help to heal you – and will help the real you flourish.

Rebalance Your Life

A more formal version of this rediscovery of who you are and what you want is to reintroduce balance into your life. This is about what you need as well as what you want and involves rebuilding a balance that may have been toppled by your abuser's actions.

Your abuser may have removed your connection to friends, they may have insisted you live and work in places that weren't really your choice, they may have chosen your hobbies for you by demanding you do the things they wanted to do. One or more areas of your life may currently be lacking equilibrium, and it's time to bring that back. The areas you will need to look at include:

- Your career (or future career if you are still in school)
- Your relationships
- Your living situation
- Your hobbies and interests
- Your beliefs

First, you will need to look at each of these areas in turn and ask yourself how the abuse affected them. Did, for example, your abuser mock your spiritual beliefs and make you feel guilty for wanting to attend services? Did they choose the apartment you rented because it was more convenient to them or suited their tastes and make you feel obliged to agree?

As you do this, it will have a secondary effect on your recovery: it will show you exactly what impacts your abuser had very clearly. This clarity can give you the strength to avoid including your abuser in your life in the future and also the strength to recognize your own boundaries in future relationships. The internal strength you are building by finding yourself and dedicating yourself to your own needs, wants and dreams is armor against allowing someone else to take control of your life in the future.

Once you have determined what changed in these areas of your life thanks to the abuse, you can think about what you want instead – and then make those changes happen. As you do, think about the boundaries you want to set.

Tell yourself what you will and won't accept from outside influence in the future. For instance, you might say you will never again allow someone to stop you from attending your horse riding classes because they are important to your happiness and your sense of self. Perhaps you will pledge to yourself that you will always attend Thanksgiving with your family and that there would need to be genuine negotiation before you broke that pledge.

This is important because controlling, narcissistic behavior is more common than we like to admit and your chances of experiencing it again are higher than zero. Falling under the power of an emotional abuser is extraordinarily easy and can be harrowing at the time and for a long while after, but the one advantage it has left you with is the ability to see such abuse for what it is.

With boundaries in place and a clear vision of who you are and what you need to be content, you will find it easier to ignore the ghosts of the past and you will also be in a better position to see the behavior of a narcissistic person for what it is – without allowing it to affect you.

Restoring balance will meanwhile help you to regain the stability you need and your enjoyment of life in general. It will help you shed the control your abuser had over you and place your focus on the future, instead of the past.

It will enable you to get back the things you had lost, even if you didn't see them slipping away at the time, and stabilize your life in the way that best suits your hopes and dreams for tomorrow.

Let Go

Recovering from abuse can take weeks, months, even years. A decade down the line, you may find yourself reacting in an all-too-familiar way to a trigger that your abuser put in place, though the person who triggered that response had no similar intentions.

As you've worked through your healing, you've placed focus on strengthening yourself and learning to look at your emotions from the outside. You have seen from a dispassionate place what effects such abuse can have on a person and identified how exactly it affected you. You have created a new balance, rediscovered who you are and slowly rebuilt your life.

None of the steps we've covered will happen overnight. Sometimes you'll take three steps backwards after taking one backwards. Do your best to be kind to yourself throughout this journey – there is a lot for you to work through. And don't hesitate to call on the help of your professional ally at any and all stages; they are your strongest support right now because they have both the ability to listen objectively and the training to help you find out your step.

Resist the temptation to engage your abuser again from this new place of strength. Yes, you are now better equipped to deal with them. Yes, you are now able to see the traps before you step in them. But no, they will not ever change and they cannot ever be a positive part of your life, in any capacity. And there will be no closure, because a narcissist is not able to see their behavior for what it is – they lack the empathy and emotional depth to do so.

Let go of your abuser forever; shed all contact if possible or keep it limited if not. Keep your emotions in check if you have no choice but to see them – remember they will be using any weapons at their disposal to bring you back in line and all of these weapons play with your emotions. Take a step back from yourself and look at the situation as though you were gazing on one of your diary entries. If it helps, remember that there is nothing so frustrating to a narcissist as not being able to elicit a reaction from you.

In time, you will feel ready for a new relationship. It's not something to be advised during your recovery because there will be too much going on inside you for you to give your heart freely and without the baggage of the abuse that happened to you. But when you do feel ready, you'll have the confidence to know that you are entering into it with the armor of self-knowledge and self-esteem.

Forewarned is forearmed, as they say, and you have suffered through the most eye-opening warning possible. You know what emotional abuse can do to your life and your self; you know how it happens and have seen the slow, insidious creep towards losing control. You can break the cycle of abuse – you do not ever need to be unhappy like this again.

Continue to practice your new skills, not only to keep that healing on track but also to keep you emotionally healthy in the future.

And finally, recognize the achievements you have made here for exactly how wonderful they are. You have rebuilt yourself from the ashes, created a new path for yourself that will make you genuinely happy and armored yourself against negative influences in the future. You are a new person – you are the real you.

What happened to you during the abusive relationship was not your fault and, as you are now better able to see, was more to do with your abuser than it was anything to do with you. But what you've achieved during your recovery was all down to your own efforts. This is an achievement to be proud of, and it's one you can and should claim as your own.

Chapter 10. Healing Emotional Trauma

Once you survive a narcissistic relationship, nothing is more important than healing. You have to learn how to regain your self-esteem and control. Recovery is not just about getting out of an abusive situation; it is primarily about creating a new emotional safety net for yourself. It is possible that it might take you a while to get over your trauma, but it is not the end of the world. Recovery is a gradual but efficient process. The following are some of the important things that you must keep in mind when working your way back into normalcy:

- Self-soothing and grounding techniques

A narcissist will confuse your concept of abandonment. If you have had issues with abandonment before, they will get worse during your relationship with them. The betrayal and subsequent abandonment makes you afraid. You feel you are abandoned because you are not good enough. There are negative emotions that can emanate from this, including panic, depression and sadness. Many victims make the mistake of turning back to their abuser because they have learned to believe they cannot survive without them.

Grounding yourself can help you overcome these problems. It is normal to feel like you lack something in the aftermath of this abuse. However, you do not have to react or respond to it by going back. Your amygdala might attempt to hijack your emotions from time to time, and the only way out is to remind yourself why you are not going back.

- Ask for help

You might not be capable of handling your recovery on your own, so seek professional support. In the wake of a narcissistic relationship, you often feel you cannot trust anyone to understand what you have been through. The rest of the world feels alienated from you. Instead of seeing people as a source of support, you feel they will judge you and you hold back.

At the end of an abusive relationship there are so many things that are left unresolved. You have a lot of unanswered questions, unfulfilled promises, unreciprocated love and affection. All these are things that you might not be able to deal with on your own. It is wise to get professional help so that you can understand yourself better, and manage your expectations better too.

The pain you feel at the end of this relationship is two-fold. You are in pain because the one person you invested everything on has turned out to be the worst investment of your life so far. You are also in pain because the relationship that you had so much faith in did not work out. You, therefore, need to heal from these two situations to completely heal and move on with life.

- Stay away from your abuser

Resist the urge to reach out to your abuser. Even if you miss them, stay away from them. Cut them off your contact list and forget about them. The confusion you experience will pass. One of the biggest mistakes that many victims make is that even after they are done with the relationship, they still leave room in their lives just in case their narcissistic partner can come back.

Forget about second chances. A lot of victims who go back to their abusers end up worse, and some end up dead. You don't have to reach out to them. Some narcissists will reach out to you after a long period of silence. They might reach out promising to change, telling you how things have been difficult in their lives since you left them. If you fall for this trick, you will never heal.

Whatever they do with their lives once you walk away is not your concern. They are adults and can make adult choices about their lives. You are an adult too, and your adult choice is to start afresh. The moment your abuser reaches out to you and you allow them a few minutes of your time, you are back to the very beginning. Never forget that narcissists always believe you need them more than they need you. They have a lot of tricks up their sleeve that will manipulate you back into their trap, if you allow them.

- Rebuilding your life

There are a lot of things that you can do to rebuild your life. Rebuilding your life is not just about reengaging people you had cut off, it is also about rebuilding your esteem and confidence. You have a lot of feelings bottled up inside. Don't keep them locked down, release them. Find different avenues where you can release your feelings.

Start writing, painting, gardening; or join a dancing class, an amateur sports team; and schedule social meetings with your close friends and have fun together. These are just a few things you can do to help you feel better again. Try and avoid risky or unhealthy behavior though, because these might end up in disaster.

- Accept your partner

You need to accept your partner for who they are. They are narcissists. They might be suffering from NPD. What acceptance does is to remind you that there is nothing you could have done to make them any different. They believe they are perfect the way they are. Since they cannot accept you as you are, it is best if you walk away and start afresh.

Accepting your partner's narcissism is another step towards forgiving yourself. You did all you could, but they could never change. There was never an intent to change in them. This will also help you overcome the feelings of self-doubt that you might have harbored for a long time.

- Forgiveness

Are you willing to forgive yourself for your role in the relationship? Forgiveness sets the tone for healing. Remember that forgiveness will only come after you have accepted your role in the relationship, and accepted responsibility for it. Everyone makes mistakes. It is normal to find yourself in a hardship situation out of your own doing. This is life, forgive yourself and move on. It is the things that you do and how you respond to these situations that will determine how your life turns out.

- Ease the pressure to recover

With your abuser out of the picture, there is a lot of pressure for you to recover and build a new life. Try to tone down the pressure. There is no time limit within which you must recover and start living a normal life. Your partner might have stolen your identity from you, but this does not mean you have to hurry to earn it back.

Recovery is a gradual process. Everything around you takes time. You have to readjust to a lot of things in life, and if you rush it, you might be overwhelmed. It is okay to feel sorry for yourself, but don't let it turn into self-pity, or you might turn into a self-loathing individual. There is no race to recovery, it is a process.

Fundamentals Of Recovery From Narcissistic Abuse

There are four important tenets that will define your recovery process, and help you survive a narcissist. Everything else you do throughout your emotional journey revolves around the following:

1.Self-esteem

Self-esteem is simply you supporting yourself. You take back control from your partner, control over your emotions, your behavior, actions, your mind and your body. Everything that your partner took from you is back in your hands.

Esteem is not just about yourself, it is also about the way you interact with the environment around you. It is about how you respond to people, institutions and so forth. It is important to get back control over your esteem, because without it, you will continue on the destructive path of self-sabotage that your abusive partner had led you to.

You have to learn to speak positively to yourself. Don't hold back from pursuing things that appeal to you. If you had resorted to substance abuse to numb the pain of your abusive relationship, talk to someone about quitting.

Having lived through a life where you were afraid to try anything, it is time for you to motivate yourself to throw your hat in the ring. You might not be selected, but you challenged for something. Take back control over your life.

2.Self-love

No one will ever love you more than you love yourself. Loving yourself is about protecting the things that are dear to you. Nurture your feelings and emotions. You have to stop sacrificing your needs so someone else can be happy. Make yourself a priority. Let go of the tendency to abandon your needs for the sake of a superficial connection with someone else.

One of the ways you can go about rekindling your self-love is to realize the things that you can control in life and those that you cannot. Remind yourself why you feel it is necessary for you to change something in your life. For most ladies, one of the things they have to deal with is body shaming when they get out of a narcissistic relationship. You have to learn to accept and appreciate your body the way it is.

In case you are worried about things that you are unable to change, teach yourself to drown those emotions and sentiments instead. Find things that you are grateful for and enjoy doing them. If possible, do them with people who are close to you so that you remember just how amazing your life should be, and embrace it.

3.Self-trust

Fear and doubt are common in victims of narcissistic abuse. Your partner made sure the only person who made decisions in your life was them. They took away your ability to decide what you want or how you want things done. They became the ultimate source of power in your life.

When you are unable to trust in yourself, you struggle to do things. You cannot make quick decisions because you are afraid you might choose the wrong thing. Your worry is that all the bad things you have experienced might happen to you if you decide for yourself. As a result, you second-guess yourself all the time.

Trust in your gut. Do something because you feel it is right. Don't hold back. To rebuild trust in yourself, you must take action. It is impossible to do this without stepping out and challenging yourself to try.

4.Self-worth

Why is it important that you rediscover your self-worth after walking away from a narcissistic partner? Self-worth is about realizing what your value is. When you understand your worth, it is difficult for someone to begrudge you what you deserve. Your value system sets you up high, and people who interact with you do so because they understand and appreciate how you treasure yourself. If you can't see your worth, no one else will. Even those who do will never take you seriously.

The challenge with lacking self-worth is that you usually end up compromising where you should not. Lack of self-worth also makes you feel ashamed and unworthy even without anyone provoking a reaction from you. You inherently believe you don't deserve the good things because you are not good enough.

Speak up for your rights. Don't shy away from the spotlight. Someone might use this to take advantage of you. Respect and take care of yourself. To rebuild your self-worth, you must embrace courage. You have to realize that even if things get difficult, you will make it.

Resetting Boundaries After Surviving A Narcissist

Emotional abuse in a relationship usually comes with breached boundaries. You love a partner who doesn't recognize your need for or respect your space. People view boundaries in different ways. Their reaction to you having boundaries in the first place might not always be what you expect.

Some people react negatively, and others even turn cold towards you when you mention your boundaries. Should you back down? No, not at all. Boundaries are the essence of who you are. They are a representation of your thoughts, feelings and what sets them apart from everyone else. Boundaries are your ethical code; they determine wrong from right and give your life direction.

With boundaries, you can protect yourself from exploitation and manipulation. You also have limits to the things you can do for people. A narcissistic partner will usually break your boundaries. They don't respect you and this makes you feel unnecessarily vulnerable. At the end of that relationship, you should find a way to reestablish your boundaries.

The good thing about rebuilding your boundaries is that you also rebuild your esteem in the process, and as time goes by, you learn to love yourself again. You learn to trust and believe in yourself. How can you reset and rebuild your boundaries after such a traumatic experience?

- Rethink your values

Your core values are the foundation of your boundaries. Take time and re-examine them afresh. These are the principles and guidelines that control your life. They are the things you hold in high regard, like respect, honesty, affection, humility and loyalty. It is important to understand your values because they help you make the right decision. A decision system should always be based on the things that align with your core beliefs. By understanding your values, you are in a better position to understand how to react or respond to different situations. You know what to do when facing a difficult situation. You know why it is important for you to walk away from someone because they don't fit in with your values.

These are decisions that do not just protect you, they also help you live a life you are proud of and you are at peace with your decisions. This way, you cannot second-guess yourself. If you have to make a big decision, you do so because you know it was the right thing to do. If it turns out wrong, you don't feel bad about it because you know it was still the right decision for you.

- Learn to say NO!

A narcissist will make you learn how to feel guilty each time you don't respond to their needs the way they want you to. Being a yes man or yes woman is exhausting. You never do anything for yourself. You never think for yourself. Your life revolves around what other people think or what they want you to do.

Learning to say no is not just about stopping someone from exploiting you, it is also about respecting yourself. It takes nothing from your humanity or personality to say no. Don't fall for the trick when someone tries to guilt you into believing saying no will appear aggressive or pushy. A subtle no is all you need, and stand by it.

To protect your boundaries, you must learn to be selfish. Your integrity is tested each time someone tries to have you go back on your no. Another problem you must overcome is the need to explain your reasons. A simple explanation is sufficient. However, if you over-explain yourself, this is a sign that you worry about what people think about you. It is a sign that you need to stop pleasing people all the time and be bold in your decisions.

At times, you don't necessarily need to explain your no. It might be a new experience for you, but give it time. It will grow on you. Some months or years down the line, you will realize it was one of the best decisions you ever made.

- Responsibility to yourself

Your responsibility in this life is to yourself. A life without boundaries opens you up to accept all manner of rubbish from your abuser and anyone else who can take advantage of you. You meet emotional wrecks who feel you can nurture them back to the person they are supposed to be. However, while you take care of them, they chip away at your personality and stability gradually.

You cannot be responsible for someone else's emotional wellbeing. If you allow them in, they will drain you. Why should you be exhausted from dealing with someone's trauma, and as they go away feeling happy and relaxed, your life falls apart because you can barely breathe?

While the emotional challenges you have experienced over the past might make you think you must take care of someone else's feelings, this is not true. Most narcissists simply project their baggage onto you and make you carry their weight alongside yours. You can understand them, but you cannot process the meaning and value of their emotions on their behalf. Step aside and let everyone deal with their own baggage.

- Respect your boundaries

There would be no point in setting boundaries if you were not going to follow through. Granted, this might be a new process for you, but it does not mean you will not hack it. For someone who has never had boundaries in their life, you must learn where to draw the line. You must be the first one to respect your boundaries before you expect someone else to do the same.

If this is your first time setting boundaries, start with simple things and learn to respect them. From there, build on to deeper stuff like your emotions. The discomfort you feel when rejecting someone because they don't respect your boundaries is normal. You are protecting something bigger than their feelings. Besides, they are responsible for their feelings. You are responsible for yours and your happiness.

Chapter 11. Taking Back Your Life

It really is simple, a narcissist isn't going to shrug their shoulders and say: "okay, see you" and allow you to walk away without anything else happening. They will probably go back to their best behavior to get you back.

They do this for one reason and that is because they hate to be rejected and they take it very badly. If you leave a narcissist, you are rejecting them, and it doesn't matter how you were treated. They won't see all the manipulation and abuse that they did to you. According to them, you were treated like a queen or king. They will view your walking away and it is going to make them extremely angry or cut into the depths of their self-conscious. You should do one of the following:

They will get resentful and angry. They will bombard you with posts on social media, texts, messages and calls about how they are better without you and before they hang up they will call you every name under the sun.

They could be the epitome of charm again and begin reminding you of all the good times you had together.

If you realize the first one is happening, ignore them and block them every way possible. This is just their pride taking over. They see you rejecting them. They view it as you are making a horrible mistake. They are trying to turn the tables on you. You can see through all their scandals. Block them any way possible; their phone number, on social media; don't go to any places that they frequent, go stay with family or friends for a week or so if you are worried they might show up at your place. They will eventually get bored and tired of no response from you.

The second point is also common and this is the way most people who are in a narcissistic relationship go back to the narcissist again and again. The best answer here is to be firm and keep in mind why you left them. If you can stay with your support group, that would be the best thing you could do. These people are going to remind you about all the bad things when your resolve is waning and it is going to at times. Yes, you had some great times, and you were with them for reasons. If you are a victim of gaslighting, then you might not be sure what your step should be since you will still be suffering from the effects of emotional abuse. Your family and friends will hold you firm but you will still need to stay firm and still block their numbers and on all social media sites. The less contact you have with them, the easier it is going to be to move forward.

What Should You Expect?

- Silence eventually
- Begging
- Insults
- Pleading
- Blame games
- Bargaining

If you think you are free and clear once the silence begins, think again. If they spot you in town soon afterward, they are going to plead and bargain with you. Getting away from them will take time but it is a process you will be glad you started.

Dating Again

After you have gotten over the “getting rid of the narcissist” process, your future will look brighter. You have to give yourself time to grieve for the “dead” relationship, and whatever you do, don’t jump right into another relationship to try to get over the narcissist. If you don’t deal with all that has happened, you are risking your future. Most people who have gotten out of a narcissistic relationship are so traumatized by what happened during the relationship that they don’t want to get near anyone else again. When a new person begins to show the smallest inkling of something that seems like narcissism, they will run.

The truth is that everyone has signs of narcissism every now and then, but this doesn't mean we are true narcissists. Everyone can lack empathy at times, we could belittle others without meaning to a couple of times, and we can act in horrible ways. The difference between us and a narcissist is that we apologize and see our mistakes, a narcissist won't. Don't make a mistake of labeling everybody with the same tag.

The best way to get your feet back in the dating pool after getting out of the narcissistic relationship is to begin slowly. Here are some tips to help you:

- Take some time to just "be". Don't try to do things. Don't try to feel things. Don't push yourself. Take time to be by yourself and unpack the events and finally deal with them. If you need someone else's opinion or to find professional help, this is the time to do it.
- Focus on yourself. Now is the time to find things you enjoy doing and be nice to yourself. You have spent a long time with someone who was constantly unkind to you. You have probably forgotten how to pamper yourself and enjoy it. Find something you have always wanted to try. Take a night class, go to movies with friends, spend the weekend being lazy, go for a walk in the park, eat your favorite foods, or read that you've wanted to for a long time.
- Think about your health. After you have focused on yourself, now pay attention to your health. Have a healthy mind and body are the best revenge ever. You really shouldn't be thinking about revenge, but being a better you after you've had bad experiences will feel great. Challenge your mind, stay away from stress, get lots of sleep, get some exercise, and eat healthier foods. You will soon realize how stronger you are feeling.
- Start enjoying your life again. When you begin to feel better, and it might take some time, just begin to enjoy your life. Don't think about dating, and don't try to meet anyone new. If it does happen, let it happen. There will be plenty of time for that.

 Once you are ready, just be open to the possibility. The main point is to meet somebody who will be worthy of your attention and time. Somebody who will give you what you didn't have before. You don't need anyone who can heal or complete you. If you think you are ready, just be open to meeting people but don't put any importance on it. People who have gotten out of narcissistic relationship might be needy since they are desperately trying not to let it happen again. If you can follow these steps and put importance on building yourself back up, this shouldn't happen to you.
 Don't think that everybody is going to act like your ex. If you do find somebody and decide to begin dating, don't put them in the same boat as your ex. This is extremely important. True narcissists are extremely rare and you need to remember this. It is very unlikely that you will meet someone else who is a narcissist twice in one lifetime. Yes, it might be possible that you will meet somebody who will act a tad bit narcissistic occasionally, they aren't a true narcissist and won't bring the same problems into the relationship.
 Recognize the signs. Don't run away at the first sign of a problem. Hold your requirements for understanding and respect at the top of your list. If anyone begins to treat you horribly, address the problem and stand firm before you walk away. If living through a narcissist relationship teaches you anything, it will be that you aren't going to let the same thing happen again.
If you are thinking that you won't ever try to date again, I am fine being by myself, it is time to ask yourself why you are feeling this way. Do you really not want a relationship and you want to be alone, you want to travel, or reconnect with friends you let slip away? Are you just saying it because you are scared of being hurt again?
Some people really don't want another relationship and this is perfectly fine, given it is for the correct reasons. If you are just staying away from romantic connections because you are afraid, this is something you need to address very early. You might find your feelings will change with time but remaining closed off to connections

just because your past is clouding your judgment is going to hurt you more in the long run.

You must remember you deserve to be loved and it doesn't matter what you were forced to believe in the past.

What Happens to a Narcissist Who Won't Get Help?

We have covered a lot of information about the victim's future but what about the narcissist's future.

It isn't a nice picture if the narcissist won't get help. If they don't, it will be likely that they will just jump from one relationship to the. If they do find a long-term relationship, their partner won't be really fulfilled and happy. They will more than likely just be putting up with the narcissist.

If during the duration of the narcissist's relationship they had children, the bad news is their children will probably develop narcissist behaviors since they were exposed to it through their growing years. Even though there isn't a definite answer to what causes narcissism, there are suggestions that experiences during childhood has firm links toward developing the disorder during their adolescent or adult years.

Narcissists are known to become bitter with time. This is mainly due to people coming into their lives and then leaving them and they can't find out why. They will always put the blame onto someone else and will never see they had a role in them leaving. Most narcissistic traits get worse with age as they experience more things through their life.

You can see it is a very bleak picture and this is the sad truth about the narcissist's life. People will only stay around if they are treated nice. If they get treated like crap, they will eventually leave. Some might not get to that point but relationships with narcissists are usually empty and don't have respect and true love.

The biggest price any narcissist will pay for their actions with time will be loneliness and not ever knowing what a meaningful relationship really is. The deepest and most meaningful relationship a narcissist will have will be with themselves.

Should We Blame Social Elements?

You almost know all there is to know about narcissists and the issues and traits that go with it. We also need to look at another area. Are social elements to blame for the increasing number of narcissists?

True narcissists are very rate but it is a term that we hear more and more. For this reason, narcissistic behaviors are more common now, so we need to find out why? Is it all the social pressures we have to deal with? Is it social media? Is it because we are pressured to own the best, look, the best, and be the best?

It is unfair to put the blame of narcissism at modern society's feet. It does make one wonder if it did have a hand in it. Social media makes us aware of the way other people live and look. The influences of social media tell us that if we want to be the best, we must look our best, and this means we have to use a certain product. We get bombarded with people constantly taking selfies and full body photos and then using filters and photoshop to change their appearance drastically. The majority of what we see just isn't real. Now, do you wonder why we have all these unrealistic expectation of what we should look like, what we should be, and what we need to aim for?

No one is completely sure what causes narcissism, so it is the things we are exposed to in life? Most of the narcissistic cases are thought to come from things we experienced during childhood, but what caused those experiences? What makes someone act a specific way? What makes someone create trauma to another human that can cause them to develop a certain personality disorder? It is hard to find out, but you have to take into account all the possibilities.

We might not completely understand what causes narcissism, and there is a specific amount of stigma attached to it. If we try to be the best, it will be a constant, fruitless task. We should try to just be ourselves.

When talking about future generations, it is our responsibility to make sure our children are brought up to be happy just being who they are, without have to constantly compete to reach unrealistic goals. If we can do this, we are going to raise a generation of young people who are fulfilled, respectful, and well-mannered. These are great boosts toward avoiding trauma and personality disorders.

Chapter 12. Self-Love

Re- finding yourself is a huge part of this as is engaging in self- therapy, healing and developing your personal boundaries. Two other things which need to be emphasized are self- love and self- care. It is very well exploring the complexity of the narcissist personality and motivations in depth, yet if you do not know how to move forward and recover through practical and realistically implementable self- love and self- care measures, it is not a very integrated approach to divorcing a narcissist.

To end this we are going to briefly explore a "Self- Love and Self- Care" plan you can integrate into your daily routine, or at least take inspiration from to create your own.

"Self- Love and Self- Care Recovery Plan" for Healing & Moving Forward

Have A Morning Routine

Having a morning routine is crucial to your recovery and moving on. It keeps you motivated, dedicated to your own self- love and healing, and fully committed to your future. Habits are instinctual, we engage in daily habits all the time. Yet, once we become conscious of our habits we can evolve and develop them into routines which can best serve us.

A morning routine can include the following:

- Saying thank you to your bed. Gratitude is one of the most powerful forces and sets you up for your day. When you say thank you with sincerity, you are actively attracting more of the things you are grateful for. You are also increasing your over- all vibration. Upon waking, show gratitude towards the bed which has provided you comfort, peace and security. This will amplify your ability to utilize the law of attraction.
- Drinking lemon water or herbal tea. Lemon water helps clear your body of toxins and herbal teas can kick start your immune system. "Your health is in your wealth," and how true this statement is! Your thoughts, emotions, physical health and spiritual or holistic well- being are all intrinsically connected, so starting your day with something healthy, revitalizing, energizing and detoxifying- cleansing has a positive impact on your mind, emotions and sense of self-esteem and self- confidence. Confidence is connected to how you feel on a physical level, therefore incorporating something like lemon water or a detoxifying green tea into your morning routine will allow you to shine within. This reflects outwards!
- Morning meditation. Meditating upon waking or not long after can do great things for your self- confidence, self- esteem and ability to stay connected to your truth, further living your best life. Meditating increase energy vitality, sharpens your mind, enhances intuition, increases powers of observation and awareness, allows for higher thinking, and opens your mind to new ways of thinking, being and perceiving. It also helps enhance qualities such as empathy, compassion, kindness, sincerity and seeing the truth or wisdom in situations. It can help you be calmer and feel both happy and content inside, also stimulating advanced levels of imagination and creative thought. Merging a morning meditation into your daily routine may also open you up to new passion projects or paths for growth, connection and meeting new people.

- Inspiring documentary or podcast. Listening to an inspiring (or motivational) podcast or watching a documentary for just 10 minutes during your morning awakening period will do profound things to your self- worth, and stimulate you into action. This activity can help remind you of your own greatness and may spark creative, artistic or intellectual interests and talents. It will also remind you of how wonderful life is and why you are lucky to be alive!
- Spiritual or inspirational literature, reading or poetry. The same is true for reading. Poetry, spiritual literature or poetry, or any which engages you and stimulates your emotions and mental thought processes in a helpful way should all be merged into your routine; or whichever one or two resonate. Anything spiritual, inspirational or motivational connects you to your own source of personal power and empowers you. You may receive memories or have flashback of joyful past experiences. You may be reminded of a past version of yourself, things you said or did or how you once inspired others. Reading not long after waking can spark you in unique ways.
- Exercise or do a martial art. Gentle exercise in the morning is known to improve all areas of life. It can move trapped energy, release stored emotions, provide physical vitality and wellness, and improve your mood and outlook on life. Engaging in a light martial art such as Chi Kung (Qi Gong) or Tai Chi is also highly beneficial. These two martial arts are very gentle and help to improve your internal energy systems.

They also stimulate your inner spirit and core strength simultaneously whilst empowering you to master your mind, emotions and health.

Chapter 13. Recovering

Despite the fact that narcissistic abuse can leave behind marks or injuries so deep that you may feel that you will never be able to truly cleanse yourself of them, you can recover from it. Of course, you can never turn back time and therefore erasing the effect of narcissistic abuse altogether is impossible but you can get yourself back to your healthy self. You can care for yourself and help yourself heal. Even though, in the throes of abuse, you may not be able to recognize the person you see when you look in the mirror, you can get that sense of identity back. You can reclaim it and if you are willing to put in the effort, you will get it back.

It does not matter how long the relationship you were in lasted, nor does it matter how much abuse you endured, you can always hope to heal. While the healing process is not easy by any means, it is possible, and you will be able to do it. This will guide you, step by step, through the process of healing, pointing you in the right direction so you can begin to work on yourself. As you work, you will get to the point where you recognize your smile in the mirror. You will feel peace of mind for the first time in ages. You will feel happier, and maybe even love, again. No matter what the narcissist has told you, you are capable of change and healing, and you absolutely deserve a life filled with happiness and peace. You are worthy of love. You are worthy of respect. You are worthy of loving the person you see looking back at you in the mirror.

Acknowledge Your Abuse

Healing begins with acknowledgment. If you cannot acknowledge that what the narcissist has put you through is abuse, you may not be ready for this process. By recognizing what happened as the abuse it was, you will be able to take the steps necessary to correct for it and heal. You will erase any of the denial you have hidden the abuse behind for however long it occurred by naming it. Naming it abuse releases your blame in the abuse. No one asks for their loved ones to hurt them the way the narcissist may have hurt you, nor does anyone deserve it. When you say that the narcissist abused you, you say that the narcissist made a conscious decision to inflict unwanted harm upon you, and that pushes the blame you may have internalized from yourself onto the narcissist. With that blame lifted, you will be able to begin working on yourself.

As you go through this process, do not forget that you only control yourself. You must be responsible for yourself but you do not control how those around you react. Even if you did something as cruel as punching someone on the street, you are not in control of the other person's reaction. You did not deserve what the narcissist did to you, regardless of how minor or extreme the narcissist's manipulation may seem to you. You were an unfortunate victim, chosen because your own traits made you desirable. Instead of lamenting that some of your traits made you a victim, you should celebrate the ones that attract a narcissist—empathy and compassion are fantastic for people to have. Being patient and seeking peace is an admirable way to live. These are not bad traits to have and they do not make you a lesser person. These are traits of a good person. In this situation, the narcissist took advantage of the good person you are and used your best traits against you. Treat yourself kindly as you consider this and remember that you did not ask for it to happen.

Forgiveness And Compassion For Yourself

With the acknowledgment of the abuse, you can then move on to forgive yourself. As you established, your traits and strengths should be celebrated, not punished. Forgive yourself for blaming yourself for the abuse so you can begin to celebrate those parts of yourself. You will be able to forgive yourself for not seeing the red flags when they happened, reminding yourself that your good nature may have been to see the good in everyone but ultimately the narcissist choosing to take advantage of that is not your fault.

You can forgive yourself for not leaving the relationship sooner, reminding yourself that you tried desperately to care for the narcissist, truly loving who he was, and that love was taken advantage of. Your good heart, your compassion and kindness when you see someone suffering, were taken advantage of. When you recognize that, you can forgive yourself.

Remember, forgiveness does not necessarily come easy but you deserve to forgive yourself. You did not intend for the situation to get as bad as it did and you are making an effort to heal the best that you can. You did your best in the situation with what you had, and that is enough. Yes, you were in a bad situation for a period of time but you *survived.* You were strong enough to cope as it happened and you were strong enough to say you are ready to get help and begin healing just by virtue of having opened this and reading as far as you have. That deserves celebrating as you work through healing.

Remind yourself to give yourself the compassion you would show other people. If your friend came to you in this situation, telling you the story you yourself have, how would you react? Would you be supportive? Would you be kind and understanding? Or would you look at her with a cold, hard look, and tell her that she should have tried harder to leave in the beginning? Would you have told her that the abuse was her own fault and that she had been asking for it? The answer is most likely no, you would not. Treat yourself with that same compassion as well. You must forgive yourself and treat yourself kindly if you hope to move on toward healing the rest of you.

Grieve Properly

Despite the fact that your relationship with the narcissist took a turn toward abusive, you still likely developed real, strong feelings for her. You loved her, or rather, the idea of her that she originally presented to you when attempting the love bombing stage, when she mirrored your heart's desires. You fell in love with an idea, which quickly was obliterated by the narcissist that was left behind, staring back at you with the face of the one you loved, as if your loved one had suddenly become possessed. You deserve the chance to grieve that relationship. Though the person that you loved was never a real person, she was real to you, and because of that, you should allow yourself to grieve. If not for the person you lost, then grieve for not getting the relationship you deserved when you fell in love with the narcissist.

Grief involves five stages that occur, though they may not happen linearly. Grief also comes and goes and while you may feel better one day, you might suddenly be shocked by feelings of sorrow when you realize that you are once again missing the narcissist. This is normal, and grief is one of those things that never fully goes away; you just learn to live with it.

The first stage of grief is denial. You tell yourself that the relationship does not need to end. You may try to convince yourself that what has happened in your relationship does not warrant breaking up. This is to protect yourself from the pain you will feel when it is officially over. You go through anger. At this stage, you acknowledge the truth in front of you: The narcissist was abusive. At this point, you recognize the narcissist for who she is and that enrages you. The thought of your abuse, or the abuser that inflicted it, is enough to send you into a fury. Third, you reach bargaining. At this stage, the anger has subsided somewhat, and you tell yourself that there are ways or reasons that the relationship could continue to work. You tell yourself that if you try a little harder, or do a little more, then the abuse would no longer happen. This would be enough to save the relationship, you tell yourself, and you try to grapple with that, even if your bargaining chip ends up being your own wellbeing, such as deciding that you are willing to martyr yourself for the narcissist because you love her. You hit the stage of depression. Here, you acknowledge that the relationship is over. You see that things can never be acceptable, and that dissipates the hope you felt. Lastly, you reach acceptance. At this point, though you may not agree with what happened or that your relationship had to end, you accept the end result and no longer try to fight it.

Release Negative Feelings

As a primary target for a narcissist, you are likely empathetic to some degree. As an empath, you likely have a propensity to absorb the emotions of those around you. You may have internalized some of the narcissist's own negativity because of the exposure to them. You may see some of the narcissist's negative traits in you, such as realizing that you are snapping at people the same way he snapped at you or that you have been thinking about yourself in the way that the narcissist thought of himself. You might feel uncharacteristically angry at the world. No matter the negative feelings, you need to develop an outlet for them.

If left alone, you may feel as though your very self is festering within you, as though the toxicity from the narcissist still threatens to overwhelm you and turn you into someone you know you are not. The solution to this is to find a good outlet for yourself. Some people pour themselves into a creative hobby, such as drawing, writing, painting, music, dance, or any other form of creating something else. They literally channel their feelings into their art, allowing the negativity to flow through them and out into the world so it can no longer consume them. Others choose physical exercise as an outlet, choosing to sweat out the negativity with each rep of the weight set, or with each mile run. Others still may decide to nurture something else, such as growing and tending to a garden, bringing back those tender feelings that were once familiar to them. No matter what you choose as your healthy outlet, what is important is that you feel better after engaging in it, and that you see that your general outlook and mood is improving the more you do it. Anything is acceptable here so long as it allows you to channel your negativity in a way that works for you and that you enjoy.

Find Support Networks

Support networks may be one of the most intimidating parts about healing. Support networks imply that you will be opening up to others about the abuse you endured in person, face to face with others. Some people are not comfortable with this idea but luckily, the internet has made finding groups of people like you easier than ever before.

Through the internet, you can locate both local and online support groups for the sorts of abuse you endured with your narcissistic partner. You will be able to find someone who has gone through situations that are eerily similar to your own, and in finding someone else, you may find that you no longer feel so incredibly, overwhelmingly alone in the world. You will find people who understand what you have gone through, and really mean it when they say they understand.

Your support group will be comprised of others who have survived narcissistic abuse. There will be people on all areas of the scale of healing, from still struggling to flee the relationship all the way to having left and thrived after years of work. You will be able to see the progression of life after the narcissist, and knowing that other people have survived and thrived may take away some of the fear and mystery of attempting to heal. You may have had doubts that you would ever feel the same but in finding a group of others who are further along in the process than you are, you will be able to acknowledge that healing is possible. You will see that some people move on to be healthy and productive and you will be able to strive for that for yourself.

You may even find purpose in helping someone else in a situation like your own in the future, realizing that you will be the one with the ability to aid others and inspire them in their own journeys toward healing.

Self-Care

Self-care will be crucial for yourself as you heal. You have spent so long catering to others, namely the narcissist, and now you deserve some pampering of your own. You deserve to go the extra mile for yourself, to treat yourself and remind yourself that you truly appreciate the person that you are, recognizing that you have one life with one body, and that you should appreciate what you have. Take this time to spend some extra money on some bath bombs, if that is your thing, and take a long, warm bath to soak and relax. You could even bring yourself a and a glass of wine to enjoy as you soaked if you enjoy wine and reading. You could spend the money to get yourself a gym membership to exercise and work on your stamina. You could decide to take a cooking class and learn to make a few new dishes for yourself now that you have the time. Anything that you have ever wanted to do goes here, so long as it is constructive and helps you feel more at ease.

When you care for yourself, you should make sure you are nourishing both your body and mind. Take care of yourself the way you would take care of your child, and your body will thank you for it. Spend time every day engaging in some level of self-care, whether it is waking up an hour before work to go on a walk at dawn or signing yourself up for a few classes in the evenings to finally learn those new skills. No matter what you choose, make sure you dedicate plenty of time to caring for yourself, as that level of self-care will eventually become your habitual default, and you will find yourself feeling far more well rested. By caring for yourself now, you will allow yourself to heal from the narcissist's abuse and begin to flourish into who you would have been without the narcissist's influence. You will begin to feel like yourself again.

Therapy

Trauma, especially from abuse from someone you loved and trusted, can be quite damaging to a person. You may feel as though you struggle to cope at times, or that some of your insecurities that the narcissist has installed are so deeply ingrained that you will never be able to get out from underneath them. Maybe you have no clear idea of where to go with your healing and you feel like you need guidance. No matter what, whether you are coping with your abuse better or worse than average, you could benefit from seeking therapy.

Nearly every single person in this world would benefit from therapy in some form. Therapy teaches us how to better solve problems, how to cope with negativity, how to think, and sometimes just helps unpack difficult, traumatic events. What you went through with the narcissist could almost definitely be considered traumatic, and you should not hesitate to take advantage of therapy if you think it could be of use to you. With a licensed professional by your side, you will be gently, and without judgment, guided through the healing process with someone that is prepared to talk you through what you are going through. You will have someone who can provide real, valuable feedback to you about why you think the way you do or what causes you to act in such a way by your side, holding your hand as you work through healing. This can be absolutely invaluable, especially if your partner was particularly abusive, or if you find yourself struggling with thoughts of self-harm, suicide, or feel as though your mental health may be suffering.

If you feel like getting involved with therapy would be a good option for you, you should start by asking your primary care physician for a referral in your area, or you can search for therapists in your area on the internet. Do not be deterred because you think therapy is stigmatized—there is nothing wrong with taking care of yourself, even if doing so involves getting a professional involved. Remember, no one would think twice if you went to a doctor if you broke your ankle and struggling with your mental health should be seen no differently. You can do this if you put your mind to it, and you should never let other people make you feel like you are making the wrong choice.

Affirmations

This goes hand-in-hand with self-care but is so important that it deserves its own category. Affirmations are small phrases you repeat to yourself in moments of weakness or when you feel as though you might make a bad choice that help you ground yourself in the moment.

Chapter 14. Power of Forgiveness

Forgiveness is an act of power. It is also an effective way to release negative energy. If you carry hatred in your heart, then chances are that you will be filled with negativity. When you forgive, you not only do it for the person who is asking for forgiveness, but you also do it for your own good. In fact, forgiveness is possible even if the offender is not sorry for their wrongs against you. You can always forgive.

The following meditation technique is a good way to extend forgiveness to anyone. The steps are as follows:

Sit or lie down comfortably. Close your eyes and visualize the person whom you want to forgive standing in front for you. Try to visualize the person as clearly as possible. Now raise your hands in the position of blessing with your hands facing outward. Think about the wrongs that the person has done to you but do not dwell on them. Just recall them into your mind. You do not even have to be attached to the memories. Now, find peace in your heart. Once you find this peace, state the name of the person whom you visualize and say, "(Name of the person), I forgive you."

Forgiveness is an act of love. The more that you forgive, the more that you turn hatred into positive energy.

As an empath, it may be easy for you to be offended. A common problem of being an empath is being overly sensitive. Negative energies may be able to affect you more than most people. If there is any person who seems to affect you negatively, you might want to extend forgiveness to them.

Forgiveness is free. As such, you can extend forgiveness to everyone, even to those who do not feel sorry for offending you. The more that you forgive, the more that you free yourself from negative energy. If you do not forgive and allow the mistakes of others to fill you with hate, then you might end up just like them, or even worse.

Forgiveness should be sincere. If you cannot find it in your heart to forgive a person, it helps if you spend some time to think about the situation. What is it that gives you a hard time to forgive someone? Sometimes by making reflections, we get to realize our own imperfections and faults.

Once you realize the value of forgiveness, you will know just how effective it is in cleansing the soul. The more that you forgive, the more peaceful you will feel.

Another important part of forgiveness is learning how to forgive yourself. Indeed, there are people who carry lots of negative energy simply because they do not let go of it. Sometimes, to do this, you need to forgive yourself. You should learn to be kind to yourself. Unfortunately, in the modern world, it has become common to be hard on one's self. This is also why so many people are stressed out. Remember that you don't need to follow what society tells you. Be in control of your life. If something gives you more stress than you can manage, then you should do something about it. When you are an empath, you're more sensitive to stress. Of course, this doesn't mean that you should not face challenges. Rather, this means that you should be more in control, and you need to manage the level of stress that you are carrying.

Healing is important. Even if you are not an empath, you will find that you need to heal yourself from time to time. Healing is a natural part of life. No matter what you do, no matter how careful you try to be, it is inevitable that you will also face challenges and hardships along the way. It is also inevitable that you will have to deal with negative people from time to time. Hence, you will have to heal yourself when the need arises. Indeed, healing is a natural part of the life of an empath. A good thing about healing is that it transforms even negative energies into something that is much more positive. Indeed, healing and forgiveness can create a substantial positive impact on your life.

Taking care of your inner child

If you have subconscious childhood wounds, you probably developed defense mechanisms early on to cope with and adapt to grown up expectations. The behaviors or tendencies that you exhibit as an adult directly reflect this molding.

Where you a relatively happy kid? But have you become a gloomy adult who's lonely or angry? Burdened by a bruised sense of self-worth?

When our parents aren't available to provide us with the proper nurturing, as children we experience anxiety and loss. We develop accommodations to fill these wounds, which then morph into defense mechanisms for getting on with life, habits in our adulthood. This is what is commonly referred to as the FALSE SELF. Very many false-self personalities make an arsenal. From the funny ones, such as the class clown, to the angry ones, such as the bully, these personas have the ability to convince us we are what we in truth are NOT.

As we grow up and develop, we forget that this false-self character, the role we play for others (and sometimes even when alone with just yourself) is not who we really are, but the mind makes such a habit of being the false self that we take it to be all we are, nothing more, nothing else. We become so engrossed by the fantasy that we need our mask to continue being safe, even when it is no longer necessary, and even when it's done so much damage to others and to ourselves. Some theorists say that we are always looking to reestablish our nurturing state, to find our symbiotic mothers in order to feel safe; much like when we were in the womb and had all our needs met automatically, without struggle, worry or anxiety. Of course, life isn't about regression and never will be, and that's where false-selves come into play. Assumed identities enable us to cope in public while we secretly burn with our failure to find a state of natural happiness once again. Most of the time, we find ourselves trying to trick others into filling these gaps. We look for mates who we tell ourselves will meet these needs. And when this fails, when these mates are unable or unwilling to meet our every need, to make us feel loved and safe at all times, it becomes the very root of relationship problems.

EXERCISE

Start doing body weight resistance exercises at home as well as cardio. If you live in an apartment, there are still things that you can do that shouldn't bother the people downstairs too much. For example, you can start running in order to get your cardio in and build up your strength and tonality. You can also start playing sports like basketball—though they may have never appealed to you before, sports can be a great and somewhat enjoyable way to pick up a hobby and start getting some exercise at the same time. They're also strangely therapeutic and will allow you to shut off your thoughts for a while and just get some positive endorphins flowing. If you can afford it, picking up a gym membership and then going three or four times a week can be a great way to start getting back into shape and improving your self-image.

There's a possibility that you aren't religious. If you aren't, then you can eschew this bit of advice. However, if you are, you may find that diving into your spirituality and being active in a church community (or a community of whatever religion you're a part of) can lead to you developing vital friendships and getting to know people that you otherwise may not get to know. Also, spirituality can be a source of great solace for many people. It can be especially helpful to a lot of people to believe in something greater than themselves and you, if you're religious, are no exception. Even the act of praying - regardless of if the individual is secular or religious - has been scientifically proven to reduce stress levels and generally improve the disposition of the individual compared to how they were prior to praying at all.

If you have time in your schedule and can afford it, you may want to start going to a community college or going back to school if you don't have a degree. Getting a proper education and getting bigger paychecks, as a result, can lead to feeling like you're worth more than you are otherwise. On that same note, don't be afraid to find something to be passionate about. Don't just go home and watch TV and stagnate. You need something to push yourself forward. Find something you care about and start researching it. Start gardening or learning about something you've always been interested in. If you can do that, then you'll make a ton of extremely important progress.

In the end, the best things that you can do in order to heal are to better yourself and focus on yourself. Don't be afraid to spend a little extra to get a therapist or a gym membership, or even to treat yourself to a nice dinner once or twice per month. These things can be massively important parts of the healing process and can do a whole lot for helping you to feel better in general. You can do this—things will be better someday! Keep a smile on your face and fake it until you make it.

The Narcissist healing cell

Healing is important. Even if you are not a narcissist, you will find that you need to heal yourself from time to time. Healing is a natural part of life. No matter what you do, no matter how careful you try to be, it is inevitable that you will also face challenges and hardships along the way. It is also inevitable that you will have to deal with negative people from time to time. Hence, you will have to heal yourself when the need arises. Indeed, healing is a natural part of the life of an empath. A good thing about healing is that it transforms even negative energies into something that is much more positive. Indeed, healing and forgiveness can create a substantial positive impact on your life.

During the first stage, denial is common. You do not want to believe that the narcissist in your life is a toxic person. You may make excuses for their behavior and not want to admit that they are not healthy for you. Start writing down your thoughts concerning their treatment of you. Every few days, look back at what you wrote. This allows you to identify the pattern.

The second stage involves getting to know more about narcissism. This allows you to see what they do, and it allows you to realize that they are not capable of empathy and healthy relationships. This is a hard lesson to learn, but it is imperative for you to heal.

The third stage starts the separation process. Write a letter telling the narcissist in your life that you are walking away. Be detailed about why you are walking away. Now, you will not send the letter. This is for you to find some closure as you end the relationship.

For stage four, you cut the person from your life. Once you say "goodbye" you have to remain strong. Cut off all contact and do not give into them no matter what. It is common for a narcissist to try and manipulate you back into their life. You should consider a clean break. This means that you just cut off contact and never go back. Since this requires taking your attention away from them, expect them to try and contact you. They can be very persistent. Just make sure that you never respond.

Stage five involves taking a deep look at why you started a relationship with them in the first place. What was it about the narcissist that made you want them in your life? This can help you to prevent a future experience with a narcissist. It also lets you reflect and determine if your reasons for a relationship with them are things you need to work on. For example, was your self-esteem low when you started spending time with them? If so, improving your self-esteem can prevent a future narcissist experience.

The sixth stage is all about you. You want to evaluate your weaknesses and your self-worth. Find places that need improvement and dedicate yourself to working on them. After having a narcissist in your life, it is common to be in a negative place. Take small steps to essentially recover from your experience. Every person gets through their step in their own time. Do not rush and do not get discouraged if you are going through the motions slowly. Every day is another day without narcissism in your life.

The seventh and final stage is accepting that the situation happened and commit yourself to learning from it. Use the pain and negativity that the narcissist caused in your life to be stronger and to drive you to put the focus on self-care. You do not need anyone in your life that contributes anything negative. Remember this. You are valuable and worthy. You also want to truly forgive yourself.

The tendency toward narcissism is quite common, and it is present in all of us. At times, you might not know if someone has a particularly high degree of narcissism until you are deeply involved with them. Only then do you realize that all the traits you were attracted to are narcissistic qualities you cannot stand anymore. You might have a parent, a sibling, a partner, or even a friend who exhibits narcissistic traits, and you may be forced to deal or work along with them. It doesn't mean narcissists are unlovable; it merely makes it rather difficult to love them at times. People with high levels of narcissism might be fun, good at what they do, and quite charismatic and charming. If you have a say in the matter, you might like the idea of reforming narcissists instead of cutting off all ties with them.

No two individuals are alike, and likewise, all narcissists aren't the same. So, the way you decide to handle a narcissist in your life will depend on the type of narcissist you are dealing with.

Conclusion

If you have ever known a narcissist you know that the only person that they care about is themselves. If you have ever been the victim of a narcissist you know that it is extremely hard to walk away from the situation. It is even harder for a person to recover from the abuse and move on with their lives. Often times when a person is the victim of abuse, they may leave the situation, but they usually find themselves in the same situation. Or sometimes, victims do not know how to focus on recovery in order to work through their feelings and end up suffering from some form of addiction.

My goal is to ensure that none of this happens to you. I want to make sure that you are able to walk away from the situation knowing that you can live the life that you want to live and be free from the pain that the narcissist has caused you.

Of course, it is going to take work and it is going to take time. Our bodies do not heal overnight nor do our emotions, our spirits, or our minds. We have to allow them the time that they need to heal. That means that we do not put ourselves in a new situation to feel more pain.

I hope that this has benefited you in some way. If you thought that you knew a narcissist, that one of your friends was in a relationship with a narcissist, or that you were a victim of a narcissist, I hope that this has given you some clarity. I also hope that by understanding the narcissist and their behavior better that you are going to be able to identify the narcissists before they are able to sneak into your life.

Stay strong as you focus on taking care of yourself and focus on creating the life that you want. Never give up on yourself and remember that you deserve everything that the world has to offer you.

PART II

CODEPENDENCY

Introduction PART II – CODEPENDENCY

Codependent is one of these oft-utilized popular expressions that imply different degrees of poverty in a relationship, or connections tinged with a dash of urgency. Be that as it may, just, the term originates from something a touch more prominent explicit to dependency and recuperating.

Codependency is an imbalanced relationship test where one friend accepts an extreme cost 'supplier rescuer' job and the option the 'taker-unfortunate casualty' job."

Codependency implies that the friends and family of addicts, in view of their fundamental, every now and again intuitive early life issue commonly tend to, as grown-ups, give excessively and love an unreasonable measure of. Therefore, they tempt, empower and entangle with dependent accomplices.

Those expecting those jobs, deliberately or unknowingly, propagate the taker's enslavement pushed bad conduct. The codependent taker is commonly a couple of blend of penniless, underneath working, juvenile, dependent, entitled or stricken. they rely upon the provider to take care of them, envision or mellow the poor outcomes for their moves, and to make up for lost time with their under-working. Meanwhile, the codependent supplier is commonly an empathic, pardoning, prepared and benevolent person. They assume the job of unnecessary guardian, rescuer, supporter or associate. They show love and being worried by methods for making penances for the taker that usually license rather than enable them.

This diverse trendy expression "empowering agent" signifies, reliable with the Merriam-Webster word reference: "one which empowers some other to harvest a stop; extraordinarily one who empowers each other to endure in self-antagonistic conduct (counting substance misuse) through providing reasons or by means of making it suitable to avoid the aftereffects of such conduct."

Healthy connections as the years progressed, have an equivalent parity of giving and ingest expressions of fulfilling wishes, rather than favoring the desires of one friend. Codependent connections are worked cycle an irregularity of intensity that needs the requirements of the taker, leaving the provider to protect on giving. Codependent connections disregard some of the basic elements of solid cozy connections since they are enmeshed in inclination to reliant, and imbalanced in inclination to impartial.

While individuals are marked as codependent, they are informed that they are looking to both empower or deal with the individual who is addicted. They put an excessive amount of spotlight on another person's lead and now not adequate all alone.

What reasons us to be us searching for out these types of connections? To the extent suppliers pass, accessible examinations show that psychological mistreatment and overlook set us at risk for codependency. on the off chance that you discovered that the best method to interface with a troublesome decide changed into to subordinate your own one of a kind wants and take into account theirs, at that point, you will be the establishment for comparative connections over an amazing span.

The time span codependency comes from something is known as "injury idea," which proposes a requesting event, sometimes happening eventually by way of immaturity, most likely coming about because of brutality or some unique state of infringement.

You can moreover have standards or character qualities that make it simpler to fall into a codependent pursuing. You can over-disguise otherworldly or social qualities that recommend generosity for other people. Being the provider in a codependent relationship can likewise fulfill needs that incorporate the need to depend on somebody, they need to encounter skilled, the need to detect close to somebody. To the extent takers go, they are once in a while narrow-minded and manipulative, flighty and entitled. Anyway, a couple is simply pained, dependent, or ailing in presence abilities.

In accordance with a more established examination inside the diary of substance misuse, the two ladies and men in codependent connections will, in general, be reliable to their friends regardless of the unpleasant strain. In any case, clearly adequate, codependent ladies demonstrated 5 of the attributes foreseen in codependency: control, overstated duty, extremely worth reliance, salvage direction, and exchange direction, even as codependent men handiest affirmed two: control and misrepresented obligation. Their feeling of fearlessness was not as identified with their accomplices as ladies.

Regardless of your sexual orientation, on the off chance that you experience you are likely in a codependent relationship, it has justified, despite all the trouble to attempt to harm the cycle. a Mexican inspect from innovation and aggregate wellbeing says codependent connections don't least complex influence the strength of the provider and taker, anyway also impacts the wellbeing in their family units. They, for the most part, will in general experience the ill effects of more weight that is prominent (and medical problems from weight), their children have a superior danger of getting to be addicts themselves, and highlight a "less fortunate top-notch of ways of life inside the psychological and physical area names" than the general populace.

Being happy and healthy is a choice that one makes, and for a codependent person, you first of all need to accept the fact that you are one then get the right steps you ought to follow in order to understand that life is majorly about you before anyone else comes in. We should always endeavor to lead a happy life that makes us take charge of ourselves other than putting the interest of other people, and ours come second. Strive to satisfy yourself and from that point, you have begun a successful journey of overcoming codependency. Some of the things one has to do in order to come out of codependency include but not limited to, the following as explained below.

Chapter 15. What is Codependency

There is more to the codependency discussion than most realize. Although codependent relationships appear to be a feature of certain conditions of mental health, some psychologists have questioned whether codependency is not something that social scientists have made up. In particular, it can be argued that some aspects of codependency may be present in otherwise healthy relationships and that it is a modern trend to pathologize behavior patterns that seem to run contrary to modern beliefs about personal independence.

But when one learns more about the narcissist and comes to understand them, codependency as a behavior pattern becomes something inescapable. The narcissist naturally forms relationships of this type: relationships that are particularly interesting in that both partners seem to have prominent features of this personality type.

In fact, despite some of the detractors of codependency, some have argued that this condition be given a more formal place in the Diagnostic and Statistical Manual of psychiatry or the DSM. Before we get into the proposed criteria, let us first present a working definition of codependency. In codependency, one individual enables the mental illness, addiction, or behavioral dysfunction of another person. One of the most significant features is that one person depends on another for their identity and self-esteem.

As we have hinted at in other parts of this page in the context of the disordered self of the narcissist (and its development), most people go through a developmental process that involves developing a "self" that recognizes the selves of others and relates normally to these. Just as the narcissist has an issue with recognizing the selves of others and seeing them as equivalent to his or her own, so too does the codependent person have an abnormality of the self, but one that lacks independence and therefore needs another self for completion.

A psychologist named Timmen Cermak actively studied codependent people and developed criteria for what he termed codependent personality disorder. The criteria that Cermak proposed for this disorder include the following:

 Association of one's own self-worth with a need to control others and oneself, or suffer consequences as a result

What children see during their development is critical in establishing the patterns of behavior they display in life. Individuals who experience physical, emotional, or sexual abuse, or who are a witness to such behaviors, or more likely to be codependent. Children are not the clueless extensions of ourselves that some adults seem to think they are. Children are constantly forming impressions based on what they see around them, and something as commonplace as seeing a parent being verbally abused by another parent can render them more likely to be engaged in a similar relationship dynamic when they get older.

Experiences during childhood is just one of the possible causes of codependency during life. Individuals who have certain traits are also more likely to be involved in codependent relationships. So people with anxiety, depression, other mental problems, emotional problems, and sensitive people are more likely to wind up in a codependent relationship. As this list suggests, the empath naturally finds themselves in relationships of this type because of their emotional sensitivity. Empaths also may have experienced abuse themselves or witnessed it, making codependency even more common.

There is also something to be said for establishing patterns in adult life. Although empaths and other highly sensitive people may be at risk for falling into these relationship types, they can reinforce these dysfunctional relationships by becoming comfortable with them and not recognizing just how dysfunctional they are. Therefore, an empath who is in a relationship with a narcissist and is discarded after being emotionally abused will likely find themselves in more codependent relationships of this type if they do not recognize the pattern.

In many normal relationships, we develop dependent relationships. This means that we prioritize our partners and rely on each other for love and in times we need support. The relationship is mutually beneficial, and neither person worries about expressing their true emotions. In a dependent relationship, both people are able to enjoy time spent away from the relationship while still meeting each other's needs.

However, in a codependent relationship, the codependent feels as though his only worth comes from being needed. He will make huge sacrifices, martyring himself out in order to ensure that the other person's needs are met. He only feels worthy if he is able to be needed. He exists solely for the relationship and feels as though he is worthless outside of that relationship. The relationship is his only identity, and he will cling to it at all costs, and within that relationship, he will ignore his own needs and wants, feeling as though they are unimportant.

Someone with codependent tendencies will struggle to detach from his partner because his entire sense of self is wrapped up in aiding that other person. It may get so bad that it begins to negatively impact the codependent's life. The codependent relationship can become all-consuming, taking over the person's life in all areas. Other relationships can weaken and fail as the codependent focuses solely on the person with which the relationship is held. Career potential may be lost, or the codependent may be fired when the relationship begins to interfere with the quality of work. Everyday responsibilities may be shirked in favor of catering to the enabler, the person with whom the codependent is in a relationship. Overall, the entire relationship is built on the faulty ground and is dysfunctional.

Like NPD, there are many external factors that are believed to cause a codependent personality to develop. You may recognize these as being quite similar to what was as causes for NPD within the page.

This is because both codependency and narcissism are similar personality flaws, stemming from the same root cause of damaged self-esteem.

Oftentimes, people who have developed a codependent personality have grown up repeatedly having conflicts with their parents throughout childhood. Their parents may have prioritized themselves, or somehow otherwise denied that the child's needs were important. By repeatedly downplaying the child's needs, the child internalizes that those needs are not important enough to meet. After all, if the child's parents could not be bothered to tend to them, they must not matter. The child learns to prioritize his or her parents instead, and feel greedy or as though a selfish decision was made when trying to commit to self-care. Oftentimes, this kind of relationship between parent and child happens because the parent has an addiction problem and would do anything to feed the addiction, or the parent never matured past the selfish stage of development as a child and focuses solely on him or herself. Because of all the time spent focusing on the parent's needs, the child never develops the independence and identity necessary to be successful in life. Feeling incomplete when not needed, these people frequently seek out other enablers that will allow them to continue living in this fashion.

When a child grows up around someone else who requires frequent or around-the-clock care beyond the realm of normal, whether due to severe illness, injury, or some sort of mental illness, the child's needs may go unmet in favor of meeting more pressing ones. As the child is pushed aside in favor of the person who needs the care, the idea of the child's needs become less important to become internalized. The child may also engage in some of the care for the dependent person as well, causing his needs to be put on the backburner as he takes care of the person who literally cannot care for herself. While living with a family member that requires extra care does not necessarily cause codependency to develop on its own and many people can make it through the caregiving stage without issue, in certain circumstances and with certain personality types that are predisposed to codependent tendencies, it can become an issue. It becomes an issue in particular if the child is younger during the time there is someone dependent on care and the parent of the child has a tendency to focus entirely on the dependent instead of spending the time the child needs to grow and thrive meeting the child's needs.

It is no surprise that abuse, regardless of physical, emotional, or sexual, leaves lasting harm on a child. While some children go on to abuse others, others may fall into a pattern of codependency. A child who is exposed to repeated abuse eventually begins to develop a coping mechanism in which she suppresses her feelings. She begins to ignore and cast aside the pain that is felt as a result of the abuse, and this ultimately teaches her to ignore her own needs in life. This leaves her only caring about other people's needs while neglecting her own.

Chapter 16. Signs of Codependency

One of the most difficult roadblocks in combatting codependency is denial. Oftentimes, one or both parties involved in a codependent relationship will have difficulty recognizing, and then admitting, the fact that the relationship has become unhealthy. Sometimes, an outside party or an intervention is required in order for codependents to recognize the issue. Moreover, there are instances in which codependents are fully aware of the unhealthiness in the relationship, but he or she is reluctant to outwardly acknowledge the issue or take action.

Luckily, there are ways in which we can identify codependency, which is the first step towards overcoming it and achieving a healthy relationship.

Firstly, it's important to separate codependency from interdependence. Within interdependence, individuals involved in a relationship are only dependent on one another to a degree. For instance, in a family environment, one parent might rely on the other spouse to help pay bills or carry out routines to help with the children. Likewise, the other spouse contributes in other, meaningful ways. This does not mean that they are codependent, or that they are relying on one another to establish a sense of self-worth; in reality, they are individualistic yet can still approach the responsibilities of a family in a shared, healthy manner.

Here's one way to determine whether or not you might be in a codependent relationship: ask yourself whether or not you are frequently second-guessing your behaviors and actions. Or, you might simply be experiencing an ever-present, high level of anxiety. Individuals in a codependent relationship are frequently judging themselves, reflecting on what they should have done or said differently.

In essence, one of the most common effects of living in a codependent relationship is low self-esteem. Oftentimes, low self-esteem isn't as easy to identify as one may think. Individuals who strive for perfectionism may actually be suffering from low self-esteem; likewise, they may outwardly appear to be confident, but it could be a façade. Inwardly, people who are experiencing low self-esteem may be ridden with guilt and shame.

Also, codependents are often people-pleasers. They feel compelled, and perhaps even responsible, for contributing to another's happiness. Typically, these individuals are fearful of saying "no" and may even experience anxiety when presented with a situation or invitation they'd prefer to decline. In many instances, people-pleasers will say "yes" to something that they may not have wanted to agree to, but felt compelled and will instead put another's desires and needs in front of their own.

Furthermore, codependents may have difficulty establishing boundaries. They often internalize others' issues, feelings, thoughts, or needs, and establish an unhealthy sense of responsibility for their partner's sense of wellbeing. Nonetheless, some codependents may become withdrawn and actively draw up their boundaries, making it difficult for others to become close to them. In other instances, codependents might vary the behaviors in which they establish boundaries; sometimes they'll let their walls down, whereas other times they might be completely withdrawn.

Caretaking is another common behavior found in codependent relationships. Oftentimes, the caretaker puts the other party in front of his or her own needs. The caretaker feels obligated to help the other individual, and might even experience feelings of rejection if the other refuses help. Moreover, the caretaker might become obsessed with the notion that he or she can "fix" the other person in the relationship, even if that individual isn't trying to overcome whatever obstacles he or she is suffering from.

Another behavior that might indicate codependency is overreaction. While most individuals do react to others' thoughts and feelings, codependents might feel threatened by adverse opinions. Instead of brushing off differing views, the codependent might absorb the sentiment and start to believer it; or, he or she might react oppositely and become extremely defensive. Either way, too strong a reaction to what should be an insignificant comment might be a sign of codependency.

Codependents also typically seek a strong sense of control. They might seek control over the other individual in the relationship, or they might seek extreme control over one aspect of their own lives. For example, codependents might become addicts in one way or another; sometimes, they'll even become workaholics to take control over one aspect of their lives in totality. Caretakers and people-pleasers might even use these behaviors in order to take the aspect of control to the extreme, using their influence over others to manipulate them.

Furthermore, codependents may try to control the other person in the relationship by restricting his or her actions. The codependent may try to give orders to his or her partner. Conversely, codependents sometimes won't let their partners participate in certain activities or behaviors that make them feel threatened.

While codependents often intrude on others' space, this can also become a physical phenomenon as well. Observe your behavior, or that of those around you: does it seem as if you're always spilling, tripping, or just generally accident-prone? Perhaps you're infringing on someone else's personal space, or vice versa. Establishing personal boundaries, both physically and emotionally, is essential to having a healthy relationship.

In many instances, codependents rely on dysfunctional means of communication. They may not be able to present their thoughts or feelings in a healthy, clear manner. Moreover, a codependent may have difficulty determining what he or she is thinking in the first place. If you notice this behavior pattern in yourself, it might be an indication that something is wrong in your relationship. Or, if you notice that you're unwilling or afraid to be honest with your partner, this could be a sign of dysfunctional communication. For example, if your partner asks your opinion on something and you're afraid to be truthful, it could mean that the communication has become dishonest, which is most likely a result of the other party's manipulation.

This is often referred to as the "doormat" side of codependents. The codependent becomes literally unable to determine how he or she actually feels about a given subject, because he or she is so used to simply agreeing with others to appease them. Nonetheless, it's important to establish your own opinions and formulate thoughts on based on how you feel. Codependents become chameleons, as their views begin to blend in with everyone else's.

In addition, at least one codependent (or both) in a relationship is usually given very few opportunities to get a word in, especially during arguments. One person may exhibit cues indicating that he or she is impatient, and simply waiting for his or her turn to speak instead of actually listening. That person has already determined what he or she is going to say, regardless of what your point is. Thus, the conversation will most likely become an unhealthy, one-sided argument in which one person's opinions or views will get squashed by the other's, instead of both parties trying to reach some level of understanding or compromise.

Finally, if you're concerned that you or someone you know could be involved in a codependent situation, assess the general emotions of the potential codependent: Are there signs of shame or rejection present? If you're suspecting codependency within your own relationship, have you sunken into a state of depression, resentment, or hopelessness? Usually, one party may develop a sense of failure: you might begin to feel as though no matter what you do, it's never enough to make the other party satisfied. Eventually, you could become numb and withdrawn.

You or your loved one may not exhibit all of the signs listed above, but chances are that if you've noticed at least some of these indicators frequently enough to become concerned, you may be part of a codependent relationship. We'll discuss how you can move forward and work towards achieving a healthier relationship.

Although codependency is not seen as its own distinctive personality disorder, there are many specific signs that can determine whether or not someone is experiencing codependency in their life. It is important that if you begin considering yourself or someone else as being codependent, you should clearly understand what the true signs and symptoms are. Unfortunately, many people loosely throw around the word "codependent," often labeling people as codependent even when they are not. If you genuinely believe that you are codependent, speaking with an informed therapist is a great way to see if you genuinely align with the signs of a codependent individual.

You will not find any in-depth information as to what is officially classified as the symptoms of codependency, because it is not yet officially recognized as a distinctive disorder. However, most therapists who are educated on codependency and who have witnessed it in the individuals that they support have come to a common consensus as to what the hallmark traits of codependency are.

If you identify with any of the following statements, chances are you are experiencing symptoms of codependency:

- You have a tendency to want to rescue other people and may find yourself taking responsibility for them, even if you know you shouldn't.
- Whenever you sacrifice your own needs in favor of someone else's, you feel a sense of purpose. Sometimes, you will sacrifice your own needs to an extreme level, and you feel a boost to your self-esteem as a result.

- You regularly find yourself entering relationships where you will need to care for or even rescue the other individual, regardless of what it costs you. You are willing to invest high amounts of money, time, or other resources into taking care of others.
- You find yourself often attempting to resolve other people's conflicts, especially if their conflicts are related to addictions or chronic mental health, despite these troubles often being beyond your means to fix.
- Although you do not fully understand why, you seem to continually attract low-functioning people who are seeking caregivers to avoid having to take on adult responsibilities or consequences. Alternatively, you might regularly attract people who appear to be in perpetual crisis, yet who are unwilling to make any significant changes to their lives.
- It seems as though you regularly engage in behaviors that have the right intentions, but that come off as unproductive or unhealthy. An example of these behaviors would be enabling.

If you recognize these statements and feel as though they resonate with who you are and how you behave with and around others, chances are that you are experiencing codependency in your life. You can also look into your childhood to see if there are any indicating factors that may signal codependency or something that could potentially trigger the onset of codependency.

If you lived a life where you had to suppress your own needs and wants to serve someone else growing up, chances are that you may be carrying that tendency into your adulthood in the form of codependency.

Chapter 17. Causes of codependency

Now that we have an understanding of what codependency is, we will now explore the main experiences which cause it.

Many of these causes are to be found in one's childhood, and then may be reinforced and experienced into adulthood. As we explore these causes of codependent behavior, thinking, and feeling patterns see if you can recognize some of these experiences in your childhood.

We will talk about how to heal the troubling emotions that these experiences have created in you in future. For now, just see which of these difficult experiences you may have encountered in your life. Know that you are not alone, that many others have suffered many of the same feelings, and that many people have been able to heal these wounds and become their fullest self.

When these core causes of codependency, the common thread is the importance of the primary caregiver. Often this is the mother, but it may also be the father, a grandparent, a relative, or a combination of different people. When the child does not receive the love and affection they require this leads to dysfunction and suffering throughout their life. Also, when the parenting of the infant is not sufficient, this naturally means that the family as a whole must also be dysfunctional. This further causes harm to the child's development and well-being.

One cannot heal an illness without a proper understanding of what caused the illness. Without this knowledge all you will be able to do is put band-aids over the wound. However, by deeply understanding the root causes of an illness, we give ourselves the opportunity to heal the core wounds and find freedom from our struggle.

Not Being Loved For Who You Are

If one was to boil down the root cause of codependency into one phrase it could be said to be "not being loved for who you are". A child needs to love more than any other thing. Studies have shown that babies born without mothers who do not receive the loving touch and attention of nurses in the hospital will die because they do not receive the most important nourishment of all - love.

The common thread of all adults to struggle with codependency is early childhood experiences which taught them in a direct or indirect way that they must change themselves in order to be loved by their parent or guardian or family. An infant baby or toddler needs love and attention more than anything else, therefore in order to survive they will modify their emotions, thoughts and needs in order to receive that love and attention. If the mother or guardian is not attentive to the needs of the child and allows them to naturally express themselves and be loved for who they are, then the child will learn to neglect their needs and desires in order to please their mother and therefore survive.

There are two main ways in which this manifests. In the case of an overbearing and overly invested mother, the child is smothered and not a loud to have the air to breathe and develop their own autonomous self. The opposite extreme is when the mother is absent and neglectful which causes the child to feel abandoned and guilty and therefore must mold themselves against their oh true will in order to receive love. In both cases the result is the same - the implanting of codependent behavior from a young age.

Individuation And The Importance Of The Mother-Child Relationship

A newborn child is extremely dependent on their mother or primary caregiver. Not only do they need food and protection, but above all they need love and the physical touch of their mother. In fact, newborn babies are hardly separate from their mothers at all – her feelings, thoughts, and moment-to-moment actions are directly shared with the child. In this way, if the mother is in psychological turmoil and her needs are not met in some way, she will unconsciously transmit these emotions to the child who is extremely empathic and connected to her.

However, soon after being born children must inevitably begin the process of individuation. This is the lifelong journey of discovering who they are and defines themselves psychologically and emotionally as they learn to take ownership of their feelings, thoughts, and actions. It is vitally important that the primary caregiver allows their child to grow and experience their autonomy without influencing them with fear, pushing or pulling, or repression of their child's natural self. The child needs to feel that their parent can fulfill their needs and allows them the safe space to separate from their parent as they individuate. The way the parent or parents respond to this requirement determines the ability of their children to mature into healthy adults who are able to have a stable sense of self as they define their own boundaries.

Lack Of Empathy And Inadequate Mirroring

In order to feel secure and safe and free to express their real self a child needs to feel loved as an autonomous individual by their parents or guardian. The mother or guardian's empathy is a crucial element of this individuation process.

One of the main ways that a mother is the formation of a solid sense of self for their child is through the mirroring of emotions.

Therefore, when the child is happy the mother smiles and laughs also, and when the child is sad and crying the mother is appropriately matching the child's emotion and comforting them. The mother must respond to the child's internal feelings and thoughts, this allows the child to feel that their mother is there for them and validates their unique perception of the world. Likewise, the mother must also keep healthy boundaries in order to not take their child's feelings and emotions personally. She must be able to except that her child will have different perceptions and needs then she may have.

Inadequate Mirroring

Inadequate mirroring is when the mother is not able to reflect and meet the child's emotional needs. Usually this is because the mother is herself distracted or otherwise unable to be emotionally available and empathize with her child. Often this is because she herself did not received this from her mother. This is how codependence can be passed down from generation to generation through the repetition of these patterns.

If the child is crying because they are thirsty and the mother ignores the child or dismisses them, this will make the child feel abandoned and unloved. Also, the mother can give their child too much attention which is just as harmful if it is not in response to the child's needs. The mother may do this as an over compensation for the lack of mirroring that she never received when she was a child. An example of this is the mother may forcefully try to play and interact with the child while he or she is tired and wishes to sleep.

Some of the most common causes for a mothers ineffective mirroring are:

- Stress
- Illness
- Sorrow and grief
- Depression
- Narcissistic personality
- Mental or emotional disorders

- Weak boundaries
- Overly rigid boundaries

While all of these causes and more can be reasons why a person grows up to be codependent, the most common is due to weak boundaries. A mother with weak boundaries cannot see the child as separate from herself, therefore she sees the baby as a way for herself to feel loved, complete, important and valuable. If her sense of self is so strongly tied to her child it often causes problems when the child is upset. This is because she unconscious the only wishes to validate her baby's actions which make her feel good and boost her self-esteem. So, if the baby is crying a mother who is unable to adequately mirror their child will get very impatient, angry, frightened, or overwhelmed as a response. She may act out in anger and either scold her child or withdraw from them.

This pattern of inadequate mirroring causes the children child to feel like their natural emotions and needs are either unimportant or wrong. This leads to the child feeling very alone and insecure. As time goes on in this pattern is repeated over and over again the child will learn to hide their own needs and feelings and instead attempt to express what they expect their mother wishes them to feel. In an unconscious way they learn to mold themselves to the environment, and in order to survive, become who they believe the outside environment or their guardian wishes them to be. This teaches them to live in a codependent manner in which they exhibit patterns of withdrawing, becoming self-sufficient, caretaking, being aggressive, being pleasing, or seeking others approval so that they may feel loved. They do this rather than developing their own sense of self and autonomous knowing of their own feelings, thoughts, needs, and worse.

If the mother exhibits a chronic inability to see to their child's needs, the child will feel lost and abandoned due to not having received that key ingredient of having their mother validate their own existence. The results of this deep winding starting in childhood often lead to chronic depression, anxiety, and a lack of passion in life. In life this often results in behavior that seeks stimulation and can manifest in dangerous risk-taking activities and a wide variety of addictions.

A mother who feels overly stressed and burdened by the practice of caring for their child sometimes will attempt to get their child to be independent prematurely. This will overwhelm the child and make them feel like they must survive at a very young age or on their own, leading to feelings of fear and abandonment which ultimately lead to a codependent personality. On the other hand, a mother whose mother is their child with too much attention and does not allow them to individuate Will only serve to keep their child dependent upon them and stunt their ability to take care of themselves. This pattern will then continue into adulthood if not rectified.

The mother or guardian must find a happy medium between not enough attention and affection on one side, and too much attention and dependence on the other side. In the cases of both extremes a child who receives too little or too much attention, or in adequately mirrored attention, this will have a deep and lasting impact on the psyche of the child throughout their life.

Dysfunctional Families

Theorist who study codependent behavior have highlighted the immense importance of the family unit. The family is similar to a living organism and therefore each part depends on every other part and the health of the whole organism depends on a healthy functioning family unit. Codependent behavior is born primarily with the mother and father, but also in how the family as a whole functions.

Many key lessons in the growth of the individual are internalized through interactions with the family unit and one's parents. Some of these lessons which are very important to developing a strong sense of self that is not dependent on others are:

Identifying and recognizing your needs and feelings

Feeling that your words, ideas, emotions, and needs matter

How you get your needs met from others. Whether this is in a positive way or a dysfunctional way such as in manipulation, crying, or lying

Self-responsibility, how to take care of yourself and meet your own needs

Your relationship to authority and if authority can be trusted.

The way in which your behavior is rewarded. Whether negative behavior is given more attention or whether positive behavior is given enforcement

Whether your true self is honored and given respect

The way in which you learn to resolve conflicts

The way in which you except disappointment in not getting what you want

Decision-making and problem-solving methods

Traits of Healthy Families

No family is perfect, and all families will have challenges, disappointments, and disagreements. However, there are certain characteristics of healthy families that lead to children in these families developing a healthy sense of self, respectable boundaries, and the ability to interact with others in a healthy and mature manner which is free of dependency.

Love-Based Relationships

Healthy and well-functioning families are based on the foundation of love and respect. This comes first and foremost from the relationship between the mother and father and is then taken on by the whole family. The whole family has a sense of goodwill and support of each other and everyone is encouraged in their thoughts and actions. Everyone in the family knows that they are loved and excepted unconditionally, even if they make mistakes or have opinions that are different than the rest of the family. There will of course always be disagreements and conflicts, but these situations are met with loving and open discussion.

Openness

A healthy family also is an open family. All members know that they are free to express themselves and share what they believe. No one feels like they need to hide their true feelings or that certain topics are off-limits and taboo. This open this allows for flexibility and adaptability also, ensuring that the family does not become too rigid and inflexible to change. An attitude of open this allows for the free flow of information and ensures the family members will not keep secrets from each other and engenders an atmosphere of trust for all. Additionally, parents do not hide their emotions or mistakes and dissenting opinions are not science but allowed to be shared so that the family as a whole can debate the merits or demerits of ideas and make collective decisions.

Equality

A healthy family is closer to a democracy than a dictatorship, and is founded in ideals of equality, fairness and respect. The mother and father treat each other as equals and this attitude trickles down to the siblings. The parents may make the rules but they are not seen as strict authoritarian. Duties and chores are divided equally and everyone does their fair share. Also, all members are held accountable for their actions, especially the parents. Everyone feels as if their voice is heard and communication between members is honest and respectful. Because everyone is listened to with respect they feel like their individuality is honored and what they are contributing has value. In this way members of the family learn to express their honest feelings and needs and learn to build self-confidence

Fair Rules

It is necessary for every family to have rules, without them children do not learn proper boundaries and responsibility. In a healthy family everyone knows very clearly what the rules are and except the responsibility of the punishment for breaking those rules. The punishment must be reasonable and consistent and the rules and punishments need to be able to be modified if necessary. Children do not feel guilty or "bad" for breaking rules, but are rather taught that punishments are merely the consequences for not following the rules which enable everyone to get along together in a safe and harmonious fashion.

Conflict Resolution

The last key trait of a functional family is the ability to find solutions to problems and conflicts. Instead of having fights over recurring problems healthy families have the ability to problem solve and work together to find solutions that work for everyone. Parents guide the younger members of the family to the ability to make their own decisions and see the consequences of their choices and actions

Traits of Dysfunctional Families

There are many reasons why families become dysfunctional. It can happen for any number of reasons such as drug or alcohol abuse, illness, the family being split apart by divorce, trauma, or depression. When a family is dysfunctional this will inevitably affect the child or children who live in the family and can lead to codependent patterns. Due to feeling abandoned or having your feelings hurt and not having a healthy and supportive environment to grow, children learn to hide their true feelings and create a false personality and codependent traits in order to cope with the stress of living in a dysfunctional family. Here we will discuss a few of the main qualities of a dysfunctional family.

Poor Communication

As one of the most important elements of a healthy and functioning family is communication, one of the first things to go in a dysfunctional family is communication. In a dysfunctional family there is no communication or communication that is done is shared in an indirect, abusive, and dishonest manner. This communication, rather than being done to understand one another is done in order to control another. Often it will restrict the free expression of the members of the family and will neglect the feelings and opinions of the children. It will also lead to arguing and shouting matches that do not lead to the individuals being heard. Additionally, the communication is often a vehicle for blame and shame. Another toxic pattern is the prevailing's of double messages, which is when a parent says one thing but does another. From this the child learns that they cannot trust their parents and that it is justified to lie.

Chapter 18. The Nature of Codependency

Codependence on Parents

Codependent parents try to make up for what their parents lacked by demanding it from their children. They expect to receive a form of love or devotion from their children, which they did not get from their parents. They blur and even break boundaries them their children and them. Mixed and confused with the love of apparent, codependency on parents may be difficult to spot. Let's look at some pointers.

1.Easily upset

Codependent parents do not precisely know how to draw limits when their child gets upset. They open up to the children and keep nursing them for a whole age, with the feeling that they are not fine because the child is not fine. While they appear to be soothing the child, they are actually soothing themselves by means of the child. When they cannot keep doing so at the moment, they may choose to return the child's words and emotions back to them, so that the child realizes that it is, in fact, the parent who is upset more.

2.Control over the child

The codependent parent will try to control the life of the child. When the child is going through an experience of discomfort, the parent attempts to take over with the thought of greatly influencing the decision of what should happen and how it should proceed. They may not promptly realize that what they want is not necessarily what the child is considering to be effective. And even when they know it, they want to insist on their course in order to relieve their emotions through the child.

3.Playing victim

The parent narrates their childhood experiences and how they negatively impacted on them so that the children can see the hurt or pains they underwent in their days. They will also tell their children to pursue certain careers in life and almost insist so when the child is not in agreement with them. If the child picks up the task to compensate for the parent's sufferings in the life, the parent wins. Similarly, if the child pursues their parent's desired career for them, the parent wins. In both cases, the child is supposed to live their life in such a way that they make up for the parent's missed opportunities or privileges.

4.Negligence over other relationships

The parent focuses on strengthening their bond with the child and obviously or subtly ignores their relationship with a partner. The parent acts with the view to eliminate the influence of their partner's connection with the child on their intended objectives. Sometime, the parent may prefer to push their partner away so that only they have attachment and influence over the child.

5.You're always right

Codependent parents are never apologetic when they are wrong. When they apologize, it is with force and insincerity. They want to always assert their authority and dominance, and apologizing could be a threat to that, or make the child rebellious, they think. This parent does not give in to their child's wish for better consideration of things or apology. They take hard stances and remain unmoved.

6.Guilt is a weapon

Codependent parents, when guilty, give silent treatments, make passively aggressive comments and projections for their incapability to handle that feeling. They deny the guilt and project it onto other people instead. They do this involuntarily without first considering what it would lead mean on the child or the other person. They cast onto others what they fear for themselves.

Whatever a codependent parent does have the view to manipulating the child to agree to their wishes or demands. What is more, the parent does it in a way that they ultimately come out as having no responsibility in the subsequent events, so it is upon the child to do what they can to accomplish them.

Codependency on Partners

Codependency in relationships is characterized by one person relying on the other for their emotional and social needs to be met, while the very person on their part maintains an irresponsible, addictive or underperforming and underachieving behavior. The other partner, in a way or another tends to be okay with doing everything to support the underperforming person, and thus the system runs in a way that seems complete in that sense.

Codependent relationships can be described to relationships that are sustained on dysfunctional helping. The codependent partner takes on the role of a helper or rescuer for the weaknesses with the hope that the relationship will keep running as long as support is accorded even in the lack of meeting other aspects or responsibilities of the relationship. Codependent relationships are unbalanced and can only go on for so long. A codependent relationship is unsustainable as it strains the helper's resources physically, mentally, emotionally, and financially leading to resentment.

A codependent relationship is one in which love and intimacy are defined contextually as one person's distress always attended to by other's rescue or enablement. The helper is the primary provider to the other's needs, showing love by giving and assisting while the other primarily receives feeling loved.

The helper's emotional fluidity makes them entirely attend to the other's struggles without trying to limit or withhold for fear of guilt. The helper's emotional needs are acceptance and closeness coupled with a fear of abandonment. Most of the helper's competencies are rooted in their low self-esteem as it is tied to the affirmation of their partner than their own.

The dependent who always needs help and assistance is bound to the helper and kept from maturing, acquiring skills of life, and developing self-confidence, but instead encouraged to stay in addiction, poor health, underperformance, and vicious neediness. Their motivation for change keeps decreasing over time until they become irreparable.

Dependent function below average and, therefore, never build more relationships beyond the current one with their partner. This adds to their resistance to change.

Let us explore the other characteristics of codependency in relationships.

Low Self-Esteem

The codependent partner regards themselves as insufficient on their own and hence constantly compares themselves with others. While some codependent may paradoxically think highly of themselves, they also imagine themselves as disguising and unlovable. They carry a feeling of shame. Their feeling good is when everything is perfect, but since this is never easily achievable by anyone, they carry an underlying sense of guilt.

People-Pleasing

Codependents go all their way and expend all their energies and resources trying to please their counterparts to the extent of neglecting their own needs. They are not capable of saying 'no.' It makes them anxious. They keep accommodating more and more their partner's demands and do not come to the point of knowing and asserting that they have enough in their hands with respect to their partner's needs.

No Boundaries

Codependents do not know how to set and respect personal boundaries. Many of them are not able to simply state what belongs to them in terms of feelings, thoughts, need, money, belongings, and sometimes even their bodies. They allow their partners to intrude into their space without permission or regard, and are thus exposed and vulnerable to exploitation. They essentially do not own anything in the relationships and do not have control over anything and themselves.

But there are also the kinds who are rigid, closed off, and withdrawn. They cannot be approached dynamically. Codependents generally have difficulty adjusting, and so they can be hard in a way to break into.

Oversensitivity

A lack of having poor boundaries makes one overreactive with everyone's thoughts and feelings. You believe everything quickly of jump into defense mode on the very instant you hear something that you do not agree with. You rarely engage reason to filter content through. A lack of boundary makes you think every opinion is aimed to describe you and comes as an insult or compliment.

Caretaking

Codependents are fond of giving excessive care to others as to rescue them from a dire situation when, in fact, it is only an ordinary occasioning that requires minimal intervention. They put their partners first. If the partner calls it enough before the assistance is in course, the codependent feels rejected in person. They keep sticking on trying to help and advice even when the counterpart is openly declining or ignoring their input.

Controlling

Codependents interpret control in quite a wrong manner. A codependent trying to control things means limiting their creativity and activity. They want to keep their paths narrower and narrower. They want 120% certainty of predictability for the future. The future ought to look like the current. They do want to accommodate risks before it causes them anxiety. In the same way, codependent want to control the people around them because they believe normal behavior follow certain structured patterns they have known all along. Their attempts to please and care for people are an instinctive attempt by codependents to control and manipulate others. They might sometimes act bossy telling others with finality what to do and what not to do.

Poor Communication

Codependents are poor communicators, be it of their needs, feelings, or thoughts. They are often unsure of or with what they think, feel, and need and there find it difficult to speak it. They also avoid owning up to certain truths especially if it would upset their partners. They might opt to be agreeable to something they totally abhor. This makes them dishonest and confusion sets in the whole communication process.

Obsessions

Codependents have tendencies of overthinking about people, relationships, and things. This originates from their dependency patterns, anxieties, and fears. They get into endless windings of thoughts when they think they made or might make a mistake. They sometimes turn their thoughts onto the ideals they desire for things or certain people who have a soothing effect on them to cease the pains of the moment. This way, they live in denial and avoid rising up to the occasion, hence being held from progressing in life.

Reliance

Codependents depend on other people's affirmations for them to feel alright with themselves. Though they can stand by themselves, they always fear abandonment or rejection by their partners. Being by themselves for a while is depressing to them, and they may choose to stick in the relationships they have, however painful or abusive they may be, trapping themselves therein.

Denial

Codependents' real problem is that they do not really get to acknowledge their problems, and, therefore, never get to face them head-on. They think that the situation or other people are the problem. They keep trying to correct situations or other people, or switch between careers, relationships, etc. not understanding that they are themselves the issue and whose habits need to be adjusted.

Codependents do not acknowledge their feelings and needs but try to understand those of the others. They focus on facilitating other people's needs than their own. They do not recognize their need for space and autonomy. Codependents may act sufficiently when they actually need help. They have trouble asking for help and accepting it. They act invulnerable and not needing love or intimacy.

Poor Intimacy

Codependents fear being open and close with the intimate partners. They fear being judged, rejected, or abandoned for their weaknesses – shame and lack of principles. Conversely, as well, they avoid being overpowered and losing their independence within the relationship. In denial of their need for closeness, codependents may begin to feel like their partner is asking or consuming too much of their time while at the same time complain they are not available for you, is denying your very wish for separateness.

Bitterness

Codependency is a precursor of bitterness. Shamed and an unvalued person lives while anxious about disregard, rejection, abandonment, personal wrongs and failures, and closeness or aloneness. They feel anger and resentment and enter into a state of depression, hopelessness, and despair. If these feelings persist for too long, the individual may become vain and detach meaning from whatever they think and do.

Examples of Codependency in Relationships

Workaholism

It is not necessarily wrong to be a workaholic; the motivation is right. However, if one overworks themselves thinking that by doing so much, they will earn the approval, praise, and respect of their partner, then that is not the right motivation. While you may earn the desired approval you need, it will not take long before you notice its effects on your health. It is likely you have a lazy partner who does not want to play their duty, and that should not cost your well-being at what you do. There is no heroism in overworking.

Taking the Blame

Your spouse out of their careless behavior lose a promising contract, and when they inform you, you do not only feel sorry for them, you also claim your responsibility in it, thinking you did not support them in a way or two, which you know would not be necessary anyway, or are farfetched. You want to take responsibility so that your spouse is relieved of their bad feeling. You fear that when they feel low, they will withdraw their love, attention, and affection from you. You want to prevent that, so you sacrifice your feelings for theirs. Then they see that you could probably have done better, not them, and that is where you go wrong. They stop looking inwards and instead shift their blame on you for what you are not responsible for. Over time, you begin to become aggressive, as it begins to overwhelm you. Your spouse will never anything wrong with themselves, but everything wrong with you and they will not improve.

Undue Anxiety

Your partner hits their leg on the wall, and you feel the pain. They do not get to bed in time, or they experience shallow sleep, and you begin to have sleepless nights. Their problems concern you more than them. You wear away while they watch helplessly. You want to show them you care, yes, but you are overreacting due to your insecurities. Your partner may esteem you for it, but that will not heal you. Everyone has their worries, and only relevant support is needed for one to be back at what they do to address their individual issues.

Manipulation

The kind here is twisting your partner's ill or evil responses to comfort yourself. Your partner called you 'stupid,' and you think they did not mean it. They were joking or playing with you, you think. By the time you realize what is going on, you have been on receiving end of verbal abuse getting worse and worse each time, and you have never tried to do anything to stop it. You keep agreeing to such abuses because you do not want to be abandoned. Your spouse, on their end, keeps throwing their abuses because they know you can only take it anyway. You accept to be nothing so that they can be everything hoping you will keep the peace that way forever. Healthy relationships require partners to regard each other with respect both on the inside and on the outside.

Feeling Unlovable

Do you really feel the love of your partner yourself, or do you just think and hope they actually love you? By the time this question begins to take a few of your thoughts, you can be sure that their commitment to you and to the relationship is decreasing. Love, when it really exists between the two of you, is not suspected, thought, or imagined, it is experienced then felt. Living in speculation of your partner's love for you is a consequent of a codependent who has less regard for themselves – abdicating their worth, esteem and dignity to promote that of their partner.

Change Your Partner

Healthy relationships are those in which partners accept each other as they are. They know the beauty of their differences. The codependent tries to change their partner. You think they will become better lovable to you when they change their identity to a certain degree. You want to improve on their version to some degree. You are trying to protect them against themselves by removing them from their current state. You think they will harm themselves in their current state. This fear is normally exaggerated, and it leads to breaking your friendship with you in the first place. No one changes unless they find need and accept by themselves.

Unnecessary Cover-Ups

Your spouse does something wrong and you sweep it under the carpet so that they may not suffer the consequences of their actions. Over time, they live expecting that they can do all manner of things and find cover in you. A promiscuous behavior such as lying in your partner, if not addressed and overcome in time will get back at and overcome you as well. Falsehood can only be hidden for a while. With time, when discovered, you will be ridiculed and judged for covering up for your partner. Initially, you thought you were doing it in good faith.

Neglecting Yourself and Your Needs

True, sometimes, you deny yourself for the sake of your partner. Codependents skip their pressing need to attend their partner's usual wants. What is more, the recipient is either not willing or indifferent. However, you force yourself on them because you consider them more important than yourself, therefore seeking their approval of you. There is no point in that. You are the performer, but you seek approval of a non-performer over what they do not even understand.

Chapter 19. Improving Empathy

When you start becoming aware of what you want and how you can do it as an empath, that is your first step towards a change. It can be mind-boggling sometimes but when you have complete knowledge about your situation, things will automatically start becoming easier. Have you noticed children when they fail to make you understand what they are feeling? They start fussing or crying but when they find the right way to express their feelings, they can easily calm down. The same thing happens with empaths as well. When you learn to build connections and convey your emotions, everything becomes easier and sorted in life.

If you want to bring about any changes in your life, you need to start by accepting your qualities as an empath. You also need to accept the entire situation that you are in. You need to see yourself as someone worthy of love and attention, and you definitely do not have to be so hard on yourself. Empaths often fear that they might end up being egotistical and that acts as a barrier not only in forming connections but also in self-love. You need to build a healthy regard for yourself and that is not something selfish.

For empaths, the world is hard to describe, and so are their feelings. They do not have faith in their perceptions or their validity. But when they start to get a grip on why they feel or do what they do, that is when all the chaos starts to smoothen out. They can understand situations now because they have identified the patterns or structures that are there. But for that, empaths first need to learn how they can build the connections with others without hurting themselves and for that, I have compiled some useful tips for you.

Understand Energy Exchange

There are several ways in which you can understand and measure energy. Now, you have to understand that one of the most vital things that keeps you alive is energy, and it can be felt in various ways. Your emotions or feelings are one way of measuring your energy. If you are an empath, you will know how exhausting it can feel after you have had conversations with a certain person. Even when you do not talk much, you can get exhausted simply by staying in the presence of such people.

On the contrary, you will also have people in your life who make you feel comfortable, and you will feel happy to be around them. This person can be your friend or even a family member. But what you have to understand is that empaths always undergo these energy exchanges whenever they communicate with someone. You absorb the energy of other people and you let them do the same to you subconsciously. What you need to do is understand that you have your own aura. It is somewhat like your own personal bubble which determines your energy limits. All your emotions and thoughts are present in your aura. All your traumas are present there too.

So, when you connect with someone, you are taking in the energy that is present in their aura, and you are sharing your aura with theirs. This energetic field exchange does not always happen through talking. Sometimes, you can experience the same with a total stranger who is sitting to you on the train.

Learn to Create Barriers

This is so important when it comes to effective communication. Empaths are so affected by what other people feel that they often mix up all the emotions and then are confused about their own feelings. They cannot separate others' feelings from their own. That is why it is so necessary to create barriers so that you learn to ground yourself. If an event or a person has bogged you down, it is in your hands to stop it, and you can do so by creating a barrier. The simplest method is to avoid people or locations that give you that feeling but as you know, it is not always possible to avoid. Sometimes, you have to interact with people you don't want to and so that is when you have to make yourself strong. You can try to meditate or practice mindfulness to create strong barriers in your mind.

Use visualization to distract your mind from the negativity and tell yourself that what you are feeling is not yours. It is someone else's emotion that you have absorbed. You need to let that toxicity go because only then will you be able to see your true self.

Another way of creating barriers is by saying the right things. But this will take some time, and you have to work on increasing your levels of self-confidence. For example, if you are in the middle of a conversation with someone and you do not like where it is headed, then you can always ask them politely to change the topic because you do not feel so good about it. Or, you can excuse yourself from the conversation and take a break. You need to prevent yourself from getting drained of all the energy you have and you need to do everything you can to keep yourself stable – that should be your ultimate goal.

Challenge Yourself

If you want to communicate better, you need to go out of your comfort zone. Communication is the key in all aspects of today's world, and if you keep yourself shut down, it is not going to do you any good. So, you have to learn to open up. Most empaths are introverts and opening up can be a big challenge for them. That is why, introvert or not, I always advise empaths to do something that is new to them because it will give you the lesson of handling anything that comes your way. You need to understand that there is room for improvement in everyone but change or improvement will only come when you take the first step. Here are some things that you can do to challenge yourself:

•Learn a new language – One of the best ways of challenging yourself is by learning a new language. Also, it won't go to waste as you choose the language to suit your resume, and then you can even earn some extra cash on the side. This is not even difficult as you have plenty of apps providing free resources and also amazing YouTube videos where you can get language tutorials.

•Pursue a hobby – Everyone has something that they always wanted to do but couldn't because they did not have enough time. So, out what your hobby is and then pursue it. You can monetize this too once you learn it well.

•Do something you are scared of – Think about what scared you. Are you afraid of public speaking or maybe heights? Then, take a small step towards your fear, and once you do that, you can take another step towards it week. Yes, the first try can be scary but don't leave it at that. You should look at your fear in the eyes and face it.

•Travel – When you travel, you meet new people from various cultures, and this will eventually help you in sharpening your communications skills as an empath. You will meet people outside your usual circle and you will come to realize that everyone is different.

Practice Active Listening

Empaths are good listeners and that is why people come to them during their sorrows. But if you want to form better connections with people, you still need to brush up on your skills. Being an empath means you are absorbing other people's energy right from the morning. If someone impacts you too deeply, you might be thinking about that particular situation the whole day, and so when you try to communicate with the person, you are not really listening as your mind has been diverted towards the first person.

Also, not all empaths are active listeners. Some empaths listen for a while, and they wait to respond. You should be really listening to the person until the very end. Your body language also plays a big role in making the person in front of you realize that you are actually listening to them and not pretending to do so. Always maintain eye contact. Keep responding to them in full sentences. Simply saying single words like 'absolutely' and 'yeah' doesn't really count. You should come up with full sentences that have your judgment in them.

Engage in Self-Love

If you want to enhance your communication skills, you also have to work on loving yourself. You show empathy to others, and you are kind to them. Now, you have to practice some self-empathy. One of the ways in which you can do this is by trying to talk to yourself just like you do with those you love. Empaths have this habit of beating themselves up for every little thing but talking to yourself like a friend might help you in solving this problem. Take a piece of paper and write down any negative thoughts that you are having about yourself and then tell yourself the positive things that you would have told a friend experiencing the same thing in their life.

You can also get rid of the endless cycle of self-judgment by practicing mindfulness. Think about your feelings and emotions, but you should not be judging them. Just let them come into your mind and then let them go as if they are free-flowing. Don't ruminate on anything and at the same time, don't push any of the thoughts away.

You should be able to forgive yourself. You need to remind yourself that you did what you could with what you had at that moment. Everything that happened has also given you some good lessons in life. But I am not asking you to shield your wrongs or pretend that they did not happen. What I am asking you is to accept that you made a mistake and then forgive yourself for it. Once you do this, you are practicing self-compassion. This means that you have learned to identify your own humanity.

Also, you need to stop comparing yourself with others. This is the era of social media where people are constantly checking through others' profiles and then comparing their life with theirs. But whatever you see on social media is just a photo. You do not know what is going on behind that. So, if you think that social media is making you upset, you need to reduce your time scrolling through the various social media accounts.

If you follow these steps, you will soon be proud of yourself the way you are, and then you will not feel shaky or tense when it comes to speaking with other people. If you want to thrive as an empath, self-love is the key to it.

Prevent Nervous System Overdrive

Since empaths are so vulnerable to negative energies or anything that can make them upset, they often experience nervous system overdrives. And when this happens, it can numb your ability to communicate or connect with someone or interact with them in a proper way. Sometimes, the overdrive can become so serious that empaths experience occasional burnouts, depression, and anxiety attacks. But if you want to prevent all of this from happening, you first have to work on preventing this overdrive from happening.

For that, you need to balance your nervous system and your energy levels. Your nervous system, as an empath, catches the energy from different people throughout the day. It might start by catching a smile from your kid in the morning and then move to a very sad friend you met on the bus and then the meaningless complaints of your boss at the office. So, there is a constant shuffle between all these emotions. In between processing all this information, your nervous system can easily run into overdrive. This results in chronic stress, as well.

So, you need to learn to identify the signs of an overdrive way before it happens. If you sense anything like increased heart rates, sweating, agitation or headaches, then you need to take a break no matter what. You can go to an empty room and simply focus on your breathing. Take deep breaths. After a moment, you will notice that your heart rate has returned back to normal, and consequently, so has your nervous system. You should also try out restorative yoga.

Fear and anxiety are two of the most common emotions that will be provoked in your time and again because of your nature of being too sensitive as an empath. And this can bring you tons of miserable experience over the years but you need to relax. You need to remind yourself that your life is a journey and there will be ups and downs. You need to put your best foot forward and the rest will unfold slowly.

If something needs to be addressed now, don't keep it buried or procrastinate about it. Your life is already unpredictable, and you need to be okay with that uncertainty. You have to understand that you cannot predict everything, even though you are an empath. Empaths who have the habit of neglecting their gifts are the ones who suffer the most. When you repress your qualities, that is exactly when your energy levels are going to become even more unbalanced than ever. You need to be more proactive and you need to embrace yourself for the person you are.

There will be times when you will be so exhausted that it is almost discouraging, but you cannot give in. Otherwise, you will have to start over once again. If you want to interact with people in a better way, you need to navigate your energy levels using multiple strategies. You need to neutralize every situation that comes your way and you need to turn every negative into a positive. The best way to thrive as an empath is to create a balance and embrace your emotional, physical, and spiritual being with open arms.

Analyze your current situation and take some time to do that. Jot down what needs to be balanced and the work on one situation at a time.

Chapter 20. What is Shame?

Shame is a common emotion that is very common in people who struggle with codependency. It is a very damaging feeling that can be ingrained very deeply in someone who has experienced what they perceive to be failures and the condemnation of their parents. Shame can be internalized to such an extent that an individual believes that shame is who they are. A person with this believes has a deep feeling that they are innately guilty, selfish, weak, unlovable, or responsible for challenging things that have happened in the past.

Unfortunately, codependent individuals have a tendency to place the blame upon themselves for the abuse that they receive or that others they care about experience. It is important to realize that there is no need to feel shame or guilt for anything. Everyone makes mistakes and as a child you have no responsibility to be perfect and live up to others' expectations.

Allowing Yourself Feel Your Grief

All things considered; they're driven by shame. It's simply the romanticized picture, which they persuade themselves they exemplify, that they respect. Yet, where it counts, narcissists feel the hole between the façade they show the world and their shame-based self. They strive to abstain from feeling that shame.

This hole is valid for different mutually dependent people too, yet a narcissist utilizes barrier components that are dangerous to relationships and cause torment and harm to their friends and family's self-esteem.

Everyone, not just those who struggle with codependency, experience grief. There is nothing wrong with experiencing this as it is a part of life; however, it is common for people to try to avoid feeling their sadness. If your grief is not fully acknowledged at the time it occurs, then it will stick with you for the rest of your life. This is why it is very important to acknowledge your grief as it is happening, but if you have suppressed grief from your past you can heal it at any time you are willing to face it again.

People develop many clever ways to avoid their grief. Some will rationalize it by saying that those who hurt them "didn't know any better". While this may be true, rationalizing it like this does not allow you to accept the very real effect these actions had on you. Connected with rationalizing is justifying. Someone may justify their abuse by thinking that "I was a challenging child to raise". Once again, this prevents you from recognizing that you have been abused. Minimizing is another tactic; many people will try to tell themselves that their abuse and neglect was very minor as a way to avoid looking at it. Some will resort to avoidance in which they use outside addictions such as food, drugs, work, or relationships to keep themselves from thinking about their trauma. Still others will engage in intellectualizing. They will mentally believe that they understand it, but they haven't incorporated the emotional aspect of being willing to feel the emotions that are necessary to fully experience the grief and therefore go beyond it. Finally, some will try to forgive prematurely by fooling themselves into thinking that they are done with grieving and can move on to the final step. Once again this is a tactic to try to avoid feeling painful emotions, and one cannot forgive someone before fully experiencing the grief and moving beyond it.

Feel to heal

It is important to learn that in order to heal you must feel. Just intellectually thinking about your grief and trauma will not allow the full experience of what has happened to you to be processed. As we already mentioned, that which is not fully experienced will stick around within you and resurface as physical or emotional pain and illness. The key is that you must feel to heal.

If you never allow yourself to feel your traumas then you will never be able to heal. It is that simple. There is never any easy time to allow yourself to feel your inner pains, but the longer you put it off the more pain you will experience in the long run and you will not be able to be free. Many people fear to feel their grief because they worry that it will destroy them and they won't ever be able to recover. It is important to know that this is not true, you are strong and have the power to face your grief and accept why it has happened and forgive yourself and others for the fact that it has happened.

Codependency don't feel a lot of blame since they think they are in every case right, and they don't accept their practices truly influence any other individual. Be that as it may, they harbor a great deal of shame. Shame is the conviction that there is something profoundly and for all time off-base or awful about what your identity is. Covered in a profoundly stifled piece of the narcissist are every one of the frailties, fears, and dismissed traits that he is continually on the gatekeeper to escape everybody, including himself. The narcissist is intensely ashamed of all these dismissed contemplations and sentiments. For instance, I had one narcissistic customer who was into skydiving, and other exceptional risk-taking practices reveal to me that he never felt fear. "Fear," he stated, "was underhanded." He was plainly on a campaign to overcome it.

Keeping his vulnerabilities covered up is basic to the narcissist's imagine self-esteem or bogus self. At last, in any case, this makes it inconceivable for them to be totally genuine and straightforward.

In view of their failure to get sentiments, their lack of compassion, and a steady requirement for self-insurance, narcissists can't genuinely adore or interface emotionally with others. They can't take a gander at the world from any other person's point of view. They're basically emotionally visually impaired and alone. This makes them emotionally penniless. At the point when one relationship is never again fulfilling, they frequently cover connections or start another one as quickly as time permits. They urgently need somebody to sympathize with their torment, to feel for them, and make everything similarly as they need it to be. Be that as it may, they have little capacity to react to your agony or fear or even your everyday requirement for care and compassion.

Mindful, helpful practices require a genuine comprehension of one another's sentiments. In what capacity will the other individual feel? Will this activity fulfill the two of us? In what capacity will this influence our relationship? These are the major questions that narcissists don't have the limit or the inspiration to consider. Try not to anticipate that the narcissist should comprehend your sentiments, surrender, or quit any pretense of anything he needs for your advantage; it's pointless.

Chapter 21. Conquering Codependency

Codependency may lead to different long-term problems such as depression, low self-esteem, health problems, career problems and relationship difficulties. Co-dependents often feel trapped, abused and they often feel that they are unable to trust anyone.

But there is hope. If you are a codependent, it is not too late. You can either end a codependent relationship or shape it to become healthier and more balanced. You can still reclaim your life and take control.

Steps On How You Could Conquer And Cure Codependency:

- Acknowledge that there is a problem – Codependents are constantly in denial. They routinely deny that they have a problem. The first step in conquering codependency is to acknowledge it. You have to accept the fact that there is a problem. Be realistic. Realize that the relationships that you are in are not balanced. You have to recognize that the people you care about are taking advantage of you- your friends, family, spouse, kids, siblings or parents. Once you acknowledge and accept this, then you are on your way to recovery.
- Make a decision to do whatever it takes to conquer codependency – You have to make a tough decision to wage a war against codependency. After you have acknowledged that codependency is your problem, this is the time to decide to take steps that are necessary to end your codependency and make your life better. This is very difficult to do, but once you have made up your mind and you made the commitment to make positive changes in your life, there is no turning back. Everything will eventually become easier, lighter and you will be genuinely happy and feel more fulfilled.

- Get some help – It is necessary to talk to someone you trust about your codependency and the steps that you will take to end it. You can talk to an emotionally healthy family member or friend or you could see a mental health professional. You can also seek the help of spiritual leader that you respect and you can trust. The support of the people around you will push you into the direction of recovery.
- Focus on yourself – This is very important. If you want to conquer codependency, you have to focus on your own needs, wants and dreams. Take time to ask yourself – what do I really want? If you find yourself answering based on what your partner wants, ask yourself again and again until you get the real answer. If you are a codependent, you have spent so much time and effort focusing on other people's wants and needs that you have already forgotten your own desires and needs. Now is the time to be in touch with your own needs and your own desire. Do you want to go back to school or start your own business or maybe travel around the world? Acknowledge your needs, feelings, emotions and your dreams.
- Practice Self-Love – Self-love is not the same with narcissism. In fact, narcissistic people may appear confident on the outside, but deep inside, they despise themselves and feel inadequate. People who love themselves, on the other hand, accept themselves unconditionally. They do not take abuse and disrespect. They do not take advantage of other people and they do not allow others to take advantage of them. They are more direct in communicating their needs and their preference. While they clearly communicate their wants, desires, opinions and views, people who profoundly love themselves tend to respect other people's wants, needs and opinions. They do not judge others and they do not feel that they should change or fix other people. More importantly, people who constantly practice self-love have healthy boundaries. They do not allow people to meddle with

their lives and they do not meddle with other people's lives. When you accept yourself completely, you do not have the urge or need to be accepted by others. Here's how you can practice self-love:

- Say positive affirmations every morning – Positive affirmations can do wonders in your life. It can fill your life with love and happiness. You can find several affirmations online or you could make your own affirmations.
- Take time to meditate – Meditation shuts off negative energy and allows you to focus on the positive.
- Enjoy life – If you are a codependent, you have spent so much time taking care of other people that you have already forgotten to take care of yourself. Enroll in a yoga class, dance class or travel. Go to the beach often, if that's what makes you happy. Take time to hang out with your old friends and take time to go to dinner parties.
- Learn something new – Expand your skills and make yourself better. You can learn a new language or learn how to play guitar, crochet or you can go to pottery class. You can also visit the local museums and libraries. Go back to business school if that's what you want or get a master's degree. Follow the desires of your heart.
- Live in gratitude – To be happy, you have to appreciate whatever it is that you have. Take time to appreciate and be grateful for your job, family and life in general. Savor that plate of baked macaroni. Stop and appreciate the view. Be grateful and you will no longer feel the need to manipulate or to let others take advantage of you just to be happy.

Always do the things and actions that honor you and respect you – Do not ever allow abusers and toxic people in your life. Do not engage with people who bring you down. Do not participate in activities that are harmful to you.

Believe in your self-worth – Understand that your worth is not dependent on someone's approval. You have to know and understand that you are worthy of love and respect. Once you realize your own self-worth, you will be surprised with how your life will change in a positive way.

Let go of the need to change and fix other people – To conquer codependency, you have to let go of your need to control other people's lives. You must let go of your need or desire to change other people. This is one of the powerful ways to heal and cure codependency. Allow people to be themselves and resist any urge to try to change them and make them better. This means that you have to stop the care taking, rescuing, controlling, apologizing and pretending. You have to also avoid making rules for other people.

Create and define your personal boundaries- This is ultimately necessary if you want to conquer and cure your codependency. Personal boundaries are basically decisions that you make about the behaviors that you will and won't tolerate.

If you have weak boundaries, you will tolerate just about anything. You allow people to hurt you and disrespect you. You also inappropriately assume responsibility for other people's mistakes, problems and experiences. If you have strong boundaries, you know where your responsibility ends and where others responsibilities begin. You draw a line between your concerns and the concerns of others. You stand up for yourself and you communicate your displeasure when someone is being hurtful or disrespectful to you.

Remember that setting boundaries is not enough. You have to enforce them. You have to communicate your feelings openly and honestly and call out people who violate them. Here are some easy steps on how you could create boundaries:

Decide what you will and will not tolerate. Take time to reflect and determine what behaviors are tolerable and what behaviors are absolutely unacceptable. Prepare a list of acceptable and unacceptable behaviors.

Watch and determine certain violations of your boundaries. Other people may not be aware that they are crossing your boundaries so it is important to communicate with others what your boundaries are. For instance, you do not want to take work related telephone calls during your day off. You must clearly communicate with your coworkers that you would appreciate it if they will not contact you on weekends about work-related matters.

Enforce your personal boundaries by calling out people who violate these boundaries. Respectfully but clearly communicate that you will not tolerate these kinds of behavior. Directly express your displeasure and then present a possible solution or alternative.

Be true to yourself – Most co-dependents have completely forgotten about their needs and desires. You have to maintain your personal integrity and be completely honest about who you are, what your dreams are, and how you feel. To heal a relationship, you have to be completely honest and become more genuine. You also have to stop caring about what other people think of you. You just have to live in the moment. Realize that it is okay not to be perfect.

Leave when you have to – Finally, when you think that you cannot change the course and the nature of your codependent relationship, it is time to leave and end the relationship. If you decide to end it, you have to end it in a healthy way. Experts say that a codependent relationship automatically ends whenever you stop responding to your partner in a codependent way. The relationship automatically ends when you set healthy boundaries and enforce it. Remember to avoid drama. Ending a codependent relationship should not be emotionally charged. Just stay calm and just communicate that if your partner could not respect your boundaries, wants and needs, then it is best to end the relationship.

Once you follow these steps, you will be surprised with the positive changes in your life. You will be happier. Your career will thrive. Your relationships will be healthier and you will be able to get rid of the diseases associated with codependency like depression, anxiety, and emotional pain. You will be able to travel more, eat in restaurants that you really like and pick out the clothes that you prefer. You will feel empowered and confident. In no time, your confidence will reach its all-time high and you can now put your painful, codependent past behind you.

As you do these small things more and more, they will eventually grow into habits and once they are habits, they can help construct your emotional foundations. You do not need to do every single one of these things. In fact, some of them may not even work very well for you. These tips are more intended as suggestions and guidance. Let them inspire you to develop your own positive habits.

Keep a journal: writing a journal is an excellent way to make the whole process of self-reflection a lot easier. You can use it as a reference and memory aid. And reading what you wrote a few days after the fact will help you to better reflect on what happened and how you actually felt in that moment. This will prevent you from minimizing pain you have felt in the past and from over dramatizing smaller events. So, as you write, remember to write down both what happened and what you feel. Getting in this habit will also help you to get better at identifying your feelings (something that many codependent personalities struggle with).

Do something creative: creative activities can be immensely therapeutic and relaxing. It can also help give your subconscious emotions a means of expression. When you don't know how to say what you are feeling in words (or aren't even sure yourself what you are feeling), doing something creative can help you process those emotions in alternate ways. Plus, you will end up with something cool in the end. So, whether it's arts, crafts, or some sort of DIY project, take the time every week to do something creative. Who knows? You may discover some hidden talents in yourself. At the very least, you will discover some hidden emotions.

Make to Do Lists: this might seem like it is coming out of left field but To Do lists can help more than you think. Each morning (or each evening before you go to bed), make a To Do list for the day. Include big important tasks as well as the little things. As you complete each task throughout the day, mark it off your list. This is a positive habit that will help you better realize just how much you really do get done in a day. It is a wonderful feeling to sit down after a long day and look at a long list full of completed tasks.

Whether it is expressing a thought, saying no, finding a new hobby, or working on any of the other steps. Starting the day with the clear intention of how you plan to work on your recovery will not only help keep you on track but also help you notice the progress you are making. Think about it, after one week of doing this, you will have accomplished 7 goals that are helping your recovery. Add those 7 goals together and you are that much closer to recovery.

Notice something beautiful: take the time every single day to stop and notice something beautiful or pleasant. It could be the sunset, a cute dog, a particularly artistic piece of graffiti, or even just an extra well-made sandwich eaten for lunch. Just remember to stop and take a moment to acknowledge how wonderful it is and let yourself just enjoy it without any outside pressure from anyone else. This is your own small moment of enjoyment and peacefulness that you can have all on your own without anybody else.

Acknowledge an accomplishment: every single night, as you are going to sleep, think of at least one thing you accomplished that day. It could simply be accomplishing the small recovery goal you had set or it could be marking off everything on your To Do list. No matter how big or small, every accomplishment count. As you are going to sleep, you can use that time to appreciate what you have accomplished. If you can think of more than one thing, go for it. But always come up with at least one accomplishment from your day.

Keep a dream journal: each morning, as soon as you wake up, write down everything you can remember from your dreams. This can be fun and enlightening. A dream journal will help you get more in touch with your subconscious and all those unexpressed emotions you are struggling with.

Plus, it can be an interesting way to pass the time to read through all the dreams you have been having the past few nights. As you reread them, look for any common symbols or themes. Alternatively, you can compare your dream journal with your regular day to day journal to see what in your life might be influencing your dreams. If you don't feel like an expert dream interpreter, you can take your dream journal (and your regular daily journal while you are at it) to your therapist to get his or her thoughts and opinions.

Start up a savings for something you want: even if you do not have very much money to put away, this can be a very good exercise. Working toward a tangible long-term goal like a vacation or a new dress can help you build emotional strength and endurance. So even if you are just putting leftover change from the day into a jar, start saving money. And start saving it for a specific goal.

Even if you do not feel comfortable telling anyone what exactly you are saving for, you can still build up a savings and know for yourself what your goal is. Let it be a somewhat long-term goal, though such as a dream vacation or even just a fairly expensive piece of jewelry or another item that you want. Part of building up emotional strength is learning to appreciate delayed gratification and long-term rewards. Saving up for things you want to get in the future can help you develop that skill.

With these steps and tips in mind, you are ready to begin your own journey to self-recovery. This is one of the most courageous and inspirational decisions you could have made so congratulate yourself for coming this far and for deciding that it is time to change. This will keep you motivated and strong as you work through the process.

Chapter 22. Detaching from Codependent Influences

The number one rule of breaking free from a codependent relationship is to recognize that you can never change the other person. Only when you come to terms with this fact can you begin to take the measures necessary to liberate yourself from the influences and effects of a dysfunctional relationship. One such measure is to practice what is referred to as detachment. Simply put, detachment is the process of removing yourself from the codependent equation. This can be achieved by avoiding arguments, ending the role of being responsible for other peoples' happiness, or by stopping any other action that contributes to the codependent nature of the relationship. This will discuss several methods for detaching from codependent influences, thereby providing you with the tools you need to begin to free yourself from the harm such influences can cause. Once you have read this you will be able to begin your journey to liberating yourself from codependent relationships and creating the healthy and happy life you both desire and deserve.

Recognize You Aren't Responsible For Other Peoples' Happiness

The first step toward achieving detachment is to change your way of thinking. This covers a wide range of areas, so it is something that cannot be done all at once. Instead, it is a process that must be achieved one step at a time. While there is no wrong place to start as such, perhaps the easiest and most important place to start changing your way of thinking is in regards to other people's happiness.

The bottom line is that you aren't responsible for how other people feel, no matter what others might say. Only when you come to this realization can you begin to move on with your life in a healthy and meaningful way.

This change in mindset will take a while to develop, as your current mindset is probably the result of years of conditioning. Subsequently, it is important that you don't look for immediate results. Instead, treat this the way you would if you were trying to develop muscle strength or lose weight. You wouldn't expect to walk into the gym one or two times and come out looking like a body builder. Similarly, you wouldn't expect to eat a salad or two and miraculously drop ten or twenty pounds of extra weight. Instead, you recognize that any meaningful results will take time. Therefore, expect these results to take the same time and effort. This way you can commit to the long game, allowing yourself the time needed to make the progress you desire.

The easiest way to begin recognizing that you aren't responsible for other peoples' happiness is to simply stop taking responsibility for all of their choices. If the taker in your relationship relies on you making the right decisions in order for them to be happy start demanding that they begin to share in the decision making process. This doesn't have to be an all or nothing scenario, rather it can be a step by step process in which you slowly turn over the burden of responsibility to the other person for finding happiness in their life. You might start by forcing them to choose between a few options rather than making all the choices yourself. For example, if you are planning to go out on a date, instead of making every decision yourself come up with a few options you think might work and make the other person choose one. This is a perfect balance that allows both parties to make decisions together, rather than relying on one person to be fully in charge.

Needless to say, there may be times when the taker puts up a fuss and refuses to play along. This is a classic attempt to maintain the status quo on their part, so don't allow them to hinder your efforts. Instead, expect resistance at first, but realize that once you cross the initial hurdle things will begin to get easier. Like it or not, the taker will have to adapt to your gradual changes or else face the possibility of more extreme changes, such as losing you altogether. They will only recognize such a choice if you stick to your guns, so don't let them bully you out of making this positive change in your life.

Recognize You Aren't Responsible For Other Peoples' Unhappiness

The step toward detaching from codependent influences is to recognize that you aren't responsible for other peoples' unhappiness. Again, this is all about realizing that every person is ultimately responsible for how they feel, both happy and otherwise. Unfortunately, in the case of a codependent relationship you will be made to take the blame for when the taker is unhappy, no matter what the reason might be. Even if you aren't directly responsible for the action or situation that causes their unhappiness, the taker will still blame you for not protecting them more effectively from those things that brought them misery. Needless to say, this is about as unrealistic a mindset as you could imagine, one that usually creates a sense of hopelessness on the part of the giver. After all, you can't possibly protect a person from everything that might cause them to become unhappy, no matter how hard you try. Therefore, the mission is as impossible as it is hopeless.

In order to put this overwhelming hopelessness behind you once and for all you need to begin to change your perspective on things.

Again, it is vital that you understand that no individual is responsible for someone else's happiness, sadness or any other state of mind. Therefore, don't feed in to the narrative that you are to blame when the taker in the relationship is angry, sad or depressed. Instead, take a step back and recognize the impact that the taker's choices had on their overall emotional wellbeing. The chances are you can trace their unhappiness to their past choices or behavior. Once you do this you realize that their unhappiness is the result of their own actions, not yours. After a while you will start to see a pattern, one that reveals the simple truth that the taker is solely responsible for their overall wellbeing. This will help you to change your perspective on things, thereby freeing you from the guilt for failing to protect others from being unhappy. The bottom line is that you didn't fail, therefore you are guilt free.

How you handle this change of perspective can be a bit tricky. The bottom line is you don't want to use this newfound information as fodder for arguments or conflict. This will only serve to make the relationship more volatile, thereby undermining your efforts to improve the situation. Therefore, the best thing is to simply not play the game of apologizing for how other people feel. After all, this is the essence of detachment. The goal isn't to change the other person, or to lead them to some sort of enlightenment. Instead, the goal is to remove yourself from the cycle of codependence, thereby allowing you to live a healthier and happier life. That said, by not feeding into the blame game you will achieve your goal, even if the taker in the relationship doesn't change their attitude.

Begin To Make Decisions For Yourself

The basic lesson to be learned with regard to how a person feels is that it all comes down to the decisions the individual makes. When a person makes good, positive choices then they are likely to be happy and content with their life. Alternatively, when they make bad, negative choices they will be unhappy and frustrated with their day-to-day existence. That said, now that you have freed yourself from the idea that you are responsible for how other people feel the step toward detachment from codependent influences is to start making decisions for yourself. This not only allows you to break free from the cycle of codependency, it actually enables you to move forward with your life, creating a life of happiness, fulfillment and meaning. By making decisions for yourself you can start to shape your life in a way you never imagined possible!

You might find this process difficult to get used to at first. This is because you have probably spent most of your life feeling as though every decision you made had to be about everyone else and not about you. The chances are you never took the time to consider how you felt about the choices you had to make. Instead, you looked at the options you had to choose from and tried to decide which option would be more pleasing to the other people in your life. In a way, it's a bit like constantly Christmas shopping for other people. Every decision you made was an attempt to bring happiness to others, never to bring happiness to yourself. In order to move on with your life you need to begin to turn that thought process around and start making decisions for yourself rather than for other people. Only then can you truly be free of the controlling influences of a codependent relationship.

In some cases the opposite scenario may play out, the one in which you start buying anything and everything your heart desires. This can have equally negative consequences, especially when the bill arrives in the mail! Such binge shopping is understandable, however, since you have years of self-pampering to make up for. Fortunately, there is a simple trick that can help you to avoid binge shopping as well as any feelings of guilt that you might experience as mentioned before. This trick is to create a wish list. Simply write down all the things you want or need, regardless of price, size or importance. Write down everything you would buy if money were no object. Once you have created this list go back through it, one item at a time, and decide which items to keep and which items to remove. Start by keeping those items that you need to buy. This will ensure you purchase only those things you can justify, which will help to overcome or even prevent any feelings of guilt.

Another effective trick is to buy one thing at a time, spacing out the shopping experience in order to keep from feeling overwhelmed. You can choose to buy one thing a week, thereby curbing your spending as well as giving you something to look forward to. Once you have crossed off all the items on your need list you can create a list of the things you want. These can be purchased on an even more infrequent basis, such as once a month, thereby helping you to ease into the process of buying things for the sole purpose of bringing you pleasure. This same process holds true for any decision making paradigm. No matter what the decisions are the important thing is to start with your needs and then extend to your wants. This will enable you to develop the habit of choosing for yourself while maintaining some level of discipline that will keep you from losing control.

Become Self-Aware

The idea of becoming self-aware might sound like some Zen ideal that requires hours of meditation or yoga to achieve. Fortunately, while meditation and yoga can help to achieve a deep level of self-awareness they aren't required for the level you need at this point. Rather than needing to out your place in the Universe, the self-awareness you are looking for right now is what your favorite color is, or what ice cream flavor you like best. As such, the path to this level of self-awareness can be a fun and exciting one, requiring more daring than discipline as in the case of meditation or yoga! The trick is to treat this as a time of self-discovery, one that allows you to meet yourself for the very first time.

Since most choices are subjective in nature there isn't really a right or wrong answer. Instead, it comes down to a matter of preference. This is especially true in the case of what your favorite color is or what your favorite ice cream is. At first you might feel anxious when trying to make decisions on such matters as you probably don't know the answers. However, rather than stressing out about it simply explore life, making one choice at a time and learning as much as you can along the way.

For example, don't be afraid to try different flavors and colors until you find the ones that work for you. The choices you make in life should bring you joy, therefore find the things that make you happy and then start choosing them on a regular basis. If you make a choice that isn't happy don't feel as though you failed or made a mistake. Instead, recognize that choice isn't right for you and don't make it again.

Another type of self-awareness you will want to develop is that of being aware of your feelings. Anyone who has been victim of a codependent relationship will have had to suppress their emotions and feelings in order to focus on the feelings and needs of others. Subsequently, you might not actually know how you feel at any given time. It is vital to develop the ability to know how you are feeling so that you can practice greater self-care in many of life's situations. Fortunately, developing this self-awareness is actually quite easy, requiring only a small amount of time and effort to achieve. The simple trick is to take a few moments during the day to ask yourself how you are feeling. At first you will want to choose a time where you are alone and uninterrupted, such as first thing in the morning or the last thing at night. Simply ask yourself how you feel and take the time to discover the answer.

You may struggle to answer the question at first since you are likely out of touch with your feelings. However, it is vital that you do answer the question, even if the answer seems a bit strange. For example, if you neither feel happy nor sad then simply state that you feel indifferent and leave that as your answer. Alternatively, if you do feel something, even just a tingling sense of happiness, sadness, or some other emotion, then state that as your answer. You don't have to feel overwhelming emotions at every point of the day. You just have to recognize the emotions you have, large or small. The important thing is to not stress about it, instead understand that you will discover your feelings in time.

Once you have mastered the ability to determine your feelings in the safe space of your home you can start extending the practice into the other environments of your day-to-day life. While at work you can ask yourself how you feel at various points, thereby recognizing the impact different people or events have on your mindset. The important thing is to become self-aware so that you shift your attention from the thoughts and feelings of others to your own thoughts and feelings. Only then can you live your own life in a real and meaningful way, making the right choices for you and taking actions that serve to benefit you and bring you the happiness and satisfaction you truly deserve.

Chapter 23. Acceptance and Forgiveness

Self-forgiveness

Just as important, if not more important than forgiving others, is forgiving yourself. Everyone makes mistakes, everyone does things that are not proud of. But if you refuse to forgive yourself this only shows that there's something you are holding on to.

You need to look on yourself with the eyes of compassion and give the same compassion to yourself you would give to another. If you look at your actions impartially, you will see that you are always doing the best you can do considering the situation. When you do things that you are not proud of you need to recognize this truth. If you cannot forgive yourself for what you have done, then you will also never be able to forgive others. And you always live controlled by this grudge against yourself.

You need to acknowledge that when you made mistakes, and perhaps hurt people. You are only acting out your conditioning and perhaps repeating the mistakes of your parents. The good news is that now you have seen the error of your ways and so you are free to change. This is a difficult and sobering realization, to come to see the depths of your dysfunction. However, recognize that it is true that it is the darkest before the dawn

Self-love

Finally, we come to the subject of self-love. As has already been stated, you must love yourself or you will never be able to love another. Self-love is often the most challenging thing that people struggle with. They may find it easy to love their mother or love their dog, but find it so difficult to love their very own self.

As with things, this all goes back to your very early childhood when you are taught that your true natural self is some way wrong or not lovable. Perhaps you are taught that it is selfish to love yourself and so you spend your whole life attempting to love others so that you can be unselfish. Maybe you feel as though you have done things that are have made you unworthy of love.

Genuine love and affection for yourself can change your life immediately. When you love yourself, you enjoy your own company and can find deep pleasure in just taking a walk or making a meal. You love your own presence and can find deep contentment in everyday life. Most importantly, when you love yourself, you do not need someone else to love you. It is only when you reach this point that you can attract a healthy love relationship with another individual who also loves himself or herself.

Do What You Love

As you begin to love yourself, accept yourself, forgive yourself, and follow your inner guidance system you then open up to a life where you are free to follow your joy and have fun. As you move beyond codependent patterns and learn to be an autonomous individual you find all of your suppressed and repressed energies suddenly free; giving you the motivation, the passion, and the free time to explore your passions.

Play!

Playfulness is key to life, but is what many codependent individuals were robbed of in their childhood. Because of chaotic home situations and the presence of addiction and trauma they were not given the safe space and support to freely play, imagine, and have fun. Play is how you deeply enjoy life without needing to compulsively try to accomplish any serious task or fulfill someone else's obligations. An important element of being free of codependency and living your truest life is being able to play. Often it is in your moments of play that you may create something and discover something new that perhaps will open up a new career for you, allow you to meet a new partner, or make new friends.

Creative Expression: Your Hobbies and Interests

As you explore playfulness you also being to explore your hobbies and interests. You can now take the time to explore the things you always wished you could do, the things you've always been interested in but never felt you were worthy of doing or have the time to do.

Life is about exploring the things that interest you. As you free yourself from codependency, it is good to make a concerted effort to explore new hobbies and new interests, and stretch yourself beyond where you had been before. Now is the time to finally do the thing as you always wished you could do but never had the time to do because you were taking care of other people, or someone else made you feel as though exploring your hobbies, was selfish

Social Interaction

A common effect of being co codependent is that your social interactions are at a minimum because you are focused on one person or a small group of people who you depend upon and feel you must give all of your attention to. As you free yourself from codependency and explore your hobbies and interests you become open to having many more social interactions. These are great opportunities to meet others on equal footing and have healthy give-and-take relationships which are balanced and do not contain elements of neediness, fear, control, trauma, abuse, etc. You will find that there are many people in the world with whom you can share friendship, collaborate, and explore life.

Meditation & Relaxation

An important and very helpful way to aid you in discovering your true self and doing what you love is the practice of meditation and relaxation. This does not need to be any complicated ritual. It is simply the practice of sitting quietly for a certain period of time each day. As you do this you allow yourself to quiet your active mind so that you may hear and feel deeper inner impulses.

Many of us are so active and busy throughout our lives that we never take time to tune in; and codependents are especially prone to this as they are always depending on another and doing things for others. Meditation and relaxation is an opportunity to go within and recognize what our heart is trying to say to us and what our soul is trying to communicate. As you take time each day, even if it is only for 10 minutes to sit quietly, you may discover impulses and feelings and desires and things you always wanted to do. This also has the effect of relaxing your body, releasing tension, healing pain, and allowing a greater sense of ease and enjoyment in your daily life,

As you allow yourself to fully feel your emotions and therefore heal, the final step is to accept what has happened and then move on. At some point you must accept that in some way it was your fate to be born into the family and situation that you were. While you may not have consciously chose it, there is no use wishing for a different hand to be dealt to you. It happened and now it is in the past. You are free to drop the unnecessary baggage of the past and move on with your life free of that weight.

Forgiveness is a critical aspect of this acceptance process. With the distance of time and space from your trauma you can hopefully come to understand that those who hurt you or were not able to provide for your needs were themselves suffering. It is likely that in your parent or guardian's childhood they themselves were not given the love and support that they needed. One thing is for sure – if you do not allow yourself to forgive yourself and others you will never be able to be free. Be careful, however, of not forgiving too soon or too late. If you try to forgive too soon then you will not allow yourself to fully feel your grief and understand why it happened. On the other hand, if you hold onto your resentment too long it will only hurt yourself and prevent you from moving on with your life.

Many people misunderstand what forgiveness is. While it does mean you are releasing your hurt and resentment as well as any desire for revenge. It does not however, mean that you are condoning the actions of your abuser. You can forgive someone while still recognizing that their actions were not right. It also doesn't mean that you need to forget what they have done and therefore lower your defenses if you must be in contact with them in the future. You do not need to still be friends or be in a relationship with them if you feel that it is not in your best interests.

Done correctly, acceptance and forgiveness free up your energy and empowers you to live the life you wish to live. You become unburdened from your past experiences and therefore are freed up to move on and build new relationships and have new experiences without them being tainted by unhealed grief from your past. This process provides you with self-esteem and the ability to be vulnerable and share your love with others.

Chapter 24. Restoring Self-Esteem

Another devastating scar left behind by codependent relationships is that of low self-esteem. Any victim of codependence will know how a taker keeps you under their power by making you feel inadequate when it comes to just about everything in life. You are made to feel inferior in terms of looks, intelligence and overall ability. Added to that, you are constantly blamed for everything that goes wrong in life, even if you had nothing to do with whatever it was that went wrong. In the end, no matter how unrealistic such accusations may be, their constancy can have a way of programming a person's mind to where they begin to believe them. Eventually the victim of a codependent relationship will see themselves as inferior in every way, and they will believe that anything they put their hand to will be destined to fail as a result of their inferior nature.

In order to create a new and healthy life it is critical that you begin to restore your self-esteem. If you don't, the likelihood of you returning to a codependent relationship is extremely high. However, once you begin to restore your sense of self-esteem you will create an ever-growing distance between you and toxic relationships of any kind. This will keep you safe from returning to the old, harmful ways of codependency and will keep you on track for creating the life of your dreams.

This will discuss several effective ways to rebuild your self-esteem, and thus rebuild your life.

Be In The Moment

A common theme in this page is the importance of being in the moment. While there are several reasons why this is important one of the main reasons is to escape the influences of your past. Any time you allow yourself to fixate on your codependent lifestyle you open yourself to returning to those ways. Among other things you allow your mind to begin to replay the sound bites of your past that tell you how inferior and incapable you are as a friend, spouse, child or person in general. The more you play these sound bites, the greater their influence is upon your mind. Therefore, it is critical to turn your attention to the present moment where you aren't being bombarded by such criticisms of your character and ability.

The bottom line is that whenever you find your mind drifting off to the negative past you need to take a moment and ground yourself in the here and now. One of the easiest practices for doing this is to simply tell yourself that those memories are dead and buried, and that your life isn't connected to that time anymore. Furthermore, you should focus your mind on present circumstances that bring you joy and fulfillment. You might have a job that you enjoy, new friends that you spend time with doing fun things, or some other aspect of your life that is totally different from the codependent existence you endured before. No matter what the specifics are, the key is to focus your attention on those things in the present moment that reflect your abilities as a friend, an employee, or just a normal, everyday healthy and functional person.

Sometimes the best way to avoid being dragged back into the past is to start the day in such a way as to create a more current and positive mindset.

The best way to achieve this goal is to give yourself about fifteen extra minutes each and every morning where you can sit in silence and contemplate where you are as a person. You might choose to list off the codependent people you have broken free from, putting them and their influences in the past where they belong. Tell yourself that those people cannot harm you anymore, and that you are a different person now, one who is happy, strong and confident. Take the time to focus on all the things you are happy about in your life, especially those things you look forward to experiencing in the day ahead. The key is to focus your mind on the positive aspects of your life in the here and now, thereby moving further and further away from the pain and suffering of your past.

Surround Yourself With Positivity

Restoring self-esteem is a goal that is best approached from every angle at once. This means that you should practice those things that fix the problem from within, as well as those things that fix the problem from without. Methods such as being in the moment are examples of solutions that solve the problem from the inside out. An example of a solution that solves the problem from the outside in is surrounding yourself with positivity. This is the practice of placing yourself in the places and around the people who create the most positive energy possible. When you are surrounded by positive energy you can't help but absorb that energy, just the same way that you can't help but become wet in a rainstorm, or hot on a sunny summer day. The more positive energy you absorb, the more positive you will become. This includes developing a healthy and vibrant sense of self-esteem.

A good place to start when it comes to surrounding yourself with positivity is to make new friends. Find people who are warm, caring and friendly, and who provide support and motivation to everyone they come into contact with. These people aren't as hard to find as you might think. Instead, they are fairly common, you just weren't able to find them while you were imprisoned in codependent relationships. Once you find these people the trick is to spend regular time with them. You don't have to move in with them or spend every waking moment in their presence, instead you just have to find time each and every day to surround yourself with people who are happy, confident and just nice overall. This will give you a dose of positive energy that will help you to build a more positive self-identity, one that is free from the influences of your codependent past.

In addition to surrounding yourself with positive people you should take the time to place yourself in positive environments. These environments will serve the same function of creating positive energy that fills you from the outside, while also helping you to discover your more positive nature from within. For example, if you love art then you could spend regular time exploring art galleries and museums. Such places are positive unto themselves in that they are full of colorful, beautiful objects, paintings and the like that bring happiness to anyone who looks at them. However, you will also create a sense of joy and value from within by engaging in something you have a passion for. This will give you a sense of connection to the positive places you go, and that connection will go a long way to redefining you as a person. By recreating your sense of self you will create a strong and robust sense of self-esteem that will enable you to create the happy and healthy life you truly deserve.

Find Something To Be Happy About

A person's self-esteem is usually a reflection of that person's experiences. As such, someone who has enjoyed positive, successful experiences will usually have a high sense of self-esteem, whereas someone who has lived a life marked with pain and suffering will usually have a low sense of self-esteem. Subsequently, anyone who has been the victim of codependent relationships will struggle to find traction when it comes to restoring their self-esteem to healthy, positive levels. Fortunately there is a simple trick that can help a person to keep from regressing into the past and begin moving forward in a more positive direction. This trick is to find something to be happy about.

As mentioned, when a person escapes the codependent influences in their life they tend to find new friends, a new job or some other new direction that gives them a newfound sense of purpose. All that you have to do in order to begin creating a strong, healthy sense of self-esteem is to begin to focus on these accomplishments. The key is to replace the negative sense of self, the one defined by failure and insecurity, with one that is optimistic and full of confidence. By focusing on the things that are going well in your current life you can begin to build a sense of self-accomplishment, one that will prove your true worth each and every day. Whether you focus your mind on the job you love, the friends you have fun with, or even your dog or cat, by filling your mind with the happy and successful experiences and elements in your life you can begin to create the healthy, confident sense of self-esteem that will heal the scars of your codependent past.

One of the most effective methods for focusing on the happy things in your life is to take pictures of those things.

Every smart phone can take a decent enough picture, and they have enough space where you can create a significant library of happy, inspiring pictures. Therefore, if you love your job, take pictures of where you work, the people you work with, and anything else that brings you joy. Take plenty of pictures of your friends, including some with you having fun with your friends. Needless to say, pictures of your pets will go a long way to making you smile if you start to find yourself struggling with the dark memories of your past. In short, create an easily accessible library of pictures that you can browse when you need a dose of inspiration and happiness. The more you focus on those things during your day, the happier you will be which will help to increase your self-esteem by leaps and bounds.

Find Something You Want To Change

While focusing on the things currently going right in your life can go a long way to restoring self-esteem, nothing is more effective than taking on new challenges. As already mentioned, experience is the key to self-esteem. Negative experiences in life will diminish a person's sense of self, whereas positive experiences will strengthen and nurture a healthy, confident self-identity. Therefore, if you really want to restore your self-esteem the best thing to do is to create positive experiences. The best way to do this is to find something you want to change and begin chasing that goal.

It can be tempting at first to take on the biggest, most daunting of challenges in order to make the most progress. For example, if you hate your job you might choose to take on the challenge of finding a better job, thereby increasing your self-esteem exponentially.

While this can be a good idea it can also be a good thing to start small and work your way up.

After all, small gains experienced on a regular basis can create the same positive self-esteem that larger gains can achieve. Furthermore, by taking on smaller challenges at first you can gradually develop a reliable sense of self-worth, one that will enable you to tackle the larger goals on. Therefore, it may be best to start with small goals that are more easily achievable yet no less significant in terms of restoring self-esteem.

Simple goals such as waking up each day, losing five pounds, or starting a new regimen such as exercising, yoga or meditation are excellent options to start with. These goals will require less effort and discipline at first, making it more likely that you will succeed in them. Furthermore, when you make these changes in your life they will begin to create positive energy in your day-to-day experience that will further develop your sense of self-esteem and self-worth, thereby giving you the energy you need to live the life you deserve. The important thing is to find things that you want to change in your life and begin making those changes. This will not only improve your life step by step, it will also give you a sense of control, one that helps you recognize that you have the ability to create your life. Once you realize that you can create your life your sense of self-esteem will reach levels beyond your imagination!

Learn to say "No"

So far the methods for restoring self-esteem have been fairly positive in nature. Staying focused on the present, surrounding yourself with positivity and creating change are all things that reflect motivation, ambition and hope. It may come as a surprise, therefore, to learn that there are some methods for restoring self-esteem that appear somewhat negative in comparison. One such method is that of learning to say "No."

Such an action can seem highly negative at first, especially when it comes to saying "No" to friends, loved ones and the like. However, this act is an essential part of breaking free of the habit of always serving the needs of others. By learning to say "No" you are developing the strength of mind and character to take care of yourself first, even if that means letting down others in the process. While this may take some getting used to at first it is an essential part of truly breaking free of the codependent life you are trying to leave behind.

The first benefit to learning to say "No" is that you will begin to put your needs first. Anyone who is in the habit of saying "Yes" all of the time will do so at their own peril. More often than not they will find themselves overwhelmed with tasks and obligations as the result of not being able to turn down requests for their time and effort. When such a person begins to exercise better management over their time and effort they avoid becoming overwhelmed by having too many things to do. This enables them to live a more confident, productive life in which they have the time and means needed to accomplish their own goals and ambitions, something which will go a long way toward rebuilding self-esteem.

The second benefit from learning to say "No" is that it places the individual in control of their lives. Rather than feeling subservient to the needs and desires of others, such a person will feel free and independent. This will give them a whole new perspective on life, one that sees life as full of opportunity rather than full of demands, obligations and the like. With this new perspective on life there will come a new sense of self, one that is comprised of higher levels of self-confidence, self-worth and most importantly, self-esteem. The important thing to remember is that you don't always have to say "No" to a request for your time and effort.

You can accept such requests as long as you have the resources needed to do so without jeopardizing your own wellbeing.

Additionally, any true friend will understand when you can't help them, and they won't hold it against you. If they do, then you have discovered that they aren't a true friend at all. Instead, they have all the markings of another codependent relationship, one that you need to stay away from at all costs.

Keep A Journal

Anyone who has ever been on a really long journey will know that at some point it can feel as though the destination will never be reached. This is especially true in the case of long races, such as marathons, where the only two markers of note are the starting line and the finish line. Once you leave the starting line there is only one destination to mark your progress— the end of the race. Subsequently, it can seem as though you are no closer to the finish despite the fact that you have run a considerable distance. This can cause a person to lose hope, which in turn causes them to lose confidence in their ability to actually cross the finish line. Needless to say, such a scenario can be devastating to a person's sense of self-esteem, and thus should be avoided at all costs.

When it comes to regular day-to-day life, this situation can be avoided by the simple practice of keeping a journal. A journal can help you to record your desires and goals, along with the steps you are taking to achieve those desires and goals. Furthermore, you can mark the progress you make in your journey to creating a happy and healthy life by recording all the victories you achieve along the way. No matter how small a victory might seem, it can be hugely significant when it comes to restoring self-esteem. Therefore, in order to keep your self-esteem and your motivation levels at their maximum it is vital to record your progress in a journal that you can refer to whenever you have to remind yourself of the gains you have made.

Chapter 25. Building excellent relationships

The unfortunate truth is that many people who struggle with codependency are not able to accurately evaluate a partner to see if they are healthy and someone that they can enter into a functional relationship with. Due to their early life experiences they associate dysfunctional behavior as being normal and perhaps even feel safe and comfortable being in a relationship with someone who is unhealthy just because that is familiar to them.

The following are some traits of healthy and long-lasting relationships. Of course, not all couples can for fill all of these requirements all the time. However, a healthy relationship should follow these guidelines the vast majority of the time.

- Both partners feel safe
- Both partners make decisions together
- Both continually develop their Self and their self-esteem
- Realistic expectations
- Effective communication
- Acceptance of the other's differences and needs
- A balance of quality time together and alone
- Cooperation and mutual giving
- Both partners maintain outside friendships
- The sharing of common vision for the relationship
- Have similar values and needs
- Both partners feel safe

Safety is an essential ingredient to a healthy relationship. Both partners need to feel that they are respected, listen to and that there is no threat of abuse whether physical or emotional. When both partners feel safe then they are free to be vulnerable and open up and experience true honesty with each other. When one or both partners do not feel safe they will become withdrawn, isolated and feel resentment towards the other. A person who feels safe feel supported to be their true, natural self. You know that no matter how bad things get you have a safe place with your partner where you can feel heard and respected. If however one of the partners is not reliable and causes the other to feel unsafe, then the relationship is bound to experience difficulties.

Both partners make decisions together

It is unfortunately common then in many relationships one individual will make a majority of the decisions. Wow it is OK for one of the participants to be the leader, if it is too unbalanced it will create problems. Sometimes couples will try to avoid conflict by pretending that problems do not exist. In the long run this leads to feelings of resentment and creates separation and distance between the people in the relationship.

However, couples who have good communication and problem-solving skills are effective at respecting and listening to each other's opinions without resorting to arguing and conflict. These couples learn how to come to a compromise that works for both of them and honors the relationship rather than being one-sidedly favoring one individually over the other. Mature couples understand that the happiness and respect of the others needs and opinions can only strengthen the relationship. They see disagreements as an opportunity to greater understand their partner and deepen their shared relationship.

Both continually develop their Self and their self-esteem

As we have touched on, it is vitally important that each individual in the relationship have a very strong sense of self. The best relationships happen when both individuals are perfectly content being alone and pursuing their individual interests, but find value and nourishment in their partnership. In this way they can both give unselfishly and without codependent neediness. One is not seeking validation and support of their fragile ego in the other, and because of this they are able to be more intimate. Couples with vague senses of self and low self-esteem will expect unrealistic things from their partner and depend on them to make themselves feel happy. One must understand that no one else can make them happy, but this is only your responsibility. As both individuals develop their self individually it makes the relationship stronger collectively.

Realistic expectations

A common trait of codependent relationships is that one or both partners will have very high expectations that are impossible to meet. They will look at the other individual as the one who will make them happy and live happily ever after. The truth is that it is only your own responsibility to make you happy and these unrealistic expectations only create impossible to live up to ideals. The period at the beginning of the relationship when both individuals are in love and infatuated with each other can never last forever, couples who have unrealistic expectations are not able to deal with the inevitable lessening of attraction and passion. A realistic expectation for a relationship is one that understands that all relationships are imperfect and will sooner or experience challenges. However, they meet these challenges in a mature and measured way.

Effective communication

A hallmark of long-lasting relationships is effective communication. In a dysfunctional relationship the open communication of one's feelings and needs is the first thing to be lost.

What is healthy communication? It is the open sharing of your authentic feelings and experiences while listening to the other person and acknowledging their experience. Both partners must feel comfortable being assertive and communicating their boundaries while asking for what they need and desire. Effective communication also does not include subtle forms of manipulation and demanding or punishing the other person when they don't agree with you.

Effective communication does not mean that you cannot have disagreements or heated discussions. It only means that these disagreements are carried out within an environment of respect and fairness with certain rules which are not crossed. At no time is attacking or abusive communication tolerated, and both partners do not resort to blame, criticizing, or personal attacks. Part of communicating affectively is knowing when to take a break and allow both individuals to cool down before attempting to discuss a topic.

Acceptance of the other's differences and needs

Differences are natural in a relationship and are what make them rich and fulfilling. A relationship between healthy individuals will contain many points of difference. The key is that when each individual is comfortable with their own differences and in being their true self they will also be more excepting of differences in others and in their partner.

After the initial honeymoon phase of a few months where there are usually few conflicts, as you began to grow more comfortable with your partner you will start to notice differences that perhaps cause conflict. The acceptance of differences in your partner does not mean that you condone or must agree with what they believe or their behavior, but you must be able to except who they are without trying to change them. That is, unless their behavior is not in integrity and causes harm. One must never expect or demand that another person change who they are to please you. If you do attempt to change someone against their will it will only be a matter of time before they revert back to their old self. You and your partner must work out together whether your differences are irreconcilable or are something you can mutually find common ground on.

A balance of quality time together and alone

Integral to a healthy relationship is having a balance of alone time and time together. As with all things, balance is vitally important. Too much time alone in the relationship will cause feelings of isolation, but too much time together will lead to one or both of the partners feeling smothered and unable to breathe and be themselves. Successful relationships happen between people who share at least some common activities in hobbies. However common hobbies aren't absolutely mandatory in a healthy relationship if you can still find time to be together. It may be something as simple as taking daily walks together or spending quality time together at meal times.

As the common saying goes, "distance makes the heart grow fonder". It is having the all-important time apart that actually makes the time we do spend together more precious. No matter how much you love another, if you spend every minute of every day in their presence you will eventually grow tired of them in need some space and time alone. All healthy relationships contain individuals who have interests, friends, and work experiences which are separate from their partner. When your only source of fulfillment comes from your intimate relationship this puts too much pressure and emphasis on it and ultimately results in strain.

Cooperation and mutual giving

In unhealthy relationships the individuals often fight over who is getting more attention or two is getting their needs met. There is a "I'll scratch your back if you scratch my back" attitude. This transactional mindset is unhealthy and leads to resentment and mutual greediness. This power struggle and competition over the reception of affection and gifts creates a very unhealthy environment of conflict.

In healthy relationships, however, both individuals acknowledge that it is their joy to make the other one happy. Both partners enjoy giving and doing acts of service for their loved one, and because of this they both feel joyful and sufficient. Due to the fact that they both know how to take care of themselves and do not depend on the other for affection, they do not feel the need to fight over the allocation of affection and acts of service. Additionally, they know when to say no if they are tired or feel that they are being asked to much of.

Both partners maintain outside friendships

Sometimes couples in a relationship becomes so focused on each other that they forget about their other friendships. This is not healthy and places too much importance on their relationship to for fill all of their needs for human interaction and camaraderie. It is not realistic to expect that only one other person can for fill all of your needs for friendship, and a healthy relationship is supported by a wide network of friends and family. Additionally, it is possible to make friendships with other couples and therefore be able to do things as a group.

The sharing of common vision for the relationship

Couples need to share a common vision for the future and for what they wish to build with the relationship. This creates a sense of cohesiveness and allows you to work towards something greater than your individual self. Couples can work together to create a business, start a family, need or build a home, etc. It is fun and exciting to see you are part of a team that is creating something new, and this is something that you can create in your intimate relationship. Couples who do not have a vision for the future can find themselves a drift without purpose or cohesion.

Have similar values and needs

While a couple does not have to have the exact same needs and values, they must have similar or compatible ones. It is important that couples except their differences, but if they are too far apart it may be a sign that the relationship is just not meant to be. Couples can have vastly different opinions and views on life and still get along well and have a very healthy relationship. It is not necessary that you have the same religious or political views as your partner, but you must be willing to compromise and respect each other's differences.

Often in relationships either opposites attract or similarities attract. When two people who are very similar build a relationship it is often not very difficult to reconcile each person's needs and values as they are quite close. However, when two people who are vastly different come together there are often many things that must be worked out and balanced in order to allow the relationship to function in a healthy manner. One way of navigating this is to sit down with your partner and list out your needs and values, together you can go over your list and have a discussion about your similarities and differences. Is this contrast between two very different personalities which can create such a rich and fulfilling relationship. But you must work extra hard to come to common ground and mutual respect for the other individual.

Chapter 26. Self-Care

Self-love goes deeper than just an appreciation of your physical beauty. Instead, it encompasses appreciating yourself as you are, appreciating your self-worth, knowing that you are loved - at least by yourself and therefore you are valuable, knowing that you deserve the best in this life... The list goes on. Self-love is akin to unconditionally loving yourself. Despite what your physical appearance looks like in the mirror, do you still appreciate yourself? Do you still accept yourself? Do you still feel good about yourself? Yes, you may be in a relationship, but away from your partner, do you still see and identify with yourself, or has the you that you once knew become lost in the relationship?

Self-love means that when you look at yourself, you see the real you, and you not only like what you see, but you love what you see. No one knows the real you except you, but if you find that you are always no longer sure of who you are, then you may be ready for a self-love journey. You cannot love someone that you do not know, and it thus follows that for you to get to a point where you can say you have found self-love, you'll need to get to know yourself all over again. Rediscovering who you are, and then learning to love yourself is not an event, but it is a process that takes patience and persistence. Keep in mind that the only thing that is constant about life on earth is that change is a given. If you take pictures of yourself from a decade ago and compare these with how you look now, you will note that you have changed. However, changes that human beings experience as they go through life are more complex than just physical changes. Every experience that you go through changes you and that also includes the relationship that you are in. That said, you constantly need to make an effort to keep in touch with yourself and to take note of the changes that are happening to you. Self-love habits will not only keep you abreast of who you are in all the hustle and bustle of relationship life but also make you gain confidence about yourself in the relationship. This will improve your decision-making process, how you communicate with your partner, and get you to a point where you can fully appreciate yourself and your partner.

With self-love, you will be on a sure path to enjoying a loving relationship with your partner. If you have self-love, you are likely to be less insecure as a human being. As such, your partner doesn't have to take on the burden of convincing you that you are worth loving, that you are as beautiful as you are, and all the drama that comes with being in a relationship with an insecure partner. As someone with self-love, you have more capacity to give love, be it physically or emotionally. Your emotional demands on your partner are likely to be less than those of someone who doesn't appreciate themselves.

Some people only have a fleeting relationship with self-love. They feel good and alive when their partner is around, showering praise and admiration, but when they're alone, all the good feelings vanish. Have you ever woken up from a deep sleep, and as you slowly come to, you feel a sense of joy and contentment radiating from your heart and slowly spreading to your extremities, and for a brief, fleeting moment, you are content, even happy? And then a brief moment, you recalibrate, and that feeling of happiness that you had is swiftly replaced with worry, self-doubt, and a whole host of other feelings that drag you down into the pool of negativity? If you are one of those people, imagine what it would be like to hold on to that feeling irrespective of what you are going through, how frustrating your day is, whether or not your partner is around, or even when you and your partner are not in a good place. Below shows the examples of self-love habits that you need to practice whilst in a relationship in order to not lose touch with yourself.

Examples of Self-Love Habits

1. Schedule some alone time to tend to yourself and your needs. As much as it is important to spend time with your partner, it is also

important to appreciate that you and your partner may have different personal needs that you can best attend to in your alone time. Although it may be uncomfortable the first few times you try it, the goal of this exercise is to get to a point where you are able to enjoy your own company. Enjoy your coffee or food or whatever it is that you like doing by yourself. You should be very good at entertaining yourself because no one should know you better than yourself, right? If you can learn to feel complete even when you're alone, then you are on the right track.

2. Go out with your besties. It is possible to get so busy in a relationship that you lose touch with your old friends. But this is important to make the effort to keep in touch with your besties from before the relationship once in a while. Not only is this something fun that can keep you looking forward to such appointments as they may spice up your life but in addition, when with your friends, you may get a reminder of who you are and recultivate your interests.

3. Set daily or weekly personal goals and a reward system. These goals may be a subset of the goals that you have as a couple or your own personal goals that you are trying to work toward. Goals give you a sense of purpose in life and can fill your days with excitement while preventing life from becoming monotonous depending on how you set them. The check and reward mechanism will give you feedback on your progress toward the things that you need to accomplish and will give you a sense of accomplishment - a reason to raise a glass to yourself at the end of the day and feel good about yourself.

4. Evaluate yourself. Give yourself credit for work done and reward yourself. Note, you don't need your partner for this, but you should be able to congratulate yourself and feel proud of yourself when you deserve it. Acknowledge mistakes and also note room for improvement. Acknowledging mistakes and doing something about them helps you grow as an individual. It is the first step toward addressing these mistakes to make sure that they don't happen again. After all, experience is the best teacher.

5. Appreciate that you are human, and you make mistakes. The good thing though is that just as much as you make mistakes, you are also capable of learning from your mistakes and can be a better person for it. A mistake does not necessarily mean that your life is ruined or that you will forever be defined by it. The lessons you learn from mistakes are invaluable and are a necessary part of growing up. Evaluation exercises thus ground you, as they require you open up to yourself and critically look at yourself, without worries about what other people, especially your partner, may think. Self-love, however, dictates that as you do this, you also should avoid being too harsh on yourself. This harshness can be identified through being too critical of yourself in certain circumstances. So, learn to cut yourself some slack. If the goals that you are setting for yourself aren't achievable given the timelines that you're on, as you evaluate, adjust these goals until you reach a point where you feel you've found an equilibrium. If you are being too harsh or overly critical about yourself, purposefully re-examine the situation using facts. You will realize that your thoughts are often not based on facts and the situation you are analyzing is not as bad as you were thinking.

6. Develop long-term plans and think of a road map that may help you get there. For example, your goals could be career aspirations, studying, a business or a hobby. These long-term plans have to be your own plans and should be things that you can accomplish with or without your partner. If done properly, having such goals can help you feel that you are in charge of your life. Having your own pet project, no matter how small it is, helps you keep in touch with the things that are most important to you. If you are also passionate about something, that could be the foundation you need to maintain a reference point of things that you have accomplished in life.

7. Acknowledge your strengths and weaknesses. This is the key to knowing who you are. You can play on your strengths and purposefully work on your weaknesses when they conflict with your

life goals. The end result will be a well-rounded individual who works hard and who you respect when you look at yourself in the mirror.

8. Don't take everything that happens in your life for granted, and one way of doing this is to be thankful for the good things in your life. You may feel good at the moment, but a few days or weeks, you may have forgotten. Keeping a journal helps in this regard, as when needed, you can relive those moments.

9. Find an exercise routine that you like and can fit around your schedule. Yoga, swimming, running, cycling, and going to the gym are good examples. You do not necessarily need your partner to do this, although some couples do enjoy exercising together. This will allow you to take care of your body, all while giving you a healthy way to de-stress and keeping you in shape.

10. Learn to say no and not to feel guilty about it if you are not comfortable with something. Sometimes as someone in a relationship, you may find it hard to say no. If a partner checks in with you to see if you can do something for them, and you can't for some reason, it's ok to say so.

11. Laugh. A good way to care for yourself is to make yourself laugh every day. Try finding a good comedy to watch, watching silly videos online, reading jokes, following your favorite comedian, etc. Laughter sends you to that 'happy place' where you decrease stress hormones and release endorphins which are the feel-good hormones. No matter how bad you thought your day was, your assessment will change after a good laugh, and you will feel much better.

12. Find a hobby. This could be something fun and creative that you used to do as a child, like singing, dancing, coloring, drawing, or painting. Your hobbies do not necessarily have to be the same as your partners, but this should be something that you like doing and that makes you feel good.

13. Pay attention to what your inner voice is saying. Whether you feel it as a tightening in your stomach every time you do something that is not right or an internal monologue in which you have to debate

with yourself in order to make yourself do something, there are times when you need to pause and listen to that inner voice. More often than not, you may get caught up in social expectations about what you should and shouldn't be doing in your relationship, but it is important to stop and find out what you want.

14. Stop comparing yourself to others. There is only one copy of you in this world, and you can never be someone else. Live your life the best way you can, given your circumstances.

15. Take what you hear about yourself with a pinch of salt. If it is praise, there is no need to puff up and walk around like a peacock, as you know more about yourself than any other person. If it's critical, know that other people's opinions of you do not necessarily define who you really are. As such, you have a right to remind yourself "that's not true" when listening to someone speak about you. In other words, learn to put a sieve in your ears and only let in information that will help you be a better person.

16. Get rid of toxic people. Once you are in tune with your inner self, you may become more aware of how being around certain people always makes you feel drained. If you always feel like you have regressed in your self-love journey after every encounter, then it might be beneficial for you to evaluate that relationship and see if you might be better off avoiding such people.

17. Confront your fears. Negative thoughts about yourself are often based on experiences and exposure to certain environments that may no longer be relevant in your current circumstances. Holding on to those fears may give you a myopic view of yourself, and the only way to address this is to acknowledge your negative thoughts, process them by gathering facts about the issue in question, and then reevaluate it in light of those facts. Throughout this process, you get to identify misconceptions that you have been holding on to and also identify areas where you think you need to improve. This process will address most of the issues underlying your anxiety, and you will be quite happy.

18. Trust yourself. When it comes to making decisions about yourself, you are the one who knows what is best for you. If you are choosing something to wear, there may be a particular outfit that just feels right despite what everyone else says. The same applies to the people that you date, the food that you eat, the career path that you choose, and all the other decisions that you make on a daily basis. Believe in your heart that no one knows you better than you know yourself. Despite mistakes made in the past, you are still the best person to make decisions for yourself, and you can't delegate this role to other people. There is a difference between asking for advice and then making the decision for yourself and simply passing the responsibility onto someone else. Once you learn to trust yourself and to make decisions for yourself, you quickly learn that you are accountable for the things that happen in your life. The knowledge that you're ultimately the one responsible will make you more introspective and cautious when evaluating situations. It also prevents you from adopting a mindset which blames other people for everything that you are not happy about in your life.

Learn to put yourself first. There are circumstances where you need to prioritize yourself. No matter how small the gesture is, be it time for a cup of coffee all by yourself, staring out the window and appreciating the sights of nature, going shopping by yourself, or running a bath with bubbles and essential oils. Other examples of doing things that you love for yourself can include a walk in the park, taking yourself out for dinner, going to the library to read, watching a movie, dancing, etc. This time can help you recharge your batteries given how hectic life can be, especially when in a relationship.

Chapter 27. Establishing Healthy Relationships

Gaining independence is a critical step toward healing the wounds of codependency, one that forms the foundation on which a healthy and meaningful life can be built. However, it is vital that the notion of independence not be mistaken for isolation or solitude. Just because a person is independent doesn't mean they have to be alone. On the contrary, many independent people enjoy rich and fulfilling friendships of all kinds. Therefore, the step toward a happy and fulfilling life is to start establishing healthy relationships. Such relationships will not only bring positive energy into your life, they will also keep you from falling back into the old habits of codependency. The more healthy and happy relationships you have in your life is the stronger your social and interpersonal skills will become, thereby enabling you to form rich, intimate relationships on all levels, providing you with the companionship that will make your life truly rewarding. This chapter will discuss several methods that will help you to establish healthy, normal relationships in your life. By following these methods you will be able to leave your codependent influences in the past once and for all.

Ensure healthy communication

One of the defining characteristics of a truly positive relationship is that of healthy communication. Anyone who has been in a dysfunctional relationship of any kind, let alone a codependent one, will know that the first thing to suffer is the communication between all persons in the relationship. Rather than being able to openly and honestly express your thoughts with one another you find that you have to keep certain thoughts and feelings to yourself in order to avoid conflict or other similarly negative reactions. In the most extreme cases this secrecy can lead to outright lying, causing you to tell lies in order to avoid tension, conflict or other negative consequences. In the end, the more you have to lie to other people, the more dishonest you become with yourself. Eventually your life becomes one big deception where even you have a hard time knowing what is real from what isn't.

In contrast, a healthy relationship not only allows for open and honest communication, it actually encourages it. A true friend, for example, will often ask for your opinion on a matter. Sometimes this matter might be as mundane as which color sweater to wear with a particular skirt, or it might be something more profound such as your opinion on relationship issues, political debates or some similarly significant talking point. While your opinion might not change their mind on any particular issue they will nevertheless take it into consideration, thereby seeing the situation from another perspective. Even if they don't agree with the opinions you offer they will always respect your opinions, unlike takers in a codependent relationship who will put you down for not seeing things exactly the way they do.

Another form of healthy communication is to offer advice to the other person.

Again, this advice might be something fairly superficial, such as which restaurant has the best food or which hair stylist is the best. Alternatively, you might offer advice on more pressing matters, such as who to avoid spending time with (in the event you detect a potentially codependent person in your midst) or how to handle a difficult situation at work or in a relationship. The best thing about offering such advice is that it isn't the same thing as controlling the other person, nor is it a form of trying to fix their life as you might within a codependent relationship. Instead, this is about offering your point of view for what it's worth. A true friend will appreciate the input as they will recognize it as a sign of concern for their wellbeing. Such communication needs to be a two-way street in order for it to be truly healthy. Therefore, in addition to being prepared to offer your insights and advice to others you must also be ready, willing and able to receive insights and advice offered to you. And, as with the advice you offer to your friends, advice you receive doesn't have to change your mind or shape your decisions. You get to remain independent in the choices you make, however now you don't have to make those choices alone. By giving and receiving honest and open insights, opinions and ideas you create a stronger, more meaningful bond with the other people in your life, a bond that will help you to become a stronger, more confident person as a result.

Ensure mutual benefits

Just as communication needs to be a two-way street in order for it to be healthy, so too, any and all benefits within a relationship should also be a two-way street. Any victim of a codependent relationship will know all too well that the nature of such relationships is all give and no take.

You constantly give of your time, energy and emotions while getting nothing in return. This creates the servile nature of the giver within a standard codependent relationship. When you find yourself in a normal, healthy relationship things begin to change. Now, rather than always giving and never receiving you begin to find that the give/take ratio is far more even. For every effort you make in order to please the other person in a relationship you will receive an equal effort on their part. This ratio may not always be exactly 50/50, however it will be pretty close, especially over the course of time. Needless to say, keeping score of who gives more is totally dysfunctional, and it is a reflection of a person's codependent past, so DON'T DO IT.

Fortunately, the chances are you will find yourself receiving more effort than you give in the beginning of a normal, healthy relationship. This is because most people are so happy to make a new friend that they invest heavily in the relationship at first. Furthermore, if people see that you have few friends, or they recognize that you are moving on from a bad relationship they will tend to pamper you at first in an attempt to restore your self-esteem and make you feel loved. The trick is to begin returning the favor once you find your feet in the relationship, that way you ensure that the efforts are mutual and not one sided. One way that mutual benefits are ensured in a healthy relationship is to share the decision making process. This usually revolves around such things as where to eat, what movies to watch or what activities to engage in when spending time together. The bottom line is that even the best of friends will have different tastes to some degree, therefore you can't always do things that bring equal joy to both parties.

That said, if you watch a movie that you choose one week you can make sure that you watch a movie they choose the week. This will guarantee that all members in a relationship enjoy equal benefits over the course of time. Alternatively, you can let one person choose the movie while another person chooses the restaurant, thereby spreading the benefits within a single outing. The important thing is to make sure that everyone gets a fair share of the decision making, thus keeping all parties on an equal level.

Another way to ensure mutual benefits within a relationship is to always celebrate each other's birthday. True friends will enjoy buying gifts for each other, so marking dates such as birthdays or other significant events will simply provide an excuse to do so. Fortunately, this ensures an equal share of the spoils as holidays and birthdays are fixed in number, therefore if you buy gifts for each other on such occasions you are guaranteed to give as often as you receive, thereby making the relationship mutually beneficial.

There is, however, a darker side to the mutual benefits of a relationship. This comes in the form of being there for each other in the other person's time of need. A good example of this is in the event that you find a new place to live and need help moving all of your belongings from one location to another. Needless to say, no one likes moving, however true friends will do whatever they can to be there for each other even in such undesirable circumstances. That said, when your friends are there for you it is imperative that you be there for them when they are the ones needing help. This ensures that the relationship is truly equal, both in terms of reward as well as the burdens shared. In the end, the best friends are those who are there for you even on moving day!

Know what and when to share

When you ask people to come up with something that defines a healthy relationship one of the things you hear most is the word "sharing". This goes back to the point just made regarding the sharing of both rewards and burdens in a healthy relationship. The idea is that the more people share with each other, the stronger and healthier their relationship will become. This includes sharing things such as time, effort, rewards, burdens, and even secrets. After all, one of the things that brings friends closer together is an intimate understanding of one another. The more a person knows about their friends, and the more they are known by their friends, the deeper the connection between all involved.

A common mistake made by anyone who is coming from a life of codependency, in which their thoughts, opinions and feelings never mattered, is to over share with their newfound friends. This is usually a reaction to having kept every personal aspect of their being suppressed for so long. The problem is that when a person over shares they tend to push people away from them, creating a sense of isolation that can lead to them returning to codependency in order to not be alone. Therefore, it is vital that you learn what and when to share in order to create and maintain healthy and strong relationships. Revealing secrets is always tempting, especially for anyone who hasn't had any close confidents in their life before. However, it is important to take things slowly at first as most people don't necessarily want to know the deep dark secrets of someone they have just met. If you feel the need to share intimate details about yourself with others the best thing to do is to start slow. Share basic information, such as the fact that you are coming out of a bad relationship. You don't have to share the specifics of what made the relationship bad, especially such things as examples of abuse and trauma. Instead, simply share the fact that you were a victim of a dysfunctional relationship and you are looking to rebuild your life after the fact. That will allow you to open up and share some facts about who you are without scaring people off in the process. You might be able to share more eventually, but that level of sharing will only come in time and should never be rushed.

Fortunately, there are signs to look for that will tell you when it is OK to share your deeper, darker secrets. One of these signs is when your friends start opening up to you. When they feel safe enough to share their darker secrets it is a sign that the relationship is strong enough to manage such a deep connection. This is another form of mutual benefit within a healthy relationship. If you unload all of your emotional baggage onto people who aren't ready for that responsibility you destroy the balance of the relationship, and that can destroy the relationship itself.

However, when both parties start to open up about their past, especially with regard to trauma and abuse, then the balance of the relationship is maintained, and the sharing of secrets will strengthen the bonds between everyone involved rather than drive them apart.

Again, the trick is to look for the signs and take things one step at a time. True friends will be with you for life, so you will have plenty of time to open up to them down the road. You don't have to bare your soul on the very first day.

Find positive people

Anyone who has ever been on a diet will know that the trick to eating right is to use healthy and nutritious foods. Eating a salad is only good if you use the right ingredients. If you fill the salad with shredded cheese product and smother it with creamy, cheesy dressings you will only be deceiving yourself with regard to how healthy your eating habits have become. In order to lose weight, gain muscle and improve your physical health and wellbeing you need to use healthy foods in the meals you eat.

The very same principle applies to healthy relationships. You can practice all of the best methods for creating a healthy and positive relationship with someone, however if that person is negative in nature then all of your efforts are wasted. While you might protect yourself from some of the harm a negative person poses, having them in your life at all is still a dangerous thing, one that will doubtlessly cause you problems at some point in time. Therefore, just as important as it is to use the right ingredients when eating a healthy diet, so too, it is vital that you find positive people in order to establish truly healthy relationships.

Identifying positive people is a fairly easy thing to do for the most part. One of the first things you will notice about positive people is a lack of negative behavior. For example, a positive person will be far less likely to lose their temper, especially over small, seemingly insignificant things.

Needless to say, everyone has a bad day from time to time, even positive people, but any incidents that arise due to a bad day will be isolated and the exception to the rule, not the rule itself. Therefore, a good way to measure whether a person is truly positive is to observe their temperament over the course of time. If they seem level headed and have a calm, confident demeanor they are probably a positive person all around.

Another telltale sign that a person is positive is that they won't be prone to spreading gossip and rumors about other people. One thing that negative people thrive on is the suffering and misery of others. That is why they spend so much time gossiping and spreading rumors. Alternatively, positive people reject such behavior as it goes against the grain of their personality. It's not as if they are simply being on their best behavior in front of other people. The fact is that a positive person finds such behavior abhorrent. To them it is like a shrill noise or a foul odor, something they want to stay far away from. Thus, any time you see people engaged in gossip or some similarly negative activity you know they aren't the type of people you need in your life. However, those who avoid such behaviors, choosing instead to engage in positive conversations and interactions, are exactly the type of people you can establish healthy and meaningful relationships with.

Make more than one friend

The final method for establishing healthy relationships is to make more than one friend. This may seem pretty obvious at first, however it is a pitfall that many people coming out of codependent relationships fall into. It can be all too easy to assume that the trick to overcoming codependency is to simply replace the nature of the other person in your relationships.

While this is a big part of the process it is just as important to change the number of relationships you have as well. After all, if you only allow yourself one or two relationships at a time you will be highly vulnerable to returning to those old codependent ways since part of codependency is relying too heavily on a small number of people. Therefore, it is vital that you begin to expand your horizons and open your heart to as many friends as you can find.

One of the biggest benefits to making many friends is that the more friends you have, the stronger your support system will be. A good way to think of this is to revisit the example of moving day. If you only have one or two friends you will only have one or two people to help you on moving day. What makes this a bad thing is if neither person is available, then you have no one to help move that heavy sofa! However, when you have a dozen or more friends in your life you will have more people to call on for help when you need it. Even if only half of your friends are able to answer your call for help that means you will have at least six people on hand, plenty to make moving day easier as well as more fun.

Conclusion

It is our hope that in reading this page you have come to understand the nature of codependency and how to free yourself so that you can be your fullest and truest joyful self. Healing from codependent patterns is a lifelong journey of recovery that takes many years to fully integrate as you make the deep and lasting changes necessary to radically change your self and your life.

Over the course of this page, we have looked at all kinds of codependent relationships because it's time to stand your own ground and to be the best person you can be. You will win admiration for your honesty and for being caring enough to discuss problems, rather than pretending that your problems don't matter. I have worked with people who suffer from codependency for some years and it never fails to amaze me how pleased these people are when they break the mold and step beyond it.

"I did something for myself today" one lady told me after having looked after her mother for the past 15 years. She had practically given up on life and her mother made no effort to make her feel she had any value at all. In fact, she has moved on and is now able to care for her mother but also care for herself. It isn't selfish. It's human and it's what makes you more complete as a person.

Yet another client lives with a drunk. When they were eventually able to sit down and talk, she was able to encourage him into a program that helped him toward being sober. She was also able to start liking who she was and enjoying her time with her family more than she had for years. She didn't have to make excuses for him anymore. She didn't have to fear the repercussions anymore because she took her stand and her remorseful husband made the changes that he needed to make.

Don't enable people who do not try to improve their lives. Don't put yourself down for not being who they want you to be. Be proud of who you are. That's the most valuable gift you can ever give anyone in the world. Kenny is proud of his wife for her strength of character, whereas in the past, he felt ashamed of what he was doing to her and to the way in which she viewed her life.

There is much happiness to be had after codependence. If you really want to get beyond it, this page holds all the clues. All you need to do is take the steps that are outlined in the page and you will gradually find your way back to health again and back to a healthy state of mind where you appreciate yourself and set boundaries that help others to respect you. This page was written with a lot of emotion because this is a very emotional subject to me and to the men and women I have had to deal with over the years who suffered from the effects of codependency. When you learn to move on and to lay down what are acceptable boundaries, you help everyone – including that person who may have begun to take you for granted.

Thank you for taking the time to read this page. I hope that you have found the information contained within its pages to be of value.

Being in a codependent relationship is hard. It is even harder to muster the courage to change your behavior and end the destructive cycle and move towards a new life.

Through this page you will have discovered what codependency is and how it differs from the normal interdependent closeness between two people. You will have learnt how to establish if you are in a codependent relationship and techniques to help you break free of codependency for good.

I hope you found the on healing and moving on after codependency, uplifting and positive. There is life after a codependent relationship and as you move past these experiences you will find new connections and encounter new relationships while re-building your self-confidence and being truly happy with who you are as an individual.

Remember, the relationship is only codependent if both parties continue the codependent behavior. If you choose not to engage,

then you are taking the first step to independence and the path to a rewarding and fulfilling life.
The step is to implement the strategies in this page to heal from the relationship and ensure you don't step back into old behavior patterns. However, the information contained in the pages of this page will have little value if you don't take action. It will work if you put in the effort.

Thank you once again for downloading this page. I hope it gave you valuable insights and empowered you to feel more confident about breaking the cycle of codependency. I wish you all the best and hope you are able to enjoy more enriching relationships in the future.

PART III

HOW TO ANALYZE PEOPLE

Introduction PART III – HOW TO ANALYZE PEOPLE

Getting to know yourself is about discovering the real you. It is more than just determining your preferences, like your favorite music or the kinds of clothing you like to wear. Knowing yourself involves a much deeper understanding of who you are as a human being. You may seem to know yourself based on what people have to say about you. But this is not a proper understanding of who you are, as it is just opinions from other people based on their limited interactions with you.

Getting to know yourself even better would mean you are understanding what your core values are in life. You will also have to take part in some self-reflection as well as get a better understanding of why you may hate someone. Sometimes the reason behind why we hate someone could be that we see a part of us that we hate in that person.

Your values are what you find to be the most important aspects of your life. They are your personal preferences on how you wish to live your life. Unfortunately, most of us don't always know what we want out of life. As a result, we end up living a life not always getting what we would want. This leads us to feel unfulfilled and unable to achieve peace within ourselves when navigating through our daily lives. In order to build a healthy and happy foundation to your life, you should determine your core values. Your values are a list of ideals and requirements that are important to your life.

Figuring out what your values in life are is not as straightforward as you may think. It is possible that some of the values that you may think are important to you aren't, because you may tend to spend more time and effort on other things. An example of this would be if you choose to hang out with your friends instead of maintaining a daily gym routine. This means that you value socializing over your health, even if you may say that health is important to you.

There will be many cases in which you will find inconsistencies between what you value and what you actually do. But this is not a major cause for concern as it can take time for you to understand what your values are in life. An example is a person that has a job that does not suit their values at all. This person prefers the freedom of choice, but they unfortunately work at a desk job that consists mostly of monotonous duties assigned from upper management. This is important to remember when analyzing people, as their choice of work does not necessarily reflect a decision that they made based on their core

values. In order to find your way in life, you should first work on finding out what your values in life are.

A simple way to start this process is to create a list of values that you find important to yourself. If you find yourself lost for inspiration, try looking for examples on the Internet. A simple Internet search will lead you towards countless websites that feature lists of common personal values. Select between five to eight of these values which you will then use to create your list. Rank these words from most important value to least important.

Once you have done so, you should then analyze each value by breaking it down even further into words that best describe the value to you. This will help you understand what a value means to you. Remember, the same value can have different meanings to different people. Once you have developed your list of values, you can then analyze this in order to find out who you are. This will help you in making relevant changes to your situation with the hopes of creating an ideal life.

There is a lot that you can learn from the people you hate. It is possible to dislike a person who has similar personality traits to yourself, especially those characteristics that you tend to deny. This denial could be a result of a bad past experience which you don't plan on revisiting.

Things that you may dislike in a person you hate could be things that you dislike about yourself. This irrational behavior can lead to an obsessive hatred towards a person who shares similar characteristics as you do. It doesn't necessarily mean that they also share the same values as you do, however.

People that have values that are different to yours will not necessarily cause you to hate them because of these opposing values. Rational behavior implies that even people with conflicting values or situations can still be able to function with one another. This is partly due to these people finding neutral ground in their differences and arguments.

But when this neutral playing field does not exist, then one cannot help but feel negative about the opposing person. A big part of this negativity is the feeling of being unable to solve an issue with that person which would have been solved if it were a neutral situation.

Observing those who we have negative feelings for can help us learn a lot about ourselves. The same goes for people who hate us. It may be a possibility that we possess similar traits to the person who hates us, a trait that may be highly frowned upon by that person.

Chapter 28. Mind Reading

Mind-reading is essentially knowing what other people truly mean, without them saying it out loud, or even despite them stating otherwise. Anyone has the potential ability to analyze others, with the right set of skills and training. It is, however, time-consuming and requires focus and patience. An open-minded approach cannot be overstated. The reader needs to be completely receptive to the subject's thoughts and nuances, far removed from any prejudices that they may have about the matter at hand or the environment in which the reading is taking place.

Particular attention should be paid to the subject's eyes, as they are said to be the window to the soul. A person's general person should be noted too, which includes but is not limited to appearance, overall behavior, physical movements, and, not surprisingly, the gut feeling you have about them. Listening to your intuition can be valuable with such matters.

There are many reasons to want to read someone's mind. Empathy is the most common reason because we long for a close connection with other people. Humans are social beings and this need is nature.

Most of the basic emotions, sadness, joy, fear, anger, surprise, and disgust are expressed in the same way across all cultures and races. This makes it easy to read said emotions in another person. The subtle nuances are what is much harder to decipher, and it takes a dedicated person to learn how to interpret each person correctly.

We all seek ease when it comes to communication with others. Reading someone's mind can help adjust how we react to any given situation. Relating also makes it possible to respond in a suitable manner.

This skill may also aid in lie detection. Being able to look past words to ascertain the truth is a valuable ability. This is most useful in criminology and law enforcement professions, where it is essential to know when and what information a perpetrator may be withholding. For example, a suspect who has an accomplice may not want to give them up. A terrorist with a bomb hidden somewhere may not want to reveal the location of the incendiary device. It is, therefore, necessary to have such analytical skills, which to decipher the information that may not necessarily be spoken. Speed and accuracy are imperative in these instances.

The situation or the environment in which a nonverbal cue applies matters. The same thing done in a different setting or as a reaction to various circumstances could mean other things. For example, a cough in a draughty room could be just that, an innocent cough, whereas a cough after an especially awkward comment could be a sign of discomfort.

One should always be careful not to pay mind to stereotypes as a mind reader. People and their body language are as diverse as the fish in the sea. One person's 'tell' may not necessarily be another's. This is well evidenced by high stakes poker players who take time and resources to research their opponents and figure out what their weakness is, to gain a competitive edge.

Considering More Than One Sign

Communication is done through multiple distinct channels; there is verbal, non-verbal, written, and visual. These are all used differently, according to the message one wants to put across. For example, someone who is angry at someone else may text or write to them in capital letters to express their anger, which would be equated to shouting if the person re actually speaking their thoughts. It is essential to understand the subject's thought process and how it applies to all these.

More often than not, it takes a combination of signs to bring the intended message out clearly. A mind reader needs to learn by constant practice how to correctly interpret a combination of signs in the subject. For example, eyes downcast could mean that someone is ashamed. The same motion while continually looking outside or away from you may mean that they have something to hide, or that they are not interested in the current topic of discussion.

Signs are also vital because, for someone who may be living with one kind of challenge or other, they may need more than one way to understand a statement or concept. Likewise, they will also communicate with more than one sense. Examples include people with failing vision, the hearing impaired, and even people within the autism spectrum, especially those who may not necessarily understand typical social cues and need help interpreting them.

Not Knowing the Person

Reading a person unknown to you can pose a challenge, but it is still possible. Meeting someone for the first time is a whole new experience that registers as a 'new file' in the brain and sets the tone for consecutive meetings. Hence the adage "first impressions are very important."

Reading a stranger's mind may require more patience and more intense focus, so as not to miss out on subtle cues. One should be careful not to make the subject uncomfortable, though, and it is recommended not to stare for too long. An initial fifteen seconds should be enough to get a general understanding of someone without making them uneasy.

A short series of basic questions, like name and address, should elicit truthful answers. These inquires can help establish a baseline for that person's facial expressions, tone of voice, and eye contact when they are telling the truth. Another generally accepted 'tell' is the firmness of one's handshake. A firm handshake may denote confidence, while a weak handshake may denote a non-committal attitude.

One should also consider other factors that could determine a person's responses. These include age and cultural background. For example, someone born in the forties or fifties may be more conservative on subjects to do with sexuality or religion than a millennial might be. Also, in some cultures, handshakes are not appropriate, especially between individuals of different genders.

Being unaware of such a seemingly trivial matter could lead one to misread a subject who does not want a handshake or who gives only a fleeting one.

When reading a stranger, it is best not to make assumptions. Such haste can lead to misunderstandings. Take the time to learn the basics of an individual. A current mood may not be that person's usual disposition. For example, maybe they had a hard time finding parking and seem flustered, which is just a momentary state. Their real character should be evident once the agitation is over.

Biases

We should also be particularly careful about applying our own judgments and perceptions to the person whose mind is being read. These are referred to as cognitive biases. On the contrary, we should consciously strive to observe or listen to the other individual objectively and rationally.

Understanding these biases helps us to avoid the pitfalls of misunderstanding or wrongly interpreting the other person's responses or intended meaning. Being objective toward others is also a wise way to conduct oneself, in general. These preconceived notions are the halo effect, the confirmation bias, the actor-observer bias, the false consensus effect, and the anchoring bias.

The Halo Effect

The Halo Effect is also referred to as 'the physical attractiveness stereotype.' It is the tendency to let our initial impression of a person influence what we think of them overall. It has the potential to cloud our vision on the person's other characteristics just because we judged them at first sight. The more physically appealing one is to us, the more favorably we are disposed to them, and vice versa, without taking into consideration the person's other character traits.

For example, a well-dressed person on the street would gain more of our attention and possibly admiration than a is shabbily dressed person, yet the well-dressed person may be a ruthless grifter who preys on retirees while the shabbily dressed one could be an honest person down on his luck. This is also very much evidenced at job interviews, where one is encouraged to attend well-groomed to give a positive first impression. We associate attractiveness with benevolence.

The Confirmation Bias

The confirmation bias is when people lean towards information that seems to confirm previously held beliefs. It is a polarizing pitfall. People may listen to the same story but only pick from it what confirms their opinions, to the exclusion of all others. For example, a presidential campaign usually has supporters and opponents, and whatever a candidate says or does is sure to be interpreted to suit either side. It will be praised and touted by supporters, while the same action will be vilified and discredited by opponents. We should be careful not to let our own long-standing ideals determine what we hear and understand from the person whose mind we are reading. Instead, we should listen logically and rationally to reach an informed conclusion.

The Actor Observer Bias

The Actor Observer Bias is when we perceive others and attribute their actions to several variables, influenced by whether we are the actor or the observer in a situation. That is, when it comes to our actions, we are more likely to explain ourselves by attributing faults to external influences while blaming other people's actions to their internal causes. For example, imagine being late to a meeting and saying the traffic was unbearable yet blaming another person who comes in a few minutes later by saying that they are just lazy. This kind of bias should be far from a mind reader's modus operandi. Otherwise, the exercise would only be clouded with endless blame games.

The False Consensus Effect

The False Consensus Effect refers to our tendency to overestimate how much other people agree with our own beliefs, behaviors, attitudes, and values. It stems from the fact that we spend most of our time with the same people, who tend to share our opinions. This leads us to believe that our thoughts are the same as the majority, even outside of our circle. Those who think like us are good and normal, while everything else is not. This is a dangerous attitude for anyone because it can easily foster intolerance.

Thinking this way limits our understanding of the subject's opinion if it differs from our own. For example, a spirited defense of the benefits of eating meat or animal protein may be unacceptable or repulsive to a vegan, who would thereby miss the subtle nuances of how the other is expresses sincerity and conviction. We must remember that the world is full of people from different backgrounds.

The Anchoring Bias

This bias occurs when we allow ourselves to be overly influenced by the first piece of information that we hear regarding any subject. This is a tricky cognitive device because has a significant bearing on how a conversation or negotiation will proceed. For example, imagine hearing that "there is ebola in Africa." This is a blanket statement, as Africa is a continent, not a single country, and the disease may be confined to only one country or one region, and the rest of the continent is ebola-free.

An over-cautious European government may issue a travel advisory to Africa, thereby affecting many other countries who are reliant on tourism, Ebola-free though, they may be. It also affects serious matters like medicine. A doctor can create an anchoring point, where his first impression on the symptoms a patient may present could lead to them giving a wrong diagnosis. This is the reason for the recommendation of a second or even third opinion, giving the new doctor a complete history of the problem, despite it all being in your medical file. Anyone trying to get to the bottom of a problem should be keen to take in all the information presented, and not be tempted to overlook important data based on the initial utterance. One who can do that will have overcome the anchoring bias.

Mirroring Body Language

This is a nonverbal and intuitive tool used to form a bond and establish a rapport between two or more persons. It helps to build a connection of mutual trust and understanding. Mirroring applies to all aspects of body language, including posture, gestures, accents, voices, and intonation. The most common forms are smiling and yawning.

Smiling when you see someone else smile immediately improves your mood. It is also very common to yawn within thirty seconds of seeing or hearing someone yawn. Even a fake yawn can elicit a real yawn in someone else!

To be perceived as being on the same wavelength or vibe as the person whose mind you are reading, it is advisable to mirror their body language. Be careful to copy only the positive gestures. For example, speak at the same tone and pace that they do. Talking too fast may make them feel intimidated or under pressure while going too slow may make you seem disinterested. Similarly, sitting upright is a positive body expression. You should not slouch, even if your subject is slouching. It could come off as lazy or unprofessional. It is also not advised to presume someone's feelings and use that to inform your behavior, as this can lead to miscommunication.

It is a documented fact that assuming a specific body language position that is identifiable with a particular emotional state makes you start to experience the said feeling. For example, steepling your fingers, which is connecting the fingertips of both hands and pressing them together, is a sign of authority and confidence. Doing this during meetings makes you feel more confident about the message you are putting across.

Men and women have also been shown in studies to have different ways of mirroring body language, generally. A person interested in reading minds should be aware of this in order to apply it successfully. Women tend to be more astute at picking up and interpreting psychical signals.

They are able to flow more easily with a conversation through multiple changes in voice, gestures, and facial expressions.

Men, however, prefer to keep a mask-like appearance, which makes them harder to read. They do experience the same range of emotions but prefer not to show it on their face or with too much movement. This allows them to feel in control. Therefore, the more effective way to mirror a man is by matching his body language as opposed to trying to imitate his facial expressions.

Another important factor to consider when mirroring body language is your relationship with the person you are following. A subordinate mimicking the boss's dominant body language may be interpreted as arrogance. Matching the movements of someone who is trying to intimidate you, may disarm them and make them more agreeable. All in all, mirroring makes the other person see their own reflection in you, making them instantly comfortable and more receptive and trusting.

Chapter 29. Analyzing People Through Their Words

Everything that a person does or says reveals something about their personality. Actions, beliefs, and thoughts of people are aligned perfectly with each other in a way that they all reveal the same things concerning an individual. Just as it is said that all methods can lead to Rome, everything a person thinks or does can reveal a lot about their personality makeup and personality. The words that are spoken by a person, even if they appear to carry less weight, tell a great deal about a person's insecurities and desires.

No one doubts that the words we speak or write are a full expression of our inner personalities and thoughts. However, beyond the real content of a language, exclusive insights into the minds of the author are usually hidden in the text's style.

From our acts of dominance to truthfulness, we are revealing to others too much about us. You can quickly know the most important of all the people in the room by listening to the words that they use. Confident and high-status people use very few "I" words. The higher a person's status is in a given situation, the less the "I" words they will use in their conversations.

Each time people feel confident, they tend to focus on the task that they have at hand, and not necessarily on them. "I" is also used less in the weeks that follow a given cultural upheaval. As age kicks on, we tend to use more positive emotional words and even make very fewer references to ourselves. A study has also shown it that the higher social class a person is, the fewer emotional words he will need to use.

According to Pennebaker, style words include auxiliary verbs, prepositions, pronouns, articles, and conjunctions.

He also goes ahead to explain the content words, which include regular verbs, nouns, and especially adverbs and adjectives. Here is the main difference between the style words and the content words. The content words are what someone is saying while the style words are how the words are said.

Women tend to use pronouns, social words, negations, as well as references to the psychological processes as compared to the male. This could be a surprise, but men tend to use more big numbers, prepositions, and articles than women. But despite all that, the way women speak implies that human beings are more open and self-aware to the self-reflection. That is, according to Pennebaker, who also discovered that there are three main ways in which people speak when they are not saying the truth. He also discovered that the health of a person is likely to improve, not with the increased application of the emotion words such as joyful, happy, and sad, but with more use of the cognitive words such as understand, realize and know. Public finds who have the tendency of addressing press briefings tend to use more first-person singular each time they are prone to committing suicide or troubled. When people tell the truth, they are likely to use the pronouns of the first person singular more often than other times. When the levels of testosterone increase in people, they will tend to drop in their use of references to other people that they are talking to.

Another study has also shown it that people who talk about traumatic circumstances or decodes to share some moments of feeling down or painful truth are physically healthier as opposed to those who kept the experiences secret.

I earned another honorary degree.

The word clue in this sentence is "another." It is used to give a notion that the speaker has earned more than one honorary degrees. The person wanted to prove to others that he/she has earned at least one honorary degree. It is a smart way of bolstering the self-image of a person. The speaker may require the admiration of others to be able to show his/her self-esteem. Professional observers could exploit this kind of vulnerability by using flattery and comments that can help in enhancing the ego of the speaker.

I have worked so hard to achieve my goal.

The word clue in this sentence is "hard." It suggests that the speaker values goals that appear so hard to achieve. The sentence might also indicate that the goals that the person has made could be more difficult to achieve than the goals that he usually attempts to achieve. The word clue in this sentence also offers other suggestions. It also shows that the speaker can defer gratification or strongly believes that dedication and hard work tend to produce a better result. A job seeker that has the following characteristics stands higher chances of getting a job because the character traits could be attractive to the employers. It is because this is a kind of individual who would accept challenges and have the determination to be able to finish up tasks in a successful way.

I patiently sat through the public lecture forum.

The word clue in this sentence is "patiently'. It can be used in many hypotheses. It could mean that the person could have been bored with the public lecture forum. Perhaps the person was forced to talk on the phone or even use the restroom. No matter the kind of reason, the person has evidently preoccupied with other things apart from the main contents of the public lecture forum. Someone who patiently waits for a break before leaving a forum or a room is someone who obeys the social etiquette and norms.

A person whose phone rings and gets up immediately and leaves the room shows that they do not have strong rigid for the social boundaries. Those who have social barriers stand higher chances of getting job opportunities because they not only respect the authorities but also follow the rules to the. Employers will analyze the characters of these people by listening to the kind of speeches that they offer.

On the other hand, someone who fails to follow the social conventions would stand a chance of getting a job that needs novel thinking. Someone who has the predisposition to act outside the social norms would make a good spy as opposed to someone who is disposed to follow the social conventions. This is because spies are usually asked to violate the social norms on a routine.

I opted to purchase that model.

The word clue in this sentence is "opted." It shows that the person weighs a few options before deciding to make the final purchase. At times, they could have struggled to some extent before making the final decision to buy what they wanted. The behavior trait showcased here is that this is a person who thinks through making the decision to buy something. The word "opted" can also be used to show that this person is not likely to be impulsive. Someone impulsive would likely use words such as "I just purchased that model'. The word clue in this second sentence is "just" and suggests that the person just purchased the item without giving it much though.

Based on the first-word clue of "opted," the listener can go ahead and develop a hypothesis that the speaker is an introvert. Introverts are the type of people who usually think before they decide. However, they tend to carefully weigh on each of the options that they have before giving their views and decision. Introverts, on the other hand, tend to be more impulsive. The use of the verb "opted" does not identify the speaker as an introvert in a positive manner, but it seeks to offer an indication that the person could be an introvert.

A detailed personality test needs a more definitive psychological assessment. However, an observer is still able to exploit a person if he is aware that the person tends towards the side of introversion and extroversion.

Extroverts are the kind of people who would get their energy from spending time with other people and look for stimulation from their surroundings. They also tend to speak spontaneously without having a second thought and use the trial and error methods more confidently. The introverts, on the other hand, tend to expend the energy that they got when they socially engage and seek some lonely time to perform other errands.

Introverts will usually look for stimulation from within and rarely speak without having a second thought. They carefully weigh the options that they have before making any decision. Before entering into any kind of business negotiations, knowing whether your opponent tends either towards introversion or extroversion can give a very strategic benefit. Salespeople should give their introverted customers to think about the sales proposals that they are presented to them.

The introverts tend to mull in the information that they got before they can come to a final decision. When the introverts are pressed to make impulsive decisions, they might be forced to say "No," even when they meant "Yes." This is because these people are not comfortable when it comes to making any immediate decision. Conversely, the extroverts can be pressed to certain levels to make quick decisions since they are more at ease when it comes to making impulsive decisions. In very rare cases do people show fully introverted features or entirely extroverted features.

The personality traits of a person tend to slide along a given continuum. There are also several people who show both the introverted and extroverted characters at the same time. In addition to that, those who are introverts appear to be comfortable with their environments and will usually showcase behaviors that are related to the extroversion behaviors. Extroverts can also display the introverted features at times.

What I did was the right thing.

The words clue in this sentence is "right." It is used to suggest that the speaker struggled with an ethical, moral, and legal dilemma and managed to overcome some degree of external and internal opposition to make a just and fair decision. According to the behavioral trait that is portrayed in this sentence, it is also very evident that the person has enough strength of character to be able to make the best and right decision even when pressed with several opposing views. The key here is to listen to what they are saying and let their words do the talking.

Open Communication

In most interpersonal interactions, the first few seconds are very vital. Your first impressions have a great impact on the success of future and further verbal communication with another person. When you first meet a person, you create an immediate impression of them; this is based on how they behave, sound, and look, as well as anything else you may have heard about them.

For example, when you meet a person and hear them speak, you create a judgment about their level of understanding and ability and their background. When you hear a foreign accent, for example, you might decide that you require to use simpler language for communication. You might realize that you need to listen more attentively to make sure that you understand what the person is saying.

Effective Verbal Communication

Effective speaking includes three main stages, that is, words that you choose to use, how you utter the words, and how you reinforce the words. All these areas have an impact on the transmission of your message and how the message is received and understood by the target audience.

It will be important for you to wisely and carefully choose the words to use. You will need to use different words in different events; even you are discussing a similar topic.

How you speak will include your pace and tone of voice. The pace and tone of voice communicate a certain message to the audience, for example, about your level of commitment and interest, or whether you are nervous about the audience reaction.

Active Listening

Effective listening is important for effective verbal communication. Ways that you can ensure that you listen more. These include:

 Be prepared to listen. Focus on the person speaking and not how you are going to reply to them
 Keeping an open mind while you avoid being judgmental about the person speaking.
 Always be objective
 Always focus on the objectivity of the message being conveyed
 Avoid distractions.
 Don't stereotype the person who's speaking.

Enhancing Verbal Communication

Techniques and tools that you can make use of to enhance the effectiveness of your verbal communication. These include:

 Clarifying and Reflecting. It is a process involving giving feedback to another person of your understanding of what has been conveyed or said.

Reflecting usually involves paraphrasing the message that has been conveyed to you by the speaker in your own words. All that you need to do is to capture the importance of the feelings and facts expressed, and communicate your understanding back to the speaker.

Reflecting is an important skill because:

 You are demonstrating that you consider the other person's opinions
 The speaker received feedback about how the message has been received
 Shows respect for, and interest in, what the other person has to say
 You can view what you might have understood the message properly

 Questioning. This is how broad we get more information from others on particular topics. It's an important way of clarifying aspects that are not clear or test your understanding. Questioning enables you to seek support from other people explicitly.

Questioning is a vital technique because it helps you to draw another person into a conversation or simply to show interest.

Types of Questions

Open question. These types of questions demand further elaboration and discussion. They help to broaden the scope of reply or response. These types of questions often take long to reply but give the other person a broader scope for encouraging and self-expression involvement in the interaction.

Closed question. They seek only two or one-word answer, often simply 'no' or 'yes.' They allow the person asking the questions to be in total control of the interaction.

Chapter 30. Types of Narcissism

In the Diagnostic and Statistical Manual of Mental Disorders, the narcissistic disorder is considered as a homogeneous syndrome, but there are so many shreds of evidence that indicate that there are variations in the expression of the disorder from one individual to the other.

According to a paper that was released in 2015, the subtypes of narcissism has two major characteristics—the overt or grandiose subtype and the covert or vulnerable subtype. For the overt or grandiose subtype, the narcissist usually has characteristics of grandiosity, boldness, and arrogance. As for the covert or vulnerable subtype, it is characterized by having oversensitive and defensive character traits.

Narcissistic grandiosity is oftentimes exhibited with the lack of empathy, interpersonally exploitative acts, exhibitionism, and aggression. Glen Gabbard, a psychiatrist, describes this subtype as the oblivious subtype that is laced with arrogance, thick skin, and grandiosity.

Narcissistic vulnerability, on the other hand, has to do with a continuous attempt to portray oneself as a helpless person with low self-esteem, shame, and emptiness. This type of narcissism is, however, expressed in their character as being socially avoidant. They cannot exhibit their self-presentation. So when they encounter such situations, they tend to withdraw. Also, whenever it seems impossible to meet their need or their expectation of getting approval from others, they also withdraw. This subtype is described by Gabbard as the hypervigilant subtype, and it has to do with those narcissists whose feelings are easily hurt and who are ashamed and too sensitive (Elsa 2016). Those people who exhibit a more severe expression of this disorder, however, always face more difficulties in life.

The Overt or Grandiose Narcissism

According to Gabbard's classification, narcissists who belong in this category are those who are very sensitive. In his work, he describes them as those who do not have any form of awareness of the impact that they have on other people. Most times, they find it easy to function at cocktail parties or any other social gathering at all. When they talk, they do it as if they were talking to a very large audience, and while they are at it, they try hard not to make any form of eye contact. They will typically look over the heads of the people who are around them during a conversation. They usually talk at other people instead of talking to them, so they hardly communicate when they talk.

Although they may not be aware of the fact that they are boring, the truth is that they actually are, so most of the time, people tend to abandon a conversation with them by going elsewhere to seek companionship. They usually fill their conversations up with many talks about their accomplishments, and they make it obvious that they always want to be the center of attraction and attention. They always indicate that they do not want/allow other people to contribute to the conversations they have.

They are always very insensitive to the needs of other people. Most times, when they are in a conversation, they are always the sender who has no receiver. It is this type of narcissist that has a very close relation to the DSM-II-R criteria. On the other hand, they are much more resistant to criticism than the ones that were specified in the DSM's criteria.

Covert or Vulnerable Narcissism

This is the type of narcissist that was described by Glen Gabbard as the hypersensitive type. According to him, this type of narcissism in the oblivious narcissism. People who are suffering from this type of narcissistic personality disorder are always very sensitive to the way people react to them as they continuously fix their attention on other people.

This attitude of theirs is in contrast with the self-absorption that is manifested in oblivious narcissists. Just like a person who is suffering from paranoia, this type of narcissist pays keen attention to the things other people have to say about them, and oftentimes, they feel slighted when others respond to them critically.

They are typically shy and inhibited people, and their attitude can get so bad that they become self-effacing. Because they always feel like they may be humiliated or rejected, they always try all they can to stay away from the limelight. Within their core, in the inner world they have created for themselves, they have a deep sense of shame, and this is in addition to their quest to portray themselves in a grandiose manner.

Although both types of narcissism always face a tough time in maintaining their self-esteem, both of them are always dealing with the issue in very distinct ways. As for the hypervigilant or covert narcissist, they are always trying to maintain their self-esteem by making sure that they stay away from vulnerable situations and also by doing a critical study of other people so that they will be able to find out what way is the best for them to behave. According to Gabbard, this type of narcissist always tries to link his own personal disapproval of his grandiose fantasies to others (Gabbard 1993). The oblivious or the overt narcissist, on the other hand, tries his best to maintain his self-esteem by always trying to impress other people with any or all their accomplishments. They, however, insulate themselves from narcissistic injuries by filtering through all the responses that they receive from others.

Countertransference Patterns

To be able to keep up with all the descriptions of narcissism as mentioned above, each narcissistic type may be considered according to the transference development with the help of a mental health expert or a therapist. In this same manner, each type of narcissism also evokes different characteristics of countertransference in a therapist or an analyst.

In the case of the oblivious patient, the therapist is forced to tolerate a satellite existence. The therapist is always very apt to feel as though the patient is oblivious of their presence in the room. Also, these patients exhibit a countertransference pattern, which involves a feeling of boredom and irritation with the patients. They usually hold forth in the office of the therapist in a way that resembles one who is addressing a crowded amphitheater. They try to avoid or ignore the therapist as a separate person who has separate thoughts and feelings.

The covert or hypervigilant narcissist subjects the therapist to struggle with several countertransference problems. They usually find faults in most of the things, if not everything, that the therapist does, from the clearing of his throat to the shifting of weight, down to every glance he takes at the clock. They typically will translate every action of the therapist as a slight.

In most cases, the therapist is subjected to an uncomfortable position of feeling coerced into sitting still and maintaining an unwavering focus by trying all he can to place his undivided attention on the patient. There is also another countertransference resentment that comes with the feeling of being controlled by the patient. This comes with a false accusation of being negligent, as well as not paying enough attention.

Although it is possible for both types of narcissism to manifest in a distinct manner, in their pure form, most times, patients who go to mental health experts for treatment or therapy exhibit a mixture of phenomenological characteristics from the two types of narcissism.

In the middle of the two endpoints on this continuum are many people with the narcissistic disorder who are very smooth socially and appear to be very normal. In giving treatment to narcissists, therefore, therapists must ensure that they first listen keenly to their patients so that they can observe and point out their transference and countertransference developments and also make a careful observation of all their responses to every trial intervention. By doing so, therapists will be able to come to a temporal conclusion about the theoretical and the technical models that are most valuable to each patient.

As for the hypervigilant narcissists, it is possible that they will not be able to tolerate any other thing aside from an empathetic approach or experience. This is a result of their very fragile self, which can quickly be fragmented. If there is any deviation from the empathetic attunement that they are used to or desire, they will greet it with a prolonged shutdown, which is a response to a perceived narcissistic injury.

The oblivious patients, on the other hand, will always protect themselves with a highly armed self that can be penetrated only with forceful confrontations, as well as events that are interpreted as contempt and/or envy. A combination of several technical strategies may, however, be of benefit to some other patients.

In summary, just as it is in every psychotherapy, the treatment for each case of NPD varies, so they must be adjusted to suit the mental and emotional needs of every patient. Therapists should not attempt to go the other way by trying to adjust the patient to suit their own methods or theories.

ven though narcissists may appear to have strong personalities on the surface, within them, they often lack core self. So to be able to get validation for their fragile and fragmented selves, they present themselves as though they have a strong sense of self-image, thoughts, and behavior. They do this to be able to stabilize their image.

On a general note, the feeling of shame, dependency, dysfunctional communication skills and showing nonchalant attitude for boundaries is not uncommon with narcissists. These, however, points to the fact that they have problems with intimacy. A study has, however, shown that narcissism and codependency have some relationships, but Darlene, a mental health expert, says that narcissists are codependents because they are always more aggressive than passive.

Although it may be a painful thing to do, the accommodation of both a narcissist and a codependent may be a perfect thing to do as the former's attributes and success may boost the latter's low self-esteem, so the accommodators will have to go through the pain of tolerating emotional abuse. Most of the time, the accommodators do not present themselves or approach the patients as authoritarian as they always prefer to be non-assertive. They take a subordinate role because the narcissists' inclination to being authoritative is always expressed through anger, which is often repressed, shame-bound, and frightening. Narcissists have a desire and hunger for those attributes they lack, so they idealize those qualities that they find in their new partners with the hope that they will be able to absorb these qualities. This is one of the reasons why it is rarely possible for two accommodators to get together.

Most of the time, those who accommodate narcissists are always astounded by their self-direction and strength. They become voracious in their image of success, charisma, protection, and power without taking the fragile persona of the narcissists, which they have successfully hidden in shame. For these reasons, accommodators get attached to narcissists because they present themselves as bold people who are able to express their anger. However, they do not usually feel the need to be guilty when they themselves become very assertive. By being caretakers and pleasers, codependents feel valued. As a result of the fact that they usually do not feel loved, they think they do not deserve receiving love. Therefore, they do not expect that they will be loved for who they are. They feel people only love them because of what they can get from them.

To keep their pride relevant, however, narcissists use other people. They are attracted to their opposites who do so well in making them feel continually relevant. Also, they are drawn to those people who are emotionally expressive and nurturing as they make up for the qualities that narcissists lack.

Narcissists always look out for partners whom they can control. They want those who will not easily challenge them, therefore making them feel weak and inconsequential. When they anticipate sex, narcissists become "distant." So becoming emotionally attached to them will mean that you have to give up your power and control such that you will begin to harbor the thoughts of being dependent. Not only does this limit their options but also weakens them. It also exposes them to certain feelings of rejection and shame, which is one of the reasons why they are not conscious of their environment, their surroundings, or even their friends. Those who become attracted to them find themselves constantly after them by unconsciously replaying an event of emotional abandonment from the past. Within the core of both the narcissist and the codependent is the feeling of being unlovable.

In order to stay away from the narcissistic abuse, it is very important to remind yourself of the fact that you are responsible for your own personal growth; therefore, when you meet a person or when you get into a relationship with someone, you need to be careful so you do not end up taking his or her responsibilities. You should not be the only one who is looking out for the narcissist's growth.

It is important to take note of the fact that narcissists are also making efforts to be better, so you should look out for the efforts they are making for themselves. Note also that boundaries are important for all relationships. For those who are empathetic, boundaries may seem harsh, but once they have come to the understanding of the fact that they can actually say no, they can then begin to find ways to protect themselves against those who are trying to take advantage of them.

To remain healthy, empaths do not necessarily need to be hardened or hard-hearted. They need to realize that not everyone needs to remain in their lives. It is normal to come across people who they will realize on are not healthy companies to keep. Therefore, it is actually very okay to let go of them.

Chapter 31. Understanding the Self

Most people live their lives without giving much thought about their existence. They concentrate on doing things that make them happy and seek to overcome any challenge that comes along. However, taking a critical thought of it can make such people realize that they do most of these things without assessing how they can impact them in the long run.

Most individuals waste time on absurd thoughts about what happens around them on a daily basis. Always seeking to improve oneself as a way of remaining real is one of the best ways to understand the self.

As you go about your daily businesses, you must be careful that you do not go beyond what you are supposed to do and that you limit your activities, fun, and learnings to acceptable levels. Freedom is always good but when not managed properly it comes with some undesirable consequences. You must be careful of your morals, ethics, and actions so that other people perceive you in a way that is reasonable.

One of the best ways to protect your image is through understanding yourself.

Who Are You?

This is quite a difficult question for most people. When coming to terms with yourself, you must first start by understanding the kind of person you are and how you compare with the rest. For instance, you may understand that you become angry quickly or that when you get too excited your communication gets careless. Although responding to such a question may not be very easy, it is important that you try as much as possible to get a solid answer for it. Doing this will help grow a big part of your life.

The art of understanding yourself as a person is known as self-concept. When you realize that you have a weakness with anger and excitement, this forms part of your self-concept. It means that you clearly understand yourself and how different you are from others. However, this is not all that is there. You must also be able to understand your motives and intentions each time you do something. This is known as self-understanding. To help you answer the above question, let us look at these two aspects in detail.

Self-Concept

This refers to having an idea of who you are. It generally refers to how you think, evaluate and perceive yourself. It is one of the building blocks of emotional self-awareness.

Several aspects work together to make the kind of person you are at one moment. Some of them are:

1.The physical self – this represents who you physically are. For instance your appearance, preferences, physical fitness and the like. For instance, one person may be physically fit and light in weight while another may be overweight and unfit for any physical exercise. Both descriptions are related to a person's physical self-concept.

2.The existential self – this is one of the most basic components of the self-concept. It explains the ability to understand yourself as a distinct entity that is separate and different from others. This form of self-concept starts when you are young and continues to build up, as you get older. It is the one that makes children realize that they are separate entities from parents and other people as they grow over time. This is what makes people learn how to survive independently.

3.The categorical self–this is where you identify yourself as a person with characteristics, behaviors and other essential attributes. This is what helps people to identify things such as their gender, height, age, hair color and many more. It also begins at childhood and keeps growing as people continue to mature. At stages of life, the categorical self also starts to include some psychological traits like a person's emotional stability and intelligence.

4.The social self – as an individual, you may have a few friends who are very close. Some people value making friends and getting to interact with them on a deeper level while others only want a few people around them. Social self-concept is the awareness of a person's ability to interact or relate with others.

5.The competent self – this refers to the ability of a person to meet his basic needs. For instance, one person may be working hard each day just to get his basic necessities while another may pride himself in waiting for others to provide for him. These are examples of competent self-concept.

A researcher known as Carl Rogers subdivided self-concept into three components, which are:

 Self-image which illustrates how you see yourself

 Self-esteem which refers to the value you give yourself

 Ideal-self which establishes how a person wishes to be like

Self-Image

In details, self-image refers to a view or mental image that you have of yourself. It describes your characteristics and includes things such as talent, beauty, intelligence, and many others. These characteristics often form a person's strengths and weaknesses.

Sometimes, a person's self-image does not reflect what is happening in reality. This means that it is very possible for people to have the wrong images of themselves. For instance, a person suffering from anorexia may keep thinking that he is fat, yet in reality, the person is very thin.

The image you have of yourself can be influenced by several factors including peer pressure, parental influence, even the media. Generally, self-image comprises of the following components:

 Physical appearance – for example tall, short, dark, brown eyes, light-skinned

 Social responsibilities – these are the roles people play on a daily basis. For example, teacher, student, housewife. Understanding your social role helps you to understand what others expect you to accomplish in the role

□ Individual traits – these are third-level attributes of your self-image. For instance mischievous, dutiful, generous, kind

Self-image comprises of those impressions you have built over time as well. It includes things like your visions, dreams, your thoughts, your feelings and what you intend to achieve in the future in terms of goals. A person's self-image may be positive or negative. A positive self-image builds your confidence while a negative self-image makes you doubt your opinions and abilities.

Your self-image may also be completely different from what others know about you. For instance, you may appear intelligent on the outside but deep inside you have a very negative image of yourself. There are individuals who believe that your self-image is determined by the events that take place around you. Others think that it is your self-image that determines what happens around you. There may be some truth about both since some activities may influence your self-image but in some cases how you view yourself will determine the kind of activities that you engage in. for example, if you fail in an activity or event, you may feel bad and rate yourself negatively. When you feel excited and confident about yourself, you may find yourself excelling in some projects or events.

Generally, your self-image affects your happiness and general outlook about life. This outlook may also determine how you view those who surround you. If you have a positive self-image, people will see your enthusiasm when working on some projects. On the other hand, if you have a negative self-image you will perform poorly on some assignments. When seeking to understand yourself, it is important that you always maintain a positive, yet the realistic image of yourself. An unrealistic image can really work against you since you may not be able to meet some of your expectations and the expectations of others.

As much as you may want to view yourself as a person who has only positive attributes, it is essential to sometimes critic yourself as a way of encouraging growth, hard work and success. In some cases, becoming too positive when perceiving yourself can result in some level of complacency, pride, and underperformance. If you want to achieve realistic goals, it is important to balance between positivity and reality.

Developing Self-image

Self-image can be obtained through learning. Part of people's perception of themselves is instilled in childhood by parents and caregivers. These influence the image you see of the world and life. The experiences you get from other people such as friends, teachers, and family members also contribute to your self-image. As stated, the image you perceive of yourself may be real or fake depending on your true nature and abilities. Most people who do not want to acknowledge their weaknesses suffer from wrong self-peception. To grow your image, you must be able to acquire information and use it to evaluate or assess yourself in the many areas above like physical appearance, relationships, and performance.

A positive self-image helps you to build on your strengths and potentials without ignoring your limitations. A negative self-image focuses on a person's failures, weaknesses, and imperfections. How you think of yourself determines how you will interact with others and your environment. Therefore, it is important to maintain a positive self-image if you want to build your social, mental, emotional and physical wellbeing.

Self-image is one of the traits that are constantly changing. The more you build it, the better image you develop of yourself and others. Here are some of the steps you can take to build a positive image of yourself.

 Identify your strengths and seek to develop them further

 Do an inventory of your self-image

 List your positive attributes and ask others to describe you based on these attributes

 Create SMART – specific, measurable, attainable, realistic and time-bound goals

□ Confront any distorted thoughts of yourself and others
□ Avoid comparing yourself with other people
□ Identify some of your childhood labels and asses their impact on your personality and performance
□ Practice self-love and learn how to appreciate yourself
□ Concentrate on your uniqueness

Self-Esteem

Also known as, self-worth, self-esteem refers to the opinion or perception you have of yourself. Self-esteem may be low, high or average depending on your abilities and strengths. Even people with high self-esteem occasionally doubt themselves. However, permanently low self-esteem often results in demotivation and insecurity. It involves the kind of evaluation you carry out on yourself and the results are always positive or negative. People with high self-esteem often display several characteristics such as:
□ Confidence
□ Optimism
□ Effective communication
□ Adaptability to change
□ Self-acceptance
□ Goal-oriented
□ Happiness and fulfillment
On the other hand, people with low self-esteem have the following attributes
□ Little or no confidence in their abilities
□ Desire to look or be like other people
□ Doubt and worry
□ Pessimism
□ Poor communication skills
□ Carelessness
Several methods and tools are often used to measure an individual's self-esteem. For instance, the Harrill Self Esteem Inventory, which comprises of 15 statements in the form of a questionnaire.

Studies carried out indicate that some uncertain situations may affect a person's self-esteem drastically. The levels of self-esteem can be maintained when people keep thinking and speaking positive things about themselves even when faced with challenging moments. This is what is referred to as the perseverance effect.

Generally, there are four main factors that impact the self-esteem of a person. These are:

 Other people's reactions – how other people react towards you may cause your esteem to go up or down. When people treat you with so much love and admiration or listen keenly to what you have to say, you will tend to notice an increase in your self-esteem. However, when people ignore and neglect you or communicate with you in an unacceptable manner then your esteem will automatically reduce.

 Comparing yourself with others – the people you keep comparing with also influence your self-esteem in some way. For example, if you compare yourself with some people who look richer, happier and better at completing some tasks then you will create a negative self-image and this means that your self-esteem will go low

 Social roles–some roles help to boost self-esteem in people than others. For instance, pilots, doctors, television presenters will always boast of positive self-esteem. Some roles like mental illness, prisoner, and garbage collection may elicit negative thoughts about self and this may translate to low self-esteem.

Self-esteem plays a very big role in influencing your life. In a nutshell, self-esteem

 Draws the difference between failure and success

 Affects your outlook about life in general

 Boosts your self-image

 Helps you to value others

 Gives you the right attitude required for productivity at work

 Promotes happiness and good health

How to Develop Your Self-esteem

1.Be kind to yourself

Make every effort to remain nice to yourself. Avoid any negative thoughts that may come your way and practice the persistence effect. Always address yourself the same way you would address others and see yourself as a great, yet unique person. To achieve this, you must also avoid comparing yourself to others. Instead, concentrate on achieving your goals and making yourself a better person.

2.Exercise

Various studies show that there is a link between exercise and high self-esteem. Exercise also improves your overall mental health. It empowers you physically and emotionally as well. When you exercise, you will be taking care of yourself and by the end of the day; you would have built your confidence and mental capacity. Working out also releases a hormone called endorphin, which is responsible for making people feel good. Doing this will increase your motivation and assist you to achieve your goals faster.

3.Do not seek perfection

Attaining perfection is close to impossible for most human beings. Therefore, do not set unrealistic expectations for yourself since it will be difficult to achieve them. The only thing you should concentrate on is building a better version of yourself and accepting mistakes when they happen. Mistakes form part of every learning process. Most people that are successful today make several mistakes in the past. By understanding this, you will be able to overcome any failures that come your way and remain positive during challenging periods.

4.See what to improve

Do not stick on things that you cannot change. Sometimes, things may get out of control. You should not focus more on theses since there is nothing you can do to change them. Instead, apply most of your energy on dealing with things that are still within your control. These must also be things that make you happy.

Spending your time on things that give you joy is one way to remain positive and with high self-esteem. Celebrate those small achievements, as this will make you continue to feel good about yourself.

5.Be considerate

Remain considerate of other people. This will boost their mood, which in turn will affect your mood as well. If you keep offending other people, they may retaliate and the result may be low self-esteem for yourself. In relation to this, always ensure that your company is full of positive and supportive people. Get support from people who feel good about themselves and yourself too. Such people will help you overcome negative thoughts and feelings easily.

Besides the above ways, you must also embrace the major pillars of self-esteem. These are personal integrity, self-discipline, purposeful living, self-assertiveness, and self-responsibility. Integrity comes in when your behavior matches your goals. Without integrity, you may have a good image of yourself but others may be seeing you differently, this can, in turn, affect your relationships and performance. Discipline is one of the aspects that give you total awareness of yourself. It helps you to withstand any challenges in life and guides you into avoiding mistakes that may bring nasty consequences in the future.

When it comes to living purposefully, it means that you apply useful strategies to your goals. Everyone has at least one goal in life. Once you achieve your goals, your self-esteem increases automatically. Assertiveness refers to the ability to do things driven by your feelings and convictions. Assertiveness allows you to remain real and authentic. It helps you to avoid copying others and keeps you on the right track in terms of focus. Responsibility, on the other hand, refers to the capability to stand by your thoughts and beliefs. It means being able to defend the truth even if others are against it. Lastly, self-acceptance is the understanding of oneself as a way of finding a solution to any arising problems. People who do not practice self-acceptance always struggle to relate with others and can easily look down on themselves. Such people experience low self-esteem most of the time since they only focus on the negative part of the lives and the lives of others.

Ideal Self

Having a mismatch between how you perceive yourself and how you would want to be in the future can affect the value you place on yourself. That is why there is a close link between a person's self-image, self-esteem, and ideal self.

As a person, seeking to improve on yourself, your ideal self may sometimes not be equivalent to what happens in your life in general. So many people struggle to accept themselves as they are. This causes a difference between the person's actual experience of reality and the ideal picture he has of himself. This difference is what is known as incongruence.

When a person's actual experience and ideal self are similar, it is said that a congruent state exists between the two scenarios. This rarely happens. Most individuals experience some level of incongruence in their lives.

Chapter 32. The Secrets to Reading People

There are many things that can cloud your judgment when reading people. Biases, intimidation, and sexual attraction are just some of the things that can make you choose to ignore your gut and misread someone. You may think that someone's harsh actions are admirable if you admire the person, while their actions would appear despicable if you did not admire them. Do not let anything cloud your judgment.

Men are more likely to judge pretty young women less harshly. They let pretty young women get away with disrespectful behavior in hopes of winning their favor. If you are attracted to someone, you are more likely to ignore red flags about the person. Try to look past sexual attraction. Understand that there are plenty of attractive people in the world, so fixating on one person's attractiveness is not necessary. You just need to view an attractive person more objectively. Try to focus on his or her character as a separate thing from his or her looks.

Status or certain jobs can also make you admire someone. But understand that someone is not perfect just because of his or her status. Do not let someone's status intimidate you or bamboozle you. In fact, they probably got to where they are today by being cruel to others. Read their character separately from their status or work.

Being in your own emotional funk can really distort your judgment, too. When you are emotionally down, you may be harsher to judge others in your state of bitterness. You may also be more vulnerable to kind actions from others. Unfortunately, manipulators are great at spotting when you are upset and offering a kind action in order to gain favor with you. Do not let your emotional state make you vulnerable in judgment.

Emotional wounds can make it hard for you to trust people. This is especially true after you been through a divorce or bad break-up. As a result, you might judge the gender that you are attracted to unfairly.

You may instantly dislike all people of that gender. Do not be so quick to write off people that you do not know. Use your scars as lessons to read people who remind you of those that have hurt you in the past, but do not make the mistake of thinking that the entire gender is bad. Give individuals a chance. Try to read them for who they are, not who your ex was.

Don't Just Base it Off of Behavior

Sometimes behavior is inaccurate because it is fake. Many people are great at creating a façade. They appear totally normal and upstanding, while hiding their horrendous internal flaws. Think of most serial killers. Often they go to work, keep nice houses, and look like totally normal people. The world is shocked when they are finally caught with a basement full of hacked up bodies and torture devices. Sexual deviants who get caught watching child porn are often politicians and businessmen with great jobs and totally normal outside appearances. While these examples are extreme, many people are adept at hiding their bad personalities under totally normal behavior. Therefore, you cannot base judgments off of the outward behavior of others, as this behavior can be faked and misleading.

Create a Baseline

Try to gauge a baseline of someone's normal behavior. Watch for unusual mannerisms that a person often displays. Quirks and habits that you frequently observe in someone over time form the person's baseline. A baseline does not take long to form once you become more adept at reading people with practice. FBI profilers will usually gather this information within the first fifteen seconds of meeting a person.

From this baseline, you are able to tell when someone is behaving abnormally. When someone is behaving abnormally, you can determine that something is going on. Perhaps the person is lying or is upset about something.

It is difficult to start a baseline on someone if you do not have a chance to observe him over a period of time and you are not yet adept at reading people in just a few seconds. Therefore, it is a good idea to watch for really odd behavior. Behavior that stands out as unusual may be a quirk or it may be a sign of something more ominous, such as deception. You may want to ask other people who know the person well if this behavior is normal for him. If you can't do that, then you simply must rely on your gut. But do not rely too much on behavior to form judgments about people.

You can start a baseline just by asking someone how they are doing today. Watch how the person reacts. From there, you can determine what his or her normal mannerisms are. The more you talk, the more you can gather about the person's baseline. Does his eye tic often? Does he often gesticulate with his hands? Does he stutter normally, or is he normally articulate? Also gauge the speed with which he speaks in normal conversation and the tone and pitch of his voice.

You must establish a baseline in order to tell when someone is behaving inconsistently. In addition, a baseline lets you know how a person is in normal settings. If a person is typically nervous, you can decide if you want to be around someone who is frequently nervous and therefore probably insecure with social anxiety. If a person is typically rude and blunt, you can determine if you want to deal with that kind of behavior in the future.

Infer Things from the Initial Reaction

Of course, strangers tend to be tense in their initial behavior toward you because they do not know you well. But a person's initial reaction to you indicates a lot of information about how he feels about himself and how he feels about other people. This initial reaction shows the hang-ups he may have and the guard that he puts up to protect himself or the façade that he erects to charm people that he meets for the first time. As a result, this reaction says a lot about who he is as a person and the things that you may expect from him as you get to know him better.

If he is initially rude, for instance, he may thaw and become nicer toward you, but you know that at heart he has his guard up against new people. You can then wonder why he has his guard up. He is probably a sensitive and insecure person with a lot of emotional baggage; he feels that he has to act tough and careless in order to avoid getting hurt.

Particularly articulate and charming people usually have a lot to hide. They are great at being around people and hiding who they really are. They have designed behavior that is intended to hook people.

Very charming behavior is often indicative of manipulative and deceptive personalities.

A person who is overly nervous usually has social anxiety and is rife with insecurities. This person will probably get more comfortable with you over time. However, you may want to avoid trusting him too much. As a general rule, people who are insecure are not reliable and will act in ways that are not always appropriate. Insecure people tend to have trust issues and they will act out in ways that are hurtful because they believe that they are not good enough. You are not responsible for the insecurities of another person, so don't allow such a person to burden you with his problems and doubts.

A person who acts too calm is probably also a sufferer of social anxiety. However, he is adept at projecting calmness to hide how nervous he is. Become suspicious of people who are just "too chill."

Also watch for people who only want to talk about themselves. People who are obsessed with themselves and don't even try to ask you questions about yourself are typically very selfish. This behavior will not change with time.

Another behavior that will not change with time is someone who is negative, even on your first meeting. People like this are very toxic and will simply try to drag you down.

A person who talks about others shamelessly when he first meets you is also probably a chronic gossip. It is not normal for someone to start gossiping when he first meets you.

Positivity and enthusiasm are great signs in a person that you have just met. However, if someone talks too much of a big game and brags overly much, you can assume that this person is trying to impress you or even make up for something that he feels that he is lacking. Mild positivity and enthusiasm is a great sign, but being overly enthusiastic is not.

Confidence and assurance of one's self is a good sign in a stranger. A person who is willing to introduce himself to you, look you in the eye, and talk to you is usually secure in himself. He has developed good social skills and hence might be a more sensitive friend, lover, or work associate. While you want to be wary of people who are too smooth and charming, someone who acts normal yet confident is usually a good person to know.

Ask Pointed Questions

If you want to get to know someone, feel free to ask him questions about himself. He will probably volunteer a lot of the information that you want to know. You don't even have to ask him things to find out a lot of information about who he is as a person, what he likes, and what he is looking for from his association with you.

But if he does not volunteer what you want to know, then ask. It is best to ask pointed questions and to not be vague. If you are vague, you run the risk of miscommunication. As an adult, there is no use or time for games anymore. You know that you cannot be a mind reader and neither can anyone else. So ask what you want to know without shame.

You do not want appear like you are interrogating someone. Asking rapid-fire questions can really put a person off. Asking overly personal questions about someone's life, family, or personality is also off-putting. But do not be afraid to ask general, socially acceptable questions whenever there is a break in the conversation.

Monitor a person in how he answers your questions. Since you have already more or less established a good baseline, you can tell when there are inconsistencies in his responses. If his gestures, tone, pitch, or eye contact suddenly shifts away from his baseline, then you can tell that he is not being truthful or that a question makes him uncomfortable for some reason. You can change the subject or pursue it more, depending on your goal in communication with him.

Word Choice is Important

How a person talks indicates a lot about what he is feeling and thinking. Listen for key words that indicate his intentions and his basic state of mind. The words that he chooses say a lot about how he is as a human being and what he is really feeling at the moment. If you are meeting someone for the first time, remember that the initial meeting speaks volumes about who a person is inside. How he chooses to speak to you right off the bat indicates a lot about who he is generally.

Someone who uses very harsh, aggressive language is an aggressive person or else he is currently in an angry mood. You never want someone to show you anger when you first meet; this indicates that the person may have an anger management problem.

Someone who uses very vague wording is possibly passive aggressive and trying to skirt around a hard subject. This type of person is not able to be direct. Expect games and behavior like shirking responsibility. If this person wrongs you, he will probably never admit to it and apologize. If he has a problem with you, he will probably never tell you to your face, but rather will hint about it or tell everyone else how he feels except for you.

Another troubling sign is when someone repeatedly says sorry or seems to take the blame for things. This type of person is very sinecure and blames himself for everything.

Someone who uses conceited language, such as bragging about how he just won "another" award, indicates how proud he is of himself. Watch for people who brag too much about themselves. These people are usually narcissistic and egotistical or else they are over compensating for feelings of inadequacy.

A person who uses very critical language is probably an overly judgmental person or a perfectionist. Watch for someone who nitpicks everything. This is a trait that will not lessen with time. If anything, it will only grow worse with time.

Most people use "I" terms more frequently than any other. This is not a troubling sign, but someone who uses more "we" terms is a better team player who is looking to collaborate with you. Someone who uses more "you" terms is focused on you. This can be a great sign that someone is focused on pleasing you and getting to know you, or else it can be a worrisome sign that someone is trying to manipulate you. Watch for other word choices in order to tell the difference. If someone is asking you about what you like or who you are, then that is usually a sign that he wants to get to know you or find out how to best please you. This is a great sign in a date, a new friend, or a person that you are thinking about hiring for a service. But if he seems to be fishing for pertinent information with overly personal questions, if he keeps trying to find ways that he can commiserate with you so that you will confide in him, or if he is using fancy language and flattery to make you feel ingratiated and charmed by him, then that is a bad sign that he is trying to get an emotional hook into you in order to manipulate you.

A good sign that someone is being shifty is vague language. Someone who refuses to answer yes or no questions is probably lying. Someone who uses confusing language is probably deliberately creating a sort of mirage of vagueness in order to hide something.

Chapter 33. How To Read Body Language

Learning body language can be easy, but at the same time, hard. Sometimes the body language of a person can confuse you to take in the wrong information. When you learn and master the body language, it will enhance your communication and improve your relationship with people. Understand the body language fully can be your second nature.

You do not need to add words; you observe and act non-verbally. There are different body languages, but for you to understand them, you have to differentiate between the negative body language and the positive body language. Like any other subject that you want to learn about, there must be channels before you learn about the issue and master it. For example, when you started schooling, you did not write your first composition before knowing the alphabets well. Same to body language, you cannot learn and understand the body language before you know the channels of the body language.

There are different channels of body language that you need to know before determining whether the body language you have seen is understandable. Below are the channels:

Facial Expressions

You must be able to understand or not understand every sign of the face of a person. The reason for this may and may not is that the neural mechanisms or controlling the front of every person may differ from time to time, giving you the analyzer a tough time. You also have to understand that different genders have different facial expressions. Children can be able to mimic the facial expressions of the persons they are close to in their environment, and this will leave you out of your analyzing unless you are a competent and experienced face reader. Knowing how to read faces will help you understand what the person is saying, how they are feeling and even their attitude towards something can also be shown through their facial expression.

Body Proxemics

This is how the distance between people affects them. There are distance ranges that speak different from each other, and only a person with an understanding of body language can get the meaning. Being too close to a person in a particular circumstance may mean wrong or right and being too far from a person under certain conditions may also drive a wrong or right message. Generally, the distance between people tells much about these behaviors. This channel of body language has four proximities, public space, social space, personal space, and intimate space. Once you understand this channel, you will be able to tell the meaning of any distance between people.

Ornaments

Ornaments are instrumental body language. This could be jewelry, clothes, sunglasses, hairstyles, makeup like lipstick and eye shadow colors; all these send a message of how you are. There is a meaning when ladies wear too short clothes or too long cloths or loose and tight things. There is a message send in your choice of sure earrings that you are wearing. Specific colors of the lipstick clothes color, the hairstyle on your head all have different meanings. For example, some hairstyles will make you look younger, and others will make you look older. Sure sunglasses send mixed messages. There is a gangster-like sunglasses and cool sunglasses. When you understand this channel, you will be able to understand the meaning of every dressing code and other ornamental things that people put on.

All the above channels will help you be able to go into your identification of the body language. You will be able to understand where the body language falls in and the meaning attached to it. A human body is like a watch. When the battery is out, it stops but when the cells are in it ticks. When a human body has life in it, everybody language has meaning unless the body is dead and nothing can ultimately be seen from it. Let us look at how we can read the body language of people or even yours at any given time.

Eyes

The eyes of a person will lead you directly to their soul. Eyes send so many signals. Looking at someone's eyes tells much more about a person or you .wearing sunglasses prohibits anyone from seeing someone's eyes and therefore it can jeopardize your analyzing or reduce the percentage of analyzing because it will be hard for you to see the eyes to tell if the person is genuine or not And for this reasons most gangsters or assassins love wearing sunglasses because it symbolizes power to them.

Looking Up

This is a sign of visualizing. When someone looks up, he is probably thinking about a particular thing or word they might have forgotten. For example, a teacher in class teaching then looks up the ceiling; he is perhaps trying to remember the words or phrases that he had prepared. When a person looks up and then turns his eyes to the left, he is trying to remember a memory. It could be something out of his experience that he is trying to recall. When he looks up then turn to the right, he is trying to imagine things. He wants to construct something out of his imagination. Most liars like doing this, and it is very confusing when you are conversing with him. It is always good for you to ask him to repeat exactly what he said and you will realize that he will have a hard time doing this because, truth is easy and loses no color, meaning at any given time, something said truthfully has high chances of being repeated with the same words and punctuations.

Sometimes looking up signifies boredom. A person could be looking up to look for more exciting things that will root out the monotony. When a person lowers his head then looks up directly at the person he is talking to, this shows that submission of attraction. For example in a love relationship, when a man asks a question then the lady looks down then raises her eyes back to him, this means she is submitted to what he asked for, and she is attracted to it.

I Am Looking Down

This shows submission. It sends a message to the other person that you are not a threat, and you do not plan to hurt him. Looking down also drives a guilty point at home. It shows that you are guilty of what you are being accused of. When a person looks down then to the left, he could be talking to himself, to understand or get what he is doing, look at his lips, a movement will show and you will fully understand what he is up to — looking down to the right show's attendance to the emotions. The inner feelings are handled when the person does this. This sign also shows respect to especially the cultures that consider direct eye contact as rudeness.

Looking sideways

This shows shifting of interests. A person looking sideways is looking at something that is interesting to him. A quick eye throws sideways can be a way to determine the cause of a distraction then continue with what you were doing. When you look to the left, it shows that you are trying to remember a certain point. Looking sideways on the right tells that you imagine a particular sound.

Lateral movement

When the eyes of a person start shifting from one side to another, this shows that the person could be lying or a person is looking for a way he can use to escape in case he is busted. Sometimes lateral movement shows a conspiracy. A person is looking out to see if anyone is listening to them before unleashing what he wanted to do.

Gazing

When a person looks at a thing for quite some time in a gazing way, this shows interest. He is interested in that thing. When a person is doing this, it is easy to follow his eyes, and you will find what he is gazing at. It could be a nice car, a person or a picture. In love relationships, a person looking at another's eyes speaks a lot. He is in love with the other person. When he gazes at the lips, he is sending a message that he would like to kiss, when he takes him down to the body in a sliding manner, he is showing lust. When you find him looking at your genital region, he wants to have a sexual relationship. When you see a person gazing at the forehead, he has no interest in the person.

If a person looks at you up and down, he is trying to size you up. He is seeing you as either a threat or a potential sex partner. However you should be keen at where the eyes stay for long, sometimes the person's eyes are showing insult when sizing you up, they are trying to tell you that they are better than you are and more powerful. This is a very annoying thing to any person. However, liars have a problem with gazing because they are feeling guilty. When they realize that they can be found out, they over gaze. In looking, there is a power gaze. It is always short but mighty. It can make one do something imposed him by the other without asking, for example, parents at home. Most mothers have power gazes. She tells you to do something and just by looking at you; you do not question, you stand up and go to do it.

Glancing

There are different meanings attached to glancing. It could mean having a desire to do something or betraying the desire. For example, glancing at a person shows a willingness to talk to the person, that is having the willingness while glancing at your car each time you are talking to someone or glancing at the door shows that you want to leave and you are not interested in what they are saying. This is the betrayal of the desire.

Maintain Eye Contact

This shows interest in the person, love, and affection and sometimes dominance.

Doe's eyes

This is when eyes seem softened, and the muscles surrounding the eyes softened. In a defocusing look, this shows sexual desire.

Making eye contact

When you directly look at a person, this shows acknowledgment. You are acknowledging his presence and what he is saying. It can also signify the attraction of attention. If a person is, talking and you were not paying attention, but after he says a particular word, you fix your eyes directly on him.

Staring

This happens when you look at something for so long with your eyes widened. It shows interest. Sometimes after receiving bad news, staring can show disbelief or shock. When a person is staring, but his eyes lack focus, he could be doing internal thinking and other times when a person stares for far too long, it shows aggressiveness. He is trying to say he is not afraid. Surprises can also be seen in staring when a person stares for a short while with eyes wide open then goes to normal.

Squinting

This is when a person narrows his eyes. He could be thinking that the thing being told to him is not right, or there are some lies in what is being said. Sometimes squinting shows lack of certainty. You are not sure if the thing is correct or not, you will find yourself looking when you narrow your eyes, your pupil size changes. They can grow wider so that you can see the broader picture of it or grow smaller because you are in doubt.

Blinking

When people are stressed, their rate of blinking goes up. They blink faster. Fast blinking can also be a say of liars because they lack what they have to say so they blink faster so that they can find the words to say, but if they realize they are doing this, they decide to open their eyes wide open and stare at you.

There are other so many signs that are related to the eyes, and this includes winking, closing, damp, tears, pupil size, rubbing, lines in the eyes and eyebrows.

The Mouth

Movement of lips tells a lot about a person. For instance, parted lips show that the person is flirting. When someone's lips are parted, and then he licks the lips, especially when gazing at someone, this is a sure sign of flirtation. On the other hands when you pull your lips inside from all direction, this is called pursed lips. Pursed lips symbolize tension. They may at the time show that a person is frustrated or in total disapproval. When you are discussing something with someone, and you see then pull in their lips in a pursed way, it simply shows that they are not agreeing with anything that you are saying. When you see pursed lips, they at times show anger. An angry person will have pursed lips, which are suppressed.

If a person is trying to decide between two possibilities, his lips will be pulled inwards. When a person's lips are drawn together in whichever the direction, this is called puckering. Puckering of lips in a kiss like way sends the desired signal. Puckering lips mainly sideways and shows uncertainty. It is always to look at the lips and the eyes when the person you are talking to is close, sometimes each might be saying different things, and this means the person is pretending. The sucked-in lips show uncertainty or deep thought. When a person's red part of the lips is dipped in his mouth he may be thinking hard about a solution to something or he is not sure if the decision took was right, his head is filled with uncertainty. This formation of lips also shows avoidance. The person is avoiding speaking when he should.

Flattened lips show the lack of desire to speak. The rims are pressed against each other in a horizontal way, which shows the person has no desire to speak. These lips can also signify a person's refusal to eat. This is common in children. If the child does not like a particular meal, they will press their lips together in denial and when they are forced after eating the lips will remain in the same position indicating their distress since they do not want to cry or turn their mouths in a sadness-showing manner. Other lips reading ways include the turned-up lips, turned down lips, retracted lips, moving lips, twitching lips, protruding lips, biting lips, and relaxed lips.

Hands

Hands-on a human body holds a lot of power that we do not know about. Hands can make you look wrong or right without your understanding. Understanding what sides say during speech is an essential thing. Below are some few ways in which hands communicate and their representation.

Palms up

This signifies a request. It is common in Christian religion when they are praying the Lord's Prayer. They believe that by palms looking up, they are God will see it as a favor and answer. However, this is true in general life. When your palms are facing up, they send a message to the people you are requesting from that, it is a favor, and your support is most likely to be granted.

Palms down

This comes out as an order. Referring to the same scenario of palms up, the people you are talking to with your palms facing down will reject your request. They will feel that you are ordering them. Nobody likes being ordered around.

Shaking Hands

When shaking hands, they should be vertical to symbolize equality. If one person's palm faces upward, it signifies acceptance of surrender, dominance, and superiority of the other person. Most politicians like using this tactic where their hands rest on top of the other person's hand. If this had ever happened to you when someone was showing dominance by turning their hands facing on top, then time that happens, cover their side so that his hand is sandwiched in yours to make it a double handshake. Doing this creates a switch in power, but you should be careful because it is annoying to the most power-hungry people. Double handshake is necessarily for power switching, especially when given by a good friend. It shows compassion and deep warmth too.

Clasped Hands Or Clenched Hands

This has different meanings. They may show nervousness, confidence, or assumption of a stance. For example, in a meeting when most speakers feel that they are being stared at a lot, they assume a confident attitude that makes them comfortable. When the fists are clenched and eyes fixed on the person speaking, it shows confidence, especially in a business meeting that you are seated at a round table.

The Steeple Hands

This is where your hands make an upward v. This shows confidence. A person is confident about what he is saying at that moment. It also signifies attitude; self-assured attitude. You are sure that the position you are portraying at that given time is the required one and you have no doubts or worries about anything.

Personal Space

The distance between two people or more tells more than you have ever known.

Intimate Space

When people are in a close relationship, the distance between them will range from 6 to 18 inches. The closeness they have will make you automatically know what kind of relationship they are sharing.

Social Distance

A 4 to 12 feet range of lengths social mile. People who are only socializing like friends or families are not so close to each other like those in an intimate relationship.

Chapter 34. Lies and Insecurities

Do you know that you are lied to more than ten times a day by the people that are close to you? When people lie, they make something that is not true seem to be the naked truth. Everyone looks at lying as a bad habit, but this does not stop them from lying. The lies start went we are still kids, and it goes on into adulthood. The sad thing is that when lying goes beyond the boundaries, it becomes a destructive habit to many people. Let us start by looking at the different types of lies.

Types of Lies

White Lie

This should be the least of your worries because people that tell white lies are polite and very tactful. White lies are more of an excuse not to do something and are told with the intention of font spoiling your relationship.

However, telling white lie after white lie will lead to conflict on when the person realizes that you have been lying to them. You will end up losing credibility in front of the family and friends.

Broken Promise

When you promise someone something, you need to go ahead and fulfill it. Broken promises refer to a commitment that you fail to a jeep. If you did not have the intention to fulfill the promise, you end up making things worse.

Fabrication

Fabricating something is telling someone something, which you do not know for sure if it is true. You just come up with something then you say it. When you spread a rumor, you will be like stealing another person's reputation.

Bold-faced Lie

This is a lie that you tell, and everyone knows that it is a lie. The signs will be there that you are telling a lie, but since you know, it is a bold one; you just say it while maintaining a straight face.

Now that you know what types of lies are there, the thing you need to know is why people lie in the first place.

Why Do People Lie?

Fear

People lie because they are afraid of the consequences of the truth. They will tell a lie because they know that they have done something that you do not like. So, they try to cover up the crime so that you do not get to know what they did.

Manipulation

A person will tell you lies so that they can manipulate the truth. The lie is motivated by the desire to get someone to say something or to do it, or to make a decision that will favor the liar in one way or another. Many people lie to get something, such as money, sex, status, or power.

Pride

In many instances, the person will lie because they are too proud, to tell the truth. They use the line as a way to display a favorable image. They will exaggerate so much that you will not know what is true.

Why Is Lying such a Big Deal?

Why is it that we focus on lying so much? The truth is that when you lie, you change so many aspects of yourself for someone else. Let us look at the disadvantages of lying.

Lying Can Affect Your Health

People that lie have to keep the guilt for a very long time. They will keep unpleasant secrets that can even lead to health complications.

You will Live a Stressful Life

People that lie get to release stress hormones.

It Makes You lonely

When you lie, people tend to alienate you because they cannot trust you. You will face the punishment that people will not believe you, and you will not believe anyone. When people alienate you, you end up having no one to share with.

It Becomes a Habit

When you lie, you will make it a routine such that even the things that do not need you to lie end up being lines in themselves. The more you lie, the more prone you become to lies.

You Have to Remember a Lot

When you lie, you have to remember what you said about the lie, how you said it and when you said it. If you have many lies, you will find it a huge bid on you, and it might cause a lot of unnecessary stress. By the time, you start remembering what you said and how you said it, you will be open showing that it was a blatant lie.

You Become Unreliable

When you lie, people will take you the way you present yourself – as a liar. Even your partner and other people close to you will not believe in you and will not trust you at all.

How to Know That Someone is Lying via Body Language

Detecting liars can be easy if you know how to read and interpret their body language. Many liars tend to use a lot of body language to convince you, but if you are keen, then you will read right through them.

Words and Body Language Don't Match

When you talk to someone, you need to make sure that the words that come out of their mouths and the body language should match. For instance, when you shake your head up and down and yet you are negating, then someone will interpret this wrongly. This is usually seen when someone is responding to serious accusations.

Folding of Lips

Remember that lips do not lie. When someone you are talking to folds their lips or curls them in a particular way, then they are trying to withhold information from you. This also happens when they hide their lips. When this happens, you need to expect a half-truth.

Tone of Voice

The biggest indicator or deception is the tone of voice. A strong voice, though I might indicate confidence, can also indicate some deception. A softer voice might indicate that someone is not telling everything right.

Big-Talking People

People that are big talkers are most likely putting on air just for the camera. The ones that try so hard to look good might be the ones that need to be checked out since they might be lying.

Jitters

If you notice that someone is fidgeting, then you might be looking at a deceptive character. You need to look at various aspects of their body as they talk including their feet as well as their hands. Any sign of fidgeting will point to lying.

While this might be true in various ways, you also need to watch out for the people that are not moving at all. The person is readying himself or herself for confrontation. When the conversation is slow and relaxed, the body usually is relaxed, but if you say, something and you realize that the person has suddenly gone rigid, then the person is soon lying to you.

Uncertainty

If you see that a person is expressing body language signs that point to uncertainty, then you need to suspect lying. You can read uncertainty in the way the person talks; the voice might go up and down in different ways.

Indifference

If you realize that someone is shrugging, lacking any expression or trying to avoid eye contact, then you need to suspect lying.

Quick Change in head Position

A person that is lying will tend to change their head position fast. They will suddenly make a change in the position when you ask them a certain question. They will retract the head; jerk is backward or bows down when you ask the question.

Change in Breathing

A person that is lying to you will tend to change their rate of breathing. Since they know that they might be caught, they will become apprehensive, and their breathing will change. You will notice their shoulders rising and falling, and then their choice might become shallow.

They are also out of breath because of their blood flow and heart rate changes.

Repetition of Words and Phrases

Repetition comes through because the person is hell-bent on trying to convince you that the lie they are trying to spin is true. They are really trying to make the lie work in their mind, but they are not getting the words to communicate.

Repeating what they are saying is a way to come up with the right words to convince you. They are trying to gather their thoughts so that they can lie to you the best way.

They Give Too Much Information

When someone rants on and on about something, especially the information that you have not asked about, then there is a high likelihood that they are not telling you the truth.

Liars mostly talk a lot because they are really hoping that when they give you too much information, you will tend to believe them.

Put Their Hands over their Mouth

The most telltale sign of lying is that the person will place their hand over their mouth when they do not want to handle questions.

When adults tend to put their hand over their lips, it goes ahead to tell you that they are not revealing everything to you, and they do not just want you to know what they are saying. Instead, they are closing off any communication they have with you.

They Cover Their Body Parts

They will cover some areas of the body, such as the chest, throat, and head. When this happens, you know that you have hit a raw nerve with the person, which in turn makes you know that the person is nervous and will lie to you.

Shuffling of the Feet

This is a way to tell you that the body of the person is taking over. When a person shuffles their feet, you will realize that the lie they are about to tell you is making them uncomfortable. It also lets you know that the person is trying to get out of the situation that has become too hot to handle.

It Becomes Difficult for them to peak

If you have ever checked out an interrogation of a suspect, then you will notice that they become more and more tongue-tied.

This is usually due to the automatic nervous system that decreases the flow of saliva during stressful situations: other signs that might accompany this is pursed lips and lip biting.

Prolonged Staring

When people lie, they try to break eye contact. But a seasoned liar will go ahead and stare at you straight in the eyes in an attempt to manipulate and control you. When many people tell the truth, they will usually shift to their eyes around without looking suspicious. On the other hand, others will maintain a steady gaze to try and intimidate you.

Now that you know when to spot a liar, we need to look at the instances when lies become acceptable.

When Is Lying Acceptable?

Have you ever found yourself in a situation where you appreciated a lie? Let us look at the various aspects that will make lies acceptable to you and other people.

The best lies to tell are white lies because they come from a harmless place. For instance, you might say to a lady you love their hairstyle yet It is no their favorite. In some situations, a little lie will go a long way to make things better for you. Let us look at when lying is precious.

When you want to Cancel Plans

More times, there is no way to cancel a plan that you have made without sounding like a very bad person. If you have something else to do rather than go for the appointment, you better go ahead and come up with a lie that will make it seem that things are okay.

If you have friends that are understanding, you would rather tell the truth than lie to them. However, at times, it is much easier to tell a lie than tell them what you feel.

This is why you need to go ahead and tell them that you are not feeling well, and this is why you need to drop a lie repeatedly.

However, if you are to tell a lie, then you need to do it in a timely way. If you cancel too early, you will not seem rude to the other person.

When Someone Asks for Personal Information

If someone is asking you for your personal information, you need to lie so that you save yourself. It is not easy to share information with someone that you do not trust. The person might not give you so many options, but try and keep the information private. You need to try and make sure that you explain to the person why you do not need to give your information, but if they insist and you are still doubtful, you can lie about the information.

When Late for Work

If you have a strict job policy, you need to know that when you get late, you will end up being fired. At first, the manager will understand, but with time, the lies will become too much, and it will make it hard for you to be believed.

Lies are acceptable when the manager that you work under will fire you sooner than put up with your lateness. If the lying means that you need to save your job, then that white lie will work.

Complimenting Someone

Have you seen your friend with a bizarre hairstyle or putting on a weird dress? If the friend is happy about it, then you will need to tell them a lie so that you hurt their feelings. Besides, it would be too late for the friend to rush back home to rectify the situation.

When Someone asks How You are Feeling

At times, you will say you are okay just to make someone feel better. Times, the other person might be in a tough situation to what you are going through, and you have to tell them what they expect to hear. So, make sure you keep it short and tell them you are feeling well even when you are not.

Protecting the Innocence of a Child

A little white lie will go a long way to keep your little ones in line. When you plan to protect the innocence of the child, you have to be able to come up with the right lies each time. They will learn the truth when the right time comes.

Talking to a Sick Friend

Do you have a friend who is sick and she looks worse the wear? Well, you can go ahead and tell the person how good she looks so that they will be optimistic that they will get better. This will help lift her spirits and make them get better.

When Eating Food Prepared by Someone Else

If your partner has prepared dinner and it does not taste so good, it is usually polite of you to say that the food is nice. At times, the situation might call for more than a single compliment. Some false truths make it easier for people to bond in most cases.

To End a Fight

If you have been arguing with your partner for many days, it might get to a point where you take your pride down and then concede. Tell them you are sorry and then tell them they are right – just to put an end to everything.

When listening to Stories from Other People

Your friend might tell you their boring stories repeatedly, and make it look as if that is the only story they know. When this happens, you will have to sit through the whole process and make sure you go along with the story just to make your friend feel good.

Go ahead and tell them how you find their stories to be great, and you can even relate to the stories so that you keep the friendship.

When You Receive a Fake Gift

Do you receive the same gift each year from the same person repeatedly? Well, even if you are getting the same thing repeatedly, you will have to make sure you pretend that you like the gift. This is the only way you can make the person happy and seem to appreciate the efforts the friend has put in.

Chapter 35. NLP

Neuro Linguistic Programming, or NLP, is the procedure by which the human personality makes a reality dependent on tactile info, sentiments and language that is then placed into perceptible examples. These examples are then utilized by the intuitive to decide how an individual ought to react to circumstances physically and inwardly.

Having a cognizant familiarity with this procedure enables an individual to make their own world. At first this may sound somewhat shocking to the easygoing onlooker, anyway its reason depends on science as we become increasingly acquainted with how the human personality works. At the point when somebody gets oneself in a circumstance that may not be bringing the ideal outcomes, the capacity to change the result in a moment is an incredible asset.

Illustrative frameworks depend on the faculties and how every individual like to acclimatize and process new data. Some want to imagine it, some need to talk about it and others may need to "feel" it. Contingent upon an individual's favored authentic style, managing them in that equivalent style may influence them in your mind. You are imparting a similar idea or thought; however, you are doing it so that sounds good to them.

Very much framed results are actualized by plainly characterizing the ideal results and expressing them in a positive way. As opposed to stating what you don't need, unmistakably state what you do need. When you have your ideal outcomes unmistakably characterized, you'll have to give the thought setting through envisioning the result with the related physical things you may understanding. For instance, you need to imagine the sound of someone’s voice, the encompassing commotion you would hope to hear or any scents or different things you may encounter once the objective is accomplished.

Imparting the result to others as such enables them to see the profit and can carry them in your mind. Making your ideal result convincing enough to others will give them the longing to accomplish a similar objective. Numerous publicists utilize this representation to allure clients to purchase their item by portraying what their life would resemble on and when they obtained a specific item. This representation encourages the client to "see" the objective of a glad life.

Displaying greatness is another system utilized under the NLP umbrella. By demonstrating yourself on a fruitful individual, or reflecting another person who has had achievement, you are taking on their conviction framework and their world. You likewise increase extra understanding into why they settle on the choices they do and how their convictions impact the decisions they make. When addressing somebody utilizing their conviction framework, you are bound to persuade them regarding the legitimacy of your contemplations and thoughts.

These strategies can be applied to numerous circumstances and are progressively being used in the business world. How effective do you find an individual could become in the event that they could legitimately impact the activities of their colleagues? Having the option to impact everyone around you isn't really a type of control yet a cooperative energy of sorts that enables people to push ahead on the whole with one reason. Having everybody in agreement and without singular wants at the top of the priority list implies that the result is bound to be agreeable to everybody

NLP has numerous utilizations in business and one of the key uses is to pick up impact over other individuals. How might you want to have the option to impart in a manner that empowered you to effortlessly communicate as the need should arise to individuals at all various degrees of an association? How might you want to have the option to persuade somebody to accomplish something just by your utilization of explicit language designs? How might you want to have the option to assist individuals with conquering their issues so as to make them progressively effective and profitable. How might you like have the option to impact client decisions by speaking with them at an oblivious level so they simply get a positive sentiment about your item or support and acknowledge your recommendations?

NLP Communication Model

How can it work? All things considered, NLP instructs you that we as a whole have certain inclinations by the way we think, how we speak to the world to ourselves. On and when we can comprehend the manner in which that we find, at that point we can impact how we think.

For instance. We as a whole have a favored framework for deciphering what goes on in our lives into our musings. We either like to utilize our feeling of sight, sound, or contact. In the event that we have a favored feeling of sight, at that point we will interpret effectively what we experience into pictures in our mind. On and when we have a favored feeling of touch, at that point we will effortlessly make an interpretation of that into interior emotions and so forth.

Let's state that we have an inclination for sight, or pictures. This will get clear in addition to other things in the things that we state, "see you," "I can see that event," "Out of the picture and therefore irrelevant" and so forth. All expressions that include the feeling of sight.

On and when we have an inclination for contact, at that point we may make statements like "look you up some other time," "you can clutch that idea," "I get a positive sentiment when I think about that" all expressions that include a physical feeling of touch or feeling.

Thus, in the event that we know this, at that point we can tune in to what individuals state, and we can determine what their favored vehicle of correspondence is. We can increase oblivious impact over them by utilizing their favored arrangement of correspondence back to them. Thus, we will utilize words and expressions that they use so as to do this.

Have you seen that individuals like individuals who resemble them? Do you and your companions have normal interests? This is the means by which it works.

Give this a shot time you are conversing with them. Watch their shoulders go here and there as they breath in and out and duplicate them. In this way, when they breath in, you breath in, when they breath out, you breath out. Notice how it gives you an oblivious association with them. They won't realize what you have done however they will feel progressively associated with them and they will like you all the more subliminally.

One of the significant commitments NLP has made to self-awareness and life improvement is its applications to correspondence both inside and outside. NLP offers numerous functional methods to enable us to participate in increasingly important cooperations with people around us by constraining a significant number of the hindrances to viable correspondence. This article will take a gander at a portion of the manners in which NLP can improve our relational abilities explicitly with others, and in doing so upgrade the nature of our lives.

Called Neuro Linguistic programming for an explanation, NLP is centered around the language designs associated with the manner in which we speak with ourselves as well as other people. Language designs, explicitly the words we use and how we use them profoundly affect our experience of consistently life. At the point when we have an encounter of any sort, at that point we give a mark to that understanding, the name, or the words we use BECOME the experience. For instance, you come back from a day at Disneyland and somebody asks you how it was. You may answer it was wonderful, fabulous, exciting, startling, energizing, fun, heart siphoning or insane... whichever word you decide to depict the experience, IS the experience. Let's assume you picked 'frightening'.

Extremely the word 'frightening' is nothing, it's only a mix of letters. And yet startling is a believing, a lot of contemplations and mental symbolism that is related to that blend of letters. Think about this: Imagine on and when you didn't have a clue about the word startling? For reasons unknown it had been overlooked from your jargon, or you'd never heard it said as a kid. OK realize that how will generally be 'terrified'? It's accounted for that some little island countries don't have a word for 'war'... Envision how that influences their lifestyle!

Words cause compound responses in our brains. The things we state or hear said to us, especially the words that they are said in, cause us to feel certain ways about things and respond in specific manners to specific conditions.

How would you answer when somebody asks "How are you?"? Do you carelessly answer "Fine" or "alright". How would you feel when you state that? How would you feel after you have said it?

Imagine a scenario where you answered "Remarkable!", "Extremely Superb", or "Awesome. Do you find you would feel in an unexpected way? Two individuals can have similar encounters every day, except one can mark them "alright" and one can call them "Great" and as an outcome one individual will FEEL wonderful and one will physically feel OK.

Do you see the intensity of words yet?

If not, consider it in a progressively outside correspondence type setting. Let's assume somebody has recently given you their feeling on something and you answer "I don't know I agree"... Do you find this would make the individual feel distinctively to on and when you said "You're WRONG". The two answers have demonstrated a similar importance... you don't concur with them, yet the words utilized make significantly various responses thus enormously impact the connection between the two individuals. Alright, OK you get it, words impact how we feel.

As a Life mentor and NLP ace specialist. NLP is a ground-breaking technique that can assist you with getting the outcomes you need in all aspects of your life. By utilizing the accompanying procedure, you will have the option to tweak your objectives, find what you truly need and the means, to accomplish it!

1. Positive

What do you need? This must be expressed in the positive as your subliminal personality doesn't have the foggiest idea about the contrast among constructive and contrary

Did you realize that residence in the negative can really be awful for your wellbeing!

2. Tangible explicit

By what method will you know when you have it?

What will you do when you get it?

What will you see, hear and feel like when you have it?

3. Contextualized

Where and when would you like to have it?

Where and when do you not need it?

4. Self attainable

It is significant that the objective must be inside your very own domain of impact for example is something over which you have control.

What assets do you should have the option to accomplish it?

What do you have to do to accomplish it?

Is this something which you, yourself, can accomplish? Or then again does it necessitate that other individuals carry on with a specific goal in mind?

5. Natural

What are the favorable circumstances and the weaknesses? There are consistently inconveniences in rolling out an improvement - being aware of these keeps you 'at cause' by settling on it your decision.

What are the upsides of rolling out this improvement?

What are the disservices of rolling out this improvement?

What will accomplishing this lose you? Become?

6. Beneficial

This is the inspiration question. Which of your qualities will be satisfied by accomplishing this objective?
What's critical to you about getting it?
What will this objective assist you with abstaining from feeling?
What is the advantage of this objective?
7. The initial step
Do you have an initial step? So as to transform your fantasy into a solid reality you pole venture out, without it you won't gather up adequate speed to make you to the following stride.
Use NLP to Create Changes and Shifts for Others During Ordinary Conversations
Discussing successfully with other individuals is a fundamental ability that couple of are extremely ready to accomplish. Since individuals learn and process data in an unexpected way, your individual style may not concur with the individual you're addressing. This dissimilarity in correspondence styles regularly prompts mistaken assumptions and hard emotions.
Consider the possibility that you had the capacity to quickly set up affinity with anybody. On and when you right now feel cumbersome when meeting new individuals, you are not conveying viably and could be losing commonly compensating connections. The capacity to make an association with somebody finishes you pretty much every part of your life. Personal, business and easygoing connections are altogether affected by your capacity to enough convey in a way that is effectively comprehended and generally welcomed.
NLP offers a few procedures that enable you to express what is on your mind just as to comfort the other party. In the event that they are in a casual perspective, they will be increasingly open to your thoughts and perspectives.
Animals in the normal world do almost no correspondence through vocal language. Just individuals depend exclusively on the expressed word to demonstrate our contemplations, emotions, thoughts and by and large perspective. While watching other living things, it turns out

to be very evident that a discussion is going on that we don't hear yet that they unmistakably get it. Not clear to most people, we also have an implicit exchange that we use to convey our perspective to other people. What we know as non-verbal communication is frequently disregarded or not taken note. NLP utilizes this implicit language now and again to build up affinity and a feeling of recognition.

This is accomplished by discreetly watching the non-verbal communication of the other individual. When you get a feeling of their stance, characteristics and manner of speaking, you can start the way toward coordinating and reflecting these practices. There is inquire about that emphatically proposes we like individuals who are most similar to us. By imitating the conduct of another person, you are comforting that person and making the person in question increasingly responsive to loosened up discussion. Along these lines, they will tune in to what you need to state with a receptive outlook and can be emphatically impacted.

Implanted directions are questions that lead with a recommendation of an idea or thought that at that point becomes planted in the audience members mind. An inquiry that starts with "What might it be like..." makes the audience picture their answer before vocalizing it. Giving an idea setting makes it a reality and by posing these sorts of inquiries, you are giving your audience another reality and changing their conviction framework.

In spite of the fact that NLP could be viewed as a training that is utilized for control and control, it ought to be utilized as a positive impact for you and your general surroundings. At the point when utilized in a valuable way, NLP can decidedly change your world and the truth of others that you come into contact with regularly. This positive impact reduces strife and fortifies connections.

Chapter 36. The Art Of Reading Every Kind Of Person

Let Go of Your Expectations

Now, because we live in a world where there is so much information and data available to you, your brain works even harder at sieving through all of those information that you receive. So, in order to make it easier, your brain establishes or discovers patterns and then it uses these patterns to predict people's behavior or outcomes of certain situations. These patterns is what we now convince ourselves have become expectations. So, you have a situation where you enter into a work environment and because you have been used to a pattern where people are nice, wonderful, warming and welcoming, you think that the office environment should emulate or match your expectations. When this happens, you become more focused on what you think the environment should be like as opposed to what it really is. If you want to really understand the true intention of people, the first thing you need to do is to give them a clean slate and to give them a clean slate, you need to let go of your expectations. That way you can truly get to see them for who they are.

Step Two: See People for Who They Really are

I can't remember where I saw this, but I remember seeing it and how the message stuck in my head. The message was simple, see people for who they really are and not who you want them to be. This is a mistake that all of us make and I think this principal here pigmies back on the step one that we just talked about. You need to learn to let go of your expectations of people. Ladies, when you meet a guy who is tall, dark and handsome, you immediately build this world around this person and rather than seeing the person as they really are you start seeing them as who you want them to be. In other words, you are projecting your own perception on them. This could play out in a positive way or negative way. For instance, you meet a girl who is rude and mean to you, but because you are impressed by a certain aspect of her and don't want to let her go, you convince yourself that maybe she's just one of those high maintenance girls who have a very strong opinion of what they want. But in reality, she is just rude. On the other side, you meet this person who is very nice and warm and open, but you feel like this person is hiding in a nasty secret because you don't trust people who are generally that way (possibly because of the experiences you had) and so you start projecting this perception you have on them. Either way, it doesn't help to really expose or reveal the mask that people hide behind. It is when you put aside your projection of people on them that you are able to unveil their true intentions.

Step Three: Trust Your Instincts

No matter who you are, regardless of your gender or social status or even your experiences in life, we have all been biologically equipped with a weapon or a programming if you prefer that alerts us to certain elements that may or may not compromise our safety and security in a situation. This alarm system extends to the relationship that we have with people. There are certain people that you meet and all of a sudden, the hairs at the back of your neck starts rising and your internal wires start going haywire. You start getting this sense or feeling that something is off. If you go through the interviews of people who have been able to escape serial killers or dire situations, they will tell you that right before that point that the event occurred, their senses were tingling. The common phrase that they use is that, they had the sense that something was off. This is called instinct. In a life-or-death situation, your instinct can save you. When it comes to relationships with people, your instincts can guide you to the kind of people who are more in tune with you or people who in the long-run would be beneficial in that relationship. In this age, we tend to want to rely on facts and logic and not gut or instinct. And it makes sense that this is how we want to live our lives. You don't want to meet a person and then have to explain that the reason you let go of that relationship or the reason you are not in that work situation is because your instincts were warning you. It doesn't make sense, but often times, it serves you well. So, learn and train yourself to listen more to your instinct.

Step Four: Ask Questions

A lot of us have been socially conditioned to behave in ways that are considered polite. And part of being polite is avoiding questions. When I talk about avoiding questions, I am not just talking about avoiding the questions that other people ask us. I am talking about avoiding asking people those questions. In this dispensation, we believe a lot in privacy and certain questions can feel like an invasion of that privacy. And so, we would rather step back and let the person come to us or hope that the person gets in that place where they would want to reach out to us. In certain situations, this is the right thing to do. But if you already have your instincts telling you that something might be off and you get a sixth sense that something different might be going on behind the scenes, by all means do ask the questions. I feel like if I had been bold enough to ask the questions I wanted to ask when Tim was alive, I might have been able to make a difference. Of course, I have learned to let go of that guilt but this is something that lives with me and will continue to live with me for the rest of my life. However, my situation is different. If you are going to improve your communication with people and you want to manage the relationships that you have with people better, you need to learn to ask the right questions. And sometimes, those questions might not be comfortable. You also need to come to a place where you are accepting that fact. Maybe apply some tact in your questioning, but do ask the questions anyway

Step Five: Take Action

There is an old African proverb that says, 'tomorrow is pregnant'. I love that proverb because it always brings to mind, the reminder that tomorrow is not guaranteed. Nobody knows what will happen tomorrow or even what will happen in the minute. The only thing we can control is what happens right now. Based on the things I have listed here, starting with letting go of your expectations, trusting your instincts more, asking the right questions and learning to see people as they really are, the final step in this process is to take action. After asking the questions, take the necessary follow-up actions. Not only does this help you manage your relationship better, it puts you in an assertive position in that relationship. If you keep waiting for things to happen to you, your role in that relationship becomes dormant. And when your role in the relationship is dormant, your influence reduces drastically. And we know that the whole point of this exercise is basically about improving your influence in a relationship. As suggested, studying people is not reserved for psychiatrists but any other person even though psychiatrists are best positioned to analyze people. Analyzing people requires understanding their verbal and nonverbal cues. When studying people, you should try to remain objective and open to new information. Nearly each one of us has some form of personal biases and stereotypes that blocks our ability to understand another person correctly. When reading an individual, it is crucial to reconcile that information against the profession and cultural demands on the target person. Some environments may force an individual to exhibit particular behavior that is not necessarily part of their real one. For instance, working as a call center agent may force one to sound composed and patient when in real life, the person acts the contrary.

Start by analyzing the body language cues of the target person you are trying to read. Body language provides the most authoritative emotional and physiological status of an individual. It is difficult to rehearse all forms of body language, and this makes body language critical in understanding a person. Verbal communication can be faked through rehearsal and experience, and this can give misleading stand. When examining body language, analyze the different types of body language as a set. For instance, analyze facial expressions, body posture, pitch, tonal variation, touch and eye contact, as a related but different manifestation of communication and emotional status. For instance, when tired, one is likely to stretch their arms and rest them on the left and right tops of adjacent chairs, sit in a slumped position, stare at the ceiling, and drop their heads. Only analyzing one aspect of body language can mislead one to come up with a conclusion correctly.

Additionally, it would be best if you lent attention to appearance. The first impression counts, but it can also be misleading. In formal contexts, the appearance of an individual is critical to communicate the professionalism of the person and the organizational state of the mind of that individual. For example, an individual with an unbuttoned shirt indicates he hurried or is casual with the audience and the message. Wearing formal attire that is buttoned up and tucked in suggests prior preparation and seriousness that the person is giving to the occasion. Having unkempt hair may indicate a rebellious mind, and this might be common among African professors in Africa, for instance. In most settings, having unkempt hair suggests that one lacks the discipline to prepare for the formal context or the person is overworked and is busy. Lack of expected grooming may indicate an individual battling with life challenges or feeling uncared for.

It is also important that one should take note of the posture of the person. Posture communicates a lot about the involvement of an individual in a conversation. Having an upright posture suggests eagerness and active participation in what is being communicated. If one cups their face in the arms and lets the face rest on both thighs, then it suggests that one is feeling exhausted or has deviated from the conversation completely.

Having crossed arms suggests defensiveness or deep thought. One sitting in a slumped position suggests that he/she is tired and not participating in the ongoing conversation. Leaning on the wall or any object suggests casualness that the person is lending to an ongoing conversation. If at home, sitting with crossed legs suggests that one is completely relaxed. However, the same posture at the workplace suggests that one is feeling tensed and at the same time concentrating. Furthermore, observe the physical movements in terms of distance and gestures. The distance between you and the target individual is communicating communicates about the level of respect and assurance that the individual perceives. A social distance is the safest bet when communicating, and it suggests high levels of professionalism or respect between the participants. Human beings tend to be territorial as exhibited by the manner that they guard their distance. Any invasion of the personal distance will make the individual defensive and unease with the interaction.

For this reason, when an individual shows discomfort when the distance between communicators is regarded as social or public, then the individual may have other issues bothering him or her. Social and public distances should make one feel fully comfortable. Allowing a person close enough or into the personal distance suggests that the individual feels secure and familiar with the other person. Through reading, the distance between the communicators will give a hint on the respect, security, and familiarity between the individuals as well the likely profession of the individuals.

Correspondingly, then try to read facial expressions as deep frown lines indicate worry or over-thinking. Facial expressions are among the visible and critical forms of body language and tell more about the true emotional status of an individual. For instance, twitching the mouth suggests that an individual is not listening and is showing disdain to the speaker. A frozen face indicates that the person is shell-shocked, and this can happen when making a presentation of health and diseases or when releasing results of an examination. A smiling face with the smile not being prolonged communicates that one is happy and following the conversation. A prolonged smile suggests sarcasm. If one continually licks the lips may indicate that one is lying or that one is feeling disconnected from the conversation.

Relatedly, try to create a baseline for what merits as normal behavior. As you will discover, people have distinct mannerisms that may be misleading to analyze them as part of the communication process. For instance, some individuals will start a conversation by looking down or at the wall before turning to the audience. Mildly, mannerisms are like a ritual that one must activate before they make a delivery. Additionally, each person uniquely expresses the possible spectra of body language. By establishing a baseline of what is normal behavior, one gets to identify and analyze deviations from the standardized normal behavior accurately. Against this understanding, one will not erratically score a speaker that shuffles first if that is part of his behavior when speaking to an audience.

Chapter 37. How To Start Hacking The Mind, Persuasion Techniques And Manipulation Techniques

The Basics Of Mind Reading

For years now, a high number of people aren't aware of mind reading, thought transference and how best to analyze people. . as time went on, there came scientists who came up with investigations and further hypothesis about the truth and everything around it. And as this went on and on, the ignorance still shielded people into not believing such things as mind-reading ever existed. These beliefs made people so skeptical about any thinker that wants to employ these tools of reading people's minds.

The world keeps revolving and today we have a different application and thoughts towards the subject. This new science has come to stay with us as the world now revolves around several relationships and the art of reading intentions. Looking back to what was the norm years ago, one would conclude that the universe is moving so close to its full acceptance and application.

To read someone's mind, there are two possible facts to uphold - the instant change in the brain of the party suggesting and the respective change in the brain of the other party B who is the recipient of the proposed opinion. Between these two occurrences, there is meant to be a pause, a pause to question whether or not to consider the suggestion of the mind. And this has a lot to do with the sequence of thoughts and how they unfold.

The structure of the brain is so connected to conceive impulses as fast as it receives it which brings a connecting channel to what one believes and what it is. As brain nerves keep expanding as it sees any iota of reasoning, it is never right to say the brain reaches a limit for thinking. However, as the action of thought gets more tedious in deciding the way to follow, there are meant to be physical vibrations that show the extreme capabilities of reasoning.

With the strange outlook of assumptions and the bewildering stances of getting what the brain is interpreting, mind-reading occurs subconsciously. This belief brings the human closer to all tools of observation, hypothetical nuances and the feeble analysis that comes with reasoning.

And as this takes a different shape in thinking, it is safe to say that the universe is about embracing the fashioned way of analyzing the mind, human behaviors and what is left behind as options. Doing this fortifies the mind into higher tasks of deciding the possibilities to rely on thereby justifying the toughness and judgment of the heart.

Non-verbal communication conveys in a split second and easily an individual's solace or distress in a given circumstance. An individual's outward appearance or position can alarm others to peril. For example, state somebody opens a fridge and takes a drink of soured milk. A bent articulation and eyes full of caution immediately send the message, "disregard this!" subsequently saving others the sorry experience of difficult the milk for themselves.

An old piece of the mind called the limbic cerebrum is for the most part in charge of communicating implicit assumptions utilizing motion, facial changes, and wild eye-widening. Miniaturized scale articulations are momentary and pass on distinct emotions even in grown-ups who can buy and considerable control their outward appearances somewhat

Techniques Used in Mental Manipulation

Persuasion Technique

Persuasion is controlling the human mind without the knowledge of the manipulated party. The manipulated party will change his or her opinion without being aware. This technique accesses your right mind, which is imaginative and creative, while the left side is rational and analytical. In persuasion, the perpetrator distracts your left brain and occupy it. It leaves you in an eyes-open altered state but still

We wish we were there with you!

Have fun and

Merry Christmas!

With so much love,
Kelvin and Bonnie

x x

conscious, making you move from Beta awareness to Alpha. This technique is famous for politicians and lawyers.

Subliminal Programming

These are masked suggestions that can only be understood by your subconscious mind. They can be suggestions in audios, airbrushed visual suggestions, and flash images on your television quickly so that you do not consciously notice them. Some subliminal programming on audio makes suggestions on low volume. Your subconscious mind will notice these suggestions, but no one can monitor them even with equipment. The music we listen to can have a second voice behind it to program your mind. In 1984, a newsletter called Brain-Mind Bulletin that 99% of our activities are non-conscious.

Mass misuse - During mass meetings, the attendees go in and out of consciousness. If you have no idea, you cannot notice what is happening to you. It is a mental manipulation of the mass through vibrations. These vibrations produce Alpha, which makes the mass vulnerable. These make them accept any suggestion of the speaker as a command.

Vibrato - Vibrato is some effect installed on instrumental music or vocal, which makes people go in a distorted state of mind. In English history, some singers who had vibrato in their voices were not given chances to perform because of the effect they had on the public. Some listeners would have fantasies, mostly sexual fantasies.

Neurophone - Dr. Patrick Flanagan invented Neurophone. It is a device that can program your mind when it gets in contact with your skin. When this device gets in contact with your skin, you lose your sense and sight for a moment. It is because the skin has sensors for pain, touch, vibration, and heat. The message to manipulate your mind is played through Neurophone, which is connected and placed in the ceiling and no speakers. This message goes directly to the brain of the audience, and the manipulator can easily manipulate their mental state.

Medium for take-over - When you know how human beings function, you get the ability to control them. Medium take-over is happening in the televisions we watch. When people are put in a distorted state of mind, they function on the right brain, which releases brain opiates and makes you feel good, and you want it more. The experience is the same as the one opium users feel. The broadcasts in our televisions induce the Alpha making us accept the broadcast easily. It makes viewers translate suggestions as commands. Every minute spent on watching television conditions us.

The Best Techniques of Persuasion

Before we indulge further into the major facets of persuasion, we will first have to comprehend the meaning of persuasion. Persuasion refers to the psychological influence which affects the choice that an individual ought to make. With persuasion, an individual is often inclined to make you buy his or her school of thought in a bid to change your thought process. In order for one to effectively achieve persuasion, there are a number of things that need to be put in mind. When we are able to go beyond the natural human framework and get a grasp of what moves others, then you are in a position to achieve effective persuasion. This is because you are aware of the pressure points and how best to manipulate them.

When exploiting the art of persuasion, there are various pointers that can come in handy. These are:

Mimicking

As human beings of reason, we tend to vary from one individual to another. The diversity of this is what makes us appear in the discrepancy of others. Owing to this particular fact, you will find that as individuals, we are more drawn to be warm and welcoming to those people who exhibit the same characteristics as us. It could be a physical trait or just the way an individual carries themselves out. This type of technique is said to elicit positive feelings that go a mile when it comes to persuasion.

When an individual has the feelings of liking towards someone, he or she is in a position to be swayed by your influence.

In a bid to elaborate on this particular type of technique, we are going to employ the use of this scenario. In the hotel industry, especially in the most advanced and high-end ones, you will find that the allocation of a waiter is dependent on the customer. High-end hotels in the industry have high customer feedback and thus they tend to treat their clients in a manner that suggests so. A client, for instance, would be allocated a particular type of waiter who matches their description. For instance, French waiters are renowned for their exquisite service. Putting the client first is at the top of the list when it comes to this particular field. Many professionals have succeeded in this area owing to the manner in which they treated clients. This is because of the clients re the main source of business. Putting the client into consideration goes a notch higher to even saying the exact words that the client has said. With this, they are able to gather that you have aptly decoded what they meant.

In order to accurately achieve this particular technique, an individual ought to do a number of things. First, he or she may consider doing in-depth research into the particular field of the question in order to see to it that what is required of them is met. Before you are able to achieve persuasion by the use of this technique, one ought to be well versed with the individual that he or she ought to persuade. This type of expertise should be keen enough to make sure that it elicits major points that may come in handy during the process of persuasion.

Social Proof

When it comes to persuasion, social proof has repeatedly proven its dominance. Before we go deeper into the technique, we first need to gather the meaning of social proof. Social proof refers to the process by which an individual's feelings and thought process are affected by the way other people have reacted to the same issue. When it comes to social influence. An individual who is the persuader, draw his or her basis from the acts that others have engaged in time and again. It could be the norm. With human beings, the danger that occurs is the feeling of wanting to be associated with a group of people. Human beings want to accrue a sense of belonging either to a group of people or to a particular act and this is what puts them at a higher risk of being influenced easily.

Employing social proof when persuading an individual will mean that you have a basis of a norm that has been used repeatedly by the people whom we consider to be in the same class. This basis must be something that most people engage in and not a few numbers. Take, for instance, there are newbies in the estate who are looking for service providers. This newbie would first be inclined to know what other people in the estate are using. Although they might not settle on the same option as the rest of the estate, this will be somewhat a buildup on to what choice they may choose to settle upon. Rather they may end up embracing what others have used. With this technique, the trick lies whereby you ought to create a distinction in the manner in which an individual sees himself or herself as per against others. You will only achieve persuasion by convincing this individual that the desired option is one that has been embraced by a large group of individuals.

Reciprocity

When it comes to this type of technique, one needs to understand that a good deed was done to another individual no matter how remote, tends to go a long way. From the wording of it, reciprocity refers to the process by which an individual is able to respond to a good deed by performing a good deed in return. With this type of technique, we will find that most people fail to notice at its onset not until you are obligated to return the favor. In the world today, it is almost as rare as the sun rising from the west as it is to find someone who will extend feelings of warmness and care towards you. Save the people whom we are closely related, we tend to feel differently when an individual who is not even in your circle of friendship extends warm-hearted feelings.

The feeling of obligation arises as a result of being extended a good deed by an individual. This is the result of being extended with feelings of warmness. At this point, you are in a position to persuade the individual in the manner that you wish. This is because he or she would be obliged to follow in the direction of the wind. It should be noted that this particular type of technique ought to be time cautious. This is because the implication of reciprocity does not last forever. There are limits to this timeline and one should be cautious enough to make sure that these limits are not exploited. With the passing of more time, it weakens the wave of reciprocity.

In order to achieve this particular type of technique, an individual ought to play in the tone of offers and obligations. If your offer is worth it, then it raises an obligation effect on the other hand. Thus creating a win situation.

Consistency and Commitment

This type of technique is wired on an already formed perception. An individual is in a position to settle on a particular choice. The choice that this individual picks would be pegged on him or her for as far as they go. From the wording of it, consistency and commitment refer to the fact that an individual is in a position to make a choice and stick to it with sheer determination and perseverance. When it comes to persuasion, not all techniques may work and you may find that you hit rock bottom once or twice in your venture. When this happens, it is not advisable to give up. Consistency is what builds our character in almost every facet in life. This type of technique is vast in a manner that cuts across various fields not limited to the field of education and business. The first approach to an individual for purposes of convincing them may or may not end up in a manner that you wish. The first approach is often one that is characterized by rejection and in some cases mental torture. The best way to respond to this type of instance is by not giving up. The second encounter of individuals who first rejected your idea will see to it that you have an audience who understands what you are talking about.

The talk of consistency and commitment is one that does not go down the throat easily. This is because these are the most subtle facets to embrace because they tend to take a toll on an individual. You can imagine getting rejected severally. In order to achieve commitment, an individual ought to operate in a manner that is relentless.

Chapter 38. How Do You Use Your Voice?

An important rapport creation tool is your own voice. The secret is the same: you imitate the interlocutor's intonations and the rhythm of his speech. Of course, this should be done carefully (not so clearly) and gradually, as with signs of body language, and it is not necessary to create a one-hundred-percent copy, because your companion will seem strange if you suddenly speak to a tee like him. Moreover, it is very difficult to imitate someone else's voice, which is why there are so few people capable of imitating the speech of famous people. But you can always find one feature that you can imitate.

Tone

Is the voice low or high? Men often have a low voice, and women have a high voice, and this is influenced by the culture of the society in which we live. It seems to women that they should speak in a feminine way, that is, in a high and clear voice, while men are trying with all their might to make their voices low and coarse. As a result, we often speak with undue effort, indistinct and inexpressive.

Depth

Interesting fact: we believe that a deep, low voice belongs to a serious person who can be trusted, while a high voice is associated with female frivolity or childishness.

Melody

A monotonous voice does not change in the course of a speech, even in interrogative or exclamatory sentences. Therefore, it is often difficult to understand what a person with such a voice really means: is he joking or speaking seriously? Asks or approves? Opposite to him is considered a melodious voice, rich in iridescent, melodious and expressive.

Pace

Does the person speak quickly or slowly? We speak at the same pace in which we think, and if you speak too slowly, your interlocutor gets tired and starts thinking about something else. In the worst case, he can't wait until you are finally done. If you speak too quickly, there is a risk that your partner will not have time to catch all the important points.

Strength Volume

I recommend choosing this particular role to follow. The one who speaks softly and gently will appreciate if you will do the same (this also applies to a loud, resonant voice). By the way, if you want your interlocutor to speak more quietly, you need to try to speak even louder—and he will immediately pay attention to the timbre of his voice (usually people do not notice this).

As you can see, there are many characteristics in the voice that can be repeated. The best thing is probably to start at a pace: rapport depends largely on the synchronization of movements—and the pace can stimulate a good result. Some argue that the pace of speech is a crucial tool in establishing rapport. I do not know if they are right or not, but the voice, for example, is very important when talking on the phone, because then it is our only tool for establishing contact with the interlocutor.

In the United States, one study was conducted, ordered by a company that sold goods over the telephone. They sold a newspaper subscription and wanted to increase the number of customers. For the experiment, the employees were divided into two groups: one continued to work, as before, the other received orders to speak at the same pace as the person on the other end of the line. With only this difference in the technology of negotiations, the second group increased the number of sales by 30 percent. The first group sold the same amount as before the experiment. Agree, 30 percent is not bad at all, especially when this indicator depends on whether you speak slowly or quickly.

Exercise On The Movement

1. When you visit a restaurant, pay attention to the people between whom rapport is established. Choose a couple of lovers or a couple of old friends and see how they talk to each other in turn, how they copy their body language, how they understand each other perfectly.
2. Pay attention to their postures: most likely, they will even sit in the same way.
3. On the bus, tram or subway car, try to guess who are traveling together. Hint: they will sit the same and move the same. You always find out a loving couple or friends, even if they were not able to sit to each other in a crowded bus.

Exercises for the Shy

If you still feel shy to repeat the interlocutor's movements, try the following exercises.

1. Watch talk shows on TV. Take the same pose as the speaker and repeat his movements. Soon you will notice that you are guessing what this person will say in the moment. There is nothing strange in this: movements express our thoughts. Repeating movement after someone, you start the same mental processes in yourself and start to think and feel like him.
2. Try to set rapport at a distance. While in a public place, select a person at the other end of the room and begin to repeat his or her body language. After a couple of minutes, he (or she) could easily come up to you and ask: "We are not familiar with each other?" But how else? After all, you are a mirror image of this person. Therefore, it is better to choose someone with whom you would be pleased to communicate, and not some nasty type. This method can be used to get acquainted with a beautiful girl (a handsome young man).
3. You can get rid of the fear of "being caught at the scene of a crime" by letting the other person talk about themselves. While he speaks enthusiastically about himself, you openly copy the signs of his body language, occasionally repeating "yup" and "uh", showing interest. When we talk about ourselves (and also when we are very

angry), we abstract away from the outside world. At such a moment we are talking about ourselves and for ourselves, not noticing anyone or anything around.

What Gives Us Away?

Our Expressions

It will be a question of directly relating to verbal communication, but once again, I want to draw your attention to this. We all use the language differently: everyone has their own favorite words and expressions, the list of which I quote below. Here they can be copied, and it is quite plausible.

Slang

Slang words and expressions are difficult to copy because their use is determined by geographic, age and fashion trends. Slang is changing every day, and the fact that it sounded so "cool" yesterday, today is sent "to crap." If you are free to navigate the expressions your interlocutor uses, then feel free to copy it. But if you have no idea what "shoelaces" means, then it is better not to: you can go crazy. Slang also symbolizes belonging to a certain group (for example, age group), and in some cases, only those who are admitted to the group can use slang words, so you risk causing the anger of the interlocutor.

Professional Slang

Often, in a conversation on a particular topic, we need special words and terms. Each area has its own professional jargon. These special words will help you gain the confidence of the interlocutor. It is only important not to overdo it: use just as much jargon as the counterpart does in conversation. If you understand computers perfectly and your interlocutor pokes a finger at the screen with the words: "This thing doesn't work," you shouldn't go into the technical details, just ask if he tried to press the green button.

Personal Features

Although we spend much of our life at school and at the university, few of us speak the way it is recommended in language textbooks. We all just adore the words-parasites. No matter how awful they sound, if your interlocutor uses them, then you will have to.

Remember, we speak at the same speed as we think. If you speak slowly, your interlocutor is bored with you. Speak too fast—he does not have time to follow the course of your thoughts. Therefore, you need to speak at one pace, convenient for you and your interlocutor.

Favorite words

We all have favorite buzzwords. We use them often and in a variety of situations. These can be slang words, jargon and even swear words. We usually adopt them from other people. Sometimes we ourselves do not like such frequent use, and, once again catching ourselves on the word "drop dead", we exclaim: "We must finally get rid of this terrible expression!" But there are other, less noticeable words. Milton H. Erickson, one of the gurus of modern hypnotherapy, calls them "trans words." No, this is not related to transvestites, but to a hypnotic trance. You can very quickly install rapport, repeating trans words of a person. Speaking in his language, you show that you are set up just like him, and therefore you understand him.

It seems to you, I demand from you the impossible? Is it possible at the same time to imitate the voice, look for special words and repeat them and at the same time not forget what you, in fact, were going to say? Believe me, this is not as difficult as it seems. I have already said that unconsciously you repeat the body language of the interlocutor, the same with voice and manner of speaking. You are already doing this, which can be demonstrated. Remember the following situation. You end up talking on a cell phone, hang up, and everyone in the room knows who you just talked to (and you didn't call your interlocutor by name). Nevertheless, they guessed it. Do you recognize the situation? They understood who you communicated with because you spoke like him that is, adjusted to his manner of speaking. Most likely it was an old friend with whom you have rapport. We all want to be accepted and respected. We are all looking for social communication. We all want to create rapport.

Breathe, Patience, Breathe

One of the main rules for establishing rapport is proper breathing. However, most non-verbal communication specialists forget to tell you how difficult it really is to adapt to the breath of another person—a breath that we do not see. This requires a lot of training, but it is possible, and it needs to be done.

Observe how a person breathes, deeply or superficially, with his chest or diaphragm—this is visible in his stomach, chest, shoulders, and neck. Listen to the interlocutor's speech: in the pauses in a conversation, you can understand how often he breathes in the air.

Why do I need to imitate the interlocutor's breath? To adapt to the rhythms of his body. Changing the rhythm of breathing, you automatically change the rhythm of speech and body movements, and this helps to establish rapport.

I have already said that you need to adapt to the body language of your partner so that the rapport between you is not interrupted. Before you copy your partner's breath, feel his rhythm, try to just breathe in that rhythm, and not repeat every breath of your interlocutor. The most important thing is synchronization at a basic level, the rest will come.

By breathing, you can also determine the mood of a person.

This may be necessary for a situation where rapport is installed, but you feel that something is wrong with the other person. Listen to his breath. If he breathes intermittently and quickly, although outwardly he seems calm, it means he does not want to give out his excitement. This can say a lot. Different emotions are associated with different types of breathing.

Cozy Exercise

If you have a person, you can hug at any time (for example, a wife/husband), then hug him tightly and listen to his breathing. Breathe to the beat. Change the rhythm. If your partner unknowingly changed the rhythm of breathing, it means that you managed to establish rapport.

Martin Nyurap and Ian Harling in their Equilibrium offer to try it without clothes. If you are so lucky that you have someone hugging without clothes, try to synchronize the breath. Now, on the contrary, breathe faster or slower than your partner. You will notice transitions in their mood—from a sense of community and almost to dislike—despite the fact that you, naked, hug each other.

Think About Energy

Imagine that you see your interlocutor from a short distance, the whole thing. Using this technique, one can determine the energy level of a person by his posture, breathing, and other factors. Some people are more passive in the first half of the day—their activity is awakened after dinner. In the morning they come to work, mumble "good-naturedly" and flop down on a chair, showing with their whole appearance that they should be left alone at least until 11–12.

And only after lunch and the fifth cup of coffee, they get out of their shells and begin to communicate with others. This does not mean that they do not work well, no, this only means that they need to warm up properly before actively contacting other people. Sometimes even five cups of coffee help. These are typical representatives of the "Oysters", and for them, it is a completely natural state.

Then there is another type of people—the exact opposite of Oysters. These people are always full of energy, like Duracell batteries. They run in the mornings, come to work half an hour before everyone else, smile widely, and at lunch run to play a game of squash.

I once worked with a colleague who had six children. He came, or rather, came to work on a bicycle half an hour before everyone else, and all this time he was engaged in recording video of children on DVDs, which he took over the weekend, printed out covers and signed to see where the movie was. He is not an Oyster, he is a typical Rabbit from a Duracell battery advertisement.

Maybe you are one of those who come to work full of energy and the desire to create and find there sleepy, tired colleagues whose help is simply necessary, then you must reduce your activity. Do not show an excess of enthusiasm, at least at the beginning. You should not suddenly fly up to a colleague and happily slap him on the shoulder so that he spills coffee on the keyboard and completely spoils the mood. If you are a slow and drowsy person by nature, then you need to cheer up in time so as not to get on other's nerves. And believe me, there are ways to deal with the problem of drowsiness.

You only need to conduct a detailed analysis of your communication tools. Remember, we talked about observing, mirroring and establishing rapport? Maybe eight in the morning is not the best time to present your ideas to the boss. It may be better to make an appointment after dinner when your partner is more inclined to talk. If this is not possible, try to adjust to the rhythm of the person you are talking to. Otherwise, you and your ideas will meet not the warmest welcome.

Chapter 39. Personality Development

All individuals possess certain traits of personality which set us apart from the rest of the world. The mix of good and bad traits tells us how you respond to the situation. According to some studies, it is stated that these traits are genetic and remain fixed throughout life.

Lastly, the third factor called character which is inclusive of emotional, cognitive, and behavioral patterns which are learned through experience determines how a person can think, behave, and feel throughout his life.

Other than this, the character also depends upon our moral values which are inherited in us through our ancestors.

The different stages of life significantly influence personality development, which is a very essential part for the person and the other human beings also. Let's discuss the stages of life: -

Infancy- The first two years of the child are very crucial in which he/she learns basic trust and mistrust. If he/she is well-nurtured and loved by the parents properly, then the infant develops trust, security, and basic optimism. If it is opposite, then the result will be mistrust.

Toddlerhood- It occurs after the first stage starts from three to four years. During this stage, they learn shame and autonomy

Preschool- In this, the child learns initiative and shame. Through active play, they start using imagination, try to cooperate with others, etc. During this stage, the parents play a very essential role in which they get a restriction on the play and use their imagination.

School-age- In this stage, the whole development of the child takes place in which he/she learns various good habits like teamwork, how to work with rules and regulations, cooperation, and basic intellectual skills. Moreover, self-discipline surges every year with the passing of school age.

If the past stages of the child are excellent, then they learn various good habits otherwise, they feel inferior in front of others.

Adolescence- It is the age between 13 to 14 years in which a child starts behaving like a mature person. The young person starts experimenting new things and if parents are opposed to it, negativity arises. Indeed, this stage starts seeking leadership and rapidly develops a set of ideals for them to live by.

Importance of Personality Development

In order to get success in both personal and professional life, a great overall personality is very crucial in the life of an individual. Every person is automatically influenced by attractive and renowned personality. Whether it is a job, interview, while interacting with other human beings, and many more sectors, you must have certain traits and features which should compel other human beings to say yes! What a great personality!

Nowadays, in every field, the personality of a person matters a lot. For instance- in the interview to impress the interviewer, in business to influence the client and make them believe in you.

Therefore, the demand of personality has surged drastically with the passage of time. These days with the advent of personality, every school is careful about it and they make their students a perfect example where they can excel in every field.

Some years ago, the overall concept of personality was very common and no one really approached towards it. Parents also rarely gave importance to it. It was just looking good while wearing good clothes, which is more emphasized in a work-related environment. Indeed, the interviewer just wanted good working skills of the person and not interpersonal skills.

But now the scenario has changed a lot in this age of competition and economic revolution. Let's put some light on the various points of personality which are considered very crucial in personality development: -

Personality development inculcates numerous good qualities

Good qualities can be in any form like punctuality, flexibility, friendly nature, curious about things, patience, eager to help others, etc. However, if you have a good personality, you will never ever hesitate to share any kind of information with others which benefit them.

According to the rules, you will follow everything like reaching on time at the office. All these personality traits not only benefit you but also to the organization directly or indirectly.

Gives confidence

Great personality tends to boost your overall confidence. If you know that you are properly groomed and attired, it makes you more anxious towards interacting with people. Other than this- in any of the situation, if you know how to behave, what to say, how to show yourself, then automatically your confidence is on the peak.

Overall, a confident person is liked and praised by everyone both in personal and professional life.

Reduces stress and conflicts

A good personality with a smile on his face encourages human beings to tackle any hurdle of life. Trust me, flashing a smile on the face will melt half of the problems side by side, evaporating stress and conflicts.

Moreover, with a trillion million smiles on your face, there is no point in cribbing over minor issues and problems which come in the way of success.

Develops a positive attitude

A positive attitude is that aspect of life which is must to face any hard situation and one to one progress in life. An individual who thinks positive always looks on the brighter side of life and move towards the developmental path. He/she rather than criticizing or cribbing the problem always tries to find out the best possible solution with a positive attitude.

So always remember, if any problem occurs, then take a deep breath-in, stay cool keeping in mind the positivity anyhow. This is because developing a positive attitude in hopeless situations is also part of personality development.

Improves communication skills

Nowadays, a lot of emphases is given on communication skills as a part of personality development. A good communicator always lives an excellent personal and professional life.

Indeed, after your outer personality, the first impression tends to fall on another person is what you say and how you say it.

Verbal communication of the person makes a high impact on another person. Individuals with good communication skills ought to master the art of expressing thoughts and feelings in the most desired way.

Helps you to be credible

It is a good saying that you cannot judge a by its cover which also applies to a person. Means people judge a person from their clothing and how it is worn. Therefore, dressing plays a very essential role in the personality of an individual.

So, be careful while picking up clothes for yourself. It doesn't mean you will buy expensive clothes, but they should be perfect and suit your personality.

How to develop a personality

I just want to ask one question from you guys that have you observed any person who is the center of attraction? They have mind-blowing qualities due to which people get attracted to them like a magnet. So, how do they manage to do this?

Actually, they are personified persons who want to learn something or everything to look unique.

Well, every individual has his own qualities and traits which make them unique. But, some of the tips are very beneficial which help the person to be a perfect example of personality. While making your personality there is no room of age, but the improvement has. It cannot happen in a day, it takes overtime.

So, there are multiple characteristics on which an individual has to work on while developing his personality. Here you will know some tips on developing personality: -

Be a good listener

If a person has good listening skills, they can make another person feel important in front of them, so be a good listener. One of the examples of this is:

This quality is very appealing in order to have an awesome personality.

Take interest in reading and expanding your horizons

The more you gain knowledge about various aspects, the more you become famous in your personal and professional life. So, read more and cultivate those interests in yourself which make you stand in front of others with confidence.

On the other hand, when you meet people, you have the opportunity to share things with the individuals by making them flat.

Dress up well

While going to the office, party, or on any other occasion, wear dress according to that which suits you. Good looks no doubt add to your personality but what matters is how you dressed up for any occasion. Thus, dressing sense plays a very crucial role in personality development and building confidence.

Observe the body language

While interacting with people, try to use positive gestures which make another person comfortable and relaxed. Some studies stated that 75% of the work is done by verbal communication in which a person's personality is judged by another person.

So, keep an eye on body language.

Remain happy and light-hearted

Try to see the joy in the world and every work that you do. Spend precious and laughing with others so that you feel happy. Always appreciate people in one way or the other. So, smiling and laughing plays a significant role in making your personality awesome.

Stay calm in tensions

Some people have good personality until and unless they come across some tense situation. Don't be that kind of person who becomes angry in tensed issues and shouts on everybody. Therefore, be relaxed and stay cool while finding out the best possible solution for a problem.

Develop leadership qualities

It is believed that good leaders have an excellent personality which can impress another person easily and effectively. However, leadership skills don't mean giving orders to subordinates. Rather, it means how well you can as a leader manage your subordinates to accomplish any task. Indeed, work hard to set an example for them who work with you so that if in the future they will get a chance to work with you, they will feel very excited.

Work on your inner beauty

Most of the people only work on external appearance, but when you behave or speak outside, everything gets reflected. So, it is true that the outer look is essential but inner beauty is also very crucial to be a full-proof personality.

Indeed, it takes only a few days to change your outer appearance but, sometimes it takes years to change the inner world. So, work on that and you yourself can see the difference.

Learn from your mistakes

As a human, mistakes are part of life which makes an actual individual. If you are learning any new thing, you are bound to make mistakes. Always get ready to learn from your mistakes while saying or feeling sorry. Saying sorry will make a significant place to make a respectful corner among your friends or colleagues.

Indeed, if you have made a mistake, forgive yourself and move on.

Always make compliments to others

If you see that someone is looking great or gorgeous, then don't hesitate to say something positive to them. This will make your image or standard up.

Be original

The essential step in making your personality awesome shows what you actually are. It is a very eminent saying that original is worth than copied things. So, follow this and be how it is; rather, pretending what you are not.

Other than this, one should not copy someone's personality. But you can adopt some habits of other individuals who are good and help you in developing your personality.

Meet new people with a smile

Try to meet new people which will make you aware of a new environment and culture by which you as an individual can learn new things. Moreover, it also broadens your horizons.

Make your own opinion

The opinion is something which cannot be changed or stolen from another person. For example, while sitting in a group when someone asks your opinion, give them your opinion which is unique and is for the betterment of everyone. This attitude will make you more interested and stimulating to be sociable.

Get out of your comfort zone

Be ready and always get prepared to challenge yourself to learn new skills. Like for most people- learning new things is quite a challenging work. But with a positive attitude and confidence in yourself, you can tackle anything.

Don't give up at any point

Whenever you try to do anything and you fail, then give yourself a second chance to improve it. So, don't give up at any cost and try, try, try until you succeed.

Create your own style

According to my personal experience, you don't need to be a replica of anyone- you need to be yourself.

So, find the best style which makes you comfortable and relaxed. This pattern of developing your personality is very unique which offers the chance to explore and develop over time. Means if you get tired of something, you can move to another style without any downturn.

Be passionate about your work

In case you are not happy with your job or work, then don't complain regards to that if you don't have the capability to change the circumstances.

Therefore, find out your passion and try to make the necessary changes in your life to change the present situation.

Don't make yourself aggressive

Well, in everyday situation there are numerous assertive situations which make you angry. But, be careful because is a big turn off to people, both in social and professional life.

If your nature is like pushy, then be honest to yourself and try to change it as soon as possible.

Don't strive hard for perfection

Keep in mind that you don't have to attain perfection in any field because no one is perfect in this world. When a person is willing to show imperfection, then he/she is putting people at ease.

Evaluate yourself

Evaluation is the best technique to change yourself towards positivity so keep evaluating yourself at regular intervals of time. In this case, take the feedback from your friends, colleagues, and other near and dear ones seriously, which will help you to improve gradually.

Conclusion

Overall, the reader is carefully introduced to aspects of behavioral psychology to understand why human behavior is complex as well what motivates human behavior. For instance, under the investment model, one seeks to maximize returns by committing certain actions. While the invokes reputable psychological theories and concepts to make the content quality and applicable, the author ensures that the is easy to read for any reader. Throughout the, the author employs simple and easy to understand the English language with the understanding the audience of the is likely to be of native and non-native speakers of the English language. We have gone through the definition of human behavior, the mind and personality types in order to understand how humans behave. This book has offered easy-to-use but very powerful and effective techniques for analyzing yourself as well as other people. You are now familiar with the concepts of nonverbal communication and their purpose in understanding and evaluating the actions of others. You have learned exercises that you can adopt to improve your ability to analyze people. You have also learned the different categories of personalities, including introvert vs. extrovert, sensing vs, intuition, thinking vs. feeling, and judging vs. perceiving.

The purpose of this title is to allow you to glimpse behind the curtain of social norms. You are now prepared to read the minds of those around you. You can discern their intentions when interacting with you. Have you ever wanted the ability to tell when someone is lying? Now you have this information. It is up to you to put these words into practice.

Additionally, the author systematically presented content and concepts allowing the reader to build familiarity and complexity towards the end.

The author presented the as a manual, guide, and informative piece of ways of reading human body language. All these were possible through extensive reading of related topics on the issue from reputable scientific journals and presenting it in a readable, relatable, and simple language. Against this backdrop, this managed to introduce human behavior psychology, discuss the role of analyzing people, ways of becoming an analyst of people, and presented different forms of nonverbal communication. Towards the end, the ways of mirroring body language, mind control, manipulation, and ways of detecting lying and deception. As such, you should find this an easy and informative guide to reading body language.

You've learned a lot in this book. If you also want to understand the balance between honoring your real feeling and experience, how to manage your emotions in relationships, how to improve your mood, and create outstanding relationships, then don't miss my second book *"Empath: Master Your Emotions - From Overthinking to Positive Thinking: How to Overcome Panic Attacks, Anger, Anxiety and Depression with Cognitive Behavioral Therapy and Dialectical Behavior Therapy."*

EMPATH:

Master Your Emotions - From Overthinking To Positive Thinking: How To Overcome Panic Attacks, Anger, Anxiety And Depression With Cognitive Behavioral Therapy And Dialectical Behavior Therapy

MELODY ANNESLEY

PART I

EMPATH

Introduction PART I – EMPATH

Empaths are incredibly sensitive to the energy of another person. Without an awareness of this gift, an Empath will have a lot of emotional turmoil and will often feel like something is wrong with them and that their emotional state is just an unfortunate part of who they are, not realizing that their state of depression, anxiety, or frustration is the result of perceiving someone else's unraveling energy and absorbing it.

Empathy is not as complicated. When you are sitting to a coworker and are an empathic listener, you might act as an available friend who will offer support while they talk about their recent divorce. You will have a very strong ability to connect with them and sense their pain, but you won't necessarily absorb those feelings and make them your own, as an Empath would.

There are a lot of people in the world who are Empaths who have studied their gifts and still struggle with maintaining a healthy balance and emotional groundedness. It can be very challenging to always identify their feelings from those of another. As an Empath myself, I have had times when I have walked into a room and sensed the angry argument that happened between a married couple just before I arrived for dinner. I worried the entire time I was eating with them that they were unhappy with my presence there until I realized that I was just sensing their feelings about each other and the fight they were having before their dinner guest arrived.

If you are an Empath, you will feel everything a lot more than other people do and it is not a bad thing. It can be a very good thing to help you understand who you are and what the world has to offer from a sensory perspective. The key is to know yourself well and to trust your instinct and intuition so that you are not carried away with fear and doubt that doesn't actually belong to your true feelings and is coming from something else outside of you.

Empathy is a powerful resource for all people and learning to develop your general empathic skills will help you to connect to others in a more impactful, personal, and meaningful way. The truth of being empathic is that you are a supportive listener and that you are able to allow another person to have their own emotional experience without making it about yourself. You offer kindness and intentional offerings of understanding while another person is given space to share their emotions with a person who might know what it feels like to be going through something like what they are feeling.

An Empath will offer the same support but will actually sense and feel it before words are even spoken about it. True Empaths are always perceiving through the senses and will pick up on the slightest intensity of feeling from the person standing just behind them at the grocery checkout. A true Empath will notice when someone is putting on a façade to pretend that they are fine but, under the surface, holding back tears of anguish and sorrow.

Empathy and being an Empath are different and it is what you need to understand about being an Empath that will help you realize how empathy works. We are all highly sensitive people and many people choose or are not capable of, being aware of that. As a human being, you have a very sophisticated internal technology that is very adept at sensing and feeling the world around you. How do you think we survived extinction? Part of our survival mechanisms is to look and listen to everything that could harbor danger or offer us safe shelter, food, and an ability to make it to the day.

Fortunately, we're no longer living in the age where death by a wild animal is as likely, but our instincts have remained intact in our brain stems, allowing us all to sense and perceive what will likely cause some kind of effect in our immediate environment.

In the case of empathy, as you are sitting to someone or something, you are sensing and perceiving their energy to determine whether they are trustworthy, kind, good, etc. Much of this actually occurs on a subconscious level and we are not always aware of the fact that we are naturally "reading" the energy output of another person. It can be very strong when you are sitting to a grieving mother who has lost her son, or to a person who is angry and frustrated by everything you are saying. You feel all of the energy with your own sensory receptors and not all people are as skilled or as predisposed to having such a strong perception of this kind.

Chapter 40. What Is Empathy?

Empathy is defined as the capacity to understand or feel the emotions of others. It can also be described as the ability to share the feelings of others. Empathy, for the most part, is a beautiful attribute. It's one of the finest qualities a human being can possess. It is associated with goodness, charity, compassion, care, and self-sacrifice. Empathy makes it easier to identify with those who are suffering, and consequently, take action to remedy the situation. The world can always do with a little more empathy.

Empathy is mostly classified into three groups:

Emotional Empathy

Here you experience the feelings of other people: sadness, anxiety, joy, pain, and so on. An emotionally empathic person catches the sensations of others, which strengthens relationships with those around her/him. Emotional empaths can do well in fields like medicine, nursing, and counseling since they deeply identify with the suffering of others and go out of their way to alleviate that.

The downside to emotional empathy is that your emotions fluctuate up and down, depending on the situation of those around you. That can be exhausting. In other instances, you feel the pain of others so deeply, yet there's nothing you can do to change their situation, and you're left suffering as well.

Cognitive Empathy

This is the ability to know the thought process of other people, and in the process, understand their perspective. It mostly involves thoughts, intellect, and understanding. Cognitive empathy helps you appreciate different viewpoints. You're able to accommodate people who hold different opinions and beliefs from those of your own. This ability also comes in handy during discussions since you understand the thought process of others and engage them appropriately.

Compassionate Empathy

In this case, you do not only identify with the suffering of others, but you're also moved to take an extra step and lend your help. This is the ideal form of empathy, where you actually take action to make a difference.

However, precaution should be taken so that you do not run yourself dry, trying to donate to every cause. A donation here refers not only to finances but also time, expertise, skills, goodwill, and so on.

Empathy isn't just towards people. It applies to situations as well. An empath will be drawn towards the state of the environment, economy, politics, international relations, animal welfare, and such other matters that eventually affect the quality of human life. People without empathy find it easy to look away, especially when others are suffering.

First, all empaths are born with the ability to experience what other people are going through, either through emotions or even their feelings. Secondly, no empath is born already skilled. They all have to learn the skills, and if not, they are prone to suffer a lot. This should not get you worried if you have no skills yet, this will help you learn some new skills that you need to know as an empath. To your surprise, you might even be more than one kind of an empath, so if you find yourself falling into various kinds of empaths, count yourself talented. These types are also referred to as the many gifts of empathy.

Physical Intuition

These are the kind of empaths who are able to know what exactly is happening in another person's body. For example, this type of an empath can easily tell when you have a stomachache or a headache. Being a skilled empath will make you able to help other people through this correct knowledge.

Physical Oneness

The way these empaths get information is always personal. These are empaths who can feel other people's physical way of being in their own body when around or with them. For instance, this kind of empath, when with Betty, they will always develop a stomachache, like this stomachache belongs to Betty. This is a confusing type of empath, but if you are a skilled one, you will be able to assist those around you with the messages you get into your body. You ought to be skilled to avoid confusion or any form of suffering.

Intellectual Empath Ability

These types of empaths are able to get into people's intellectual abilities. For example, they might find themselves using long words while speaking to Joy, but then, they come to realize that Joy also likes using long words.

Emotional Intuition

These types of empaths are able to tell what is going on in someone's body, specifically their emotions, even when other people are trying to hide or fake their emotions. For instance, an empath will note that Betty is always cheerful, but she is hiding worries behind her smiles. Skilled empaths will know how to cut through the fake and real emotions since they all have the ability to differentiate what is real and what is fake. This helps you become a better friend since your friends get to realize you know them better.

Emotional Oneness

This is the type of empath where you get to learn the reality about what is cooking in other people's feelings. The difference of this kind of empath with the Emotional Intuition is that an empath in emotional oneness is able to feel what others are feeling. Your emotions and those of your friends will tend to merge. And as a skilled empath, you should not be carried away by the absorbed emotions since most of them are always negative. Instead, you should help your friends come out of this negative emotion or feeling, for instance, worries or anger. Being skilled means, you will have a stable emotional foundation to help out.

General Types of Empaths

Spiritual Intuition

This is a kind of empath where you get to experience how someone else connects to God or other spiritual beings. For instance, accompanying Betty to church and getting to hear what her pastor preaches about God, you get to feel the flavor that Betty gets from the teachings about God. This can happen in the case where you know nothing about your friend's religious views. Skilled empaths use this chance to know the many faces of God and even develop interests for religions and spiritual lives.

Spiritual Oneness

This kind of empath is different from that in Spiritual Intuition in that, in Spiritual Oneness, an empath will experience directly how their friends are connecting to their Supreme Being. This can be through the hymns that are being sung and relating the inspiration behind them. This helps skilled empath grow more spiritual in various ways.

Animal Empath

An animal empath will experience what it feels like to be a certain animal. A skilled animal empath is totally different from an animal lover in the sense that an animal empath is able to tell the difference between two animals that an animal lover thinks are identical. A skilled empath will help animals locate their groups or even help pet owners.

Environmental Empath

Environmental empaths are able to tell the difference between landscapes in certain environments. To them, each landscape is scenery. Skilled empaths enjoy walking through forests, and this can even make them emotional.

Plant Empath

Plant empaths get to feel what it is like being a certain tree, leave, or even flower. Skilled empaths use this gift in their agricultural farms or even in gardening.

Mechanical Empath

Mechanical empaths experience what it is to be a certain machine and their needs. This can even make them fix machines without the necessary qualifications due to the increased interest in machines. As a skilled empath, you are advantaged because you will not need a mechanic to identify what your machine needs, you will be able to tell it yourself. It may lead to more research into machines and technologies.

Medical Empath Talent

This gift helps identify any sickness or anything about your own or other people's health matters. Skilled medical empaths help give support, can even end up developing professional skills and become nurses, or even help in preventing any burnouts.

Empath Talent with Astral Beings

These empaths have direct experiences with astral beings such as angels and fairies. Skilled empaths will use the experience to grow themselves or enjoy more of these adventures.

The Difference Between Cognitive Empathy, Emotional Empathy, Compassionate Empathy

Empathy is one of those buzzwords continually put on everyone's lips. There is no doubt about it, but the continuous use of this wonderful quality that facilitates relations between human beings causes, on occasion, there is confusion regarding the term, which ends up losing meaning.

We probably all know that through empathy, that ability that allows us to recognize and identify with otherness, we are able to perceive what the other can feel and think. But what surely know of this quality which has been so positive over centuries of evolution for unity and survival of the community, it is that there are three different types of empathy: the emotional, cognitive, and compassionate.

Firstly, we have emotional empathy. It is a dimension that can be contagious and even dangerous when we do not know how to impose limits, and we are impregnated" with the suffering of others. It is to feel what others feel and to understand their personal reality. In this process, mirror neurons, our feelings, and even our physiological response come into play.

Cognitive empathy, in turn, implies making use of the intellect, cognitive processes such as attention, reflection, communication, inferences, etc. It basically means knowing how the other person feels, why they feel this way, and figuring out what ideas and thoughts might be in the other's mind.

Also, we have this great unknown, this dimension that is often overlooked: compassionate empathy. With this kind of empathy, we not only understand what the person feels and what their problem is, but we mobilize to help them if we believe they need help.

However, when we apply emotional empathy, there is an emotional reaction through which we identify so much with the feelings of the other person that we can feel them in their own flesh. Sometimes, if this emotional empathy is extreme and the identification with the other person is total, it can paralyze us and prevent us from being able to advise and be a useful help for the other. However, emotional empathy is about a noble and deep feeling that, beyond compassion, allows us to give sincere support without being condescending.

On the other hand, through cognitive empathy, we can understand and recognize what the other person is feeling, but always from the intellect, never from the emotion itself. In this type of empathy, there is, therefore, no emotional reflex and can be learned through social imitation. Psychopaths, who by definition are unable to identify themselves emotionally with another person, could fake emotional empathy for a manipulative purpose; to get what they want from others.

Thus, this is the kind of empathy that allows us to offer others a useful response since with it, and we take action: we propose or execute a plan to help the other. Usually, when we put empathy into practice, we usually apply a balance between the two, being able to recognize the feelings of another person in us and to understand what happens to them to give them effective help.

Empathy is a fundamental quality in communication and, therefore, it is a skill that we work continuously in point of discussion. We often associate it exclusively with the peaceful resolution of conflicts, in which knowing how to understand all the parties involved and addressing them as assertively as possible is essential to mediate successfully.

On the other hand, the role of empathy in communication goes much further: it is essential to really reach those who listen to us, connecting with their feelings and their needs. Being empathic with our audience guarantees us to opt for the only possible way to have communicative success: to carry out an intervention adapted to the interests of the audience, making it the protagonist.

Empaths, Intuition, And Perceptions

Being an empath is a beautiful gift. You are wise and caring, insightful and perceptive. You take care of those you love and have a deep consideration and respect for all life on earth.

It is important when looking into how you can live your best life and thrive psychologically and spiritually that you first have a sound inner standing of what it truly means to be an empath. There are different levels to being an empath as we will explore in the , however, for now, let's break down the empath personality so you can inner stand it holistically.

All of the following are aspects to the empath personality however in varying degrees. For example, there may be elements you strongly resonate with and others which you only see a small part of yourself embodying. This knowledge is not taught in school, nor is it widely accepted, and many unique abilities that accompany being spiritually aware and connected and existing in a higher frequency or vibrational state of being are intuitively felt. Your empath nature connects instinctively to something beyond the everyday 'I' and often separation based reality which many people still reside in. Looking at the varying aspects to being an empath, therefore, can be a healing journey in itself.

It is OK if you only resonate with a few. Not all empaths display all of these qualities or characteristics. As you read the different aspects of the empath personality, spark your awareness back to memories or a memory where you may have been displaying some of these abilities without being conscious of what was occurring at the time. With each, there is a description of what it means, followed by how you may have been subconsciously or unconsciously displaying and embodying it.

The Artist, Creative, and Visionary

You are an artist. Due to your ability to connect to something above and beyond you through your deep and rich emotional wisdom and intuitive sight, you can also tune in to universal archetypes, ideas, concepts, and often ingenious images and thoughts in a unique way. This makes you a natural artist, creative, and visionary. Whether you choose to express yourself through song, dance, art, painting, drawing, poetry, writing, photography, film making, or directing, you can achieve great things. The visionary aspect to your nature can, literally, connect on an unseen level to some concept or archetype beyond the physical realm, and further bring it forth into the physical. Alanis Morissette is one of the most well-known empaths and even if you have not yet heard of her, her music inspires many people around the world.

Practical Implications of being the Artist, Creative and Visionary: If you embody the artist, creative, or visionary you may have found yourself as a child daydreaming and letting your mind wander to unseen worlds and ideas. Your imagination was rich and you may have been bored in social or overly externally stimulating situations. You also may have naturally had a strong inner knowing that you could come up with better or ingenious ideas and solutions to ones being presented in school, or by your teachers and peers. Your abstract and creative ways of thinking may not have been appreciated or understood by others.

Importance of Empathy

Without empathy, people would go about their lives without considering the feelings and thoughts of other people. Every person has differing perspectives on life; therefore, if we did not have something that made us accommodate each other, life would be very complicated. We all experience moods, joy, sadness, pain hurt et cetera, and if we focus only on the things happening in our lives, we will limit our capabilities. It is easy to jump into conclusions if we do not take a moment to truly understand what the other people stand for. Lack of empathy normally leads to bad feelings, misunderstandings, poor morale, conflict, and even divorce.

When one uses empathy in real life to understand why a person is angry, or a child is throwing a tantrum, he/she might learn about things in their lives that trigger the behavior. For example, one might find that something happened at home, thus pushing the angry person to act out or that the child did not have a meal in the morning thus they are not okay.

Empathy enables one to ask questions about the situation or behavior of another person before taking a defensive stance or reacting to some emotions. There may still be the need for disciplinary action, but one should use empathy first. Empathy makes a person feel valued and understood even if they are punished for the wrong deeds, and as such, they will accept responsibility for their action. Empathy is currently the missing link in schools, families, workplaces, and the world at large.

There are a few misunderstandings that arise when one is applying empathy in real life. Some people believe that being empathetic involves agreeing with the opinion of everybody else. That is wrong and will only lead to exhaustion. Understand the perceptions of the other person, acknowledge them but you do not have to sing along every tune.

Other people believe that being empathetic involves doing what everyone else wants or doing anything to make others happy.

That is wrong. You are not obligated to please everyone; you do not have to cooperate in every other situation. Just because you fail to accommodate every other matter does not mean that you are evil. The world is complicated; therefore, use empathy but do not agree with everything.

Empathy does not mean being there for someone for a lifetime. After listening to a person and offering a solution, you do not have to always be there for them, you have other tasks to accomplish and if you feel that the person is just using you, walk away. Empathy does not mean you should have no ego or intention. Once you assist someone, allow your ego to help you walk away or change the discussion.

Chapter 41. Are You An Empath?

Your journey towards identifying your empathic nature starts with self-awareness and being able to identify the unique characteristics that make you who you are. While we can all display different features based on the situation, it's easy to identify the patterns of behavior that we routinely engage in.

It's important to remember that most people, empaths or otherwise have a natural level of empathy and consideration for others. Empaths are set apart by their higher sensitivity and ability to not just understand but also feel the other people's emotions. The following test should help you determine whether or not you are an empath and to what extent.

You Are A Great Listener

Empaths are known to be incredible listeners. In fact, many tend to be the "counselor" in their friend group. You may notice that your friends, family, loved ones, and maybe even complete strangers come to you with their problems and want to talk. At times, it may also feel like you are an emotional dumping ground for people's thoughts and emotions.

As an Empath, you have a strong ability to listen to others and truly feel what they are sharing with you. They especially like talking to you because people feel like you hear what they aren't saying and know the problem better than they do, which can be a great relief for many. Modern society is not overly accepting of many thoughts, feelings, or emotions. As a result, many people are uncomfortable or seemingly incapable of sharing these things. Because you seem to "just know," people may be drawn to you because it feels like a breath of fresh air being understood in ways that no one has likely ever understood them before.

You May Struggle to Connect to Standard Religion

Many Empaths find it extremely challenging to connect to the teachings of the majority of modern religions. Although most Empaths will see and appreciate the underlying messages of connection and unconditional love, they tend to pick up on the reality that most religious organizations do not actually live or operate in alignment with these teachings. This can lead to a deep inner sense of struggle for any Empaths who have been raised in or around a religious community. They want to see the good in it all and connect with their loved ones, but many see right through the teachings and find themselves feeling frustrated with the deception that seems to go on with many religious groups. Furthermore, Empaths highly value freedom and free will, both of which are rarely honored in spiritual teachings. For this reason, most Empaths will find themselves being heavily drawn away from religious teachings, perhaps even growing a deep sense of resentment toward them and all that they stand for.

You Are Drawn to Spirituality

Despite not being attracted to religious teachings, many Empaths will be attracted to spirituality. Spirituality tends to be more accepting of and understanding toward Empaths, allowing them to feel understood and recognized by others. This also allows them to facilitate deep connections toward the teachings and the others who follow similar paths. This type of connection can be heavily empowering for Empaths, allowing them to feel supported in their journey as they also support others. Since the spiritual path is filled with Empaths, many Empaths trust that the individuals in these journeys will think similarly to them and, therefore will be more accepting, understanding, empathetic, compassionate, and caring towards them. This allows them to feel reciprocated, making it far more inviting than many standard religious teachings.

In addition to supporting them in feeling understood, many spirituality-based teachings actually elaborate on the meaning of being an Empath and support Empaths in understanding themselves and refining their talents. This means that through these teachings, the Empath can further their own sense of self-understanding and work more passionately alongside their life and spiritual purposes with clear direction, guidance, and support.

You Struggle to Keep Healthy Boundaries

One symptom many Empaths face is struggling to keep healthy boundaries. Because an Empath can sense exactly what another person is feeling or experiencing, they may find themselves regularly making excuses for the other person. Things such as "oh, they didn't mean to" or "they only did this because deep down they are hurting" regularly come to mind. Although having these deep understandings of others can be valuable, they can also result in the Empath being taken advantage of and used by others with less empathy, or none at all.

The difficulty of maintaining healthy boundaries, or any limitations at all, for Empaths, can be a major point of trauma. Because the Empath strives to see the good in others, they may let people repeatedly take advantage of them or abuse them because they struggle to connect to the reality that you cannot help someone who does not want to help themselves. You may feel like you have to be the "savior," even though the chances of this panning out are extremely slim.

You May Struggle with Addictions

Empaths are known to struggle with addictions. Many use addictions as a coping method to attempt to "shut off" their empathy or numb them toward the world around them. While this may seem to work, the reality is that nothing can actually shut off their gift. Instead, what often ends up happening is that they begin to dissociate from their feelings and ignore the reality of their empathic abilities. Over time, this leads to a deep sense of depression because they take on an excessive amount of energy and emotion, create even more within themselves, and never effectively deal with or release any of these energies or emotions.

Addictions within Empaths are not restricted to substance abuse. They may also be drawn to overeating, oversleeping, or never sleeping to avoid nightmares and restlessness, video games, or otherwise obsessively attempting to draw their attention away from reality to avoid the pain that they are experiencing and suffering with.

You Are Likely Highly Creative

Empathic individuals are almost always highly creative. They perceive the world in an entirely different way and tend to see art where others see virtually nothing. For example, an Empath may look at a blank page and see an entire image come to life, thus drawing them into wanting to create that image and bring it into reality. Empaths have visual gifts unlike any other, allowing them to quite literally think things into existence. An individual who is not empathic would likely see just a blank page. Empaths are known to become artists on varying levels. They may create art through words, objects, perception, photography, or virtually anything else. The entire world is a canvas to Empaths, and they just want to create. Creating allows them to express themselves in ways that words and emotions do not always allow for. Additionally, it allows them to feel incredible self-worth, empowered and inspired by the world around them.

You Can "Feel" Others

Empathic people can "feel" others. As you may have picked up on in, this is actually one of the first things that identify an Empath. If you can feel others either emotionally, mentally, or physically, or any combination of these three, there is a good chance that you are an Empath. These symptoms allow you to step into the reality of others and experience what they are experiencing in a way that the average person cannot.

When it comes to Empathy, average people experiencing Empathy can relate what someone else is experiencing to something that they have experienced themselves in the past. However, for an Empath, it is much deeper than that. You do not relate people to your own experiences. Instead, you directly feel theirs. This is what allows

Empaths to feel things that they have never personally experienced before. For example, if someone were to tell you that they had a concussion, you may feel the exact symptoms they are experiencing, even if you have never had a concussion before.

You May Have Suffered from Narcissistic Abuse

Narcissists are drawn to Empaths because they have the one thing that the narcissist completely lacks: empathy. Empaths, as you know, have a heightened level of empathy that is above average. This makes them more desirable than the average person because they have enough to substitute for the lack of empathy that the narcissist has. Furthermore, Empaths are more likely to forgive and desire to see the good in other people. This means that it is easy for a narcissist to draw Empaths into their abuse cycles and quickly turn their empathic gift into a burden that they long to destroy so that they can step away.

You May Feel Extremely Close to Plants and Animals

Empaths, especially plant Empaths and animal Empaths, have a tendency to feel extremely close to plants and animals. Even if you are not a plant or animal Empath, you may still find yourself feeling extremely drawn to them. This is because they tend to have much purer energy, filled with unconditional love. For many Empaths, plants and animals are a breath of fresh air from the corrupted society that many of us live in.

If you find that you are heavily drawn to plants and animals, and especially if you feel like you can communicate with them in a paranormal way, this may be an indication that you are experiencing your empathic gifts. The unconditional love you feel between each other is simply amazing and blissful. You may even think that your plants and pets are the only things that can make you feel better when things are not going well. If you feel that you receive wisdom and advice from plants and animals, this is your claircognizant gift arising from your empathic abilities.

You Might Have Experienced Mental or Physical Symptoms

Empaths often experience mental and physical symptoms relating to their gift, in addition to the more commonly talked about emotional symptoms. These are not always directly borrowed from someone else, but may actually be the symptom of feeling so many other people's energies so deeply. Many Empaths may actually experience psychotic attacks or episodes because they feel overwhelmed by the amount of energy around them that they are always picking up. Often, Empaths feel like they are a "sponge" to the world around them, which can result in them picking up and holding on to a lot of different sensations.

Some of the common mental or physical symptoms that you are likely to face are those that are related to experiencing chronic high stress. The body can only carry so many different energies and emotions before it becomes too much for it. Then, it begins to maximize its output of cortisol, the stress hormone, causing you to start experiencing emotional, mental, and physical symptoms related to personal stress. This could be anything from physical pain to anxiety and depression, and even recurring thoughts based on suicide or self-harm. It is important to understand that these symptoms are often in relation to your empathic gift. They are generally heightened by both you experiencing other people's stress, as well as the stress from feeling these feelings without properly managing them within yourself. In other words, you are not stepping out so the stress is getting blocked within you.

You May Experience Psychic Attacks

Psychic attacks are a common experience for Empathic individuals. Psychic attacks are an attack on Empaths with negative energy. This energy is sent either consciously or unconsciously by another individual or entity to create or inflict harm upon said person. These attacks can be felt by anyone in your life, including family and friends, an acquaintance, or in some cases entities that we cannot see. This harm can be intended to create turmoil in the emotional, spiritual, physical, or mental state of the individual receiving the attack.

If you have ever had a psychic attack, you would recognize it through a multitude of symptoms that you might face. One of these symptoms includes feeling exhausted and then having a deep sleep where you may or may not remember having a nightmare. You may have fears in your dreams of being attacked by someone, typically with quite a large amount of violence. You may also feel extreme and unrealistic fears that feel debilitating. There may be no rational explanation as to why you have this fear or why it is so strong for you, all you know is that you suddenly have it. You may also begin feeling much better following a bath or shower as they support you in protecting your energy and freeing yourself from psychic attack. It may feel like you are not in control over yourself or your thoughts, which may lead to increased fear.

Psychic attacks feel a lot like psychotic attacks, causing you to feel like you are no longer lucid and in full control of your own body. Many reports they feel like they are standing to themselves, watching themselves go through the motions.

While this may be medically rooted, if you are an Empath, there is also a big chance that you are experiencing a psychic attack.

You Are Sensitive to Food

Empaths are known to feel their food in a way that no one else can. Many will become vegetarian or vegan because they feel too much negative energy in meats and animal byproducts. However, this is not always the case. Other people find that they can eat meat just fine as long as it has been ethically sourced. Some also like to bless their meat before eating. How you choose your diet will be highly personal, but you may find that it is chosen based on the feeling and energy of the food more so than anything else.

When you are empathic, you may find that you can literally feel what you need. For example, say your energies are feeling off, you may feel that you need the energy that is within carrots, sweet potatoes, or other foods. This comes from your energetic capacity to read your own energy, read the energy of your food, and discover what it is that you need exactly. You may also feel energetically averted to things that may be causing chaos or destruction within your body. For example, you may be naturally averted to sugars and sweets, especially when you are feeling under the weather because your body knows what energy it does and does not need at any given time.

Other Empaths report feeling emotions from their food. For example, they may feel joy and a surge of love and passion when they look at a plate full of foods that give them positive energy.

However, they may feel dreadful and even nauseous when they look at a plate of food that seems to radiate negative energy. Being able to feel the energy in their food means Empaths can intuitively eat in a way that nourishes their body well.

Chapter 42. Realizing The Gift Of Empath

Empaths are unique individuals who possess a powerful gift that can greatly change the world around them. Aside from being able to help others through difficult times, their innate abilities can help them better navigate difficult times and better care for others. Unfortunately, this gift is often looked at as a burden. Many empaths feel weighed down, resented, and feared because of their special gift. When you learn how to fully utilize your empath gift, you will begin to change your opinion of them. Instead of being a burden, they will become your unique superpowers.

What Is the Empath Gift?

The most vital gift of an empath is what makes them an empath. Their ability to feel and understand what another person is experiencing can serve a number of positive purposes. This gift, however, is looked at both as a blessing and a terrible burden for an empath. Not only is it the emotions that an empath takes on, but they also absorb the energy attached to these emotions. They also absorb the energy from their environment. This ability to absorb energy is where many empaths fail to understand how to protect themselves or what to do with this energy they absorb.

For many empaths, the energy they absorb tends to stay bundled up inside of them. When an untrained empath absorbs this energy, it can cause a block in the flow of their own natural energy. When this energy is positive, it does not cause much of a concern, but when this energy is negative, it can cause a number of disturbances for the empath as well as for those around them.

When an empath absorbs negative emotional energy, their own energy will be drained. This becomes an increasing concern if the empath is unable to let go or let this negative energy flow from them. When negative energy empaths tend to be trapped by it. They ruminate over it, and this can lead to anxiety and depression rather quickly for the empath.

But when an empath understands how to manipulate and read this energy properly, they can turn it from negative to positive and release this positive energy back into the world around them. This ability to feel others' emotional energy gives the empath the gift of being able to transform negative energy into positive energy. When an empath is able to train themselves and develop their gift, not only can they transform negative energy into positive energy, but they can also help heal others and project more positive emotions into their environment.

An empath's gift can vary in degrees. This is dependent on the empath. One's ability to utilize their empath gift lies in their willingness to embrace it. Many empaths block out a lot of energy so as not to suffer through the pain of others or to go through to confusion of trying to sort out the mess. This diminishes their gift. On the other hand, those that look at their gift as an actual gift are able to understand how to utilize it in a proactive way. Instead of letting their gift diminish them, they use it to empower them and lift up those around them. They use their gift to heal others and to bring more light into the work.

How Can You Develop the Empath Gift?

Many empaths suppress their gifted abilities, which can come across in a number of physical, mental, and emotional symptoms. When an empath suppresses or blocks their abilities, they often suffer from an increase in aggression, addictive behaviors, poor health choices, negative self-talk, weakness, chronic pain, and more. These symptoms are due to the blocked energy you may be holding or due to the fact that you are going against what is in your very nature. While it is understandable why an empath would want to hide their ability, this is often because of a lack of understanding them. When an empath can fully understand just what they are capable of, this gift will no longer feel like a burden but something unique that they are willing to use and share with the world.

One of the first steps in helping to develop your empath gift is to first understand and accept that while you can feel other people's emotions and energies, they are not your responsibility. Yes, you may fully understand what they are going through, and you can provide them with ways to heal or overcome these things, but that is all you can do. It is up to the other person to accept the guidance you provide, and it is their choice alone as to whether or not they do. You may be feeling a great need to be persistent in helping people, but they are the ones that have to take action. You can only do so much, and once you become fully understanding of this, you will be more willing to embrace your gift. You won't be able to help everyone, but those you do help will take it with grace and gratitude.

On top of understanding that others will need to take responsibility for making the changes necessary to better their situation, you must also understand that you are responsible for your own emotions. As an empath, you have the ability to project more negative or more positive energy into the world, and the choice can ultimately be yours. You need to understand that you also have a tendency to play the victim and, at times, use your abilities as a way to escape from everything you are feeling. This is not an easy task for an empath as distinguishing your own emotions from others can be hard to identify. This is where having high emotional intelligence as an empath can be highly beneficial.

Increase Emotional Intelligence

It may seem as though empaths would have a rather high emotional intelligence naturally. Emotional intelligence refers to one's ability not only to understand their own emotions but also to understand the emotions of others. It also refers to one's ability to properly manage and emotions and process emotional cues of others so as to react appropriately to them. While empaths may be able to understand emotions on a deeper level, this does not always translate to their ability to properly manage or separate their emotions from others. In order for an empath to develop their abilities, they need to first increase their emotional intelligence. This will allow them to distinguish their own feelings from those of someone else, this will allow them to react and manage these emotions in an effective way. To increase emotional intelligence, one must focus on five key components of emotional intelligence.

1. Self-awareness. Without first developing your self-awareness, you will not be able to effectively develop the other components that will increase your emotional intelligence. Self-awareness for an empath is especially important as it relates to your ability to recognize your own emotions, how you handle your emotions, what triggers them, and how their emotions can impact those around them. Being able to fully understand your own emotions will make it far easier to distinguish between your emotions and those you feel from others.

2. Self-regulation. Self-regulation is a crucial factor for increasing emotional intelligence. When you are able to self-regulate, you are able to respond appropriately to the emotions you are feeling. For an empath, this is a valuable skill to develop because it focuses on being able to regulate not only the effects your own emotions have on you but also the effects of others' emotions. One of the best techniques for self-regulation is to focus on your breathing. When you become overwhelmed by emotions, yours or others, it is best to turn your attention to your breath. Focus on keeping it steady and calm. This will allow you to let the emotions run their course and keep a clear mind. When the intensity of these emotions dissipates, you will be able to better recognize which were your own and which ones are from others. As an empath, this can be a helpful and quick way to remain calm when confronted with intense emotions from multiple people. Remember to keep your focus on your breath; when you notice you are putting too much attention to the emotions you are feeling, remind yourself to return to your breath.

Self-regulation is what can make the increase of the other areas of your emotional intelligence possible. It is through self-regulation that you can truly begin to understand the control you have over your own emotions, and this understanding as an empath will allow you to better control how you let other people's emotions affect you. If you do not develop your self-regulation, you will constantly feel overwhelmed and bombarded by emotions and react in unhealthy or unproductive ways.

3. Motivation. There are many factors that can motivate individuals; most empaths are motivated by the desire to help and heal others. In order to increase your motivational skills, you need to keep track of what you have accomplished even if it didn't turn out the way you anticipated. For an empath, this can be a list of ways you were able to comfort others or how many times you turned the negative energy you absorb into positive. Motivation can come in many forms, but you have first to be able to recognize and celebrate the things you accomplish. Empaths can be challenged by this when they are confronted with an overwhelming amount of negative energy. It is through this component that many empaths can learn to see how they have been able to overcome these negative situations and focus on the positive outcomes of the day.

4. Empathy. Empathy is a skill most empaths will not need to work on much since they naturally are highly empathic individuals. This doesn't mean there might not be room for improvement. Having empathy allows you to step into the other person's shoes, but it is also about being there to help the other person work through what they are feeling. This is the desire for all empaths, but this is where things can get off-balance with the empathy component. Most empaths take empathy to the extreme, which is what will cause their energy levels to drop and is what causes empaths to shut off their gift abilities. Finding a balance between fully understanding how another feels and effective ways to help is a fine line. What can help an empath gain better balance is to practice loving-kindness. This is a simple process

that allows you to send love and kindness to those who need it in your life or to those you are grateful for. This can be an effective practice that will help empaths release the negative energy they absorb from others and transform it into loving and positive vibes. This also helps you build up your compassion for others, which is a slightly different trait that empaths can develop.

5. Social skills. For an empath, developing healthy social skills can be overwhelming, but in working on this key factor of emotional intelligence, you will be able to put to use all the other skills you have been developing. When you develop your social skills, you will find that using your empath gift to help and heal others becomes much easier. Social skills refer to your ability to manage and maintain not only relationships with others but also the impact you have on them. How can you influence a more positive way and move them in a direction that is beneficial for both of you?

Increasing your emotional intelligence as an empath can greatly help in distinguishing your emotions from others, as well as give you a better idea of how you can use your abilities in the most beneficial way. But increasing your emotional intelligence, as with everything in life, requires having balance. If you focus too much on improving one area of emotional intelligence over another, you can lose sight of your goals, self, and confidence in your abilities.

Aside from increasing your emotional intelligence, empaths can also develop their gift through other practices and techniques.

Tips to Develop Your Empath Gift

1. Openness. Discussing emotions is an ideal topic of interest for an empath. Being able to talk about feelings as just a way either to gather knowledge or to specifically discuss someone else's emotions or their own gives an empath great understanding of emotions. The more they talk about emotions and feelings, the more they are able to develop their abilities.

2. Self-development. Self-development can come in many forms. As an empath, self-development is vital to help develop your abilities. It

requires you to focus on things such as habits, behaviors, knowledge, or other areas of your life you want to see an improvement with. This also refers to your abilities as an empath. Self-development should be utilized through all stages you find yourself in as an empath as well as to help move on from the experience you have as an empath. While self-development might not sound exciting as you go through the process and notice the benefits, it is something you will eagerly and regularly incorporate into your empath development.

Tips for Self-Development

1. Plan. In order to first take action on making improvements, you need to create a plan that will know which steps you need to take. Be careful with your planning. Many people get caught up in the planning that they never start taking action. You may be waiting for the perfect time, but there is no reason why that time cannot be now. Write the things you want to work, commit to starting now, then take the first step to make those improvements.

2. Start small. Self-development is not something you will see drastic changes overnight. But that doesn't mean any change is insignificant. Remember that taking the first small steps is what gets you moving. When you have bigger goals in mind, you need to break that big goal down into small, manageable steps, then take the first one. For instance, if your end goal is being able to attend a big event or be around larger groups of people without letting your gift overwhelm you, you wouldn't just go out and plant yourself in a large social gathering. This would only set you up for failure. Instead, you might start by going to a park and sitting while watching the people go by, or you might agree to hold a small get together at your house with people you feel comfortable with. The point is to start small; once you feel comfortable with the small steps, you can move forward to bigger ones. These smaller steps lead you to your bigger end goal, but if you just jump right into the bigger goal and are not successful, you will find yourself discouraged. Moreover, you will give up before you even give yourself a chance to be successful.

3. Study others. You are not the only empath to struggle with developing their skills or understanding the full extent of their gift. Many empaths have struggled and stumbled on the way to becoming empowered. You can learn a lot from those who are now successful and are able to manage and use their gift to the fullest. There are plenty of, videos, lectures, blogs, and other resources that you can consult to learn more about your empath abilities. While this won't guarantee that you won't make mistakes on your own empath journey, reading and learning the lessons from others can help you find a better way to develop your gift. Learning what has and hasn't worked for others will help you know what may or may not work for yourself.

An empath gift is unique and can take time to develop. In order to fully utilize your abilities as an empath, don't feel burdened by them. You need to become more aware of your own emotions. The reason many empaths struggle to accept their abilities is they struggle to separate their own experience from another's experience.

Increasing your emotional intelligence is the first step in accomplishing this. Creating a self-development plan to aid in this is a way to help you increase your emotional intelligence while also allowing you to further explore your gift.

Chapter 43. Understanding One's Energy

If you are in the presence of people like we described above, you need to understand that to maintain a calm state of mind you need to untangle yourself from them, if possible. Empaths refuse to accept that not all people are good and will want to fix everyone who has a mistaken view of life and treat others with no respect for their feelings. However, this will backfire and will only harm you. If you can't cut them off completely, there are things you can do to protect yourself.

To start with, you need to accept that Emotional Vampires are real and are extremely dangerous to Empaths. Empaths have the tendency to stay in a friendship or romantic relationship that is toxic because they start coming up with excuses for Emotional Vampires. Sometimes, they refuse to believe that there are people so close to them that choose to be with an Empath for selfish reasons. But this is true and you need to know what you are up against in order to protect yourself and deal with the situation accordingly.

Always listen to your instincts. At first, your instincts will tell you how wrong it is to be in the presence of Emotional Vampires, but if you choose to ignore it and stay with them, those people may make you question your abilities. If you are in this state, you should start writing down everything your instincts tell you about someone. Write down when a person lies or causes problems due to his or her hurtful behavior. Do this thing for everyone you meet even if you don't associate yourself with them. This way, you will eventually learn to identify them without the help of a notebook since you will be able to recognize the clear signs that you are dealing with an Emotional Vampire.

When things get too overwhelming because of Emotional Vampires you could always ask for help from a true friend of yours. Someone you trust and resort to whenever you start to doubt everything.

Arrange a meeting with him or her and pour out your problems. Then, you will either get a piece of extremely helpful advice from your friend or you will listen to yourself talking about your problems out loud and the solution to your problems will dawn on you.

Energy vampires will always try to keep you under their control. They want your energy, your soothing words, and the calmness you project. They will manipulate you or be frustrated with you whenever you try to place some distance between the two of you. It doesn't matter; you are entitled to please yourself first and not everyone else for a change. But don't do this once a year; Energy Vampires do it often, most especially. You have a right to be happy and when someone is angry because you need some alone time, they can stop thinking about themselves and let you have a relaxing time.

It is apparent that one of the most effective ways to protect yourself from an Energy Vampire is to cut down the times you see and talk to this person. Whenever he or she asks to go out with you or starts long conversations, you can refuse. As an Empath, you have to stop saying yes all the time, particularly to toxic people. You may think you can help them, but you will rarely succeed in nurturing empathy for these people. Practice saying no and if you find that too difficult try to give them vague answers that will turn into negative ones.

Protect yourself by limiting the time you spend with things that can drain you of energy. You could spend less time on social media, watching the news or limit the time you spend in your relationships if you feel drained. These measures are important for all people and Empaths should adhere to them by the due to their sensitivity. For example, if your friend goes through a tough time, you can go out with them, but stay for as long as you still feel alright. Don't stay too long as to get exhausted by trying to make them feel better. Your partners, friends, and family exist to make you feel better, not constantly drain you of your energy. Even though we all have gone through difficult times, if you realize that someone is draining you more times than you can count, then the time has come for you to set some boundaries. Take some hours out of your day and dedicate them to yourself, to do something that relaxes you and pleases you.

Chapter 44. Empaths And Narcissists

Protecting Yourself From Narcissists

Escaping and healing from a narcissistic relationship is one of the most challenging things that we can do. There are many things emotionally and psychologically that keep us trapped in the relationship. Some victims may fear being physically abused by the narcissist as well. Having the ability to break the trauma bond, safely escape, regain your independence and heal the trauma is essential but challenging.

Breaking the Trauma Bond

One of the biggest reasons why it is such a challenge to escape from a relationship with a narcissist is because the victim forms a trauma bond with the narcissist. Trauma bonding is a form of strong emotional attachment that an abused person forms between his or her abuser. It is perpetuated by the cycle of abuse and reinforced each time the abuse-cycle is successfully completed. While bonding in and of itself is natural and healthy under the right circumstances, bonds developed in the process of abuse are unhealthy and traumatic to the victim. People who have grown up in abusive households are more likely to develop these bonds with multiple people because, to them, this is a "normal" bond to have.

In addition to the trauma bond itself, there is also damage that occurs within the brain when we are exposed to abuse for a long period of time. When you have been abused, you will likely suffer from some degree of Complex Post-Traumatic Stress Disorder (CPTSD). CPTSD is a psychological condition that is stored in various places throughout the brain, making it challenging to release and eliminate. This disorder will actually rewire your brain, causing you to chronically live in a state of fight or flight. While you can still resume a relatively normal life following the breaking of the relationship and abuse cycles, if CPTSD is not properly healed you will carry it with you for life. Because it will rewire your brain, you will essentially train yourself to live around the symptoms of CPTSD, which can result in you losing your quality of life and feeling like you are trapped even long after the break.

Breaking the trauma bond is an essential part of leaving your abusive relationship. It can be a challenge, but it is possible. The first step is to consciously decide that you want to live in reality and not within the falsehood of the abuse. It starts with confronting all of the denials and illusions that you have lived in, including the ones the abuser made for you and the ones you made for yourself. It is essential that you realize that this person is abusive and will never change. Of course, it is okay to grieve this as it truly does feel like a real loss. You are losing a person whom you thought you had, but you never truly did.

In addition to choosing to consciously live in reality, you need to create boundaries. There should be a no-contact boundary between you and your abuser. You do not contact them, ever. If for some reason you must keep them around, such as if you share custody of children, minimize the contact and keep it very focused on necessary topics and nothing else. Breaking your habits and changing these patterns can be a challenge, but they are necessary. It can be extremely helpful to seek external support to assist you in relieving yourself from the trauma bond, and other aspects of trauma that linger in your brain. Healing does take time and having professional support is extremely beneficial for your long-term health. Be sure always to choose a therapist who is trauma-informed, so they genuinely understand what you are going through and what you need.

You should also understand that breaking trauma bonds takes time. Be gentle and patient with yourself. Remember, the creation of the bond itself was not overnight. It took time to build so it will take time to unravel and eliminate as well. Stay intentional and focused but be patient with yourself and all of the challenges that you may face in the process.

Escaping Safely

The very first thing you absolutely must know before leaving a relationship with a narcissist is that they will continue to try and manipulate you. They will pressure you into believing that you are overreacting, blame you for everything that happened, and attempt to con you into believing that they genuinely miss you and that they want you back. An abuser will always make false promises of a better future to draw their victims back in. It is essential to understand that you cannot trust anything they say, ever. Anything they attempt to do is in an effort to manipulate you back into the relationship. You must try to look at the bigger picture and understand the narcissists end goal. It may take you a few rounds of the entire abuse-cycle before you finally realize.

It is also essential that you leave cold turkey and allow yourself to endure the pain that comes with it. You may feel as though you are unable to, but trust that you can. Again, seeking support from understanding loved ones and trained therapists can be incredibly helpful at this point. Instead of contacting the narcissist in a moment of weakness, contact a loved one or a professional instead.

The Extreme Importance of No Contact

To successfully escape and stay away from the narcissist, you must enforce 'No-Contact.' If you feel that you are in serious danger from this person, having a legally enforced law surrounding the No-Contact order may be required to ensure that you have the support of law enforcement in this clause.

If you have any contact with the narcissist whatsoever, you are giving them easy access to manipulate you and keep you in the relationship longer. No matter what you think, this will be true. Any time you communicate with the narcissist, every single piece of communication will be designed to manipulate you and lure you back in. If you communicate with the narcissist, you are allowing your own mind to justify and rationalize why it may be a good idea to go back to the narcissist. You have to realize you are in a very vulnerable and weak position at this moment of time. You must vanish from the narcissist and focus on your recovery. You have to refrain from contacting them for any reason whatsoever, unless it is absolutely mandatory (such as if you share children with them.) And even if you do share children, you must work towards creating an understood schedule between both parties, where no communication (or very minimal) is needed.

Whenever the narcissist begins the hoover phase and starts trying to lure you back in, you must also understand that they are doing so only because they are lonely and they want to exploit you for their own needs. There is nothing genuine here. They do not miss you, love you, or need you in their life no matter what they say. This can be extremely challenging to understand and to embrace on an emotional level, especially because of how you have been abused and lead on by the narcissist. Because of the number of emotions that may arise any time you feel the need to contact them, or anytime they contact you, having a trauma-informed therapist and empathetic friends or family members that you can turn to during these times will be extremely supportive in helping you stay away from the narcissist.

Realize that no matter how good your intentions are in leaving the relationship, you will have to fight temptation. It is very easy for your mind to replay the good times from the relationship and to convince yourself that things may be different the time you go back. Many victims will leave the relationship with no intention to go back, only to be lured back in dozens of times before hopefully realizing that things will never change. This is because you have a trauma bond, which keeps you seeing the "good" in this person and justifying your return. What you are actually seeing are the lies and manipulation, but as a victim, it can be extremely challenging to decipher the difference. This is because it would require you to admit and endure the reality that every aspect of the relationship was a self-serving lie fed to you by the narcissist. Which, understandably, is extremely challenging for anyone to admit, let alone endure the aftermath of the admission. This aspect can lead to complex PTSD, that makes it mentally devastating for any victim to attempt to endure or leave.

Another reason why your No-Contact order is absolutely necessary is that the hoover and idealization phases are so well-refined with a narcissist, and you are already so mentally destroyed from the CPTSD and trauma bond, that there is virtually no other way to overcome this aspect than to seek professional support and break contact. As a victim, you have become addicted to the idealization phase. What leads you back and causes you to justify the rekindling of the relationship is generally the fact that you desperately want to have that deep, passionate, tailor-made love once again. It is something that is rare to find in organic relationships, thus meaning that you have likely never experienced anything like it. It gives your mind a high with the hormones of dopamine and serotonin that actually physically leaves you addicted to this phase. You become so addicted to it that, like anyone addicted to anything else, you easily overlook the dangerous and damaging parts of the addiction in favor of your "fix." This only further supports the narcissist's hoover phase, which ultimately leads to a relapse every single time.

When leaving the relationship with a narcissist, ensure your physical safety and maintain absolutely no-contact. I cannot stress this enough. During this time, you will be extremely vulnerable to "relapse" into the addictions of the relationship and the only way that you can completely avoid this is by quitting the relationship cold turkey and never looking back.

Healing from Your Narcissistic Relationship

The healing process is not fixed within any particular time frame. How long it takes varies from one person to the. There are many things that you can do to promote healing, however. The following practices will help you hugely with healing yourself and healing the trauma within your brain. It is important to understand that healing trauma in your brain is a lengthy and challenging process and that it is best not to do it alone. Seeking support is always the answer, and it is also essential to make sure that the support is empathetic, caring, and genuinely invested in your healing. You are vulnerable at this time, so be cautious not to jump into another abusive situation when seeking support.

Having boundaries is essential. You should begin practicing boundaries with yourself and with other people around you. When you have been abused by a narcissist, boundaries are something you have been conditioned to eliminate so that you can be fully available to the abuser. It is time to start practicing saying no and being very choosy about who you let into your life. Be picky with the energy that you let into your life.

You need to spend some time eliminating the toxicity from your life. Since you have been very isolated during this experience, externalizing can be helpful. Practice journaling, speaking your truth, and talking to a trusted loved one. Getting out everything you have been holding in can be very therapeutic in helping you release everything built up inside of you and moving on.

After a long time of lies, it is essential that you take this time, to be honest with yourself. As well, you need to forgive yourself. Realizing that part of you knew and forgiving yourself for knowing but not feeling strong enough to do anything about it is essential. You should also forgive yourself for anything you hold against yourself regarding your relationship. Trust that if you could have done better, you would have done better. Abuse can be tricky, and you are the victim, not the abuser.

Doing the deep work is important. When we are abused, we carry a lot of damage within us. This is where you are going to get to work through your inner trauma and heal everything inside of you. Spend time going through the pieces of you that feel broken and addressing them one by one. This is where having your therapist on board can be helpful, they can listen and provide you with professional support when addressing the particularly painful parts that you have been holding on to. You can also use other practices, such as yoga or spirituality, to draw you into yourself and help you explore the parts of yourself that have been hurt and hidden for a long time.

Shifting your focus is another essential part of healing from abuse. You need to make sure that you are engaging in your reality and focusing on the world around you. Be patient with yourself and practice engaging bit by bit. This is a good time to practice rebuilding your independence, going out on your own and with loved ones without the abuser, and being your true-self. The parts of you that were dormant for so long can now be appreciated and adored again. Ask people how they are doing, get involved in the lives of the ones you love, and begin integrating yourself with the world around you again.

It is time to start bathing in self-love again.

Chapter 45. Empaths In Codependent Relationships

In your own life, you have a lot more power than you think. The relationships in your life have been placed there on purpose—either to help you grow, to help you learn more about yourself, or to help you feel nurtured and supported. Chances are, you will find that each relationship in your life serves as a "test" of sorts, so you must be able to understand what those relationships are about and how they are currently impacting your life.

If you have relationships in your life that feel as though they are meant to help you grow or learn more about yourself, you may find that these are either positive or negative. In some cases, you may have these friendships with other empaths who teach you about who you are and what is possible for you and who encourage you to grow into your gifts and become stronger with them in general.

In other cases, you might find yourself in negative relationships where the purpose is to learn about your weaknesses and where you may not presently be taking care of yourself with stronger boundaries. In these cases, you should consider these relationships as an opportunity to understand how you are allowing others to take advantage of you and harm you. Take the opportunity to know how you can eliminate that by being more present and available for yourself. As you learn to navigate these negative relationships and set boundaries for yourself, you may find that some naturally grow into healthier relationships, and they become more enjoyable and safe for you to navigate. On the other hand, some may become even more toxic, and you may find yourself with the need to eliminate your relationship with that person so that you are no longer being entrapped by that relationship and all of its toxic elements. Sometimes, learning to let go and give yourself space to decline toxic relationships is an important lesson for an empath.

In relationships that are meant to help you feel supported and allow you to feel safe to be yourself, these are naturally healthy and positive relationships that you should continue to nurture in your life. These are the ones that are meant to support you with understanding the value of strong relationships and the value of who you are. Typically, nothing needs to be done in these relationships aside from possibly asserting some of your new boundaries more clearly if you find that some of them are not being respected. Often, you will find that in these relationships, the boundaries were not being respected, not because the other person is not respectful, but because the other person had no idea they existed. Once you begin to assert your new boundaries, these individuals will often shift their behaviors immediately and celebrate you by choosing to honor yourself in a deeper way.

While we may agree that being in love requires vulnerability, the experience can be heightened when one or both partners are sensitive. In discussing this, we must remember that relationships are not necessarily a happy place for highly sensitive people—mainly because they are more aware of their surroundings and of the people they are relating with. As such, they are more likely to become unsettled by their partners' behaviors or the possible outcomes of such behaviors. Generally, an HSP will often feel more stressed and will need more downtime—a combination that can strain and bring down any relationship.

In spite of the challenges involved, many people are attracted to HSPs and their sensitivity. They like them for their openness, compassion, empathy, and concern for other people. The tendency of HSPs to foster deep, meaningful relationships and their distaste for superficial stuff makes them even more likable. Their authenticity in their dealings in life is a breath of fresh air.

Unsurprisingly, highly sensitive people tend to be attracted to people who need their help, but sometimes, this attraction can be deceptive. Sometimes, they fall into the arms of others who never give a thought to taking advantage of the caring and giving nature for their benefit. Because of these characters, highly sensitive people become the doormats of their circles and end up in the therapists' office.

The lack of acceptance and appreciation for the sensitivity of HSPs causes sensitive persons to suffer from low self-esteem and self-doubt. When it comes to establishing a romantic relationship, the HSPs tend to become more helpful, empathetic, compassionate, and sensitive to the needs and feelings of other people trying to gain love and acceptance from them. In particular, HSPs have a distinct characteristic called mate sensitivity, which is the ability to quickly decipher a spouse's needs and making an effort to resolve the problem so that they may be happy again. HSPs do this all the time, and sometimes make it their daily goal.

As you would expect, there are bound to be problems when one party is giving too much. The reality is that the more you give, the more your partner takes. When you focus more on giving without receiving anything in return, at the end of the day, your own needs will be unmet, and you end up feeling unhappy, resentful, and exhausted. Unfortunately, when this happens, you begin to blame yourself again but remain unfulfilled.

Relationships can be quite a challenge to a highly sensitive person. However, the following tips can help HSPs derive more satisfaction from relationships. They include:

1. Set Aside Some Alone Time

Among the significant needs of an HSP are the desire for a meaningful connection and the desire for some downtime, but the secret is in finding a perfect balance between the two. You need to strike a balance between the time you spend with your wife and the time you withdraw to your spot for some personal time. If you fail to balance and you fail to spend some time alone, you will end up feeling overstimulated, which leads to anxiety, illness, anger, and burnout, among other struggles. However, the way to work out a balance is to develop a consistent routine that allows you to have a little of both worlds.

2. Be More Direct

To ensure that your needs are met in the same measure as you respond to the needs of others, you're going to have to be more direct. You ought to realize that while your intuition and perception allow you to anticipate the needs of other people easily, others do not have the same ability.

Naturally, you anticipate receiving the same level of care and concern as you give to others, but the reality is that the non-HSP partners may not even come near to meet your expectations because their brains are not wired to be as perceptive. When your partner is not responding to your call for a connection repeatedly, resentment and disconnection are bound to build. For this reason, you need to voice your wishes. If the volume of your voice has not been loud, make it louder (not harsh). Express your needs directly.

3. Take Some Time Off During a Conflict

Conflicts are a sticky situation for highly sensitive persons because they quickly are overstimulated and shift into the fight or flight mode. Whenever this happens, both partners begin to express anger on each other or will have an urge to leave during the conflict. This is the fight or flight reaction.

A conflict situation brings about a high physical and emotional degree of discomfort, and when this happens, the HSPs start to retreat to their shells, understating their needs, and opting to initiate a truce. Although burying the conflict can bring about some temporary solution, it does not keep the conflict from recurring; it only opens the door for some more resentment and conflict.

Instead of burying the conflict, take a breather, and allow the heated emotions to thaw. Once you are relaxed, with your partner, come up with a plan on how to manage the conflict moments. Come up with the rules that you will be following when you want to speak to each other, when you should be taking breaks, and how you will be communicating with your partner to have your needs heard, especially when emotions come flooding. Having set the rules of engagement, it will now be easier for you and your partner, HSP or non-HSP, to navigate any conflict or uncomfortable situation with ease.

4. Allow There to Be Some Differences

Differences between couples are the primary source of conflict, added to the fact that people have different empathy capacities, sensitivity, and emotional responsiveness. Our humanity causes us to weigh situations based on our experiences, and sadly, the people we deal with have not had the same experiences, yet we expect them to have learned the lessons and rhythms we learned through our experiences. It does not matter if both partners are highly sensitive or not; they must remember that they have differences in sensitivity and preferences.

5. Create Intentional Connections by Sharing Experiences

HSPs are easily put off by the lack of connection, the misunderstandings, and the conflicts that occur in relationships that lack proper communication. The situation is aggravated by the myriads of things happening these days, the kind that takes your attention away, causing them to feel as though they are taken for granted. For example, these days, people are so committed to finding ways to make money that it's all they think about all day. When doing this, we assume that once we have money, the rest, including the relationship, will iron out and maintain themselves. Conditions like these are the perfect breeding ground for emotional distress with your partner, friends, family, and other relations.

Without actively connecting with those around us, the bond we have with them weakens quickly before the eventual break, and this makes both parties in the relationship susceptible to stress and conflict.

As an HSP, you should set clear priorities of what is of most importance to you based on your limited capacity to create connections with other people. Perhaps you and your partner could set aside some time to sit down and engage with each other either through communication, playing a game, or some other fun activity, without interruptions.

Take this time to know your partner at a deeper level. What are his likes, dislikes, joys, hopes, worries, and goals? Ask him what he or she is most grateful for, the things he or she has been up to, the challenges encountered, and any such information. Talk about what has been happening in your area, in the country, and across the world. Get to know each other's opinions about different things in life; it is by learning about how a person's mind works, his outlook of life, the growth he has undergone, the new knowledge he has and other like information that you begin to understand the person and what he is about. You also get to share with him or her in-depth knowledge about yourself. In the process, you create an intimate relationship with the individual from which you can build a lasting relationship.

6. Celebrate the Successes

Human beings suffer from a "negativity bias" that causes them to give more attention to the things that are going wrong in their lives rather than the things that are working well. This tendency has served as a survival technique for a long time, but unfortunately, it keeps you from noticing the good that is happening within and around you. Focusing your attention on the difficult things of life will only make you feel more helpless, angry, misunderstood, and many other negative feelings. The negativity is a threat to your physical and emotional wellbeing.

In all relationships, as an HSP, remember that you feel things much deeper than the average person, and when the situation is bad, you will suffer more than the others will. On the other hand, when things go well, you will enjoy and savor joy better than they do. Therefore, strive to make everything around you positive, as far as it depends on you so that you can lead a happier, peaceful life.

How to Be Yourself in Relationships

While there are many things you could do as a couple to make your relationship better, as described in the previous, there is more you could do as an individual to help yourself and secure your place in your relationship. You could do the following:

1. Know Yourself Well

The essence of this is to help you and others around you learn what the state of being a highly sensitive person is about. However, more importantly, before others do, you ought to have an explicit understanding of who you are. You must first understand your nature and your needs so that you can have them met, be it some quiet, peace, downtime, or a personal conversation. Whatever is important to you, take note of it and prioritize it in your relationship.

2. Accept Who You Are

When you learn to appreciate and accept who you are, others around you are likely to do the same. Do not be in the company of people who claim that you are 'too sensitive' or that you need to relax. There will be many people claiming that you are making a big deal out of things and that you ought to 'chill.' You shouldn't have people like these around you because the nature of a highly sensitive person is that of being expressive, and you cannot change anything about that. You must understand who you are and what you're about. As a sensitive person, you cannot help but show your feelings, whether joy, fear, or anger. Your partner must know and understand that fact too. An HSP may understand you better and quicker than a non-HSP, but either way, a person that loves you will make an effort to know more about and to appreciate you for who you are. Sensitivity is not a flaw that you should correct or hide; it is a gift that we ought to value and nurture, and the person that will teach others to do so is you.

3. Be Responsible

Everything you want in life, you must go for because nothing will ever be dropped onto your laps. Of course, there are windfalls in life, but the things that matter to you, you must work for. It is up to you to ensure that your needs are met, especially now that your needs are different from that of your partner. You see, most people only lean towards the fulfillment of their needs while you, as an HSP, are always looking to help others. However, the key to a successful relationship with yourself and with other people is to take responsibility for what you and others do to yourself. Endeavor to care for yourself as much, if not more, than you care for others.

4. Love Yourself

Loving yourself causes you to value yourself so that you appreciate the attention, time, love, respect, and care that you give yourself. Do it as you would to your child. Loving yourself does not mean that you will be selfish or unable to love others—it only means that you will not have to depend on others to give you the love and attention you desire. You have to give it to yourself first.

To an HSP, giving yourself this much attention can feel very wrong because you are used to directing these emotions to another person. However, you must understand that by loving yourself, you are only ensuring that your needs are met, before proceeding to meet the needs of others, without feeling left out. Only then will you give freely and lovingly from the store of love you already have going on.

5. Defend Yourself

HSPs tend to avoid conflict situations rather than face them, which means that in a conflict situation, their attention is turned towards calming and soothing their partners rather than standing up for their ideas. Of course, they know that they should speak their mind, but the thought of discouraging the other person or receiving a harsh response outweighs the need to speak up. However, you need not fear disagreements because they do not necessitate a sharp reaction;

people can still disagree while maintaining the utmost respect for each other.

Whenever you want to say something, say it clearly and calmly, and your partner will do the same. Take responsibility for the contribution you made towards the conflict and apologize for the wrong you have done. If the conversation gets heated, pull yourself from it, and spend some time away from your partner. When things have calmed down, return to your discussion soberly, and try to see if you can reach an amicable solution.

6. Don't Become a Nag

While you may want to be heard, avoid making several attempts to make your partner listen to you, love you, or be there for you while they would rather not. You might have already spoken your needs, have been there for your partner, have given him or her enough time to change—but you are yet to receive the love, respect, valuing, and appreciation. If this is the case, do not keep insisting. Move on—you will find another partner who will have the will and the capacity to meet your needs.

Chapter 46. Empaths And Work

Depending on what type of job you have, the office environment can be an interesting dynamic between coworkers. There may be cliques, there may be those who keep to themselves, and there may be those who do not do what they are supposed to do. The workplace can be an odd collection of different types of personalities and work ethics.

Empaths may work a wide array of jobs, some more depleting than others. In order for an empath to feel fulfilled with both their individual and communal senses, they could potentially have a difficult time finding the right job for them. Here are some positions that would work best for an empath to use their gift:

 Nurse: Since empaths are caregivers, being a nurse would be a great fit for an empath. Empaths want to help, and using your gift to help comfort sick patients would fulfill your needs as well as the patients.

 Writer: Empaths can also have a way with words, and it can be quite therapeutic for them to get their feelings out and on paper. When an empath is able to get creative, they release the powerful emotions that they may have held inside. People would most likely relate to them as they have plenty of feelings and emotions to relay.

 Psychologist: A psychologist is also there to help those who have an illness of sorts, just on a mental scale. Since empaths can feel so deeply and understand what others are thinking, they are able to help those who have a mental illness on a better level.

 Artist: Many artists see things differently than the rest of us and have a unique collection of perspectives. Since an empath is more connected to their surroundings, they tend to be more creative than others when it comes to art and the emotion that goes into it. With that, their creativity will be second to none when it comes to being an artist.

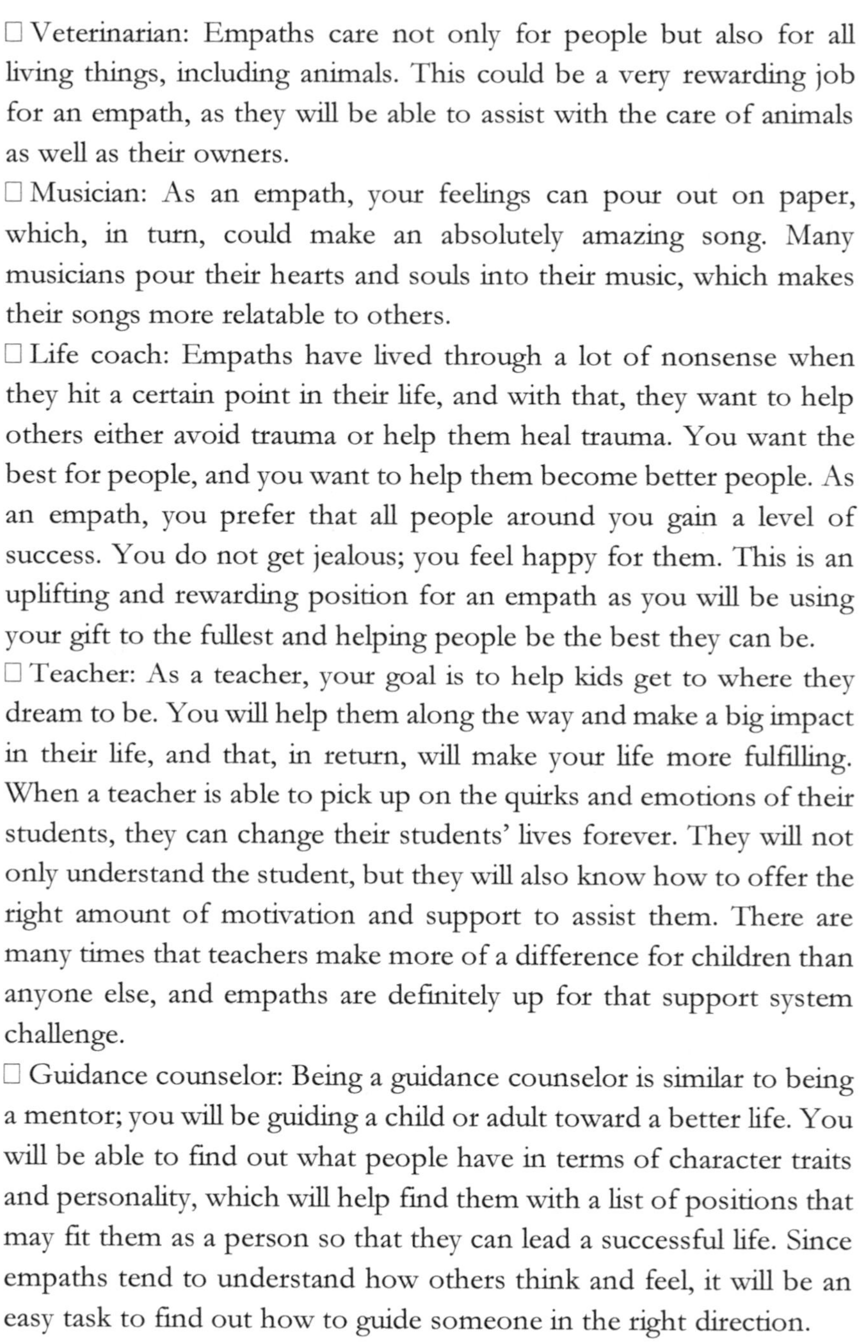

□ Veterinarian: Empaths care not only for people but also for all living things, including animals. This could be a very rewarding job for an empath, as they will be able to assist with the care of animals as well as their owners.

□ Musician: As an empath, your feelings can pour out on paper, which, in turn, could make an absolutely amazing song. Many musicians pour their hearts and souls into their music, which makes their songs more relatable to others.

□ Life coach: Empaths have lived through a lot of nonsense when they hit a certain point in their life, and with that, they want to help others either avoid trauma or help them heal trauma. You want the best for people, and you want to help them become better people. As an empath, you prefer that all people around you gain a level of success. You do not get jealous; you feel happy for them. This is an uplifting and rewarding position for an empath as you will be using your gift to the fullest and helping people be the best they can be.

□ Teacher: As a teacher, your goal is to help kids get to where they dream to be. You will help them along the way and make a big impact in their life, and that, in return, will make your life more fulfilling. When a teacher is able to pick up on the quirks and emotions of their students, they can change their students' lives forever. They will not only understand the student, but they will also know how to offer the right amount of motivation and support to assist them. There are many times that teachers make more of a difference for children than anyone else, and empaths are definitely up for that support system challenge.

□ Guidance counselor: Being a guidance counselor is similar to being a mentor; you will be guiding a child or adult toward a better life. You will be able to find out what people have in terms of character traits and personality, which will help find them with a list of positions that may fit them as a person so that they can lead a successful life. Since empaths tend to understand how others think and feel, it will be an easy task to find out how to guide someone in the right direction.

 Social worker: Social workers have a difficult job, but they are around to help their clients through terrible situations. This type of position is great for an empath as they love to make a difference in other people's lives. When this position works out well and there are times it will not, the empath will be involved in the achievement of happiness for those around them as well as themselves. The only downfall would be that, when something does not end very well, an empath may deplete all energy and emotions due to an unhappy ending. Empaths who are very secure and have thick skin would be best for this type of position.

 Nonprofit organization volunteer: This could be many things, but all of which are set to help someone or another. For example, if someone has a child in an ice hockey organization that they have also played back in the day, they may love to sign up to help coach a team. There may also be board level positions that could provide a lot of fulfillment by helping educate the parents about the programs they offer at the organization. These types of organizations need workers that are empaths as they strive to make a difference. They need people who want to make a difference to fulfill their level of happiness as opposed to those who are money-driven. Volunteering is more fulfilling as it will let you help without expecting anything in return, and that is typically where empaths thrive.

 Self-employed: Since an empath may battle ups and downs, with bouts of isolation, being self-employed would help them as they could make their own schedule. Being self-employed, they are on their own to make decisions; empaths would thrive in this type of environment. There is no need to risk having toxic people around them as they would be in control of their environment. This is the perfect work for empaths who have waves of needing isolation or do not have enough energy to deal with coworkers.

 Lawyer: This job is not typically where an empath would excel at. It seems that there are more snakes as lawyers than those who want to look for others' best interests. Because empaths do love to help, can be assertive, and can look out for the best interest of their clients, a position like this is great for them.

While this list is not all-inclusive and some of the positions may not seem like they would be a good fit for an empath, many do utilize their strengths.

How to Manage Your Work Environment and Boost Your Productivity as an Empath

You may have heard the expression "nice guys finish last". In my experience, those with higher empathy are far more effective in the workplace than those with lower empathy. Different companies tend to reward and promote differently, and sometimes sheer cantankerousness is the only dimension that matters, but in general the modern team-oriented workforce requires employees and managers who can get along with others. Deadline pressures and high stakes can make some people forget the value of empathy in the workplace, but that doesn't mean it isn't an attribute worth cultivating. Empathy can also be good for business, especially in industries offering premium services with a personal touch.

Being an empathetic manager doesn't require sacrificing productivity. It's possible to be both person-focused and task-focused. In fact, as employees feel valued, their contributions may increase. Attending to their emotional needs and ensuring vacation and rest are part of the equation can lead to increases in overall productivity. Accountability is an essential part of the equation, too. With good accountability, employees know exactly what is expected of them and can be rewarded for meeting or exceeding expectations. They can also know in advance what the consequences of poor performance will be, so there are no surprises.

As a manager in a technology setting, I once had an employee who was ineffective in his work. Instead of holding him accountable, I focused on becoming his friend. His work continued to be poor. It affected our relationship and created resentment, leading to an unfortunate confrontation.

After learning from this experience, I had another employee who did not show up for work and didn't contact me to say he would be out of the office. This happened three days in a row. It was an offense that could have resulted in immediate termination, but I decided to give him another chance. I clearly explained the consequences of a repeat occurrence. When it happened again, I let him go. I'll admit it was hard for me to do, but I owed a duty to the company and the consequences had been clearly explained. Accountability and integrity both required me to act decisively, but I did not act out of hate or malice. I simply did what I said I would do. He told me that he had a drinking problem and being fired was a wakeup call. He got into a treatment program after that, and I hope and pray he found the help he needed.

I've always enjoyed watching outtakes. Those moments when even actors in serious dramas find themselves laughing intrigue me. I've often wondered what would happen if a director or producer decided to lecture those actors and actresses about wasting time and money instead of using the breakups as material for a gag reel.

It seems the work of acting requires a certain amount of artistic freedom, and repressing such jovial behavior would likely limit a person's ability to get into character and deliver a quality performance. If that's the case on the big screen, why do other industries insist on belittling employees? The best work cultures I've seen treat people like people, not dollar signs. Policies are procedures are in place, but they are not oppressive and camaraderie among employees is valued.

Good working relationships with co-workers can be one of the more fulfilling aspects of the workplace. It can be difficult, though, to balance the various demands of a job with making investments in quality working relationships. It can also be difficult when boundaries are crossed between work and personal life.

Avoiding gossip and negative talk about co-workers, especially those in management positions, and the company itself can lead to greater workplace fulfillment. Everyone has strengths and weaknesses.

There's a time to address problems in the workplace, sometimes directly with the person, or with the person's manager, and there is a time to walk away from the drama.

One challenge I've experienced is overly talkative co-workers. I work in an office setting, and friendly people sometimes stop to visit with me for long periods of time. I love talking with people, but it can keep me from being productive. Sometimes, however, I'll find myself needing to politely end the conversation, which can be difficult with some co-workers. It's important to establish appropriate boundaries so resentment doesn't build.

When an employee leaves a company, it can be tempting to take the departure personally. After seven years of hard work for a grocery store, my accountant friend gave her 2 weeks notice and was told to leave immediately, because they didn't want to see her disloyal face there anymore.

As a manager, when I saw employees leaving, I was happy they had found something better. Though at times it left a hole to fill, growth and change is only natural. When employees leave, celebrate them, thank them, and honor their contribution. The ability to transcend ego is an essential management skill. Empathy and leadership go hand in hand.

Those who work in customer service are fully aware of the difficulties that can arise when a customer is angry. Showing empathy in such situations can be extremely difficult, especially when customers are being completely unreasonable. Here are some techniques that can help in these situations. These techniques can be used in other situations as well, such as when a spouse or child is upset.

- Make sure the customer is heard
- Acknowledge the customer's concerns and repeat them back
- Find out what the customer feels would be a fair resolution to the problem
- If the customer is asking for something that cannot be offered, negotiate with the customer to determine a compromise

These steps may not always diffuse the conflict or resolve the issue, but they're much more effective than responding with anger, which will simply make the problem worse.

On the other side of the equation, as you work with customer service personnel, try to remember there's a human being on the other end of the phone or screen.

Companies can, at times, be extremely frustrating. They often have blanket policies in fine print and, being imperfect institutions, may fail to deliver on their promises. Lawyers and judges make good livings prosecuting contractual violations, and there is a time and place for litigation. However, there is also a time and place to cut losses. Some things simply aren't worth sacrificing peace of mind.

Everyone has a breaking point. What we do when we reach ours goes a long way towards defining our character. When we are angry at a company or policy or circumstance, we may mistakenly direct our anger at the messenger. This serves no one. Before making that angry call, take a moment to reflect on how you might act if your best friend worked at that company and happened to answer.

Chapter 47. How to Stop Absorbing Other People's Anguish And Negative Feelings

Empaths and intuitives are like sponges in water. A sponge can't help but absorb what it's put into. If it's dropped into clear, clean water, it can be used to make the environment around it clean as well. If it's dipped into water that has bacteria like salmonella, however, it is no longer useful, but dangerous until it's been fully sterilized.

Even though it's impossible to guard against being in any negative situation ever, there are steps we can take to filter out negative energies trying to drain us.

Visualization

This sounds a bit "out there," but if practiced before stepping into a potentially negative environment, it can serve you in fantastic ways. Take time when you're alone to sit or stand quietly and envision a protective sphere around your whole body. Imagine anything that's bothering you as particles floating around in your safe space, then imagine them moving out of it. Once your safe space is clear, focus on your breathing: six seconds to inhale, six seconds to exhale. Do this for a minute several times a day. Your own energy will begin to shield you from negative external influences. When you've got this weapon in your arsenal, you can take it and use it anywhere.

Tokens

A token is a physical object that you can keep on your person and touch to help you remember to be present in your body and maintain your energy. In the film Inception, Leonardo DiCaprio's character Cobb keeps a top that he would spin to determine if he was awake or still dreaming. Other tokens, or totems as they are called in the film, were a weighted red die, and a golden bishop chess piece that is hollowed out to feel different than others. A token for an empath could be a rosary, a scarf, a foreign coin, a crystal, or a piece of jewelry.

Nearly a decade into their estrangement, their father passed away. Ana knew that Maria would be present at the services, and she knew that her own energy was at jeopardy just going into the day. That morning, Ana dressed very deliberately. Once her black dress was in place and her shoes on, she carefully selected two necklaces: one her father had given her, and a longer pendant featuring a happy unicorn that her daughter Paloma had gifted her. She tucked the unicorn pendant into her dress and went about the other preparations for the day.

As soon as Ana arrived at the funeral site, she found Maria already in singular histrionic form. Ana navigated the services that day gingerly, giving her sister a wide berth. Maria tried to make a scene a few times, even falling to the ground as they walked away from the burial mound. Ana didn't react except to reach up and touch the unicorn, then to tuck it back into the top of her dress. The simple act of responding physically to herself via something with a pleasant memory attached to it, like the unicorn pendant, helped Ana to stay within her own energy so that she could support her mother and other family members during a particularly trying time. She had maintained enough positive personal energy that their grief did not have negative effects on her.

Move Something

If you are assaulted by negative energy in a certain place, say your office at work, it can help to rearrange things drastically. If you usually reach up to your left to get a piece of tape, put the tape dispenser on top of the cabinet to your right. If small items are cluttering the top of your desk, get an attractive container to corral those things and put the container somewhere new. The act of reaching in a different way should act as a prompt for you to remember that your office isn't what's different, but your mind is. Use it as a reminder that you are making new, better decisions for yourself.

Declutter

Because empaths tend to spend a lot of time in their own heads, clutter tends to take over their workspaces. Take time to declutter those places. At home, the kitchen counter and sink may fill up with dirty dishes and foodstuffs. Your bedroom may not collect dirty laundry, but it may collect clean, unfolded clothing just the same. Taking the time to find homes for all of your belongings and creating clean surfaces will go a long way for your ability to deal with intangible problems.

Tap into Marie Kondo's wisdom and lovingly let go of things you don't have active use for or don't spark joy. For many empaths, hanging on too tightly to clothes and objects is intertwined with guilt. We feel ungrateful for giving away unwanted gifts. We feel selfish if we don't like a perfectly good sweater. We feel foolish for having bought something that broke too soon, and not either getting it replaced or fixed quickly enough. The best way to free up that emotional space is to take the time to downsize.

Recognize Threats

If a person walks into a convenience store brandishing a gun, they don't have to issue threats for the store's customers and employees to recognize a threat. People without special training to handle this sort of situation are likely to freeze up and want to get as far away from the threat as possible.

If a man is walking through the forest in the deep South and happens across a large snake in his path, he won't just continue walking. He will pause and assess the situation. What kind of snake is it? What are his routes of escape? Is there a better way to continue to his destination? He may weigh his odds and consider stepping over it. He may recognize it to be a non-venomous breed and feel comfortable either moving it or crossing over it.

Chapter 48. Maintaining One's Gift

Now that you have learned how to embrace and leverage your gift, the step is to normalize it. This involves learning how to make the gift a normal part of everyday life. At this stage, you will no longer need to think about how you plan on responding or how you intend to use your gift, you will just be able to use it and reap the benefits from it. There will be no need to put any effort into the thinking about tapping into your gift; it will become like the air that you breathe.

The normalizing process is a crucial part of fully stepping into your gift as an empath. It will free you from worrying about the fact that you are an empath because now you are capable of managing it consistently. Never again will you have to worry that your gift has some type of hold over you because you now know what you need to do when things get out of control. You will be able to tune in and out of energy when you want to.

You will never become void of all the emotions that you used to feel; when you are normalized, you will only feel the emotions and energy that you want to feel. You will no longer pick up energy from other people or feel an immediate negative reaction to the energies that you are exposed to. Once upon a time, you might have lost your temper or become exhausted and drained because of negative energy. You may have avoided crowds, public places, certain people, dinner parties, family gatherings and house warming parties because you knew that you would leave feeling drained, overwhelmed and exhausted, which could last for several days. During that time, you were perplexed as to where these feelings were coming from, leading you to feel frustrated and irritated as a result.

Now that you have become accustomed to life as an empath, you no longer experience these negative feelings. You can walk into a room full of unfamiliar or familiar people and feel energized and empowered. You no longer absorb the emotions and energies from other people; you are still capable of reading their emotions but they no longer have the power to hold you hostage. You know how to ground yourself and deflect the feelings, energy and emotions that are not beneficial to you.

Maintain Your Gift

Maintaining and mastering your gift are two completely different processes. When you have mastered your gift, you find it easy to live in harmony with it and as above, you have normalized it. However, don't get comfortable once you have reached the normalization stage because now you need to maintain your gift to ensure that you don't regress to the beginning stages of learning that you were an empath. There are several things that you will need to do to maintain your gift. This process will enable you to live in perfect harmony with your gift.

Regular Check In

To maintain your gift, it is important that you check in on a regular basis. You should do this a minimum of once a day, but you should really aim for twice a day. The best times to do so are first thing in the morning and before you go to bed. This will enable you to reflect on the things that have had the most effect on you throughout the day. In the morning, you are capable of recognizing residual experiences that you have been unconsciously holding onto. Much of what attaches itself to our minds often comes to life in our dreams; you can then let these feelings go and get on with your day in peace and harmony.

It is a good time to check in before going to bed because the experiences that you have had throughout the day will be fresh in your mind. You will be able to detect how these experiences have affected you and release them so that you can have a peaceful and restful sleep.

Daily Meditation

The best time to meditate is as soon as you wake up in the morning and just before you are going to bed at night. However, make sure that you don't make a habit of meditating until you fall asleep because this can have a negative effect on your meditation practices. It can leave an imprint on your unconscious mind causing you to associate meditation with sleeping, which will lead you to fall asleep during your meditation times in the morning and throughout the day. Meditating gives you the opportunity to rest with your energy. You don't have to feel as if you are in control; there is no stress and you can enjoy your energy at that moment.

Deep Breathing

It is important that you relax often, but at the same time, you should make sure that your breathing follows a certain pattern. Deep breathing allows you to relax completely by achieving a state of rest within your body. A good breathing exercise that you can try is to breath in for 4 seconds, hold your breath for 6 seconds and then breathe out for 8 seconds. This will help you eliminate any excess air from your body. At the same time as taking deep breaths, you can imagine any negative energy or stress leaving your body with the air.

Deep breathing is an excellent way of centering yourself and quickly gaining harmony within. If you ever find yourself struggling with your grounding exercise, begin to intentionally center your breathing. This will help you gain complete control over emotions and come back to your power center. It is advised that you practice breathing deeply daily and anytime that you find yourself in a distressing situation.

Intentional Grounding

An important part of normalizing your abilities as an empath is that you ground and shield yourself on a regular basis. The process of grounding allows you to regularly eliminate unwanted energy and intentionally come back to your center.

You should never leave maintaining your energy on autopilot because you will fall out of alignment very quickly and become unbalanced. Even when you have managed to master your abilities as an empath, you will still find that you get into situations where you are absorbing energy from other people.

Chapter 49. Build Your Self Confidence

Building self-confidence is an ongoing process that needs determination and energy. Here are some steps to think about when you are trying to build yours:

Step Out of Your Comfort Zone

If you are going to have unshakeable confidence, you have to be willing to step out of your comfort zone so that you can do things out of the ordinary. You have to stir up that urge burning within you to be extraordinary.

Perhaps you have a brilliant idea that your belief could benefit your company, but you do not know how to share that with your boss. Perhaps you have a crush that you never dared to approach.

The problem that comes with not acting on these desires is that you will stagnate right where you are. Truth is, when you fail to explore new experiences, you are letting fear take away your sunshine. You are simply digging deeper into your zone of comfort. The hole that you have been sitting in for several decades now.

Yes, it may be intimidating to make the first approach into the unknown, risking being embarrassed by failures. But if you think about it, it's just 'FEAR' – False Evidence Appearing Real. What is the worst that could happen? Often times, you are just overthinking. Stepping out of your comfort zone can be so daunting, but it is important if you wish to fulfill your life's purpose and have unshakeable confidence. This could be the way you can finally prove to yourself that you can achieve anything you set your mind to.

After all, what is the worst that can happen? You can share with your boss and steer the company to success, or the boss simply turns it down. You could ask that girl or boy out, and they could say either yes or no – You also get your answer without wasting too much time guessing. Either way, it is a win-win situation.

The secret to having solid confidence starts with you!
One thing that I will tell you for sure is that to get out of your comfort zone; you have to start by setting micro-goals that will all eventually add up to the bigger picture. Micro-goals simply refer to small pieces of the larger goal you have. When you break your bigger goals into chunks, accomplishing them becomes quite easy, and you will have so much fun while you're at it. This will also build up your momentum to keep pushing until you have reached your target.
So, we suppose that you have a business idea or strategy that you would like to share with your boss but haven't gotten the courage to do it. What you can do instead is break your major outcome into smaller goals that eventually yield similar outcomes. Take small steps to get started, no matter how small it is. Instead of taking the big leap and feeling overwhelmed, starting small will take the pressure off you. When you do this, you simply make things quite easy to digest and make follow-ups easy.
So you like that girl or boy and have no courage to tell them how. But he or she may not be single in the first place. So your micro goal should be to establish a rapport with them first before you dive into the deepest end of things. Even before you ask them out on a date, get to know who they are by just initiating a short conversation with her/him. Isn't that better? This does not sound like you are stalking them.
That said, you have to appreciate that when you set micro-goals, it allows you to step out of your comfort zone. As you achieve your micro-goals one after the other, you will realize that every small wins can help you get the confidence you need to move forward. Challenge yourself that you are going to do something out of the ordinary every day and see how that grows your confidence.

Know Your Worth

Did you know that people with rock solid confidence are often very decisive? One thing that is pretty admirable with successful people is that they do not take too much time trying to make small decisions.

They simply do not overanalyze things. The reason why they can make fast decisions is that they already know their big picture, the ultimate outcome.

But how can you define what you want?

The very first step is for you to define your values. According to Tony Robbins, an author, there are two major distinct values; end values and means values. These two types of values are linked to the emotional state you desire: happiness, sense of security, and fulfillment among others.

Means Values

These simply refer to ways in which you can trigger the emotion you desire. A very good example is money, which often serves as a mean, not an end. It is one thing that will offer you financial freedom, something that you want and hence is a means value.

Ends Values

This refers to emotions that you are looking for, like love, happiness, and a sense of security. They are simply the things that your means values offer. For instance, the money will give you security and financial stability.

In other words, the means value is the things that you think you desire for you to finally get the end values. The most important thing is for you to have clarity on what you value so that you can make informed decisions much faster. This, in turn, will give you a strong sense of identity, and that is where you draw everlasting confidence from. You have to be in control of your life and not the other way round.

One way you can do that is ensuring that you define your end values. You can start by dedicating at least an hour or two each week to write down what your end values are. To get there, start by stating what your values are that you'd like to hone to get to your dream life.

Some of the questions that might help you put things into perspective include:

 What are some of the things that matter most in your life?

 Are there things that you do not care about in your life?

- If you were to make a tough decision, what are some of the values that you will stand by and what are those that you will disregard?
- If you have or had kids, what are some of the values you will instill in them?

Create your own happiness

Happiness is a choice, and also the best obstacles are self-generated constraints like thinking that you're unworthy of happiness.

If you do not feel worthy of joy, then you also don't believe you deserve the good things in life, the things that make you happy and that'll be precisely what keeps you from being happy.

You can be happier. It is dependent upon your selection of what you focus on. Thus, choose happiness.

Happiness is not something happens to you. It is a choice, but it takes effort. Don't wait for somebody else to make you happy because that may be an eternal wait. No external person or circumstance can make you happy.

Happiness is an inside emotion. External circumstances are responsible for just 10 percent of your happiness. The other 90% is how you behave in the face of those conditions and which attitude you adopt. The scientific recipe for happiness is external conditions 10%, genes 50 percent and intentional activities - that is where the learning and the exercises come in - 40%. Some people are born more happy than others, but if you're born unhappier and practice the exercises, you will end up happier than somebody who had been born more joyful and does not do them. What both equations have in common is that the minimal influence of outside conditions on our happiness.

We usually assume that our situation has a much greater impact on our happiness. The interesting thing is that happiness is often found when you quit searching for it. Enjoy each and every moment. Expect miracles and opportunities at each corner, and sooner or you will run into them. Whatever you focus on, you may see more of. Pick to concentrate on opportunities, decide to focus on the good, and choose to focus on happiness. Make your own happiness.

Be Ready To Embrace Change

Have you ever found yourself obsessing about the future or the past? This is something that many of us find ourselves doing. However, here is the thing; the person you were five years ago or will be five years from now is very different from who you are right now.

You will notice that five years ago, your taste, interests, and friends were different from what they are today and chances are that they will be different five years from now. The point is that it is critical when you embrace who you are today and know that you are an active evolution.

According to research conducted by Carol Dweck, it is clear that children do well at school once they adopt a growth mindset. In fact, with the growth mindset, they believe that they can do well in a certain subject. This is quite the opposite of what children with a fixed mindset experience because they believe that what they are and all that they have is permanent. Therefore, having the notion that you cannot grow only limits your confidence.

What you should do to embrace all that you are is stopping self-judgment. Most of the time, we are out there judging people by what they say, how they say it, what they wear, and their actions. In the same way, we judge ourselves in our heads comparing our past and present self.

For you to develop a strong sense of confidence, it is important that you start by beating the habit of self-judgment and negative criticism. Yes, this is something that can be difficult at first, but when you start to practice it, you realize how retrogressive that was.

You can start by choosing at least one or two days every week when you avoid making any judgment at all. If you have got nothing good to say, don't say it. If there is a negative thought that crosses your mind, you replace it with a positive one.

Gradually, your mind will start priming to a state of no judgment, and it will soon become your natural state of mind. This will not only help you embrace others but also accept yourself for who you truly are.

Be Present

Sounds simple, right? It is important and necessary that you build your confidence. By being present, you are simply allowing your mind, body, and soul to be engaged in the task at hand.

Let us imagine speaking to someone that is not listening to what you are saying. This is something that has probably happened to a good number of us. How did you feel? On the other hand, imagine speaking to someone, and you feel like you were the only person in the room. Feels pretty special, huh?

The reason why you feel special is that they were present at that moment. They paid very close attention to what you were saying, feeling every emotion with you. They were engaged in the conversation at a deeper level. This way, you can retain information while still experiencing empathy.

To be present, you have to develop a mental double-check. This simply means that you should mentally check-in on yourself regularly. To do that, you have to develop a mental trigger or calendar when you ask yourself where your mind is. This is the time when you act as an observer of your mind.

Are you thinking of dinner reservations while in a meeting? Do you think that you are not good enough? To call yourself out of these negative thoughts means that you mentally check in on yourself every often. Once you have the answer to your question, take in a deep breath and bring back your focus on your most important things.

Chapter 50. Understanding Fear And Negativity

The sad truth is that empaths feel negative energy the most and they also get intensely affected by it. People see the empath as a reliable and grounded character and a person who can help them release all their burdens. Empaths are highly sensitive but from the outside, people will see them as someone who is used to handling all the negativities and emotional turmoil. On the inside, an empath is a raging soul who is troubled with all the contrasting feelings inside them. All of this results in an uncontrollable and never-ending noise inside their heads.

Things can get quite overwhelming from time to time and you can even feel like someone has clasped your neck so tightly that you are unable to breathe. You will need every ounce of your strength if you want to fight against this tremendous pressure. Empaths have this unique ability to feel every bit of energy that is present in their surroundings and this constant sensitivity makes them feel like someone is plucking the chords of their soul.

But the worst of it all is when the sudden negative forces come and surround the empath and pull them down. Having heightened emotions at all times is both mentally and physically exhausting. Although empaths give the illusion that they have it all together in their grip but it is often quite the opposite from the inside.

Despite all these things, empaths will still go out and do their best to help others because that is in their very nature. They choose to oversee the malicious intentions others have and always prefer to see the good in others. Are you suffering from the same problem? Then the following ways will help you fight the fear and negativity in your life.

Find Something That Makes You Feel Good

Accumulating negative feelings inside of you can become quite toxic as an empath. All these feelings of negativity will start dragging you down and you will not be able to achieve all those beautiful things in life that you wanted. So, if you have recently gone through a situation that has left you in a negative loop of emotions, then you need to take some step right now and come out of fit. The first thing that you can do is find something in your life that makes you feel good about yourself. Find something that instantly puts a smile on your face. This can be anything. It can be spending some quality time with your pet or it can also be reading a novel that you wanted to for quite a long time.

Feeling good is not about having a smile on your face. It is something more than that. It is about feeling happy from within. Just pick up anything that interests you and keep some amount of time in your day when you will not let anything else disturb you. Choose something that you can do daily because maintaining it daily is what will give you long term effects.

Always Remember That People Don't Really Care About What You Do

This is one thought that you need to understand and set in your mind. People constantly think about what society is going to say or think about their actions. Empaths feel this even more because every emotion for them is heightened. But in reality, people don't really give that much thought into what you do or not do. But when you keep having such thoughts in your head, it will keep you stuck in one place and drag your down from your success ladder. The truth is that people, in their busy schedule, don't have so much time to think about what you are doing and whether you are doing it right.

Everyone has their jobs and tasks to complete and even kids to look after. They have already got their hands full with their life. You need to realize that all these thoughts about people's perception of you are in your head. And when this realization will start setting, you will be reminded of how beautiful this life is. You will be able to set yourself free from all the fears and constraints that are holding you back.

Question Your Thoughts

Whenever you find any negative thought creeping into your mind, you need to take a moment and question it. This is the first step towards eradicating all negativity in your life. Ask yourself whether you should take that thought seriously or not. In most cases, you will find yourself answering that you shouldn't take that thought seriously. It might be that at that moment you are too overworked or tired and thus you are having negative thoughts. But when you start thinking about it with careful consideration, the thought might seem baseless altogether. So, extreme emotions can always cloud your mind but you should not let it cloud your judgment.

Another mistake that every empath makes is that they start focusing on one small mistake rather than the entire day. No one's day is all negative. So, you should focus on the good parts rather than the bad ones. That is where the questioning comes in. When you question yourself, you will understand that one bad mistake does not define your day. You should start looking at the bigger picture. You will also start realizing that one small negative thing does not mean that all your future ventures are going to be negative. Be an optimist and see the glass half-full instead of seeing it as half-empty. Whenever you question your thoughts, you will be performing a small reality check on yourself and you will be quickly back on track.

Identify the Sources of Negativity and Replace Them

Whatever is going on in your mind will have a direct effect on your actions and your life in general. So, you need to start assessing your thoughts. Are they mostly negative? Are you finding it difficult to get out of that endless cycle of negative thoughts? If the answer to these questions is yes, then you need to take some action and eliminate this negativity. The best way to do this is to replace it with all the positive things in your life. But first, you need to identify what are the top sources of negativity. These sources can be anything. It can be the current or magazine that you are reading, it can be a TV show or it can also be a person.

Once you have identified the source, your step is to try and spend less time with these sources. If it is a magazine, then you can cut off the source entirely. But if you cannot cut off the source completely, you can take small steps towards reducing the time with these sources. If handling all the sources at once seems problematic to you, then try focusing on one source at a time. Once you have freed some considerable amount of your time by cutting off these sources, use that time on more positive things.

Don't Make a Big Issue Out of Petty Things

You need to understand that every single incidence or matter in your life does not have to be something that needs all your attention. So, whenever you are faced with a situation, you need to ask yourself how much attention it really needs. If you see a negative situation brewing, which you can sense as an empath, you need to nip it in the bud. This will prevent that situation from taking the shape of something huge and uncontrollable. Alternatively, you should not worry too much about minute things. This will only drain you of your energy.

Whenever you are at such a crossroads, ask yourself whether that situation or issue will matter to you in the long run. If it doesn't then you shouldn't be wasting your time on it as well.

Don't Accumulate Your Thoughts Inside

This is one of the biggest mistakes that every empath makes. You shouldn't be stuffing all your emotions inside you. You need to let them all out. If you keep them unshared, then they will magnify and hold you back in life. If you have fears then share it with your trusted friend. If you are having negative thoughts, share them with your family. If you think you do not have anyone to share them with, then you can always go for professional help or join communities. Venting out your thoughts that are making you feel suffocated will take the pressure off your shoulders and you will automatically feel a lot better.

The moment you share your feelings with someone, you are also opening your heart to them. When you keep your emotions buried for a long time, they can even change your behavior and you might start giving inappropriate reactions to various situations. But when you start sharing, you will find it easier to solve your problems and relationships will become simple. When depressive thoughts are kept buried, they will start distorting your thoughts. Letting them out can make a huge world of difference to the way you feel.

Live in the Present Moment

When people think about their fears and negativities, they often tend to deviate from the present and start living in their past. On the other hand, if they are worried about something that might happen as a result of their actions, then they are existing in their future. Their time gets jumbled up and they lose a grip on their present. They have a puzzling mood and all of this affects their present life adversely. They start sinking. But if you are in such a situation and you want to snap out, then for starters, you need to come back to your present life and not let your mind wander off here and there.

The moment you start spending time in your present, you will see how different your perspective of life becomes. In case you are finding it difficult to achieve, then you can also practice deep breathing as it is often helpful in these cases. Take deep breaths and make sure you breathe into your stomach and not just your nose. When you breathe out, focus on your breathing only. Don’t think about any other stuff in your life.

Keep Some Time for Workout

A physical workout on a daily basis will help positive energy flow through your body and keep all the negativity away. As already mentioned previously in this, exercising also helps in the release of endorphins, which are the feel-good hormones. Moreover, working out can also clear your mind of all the things that were clouding your thoughts and not letting you think properly. You do not need to indulge in some extensive workout schedule for this. A 15-30-minute session of freehand workouts or a simple walk in the park would be enough. But if you are a fitness lover, then you can get a gym subscription and hit the gym at a suitable time in your day.

According to research, working out before you start the day proves to be way more fruitful that working out at some other time. This is because you can start your day on a positive note. You can release all your worries and the tension that was accumulating in your body. You can achieve a constructive state of mind before you start your work for the day.

Don't Let Vague Fears Cloud Your Mind

The first reaction that people have for their fears is to run away from them. But that is the mistake that you are making. You need to take a minute and have a closer look at your fears instead of simply running away from it. The natural impulse of any human being is to avoid what they fear the most and this is exactly what makes the problem even more complex. This is also what makes the situation scarier than it actually is. But have you ever thought about facing your fears? If not, then today is the right time to do so.

If you don't know where to start then start by asking yourself what could be the worst scenario even if you faced your fears. When you realize that not much can really happen, you will be able to gather some courage. Once you find out the worst-case scenario that can happen, you can also start listing measures that you can take in order to prevent that scenario from arising altogether. This will assist you in achieving complete clarity of the situation you are currently in. This will reduce the occurrence of any vague fears in your life that are hindering your success.

Help Others Feel Positive

Another great way to feel positive is to help others who are struggling with the same thing. When you bring the light of positivity into someone else's life then you will start feeling optimistic about your life as well. This will also help you get out of your head and socialize with the rest of the world. The more time you spend being stuck in your own head, the more depressed you will feel. As an empath, helping out others is your second nature but you need not give up all your time to do that.

A simple compliment on how good that person looks will bring a smile on his/her face. It will also make you happy. It might be a very small gesture but when you add these small gestures together, it will fill the hole you feel in your life. You can also help someone who is moving to a new place or someone who is house hunting as they are new in the city. Or sometimes your friend might just need you to be there and listen to what they have to say.

Be Grateful for Everything

Practicing gratitude is also one of the most effective ways to keep negativity out of your life. Did you have three proper meals in a day? Did you have a comfortable bed to sleep in? Do you have enough amount of clean drinking water? Then what else do you need? These are the three basic amenities that others struggle to get and if you have them, then you should consider yourself quite lucky. Things that are a normal part of life are often taken for granted but these are the things that no one can live without.

Follow the above steps and you should start seeing some difference right from the first week. In addition to these, listen to some good music or some motivational podcast to keep you going through the week. You can also try reading a humorous and have a good laugh or you can also watch comedy shows. You can even set a small motivational reminder on your phone and set it as your alarm so that every morning when you wake up, you see something encouraging. Engage in uplifting conversations and keep fear and negativity at bay.

Chapter 51. Taming Your Tools

You have already findd out some of the important ways you can save time or make more use of your time. You probably have some tools in place that can guide you through it. The challenge, however, is how to tame these tools, how to use them effectively to help you become successful in your venture.

The thing about time is, you have very little of it to work with. Therefore, you cannot afford the luxury of doing things over and over. You should start doing something once and getting them right first time around. You should avoid instances where you have to repeat tasks because this never bodes well. You end up using the time that should have been set aside for something else. However, busy you are, you can still make sure you give everything your best effort.

You have to increase your productivity in each task you take up. This allows you to perform more in the limited time you have. At the same time, try not to rush your work because no one pays for shoddy work. You might lose your contracts, or lose your job altogether.

What you need to do is find the right mixture of techniques and tools to help you become more productive. You have many tools that you can use to help you live an organized life. You must learn to block distractions from your busy time, set schedules that you can follow, and allow yourself enough time to rest.

The following is a guide on how to achieve the perfect mix. If you already have a system in place, you can use this to refine your system.

Choosing the Right Time Management System

The time management business is thriving, and rightly so. Today, many people have realized they are not making the most use of their time, and, as a result, they look for options, tools to help them become more productive. There is nothing wrong with that. There is also nothing wrong with entrepreneurs who realize this need and do something about it. What you end up with, however, is a market where there are so many tools you are spoilt for choice.

Your time management skills might not be the best out there, but realizing this and admitting it is the first step towards a better future. Without proper planning, you might find yourself jumping from one crisis to another without getting time to refresh.

There are lots of systems that you can use to help you manage your time better. Do not jump the gun and pick the first system you come across. Take your time. Research, read, brainstorm, find out as much as you can about the tools you come across. At times all you need to do is be more organized. Have a look at the way you go about your day and change things around.

Have a to-do list. It might not be one of the most innovative suggestions, but it is something that can guide you on what you need to get done throughout the day. This list gives you structure and order in which to do things. You can use a straightforward list, where you check items off one by one, or depending on the level of complexity of your schedules, you can find a more elaborate list. These days you have lists that you can share with a team in case you are collaborating on projects. This will also help you stay focused because there are a lot of people involved in the project you are working on.

Remember, just because a system works for someone you know does not necessarily mean it will work well for you. You must keep an open mind when going about this.

Organization

For any of the tools you are using to be effective, you have to understand how important the tasks at hand are. The organization is, in fact, one of the most important things. It will help you establish and organize your list of priorities. There is no use coming up with a list, only for you to push the difficult tasks to a date, and instead spend most of your day working on simpler things. This level of procrastination will lead to your ruin in the long run.

Determine the critical tasks for the day. Tackle them as soon as possible. The you get them out of the way, the sooner you can start working on simpler tasks, and free up time. You can also create categories for your work. Identify things that have to be completed by the end of the day, others that need to be completed over a certain period of time, and apportion your time for them accordingly.

However difficult or boring the tasks set for the morning are, try to power through them. This is the time you are at your best, and you have the energy to handle them accordingly.

Respect Your Productive Time

One of the first things you do when you wake up in the morning is to find your phone and go through your emails or your social media accounts. You go through this until you have cleared all the notifications, or until you have something pressing to deal with. You might think it is fantastic being in the know, but in the real sense, you have started your day a distracted fellow.

Checking these platforms very early in the morning means your mind is already interested in some story that you have come across. After all, there is always something exciting happening on social media, something that piques your interest.

Social media companies spend a lot of money, creating and refining their algorithms to make sure that they deliver content that is tailor-made to suit your needs. They trawl your account, the things you like, the conversations you have online, track the words you wish to use, and through their algorithms, they use this to send you updates about things that can keep you hooked long enough.

Checking your emails or social media notifications is not supposed to be a top priority task, but unfortunately, most people treat it as such. If you want to be and stay productive, create a time in the day when you check your emails, social media accounts, and respond to whatever needs your attention. The best time for this is in the afternoon. This is the time when most people are not attentive, people are bored, and the energy they had at the beginning of their day has dissipated.

Even as you do this, try not to spend a lot of time on it. Glancing at your phone for 5 minutes can quickly turn into an hour. Those notifications will not make a difference in your life whether you respond to them immediately or two hours . So what if you miss out on some celebrity gossip? They are living their lives. What if you have not seen the banter going on about the game last weekend? It does not change the results, and might not even affect the results of the game. Keep your head in the game.

Time management is about organizing your time between some of the challenging tasks you have to accomplish by the end of the day. A critical aspect of time management is planning. If you have a plan and you stick to it, there is very little you will struggle to do. Hard work is overrated. To succeed in life, you have to be smart about the way you work.

Hard workers spend a lot of time sweating and toiling to make sure people see them putting in the hours. Smart workers, on the other hand, do so much in very little time. Even when you are running out of time and the pressure to deliver is intense, your effectiveness depends on how well you manage your time.

Spare the time to talk to some of the high achievers, you know. One thing common between all of them is how well they manage their time. You have to be exceptionally good at this. You should be a result-oriented person.

There are benefits of proper planning that you can look forward to, including reduced stress, being able to use the opportunities that come your way, and improved professional outlook, efficiency, productivity, and confidence.

If you cannot manage your time well, some challenges will become part and parcel of your day. These include things like poor quality of work, missing deadlines, inefficiency, increased stress, a stalled career, and a deteriorating professional reputation. Very soon, no one will want to associate with you.

The lessons you learn in time management and planning are things that will help you for the rest of your life. The experiences are not just about your career, but also about your personal life. These are lessons you can also share with your loved ones, your children, and coworkers.

How can you manage your time properly such that distractions become a thing of the past? How do you become impenetrable to distractions, internal, personal, electronic, or otherwise? Here are some useful ideas that will help you to establish boundaries during work hours and eliminate the risk of procrastination.

Chapter 52. How To Control Your Emotions With Meditation And Grounding

As an empath, you have consistently been to some degree 'ethereal' in nature. Being ethereal can feel rather happy, far-reaching, and free – an invited alleviation from the power of being an empath. The ether is the space where unadulterated vitality thrives. It is the place life-power, chi, nourishment, widespread life vitality streams. Since empaths are about energy – feeling, detecting, transmuting and vibrating vivacious frequencies – the ether is somewhat an asylum for delicate creatures. It tends to resemble washing in an ocean of light. It is serene, quiet, and unlimited. Etheric vitality is a language that empaths get it. It just bodes well. It feels like home. For you, being ethereal ought to consistently be the simple part. Being encapsulated and grounded as a person, in any case, while feeling and detecting the majority of the energies around you is all that you need!

Gliding Around and Crash Landing

Try not to be accustomed to being grounded by any means, frequently feeling floaty without a stay. You can be imbued with a mind-blowing feeling of softness, yet you could thump somebody over with a plume. This is the place the issue may begin from. It can bring about ceaseless 'crash arrivals' – back to earth! These unexpected, brutal shocks can even send you in turn. You may feel overpowered and thoroughly washed through with disorderly energies, an inclination that is so natural for empaths. Without being grounded, it tends to be hard to release the strengths that you had accepted. Without a firm ground to remain on, you cannot understand that feeling of steady quiet that usually happens when anybody is earthed.

There may be a moment that it occurs to you that without imbuing your experience of being an empath with an Earth association, you could be merely drifting around like a tumbleweed in the breeze; which is all great. However, it cannot generally fill a need. Your otherworldly encounters can be astonishing, with the most dominant of acknowledging; yet you could be floating. You may understand that your endeavors to acquire the heavenly and genuinely fill your need can be pointless except if you give it a firm ground to arrive upon. In this way, you ought to before long become familiar with the imperative significance of being grounded.

Why Is Establishing So Significant for Empaths?

One of the issues that empaths and exceptionally sensitive people face is feeling exhausted and fatigued because we take on an excessive amount of vitality from outside of ourselves. Here is the reason establishing is significant.

- Grounding offers a moment approach to release undesirable energies
- Grounding bolsters you enthusiastically
- Grounding reestablishes and revives your vitality field
- Grounding advances a moment feeling of quiet
- Grounding improves mental, passionate and empathic clearness
- Grounding gives your life's motivation someplace to arrive

The Mother Earth Association

Even though you may feel the profundities of empathy for Mother Earth, being grounded does not work out efficiently for some Empaths. It is typically a procedure that must be educated. The brilliant incongruity for you could be, that regardless of your tendency towards the etheric domains, Mother Earth can be probably the best motivation. With the unlimited love of a genuine Mother, she can continually be close by, controlling you through this manifestation. You could not need to request a superior instructor. She addresses each individual, managing individuals with her antiquated shrewdness – all you have to do, is tune in.

Physical bodies are made of similar stuff that Mother Earth is. In this sense, individuals are all likewise offspring of the Earth (regardless of were known to humanity individuals feel they may have recently originated from). When you go out into nature, your vivacious recurrence starts to sway a similar recurrence as the Earth. This breathes life into you. It inhales everybody. It reestablishes and revives your vitality field. The reappearance of Mother Earth is amazingly mending. It is superbly designed for an ideal person.

Getting to be Earthed

Studies have since found numerous methods for establishing. The best is regularly the most basic. Strolling in nature is fantastic, just as anything that encourages you to feel your bodies (that is, moving, development). You may find that being shoeless and touching the ground underneath your feet, in a split second revives your proclivity with the Earth. You may love to invest energy interfacing with anything familiar; communing with the trees; venerating untamed life; feeling the loftiness of the moving slopes and mountains.

Basic Hints for Establishing

- Acknowledge the significance of creating for yourself
- Commit to intentionally interfacing with nature at whatever point conceivable
- Use a reflection to enable you to ground and interface with Mother Earth

An Establishing Reflection

(While regarding your etheric nature)

Here is a straightforward technique for establishing any place you are – regardless of whether you are not out in nature. In this reflection, individuals additionally respect your unique ethereal quality as well. Preferably, locate a particular spot, associated with the Earth, in any case, if you cannot do that where you are at the time, envision your association with the ground.

Close your eyes and carry your attention to your association with Mother Earth.

Feel your vivacious 'roots' sink into the Earth, through your feet (if standing) or base chakra (whenever situated).

When you feel associated, get a feeling of Mother Earth unadulterated vitality ascending through you. Enable her spirit to stream up through your base, permitting the implantation of Earthly energies all through your body.

Feel the completion of your body as you feel grounded and associated with Mother Earth.

Allow your ethereal self to imbue into your body while keeping up your feeling of 'groundedness.'

Your ethereal and natural energies will start to move together and inject.

Carry on with your day feeling the completion of your groundedness. Feeling alert, associated, present, and mindful.

As an empath, this will keep up a feeling of yourself, without getting excessively lost in other individuals' energies.

Grounding Methods to Help You Center Yourself

These days, with the consistent assault of negative energies, it is a test for the Empath to remain grounded. Notwithstanding when staying at home, inside their asylums, their empathic radio wires are continually exchanged on, getting passionate vitality from the outside world. Along these lines, they effectively become depleted, overwhelmed by disregard, and diverted from their actual Empath jobs. To battle the consistent overpower, the cutting edge world engravings on an Empath, they have to secure themselves and work to remain grounded. Everybody is extraordinary, and what works for one Empath won't generally work for another. Be that as it may, it must be stated, the best type of assurance and approach to remain grounded for any Empath is to make a flexible, solid body, calm personality and solid vitality field. The following are probably the ideal approaches to accomplish this:

Water

The body is comprised of seventy-five percent of water (somebody tissues have ninety-five percent), so it should not shock anyone this is far up there on oneself mending scale. Numerous individuals are unconscious of exactly how got dried out they are. Lacking supply of water makes issues with the working of the enthusiastic and physical bodies, influences general prosperity and quickens the maturing procedure. Water is a fantastic defender for the Empath, and they need loads of it, both inside and outside of their bodies. Most ought to drink in any event eight glasses of unadulterated water multi-day to recharge what the body usually loses through perspiring or pee. The heavier you are, the more water you need. There is an old religious saying that: 'Neatness is an underdog to righteousness.' Water washes something other than earth away; it can rinse the animated body and evident cynicism. If you are doubtful, when you get back home from a hard day at work attempt this: rather than going after the wine, bounce straight in the shower and see what an elevating and clearing impact it has. Or on the other hand when feeling genuinely fatigued beverage a half quart of lukewarm crisp water and perceive how it weakens the effect.

Diet

Perhaps the best thing an empath can do, for establishing as well as for all-round equalization, is to incorporate all the more establishing, nutritious sustenance to their eating routine and evacuate any medication like nourishments. Wheat is one of the most exceedingly awful guilty parties. Stopping a long story: grain acts as a medication in the body. Empaths respond more to medicate like nourishments than those not of a delicate sort since they are profoundly receptive. High reactive are sensitive to various vibrations of vitality. Everything is vitality vibrating at multiple frequencies, and that incorporates sustenance, medications or liquor: the quicker the wave, the higher the recurrence. Empaths are contrarily influenced by anything of a low vibration. Most drugs and alcohol have low vibrational vitality and cut the Empath down quick. Wheat is not classed as a medication, even though it demonstrations like one, and in this manner conveys a similar mark. You may not eat bread but rather still devour loads of grain. It is covered up wherever for a reason it keeps everybody swallowing a more significant amount of it.

Sea Salt

It is said that the 'father of drug,' Hippocrates, was among the first to find the, practically otherworldly, mending capacity of ocean salt, after seeing how rapidly seawater would recuperate injured anglers' hands. In addition to the fact that sea is salt an incredible restorative healer, it is additionally profoundly decontaminating. It can draw out and break up negative energies from the passionate and physical body. This is particularly useful if your day includes interfacing with others, where over and over again, you wind up picking their pushed or on edge vitality. Salt is not establishing, for the Empath, yet an immensely valuable vitality clearing apparatus.

How to Balance Your Energy

By adjusting your manly and female vitality, it works exceedingly well to help keep you grounded and enthusiastically steady.

Smudge

Smearing helps clear your Empath vitality field of undesirable vitality and furthermore offers extraordinary insurance.

Exercise

In the Western world, many go to practice for the advantages of weight reduction and a conditioned body. Be that as it may, the practice offers quite a lot more, particularly for the Empath. It discharges repressed feelings, evacuates debasements through perspiration, improves and elevates states of mind, stimulates, expands joy, assembles a ground-breaking vitality field, and is likewise establishing. With regards to exercise, do what you adore. If you do not care for guidelines, schedules, or set occasions at that point, go free-form. Make the principles yourself. Get the music turned up and move like no one is watching (which it is most likely best if nobody is while tossing shapes out). Move, stretch, and bounce your considerations away and get a sweat on.

Meditation

This is an absolute necessity on the off chance that you have a bustling head with interminable personality gab and dreadful musings, as most Empaths do. A bustling disordered personality is un-establishing. Reflection encourages you to manage distressing circumstances and gives you a more precise understanding. There are numerous types of contemplation. It is only an instance of finding what suits you.

Example: The Jaguar Protection Meditation

When you need additional security studies to prescribe this reflection to approach the intensity of the puma to ensure you, you should utilize it when there is an excessive amount of antagonism coming at you excessively quick. The panther is a savage and patient gatekeeper who can ward off dangerous vitality and individuals. In a quiet, thoughtful state, from your most profound heart, approach the soul of the puma to secure you.

Feel her essence enter. At that point, envision this flawless, incredible animal watching your vitality field, encompassing it, ensuring you, keeping out interlopers or any negative powers that need to get past. Picture what the puma resembles: his or her lovely, wild, adoring eyes; smooth body; the agile, intentional way the panther moves. Have a sense of safety in the hover of this present puma's security. Give inward gratitude to the panther.

Realize that you can approach her at whatever point there is a need. Feel the intensity of that. As a touchy people, you should learn the way to manage tangible over-burden when an excess of is coming at you too rapidly. This can leave you depleted, on edge, discouraged, or debilitated. In the same way as other of us, you may feel there is no on or off switch for your compassion. This is not valid. When you think ensured and safe, you can assume responsibility for your sensitivities as opposed to feeling defrauded by them. To pick up a feeling of security, perceive some regular factors that add to sympathy over-burden. Start to recognize your triggers. At that point, you can rapidly act to cure a circumstance.

Creativity

In a universe of standards and schedule, individuals only here and there persuade time to be imaginative; however, this is perhaps the most straightforward approaches to delight in the high vibe factor. When you feel great, you likewise feel grounded. When you make from your interests or interests, it has an inspiring impact on your mind, and when participating in something you adore, it wards off the brain from dull contemplations and sentiments which is an unquestionable requirement for all Empaths.

Chakra Balancing

You have seven primary chakras which are a piece of your enthusiastic body. They are your focuses of otherworldly power that run the length of our organization, from the lower middle to the crown of the head. The chakras are spinning vortices of vitality lined up with the endocrine framework (organs which emit hormones, for example, adrenalin, cortisone and thyroxine into the body). At the point when any chakra is out of equalization, it can make infection (dis-ease) inside the body. Discovering approaches to adjust the chakras assists in being establishing just as being extraordinarily advantageous to the strength of the body and psyche.

Yoga

Numerous individuals claim that yoga is not for them, yet it is the very individuals who get some distance from yoga who are the ones that need it most. Yoga is fantastically establishing. It takes a shot at the physical and lively bodies and serves everybody, regardless of what age or capacity. Yoga ought to be a staple in each individual's life. There is a yogic saying that: 'We are just as youthful as the spine is adaptable.' Because yoga attempts to make a supple spine, it could be classed as a mixture of youth. The very center of yoga is based on the breath. By taking all through stances, it stills and quiets the psyche, and makes a solid, supple body. Yoga is likewise classed as a moving reflection.

Nature

Being outside in life has a recuperating and establishing impact on each Empath. As an Empath, on the off chance that you invest little energy in kind, you will battle to remain grounded or discover balance. If you work in a city, with no entrance to parkland, ensure you get out at ends of the week from autos and air contamination.

Laughter

As adults' individuals invest a lot of energy being grave and genuine, and too brief period having a ton of fun (particularly in the present occasions). Do you recollect the last time you had an appropriate paunch snicker? Imprint this, 'You do not quit playing since you develop old; you develop old since you quit playing!' You hear youngsters snicker always. They do not have a clue how to pay attention to life; it is about play and fun, which helps keep them grounded. Everybody ought to endeavor to remain untainted. To see the world in surprise or more all have a ton of fun and chuckle. Anything that makes you giggle will make your spirits take off. It truly is a treatment.

Crystals

The mending intensity of precious stones has for some time been known in various societies, from Atlantis to old Egypt. It is accepted that the people of yore had costly stone chambers they used to mend physical, profound or lively infirmities. Precious stones can be utilized related to the chakras to help balance them and expel blockages. Detecting their normal mending vibration, many Empaths are instinctually attracted to precious gems for their establishment and defensive capacities.

Essential Oils

As with gems, the mending intensity of first fuels has been known through the ages. It is through the olfactory faculties that a large number of the advantages of essential oils are gotten. There is an organic oil to suit each Empath for either: assurance, establishing, re-adjusting, unwinding, and that's only the tip of the iceberg.

Earthing

Even though this is a late expansion to the rundown, it is one of the most useful with regards to Empath establishing. Earthing includes setting exposed feet on characteristic earth or strolling shoeless! You may frequently underestimate the remarkable recuperating intensity of Mother Earth yet associating with her is perhaps the simplest ways for the Empath to discover balance.

Chapter 53. Ways to Find Serenity And Live Happily

If you want to achieve serenity in life, then you will have to put enough effort into it as well. Just like you have to maintain a proper diet and exercise regime to get into shape, you need to build some good habits if you want to achieve peace of mind. For some reason, everyone thinks that serenity is something that can only be achieved by yoga instructors and monks. But is that the truth? Of course, not! Anyone can achieve serenity by following the right path. When you attain serenity, you will be able to enjoy life in a much better way.

Attaining peace of mind and happiness in life is essential for empaths because of their nature of absorbing others' emotions. If you keep getting engrossed in the negative energies of others, you will stop enjoying this beautiful life. But when you attain serenity, your problems will no longer seem bigger than they really are and you will stop heightening every feeling that you get. And when you face some real crises, you will be able to maintain your calm and deal with it properly. Here are some ways which can help you find serenity and give the key to a happier life.

Say Thanks for The Things You Have

If you want to achieve serenity in your life, practicing gratitude will take you a long way. Hustling towards your goal is all fine but will that make you happy at the end of the day? Not always. But what will make you feel happy is if you think about all the things you have and how blessed you are to have them. The moment you start practicing contentment in your life, practicing gratitude will become way easier. You will feel thankful for all that you have the moment you train yourself to become content with what you have achieved in life. Accept yourself the way you are and learn to let go of perfectionism.

Stop fretting over the things that happened in the past because that will be of no use. What has happened has already happened and there is nothing you can do about it. So, you need to start living in your present. Focus on those small joys in your everyday life. Another way of ensuring a greater sense of gratitude in life is to offer moral support to others in need. But since you are an empath, you should be careful about not absorbing all their emotions. All you need to do is listen to them. You also need to stop overthinking about your future. No matter how many plans you make, life will happen. Don't spend hours thinking about that dream home because it doesn't really matter now. Revel in your present and think how blessed you are to have all that you currently possess.

Learn to Accept

Some people interpret acceptance to be something it is not. You need to understand that practicing acceptance does not mean that you have to endure every injustice that is being done to you. If you are being poorly treated by someone then that is not the place for acceptance. Acceptance means that you need to learn how to accept people the way they are without wanting to change them at all. If someone in your life is a jerk, then you need to accept the fact that it is in their nature. But it will always be in your hands whether you want to spend time with them or not. The thing that you have to accept is that you can't really change people.

One the other hand, implementing acceptance in your life does not mean you will not find any room for improvement. Read this example and you should understand the concept better. You might be living in an apartment that you are not quite happy about. But you can't just go out of your house and start living somewhere else, right? First, you need to see whether you can afford your dream house or not. And if you cannot afford it right now, then the best way to deal with it is to accept your situation for now and continue living in your old house. At the same time, find out ways in which you can save money for your dream house so that one day you can move in there.

Keep Your Mind on the Right Track

Your mind can get off track from time to time and that is completely normal. Do you find yourself getting frustrated over very small things in life? Do you find yourself imagining that it is always your job to fix someone's behavior if you think it is not right? Well, if you are someone who does all these things, then your mind is definitely going off its course at times but you can also bring it back on track with a little bit of practice. The moment you find your mind going in the wrong lane, you need to stop it then and there.

If you find that someone is not behaving properly, you might feel that you are obliged to help him/her just because you are an empath. This is not true. If you want to find serenity then the right way would be to move away from that person. Then, engage in any activity that you think might help you to get yourself back on the right course. It can be something like listening to music or it can also be talking to your best friend. When you start re-directing your mind, your focus will no more be clouded by other things and you can think with clarity.

Make Amends

Do you think you have treated someone unkindly? Don't sleep over it as some might suggest. The moment you ignore your guilt, it will start accumulating in your subconscious mind. So, you need to accept the fact that you have treated someone in a way you shouldn't have and you also need to take proper measures to make amends. Moreover, try to make amends as soon as you can because this will help to keep the guilt at bay.

If you keep the guilt buried in your heart for a long time, it will take a toll on you. They can even fuel negative energies and cause you to be in denial. Sometimes, people get into a vicious cycle and instead of making amends, put the blame on others. This is an example of a self-destructive attitude. There is nothing wrong with apologizing and coming clean about what you have done because it will help you clear your conscience. It will also assist you in repairing your broken relationships. The first step to making amends is to forgive yourself for what you have done. If you are not able to do that, you will not be able to ask for forgiveness from someone else as well.

Be Kind

In no possible situation can an unkind behavior benefit you. You must be extra careful about how you are behaving because this will also have a direct impact on your mood. This is even truer for empaths. When you say or do something bad to someone, it affects them adversely and if you are an empath, then you will pick up the feeling or emotion of the person in front of you and start feeling the exact same pain they felt. So, whenever you are hurting someone in front of you, you are also hurting yourself indirectly. If you are experiencing this in your life, then it is time that you take a long hard look at yourself and what you are doing and analyze your actions.

Be kind to everyone consistently. Help them overcome their sorrows in life. Build their confidence levels. When you are kind to someone, you will see that you are making a social connection with that person. You will automatically have an improved mood when you help someone. You can also try volunteering at various camps. Moreover, kindness always comes back around in some way or the other. If you are kind to others, the world will be kind to you as well.

Clean Your Home

Have you ever noticed any dirty towels or dirty floors in any spa? I'm sure your answer will be no because there is a psychological connection between staying clean and staying happy. If your place is messy, you cannot relax there because there is a lot of pent up energy in the room that you, as an empath, can feel. Moreover, it is said that whenever someone has a cluttered room, it directly portrays their state of mind which is also in a state of chaos. So, you need to make your room or your house clean.

The moment you clean away the mess, you will be able to de-stress. Empaths become exhausted from bearing all those emotions in a day and if you come back to a house that is messy and full of things lying around here and there, your mind will not be able to attain the peace it wants. You don't need to burn yourself out by trying to clean the entire house in a day. You can start by cleaning one room or one portion of a house in a day and by the end of the week, your house will become all sorted. Keeping your bedroom clean should be your first priority because that is where you come at the end of the day to crash. So, a better idea would be to start the cleaning from your bedroom itself.

Mix with the Right Kind of People

Everyone has some people in their life who are of no support but rather a problem. They always carry some drama with them wherever they go. They are always upset about something or the other in their life because someone has broken their heart or someone has said something insulting. Or probably these people simply can't say anything nice to you. These people can leave a very bad emotional impact on empaths. There are some people with whom you can stop mixing with but there will always be some who cannot be eliminated. In that case, you can try and limit your exposure to such kind of toxic people. There is nothing to feel bad about it because it will be for your own good. It will be the right step towards attaining serenity and happiness and thus a matter of self-preservation. When there is chaos in your life, you cannot concentrate on anything else and doing things for your own happiness starts seeming like a far-fetched concept. You have to remember that even though you are an empath, it is not your job to solve others' problems or to make them feel better. When you spend time with people who motivate you, you will automatically feel more energized and you will always be in the right mood.

Get Exposed to the Right Kind of Media

The different kind of media that you get exposed to in a day plays a huge role in your life too. This includes the TV shows you watch, the movies you see on Netflix or any other web platform or the you read. All of these leave a mark on your thinking process. If there is a certain type of genre that you love specifically, it doesn't mean that you have to watch everything in that genre. Filter what you watch or read.

Sometimes, these media will impart pointless junk that can influence you negatively. If something is too strenuous for you mentally, don't watch just because your friends asked you to.

Watch or read things that make you feel happy or interest you. Don't get involved with media that invokes fear or negative thinking or puts you in a situation of self-doubt. When you watch or read something that imparts a positive vibe, you can benefit from it in numerous ways. If you have free time in your day, why waste it by filling it with garbage when there are so many helpful and uplifting contents out there? It is better to not watch anything than to watch something that demotivates you.

Validate Yourself

Do you want to experience peace in your life? Well, the first step to peace is self-validation. The most common misconception about the concept of validation that everyone has is that they believe it somehow means that you agree or approve of something. But this is not how self-validation works. Instead, it is about acceptance of the internal experience of a human being. It has nothing to do with the justification of the person's thoughts or feelings. Many a time in your life, you will find thoughts cropping up in your mind that you don't fully agree with. You will know it in your heart that the thoughts that you are having are not justified in any way. But judging yourself for having these thoughts or being hard on yourself will only cause a toll on you emotionally and you might also miss out on some important information.

But, if you practice self-validation, then you will be looking for ways in which you can stay calm and at the same time, manage the situation more effectively. You will see that you have started to understand yourself in a better way and this, in turn, will help build a strong identity. You will also improve when it comes to handling intense emotions in life. This is often difficult for empaths but once you start validating yourself, even this should seem easier. You will find wisdom through the process of self-validation. Another thing that you should keep in mind is that validation and mindfulness are two very related things and they often go hand in hand.

Accurate reflection of your current predicament is a very crucial part of self-validation. You need to label your internal state of mind accurately to validate yourself in the right manner. You also need to start normalizing your emotions. Empaths tend to think that whatever intense emotions they are feeling are not normal. But everyone has their own emotions and having them at intense levels is also completely normal. Never lie to yourself about anything and stay true to yourself. This means that you should never be an imposter or try to be someone you are not. Being in denial of who you are as a person is one of the biggest reasons why people invalidate themselves. So, in case you are facing this, you need to start accepting yourself right from today. You also need to realize that what you do does not define who you are as a person. But yes, in case changing some of your behaviors for the positive alleviated your pains then you can do so.

Self-validation is a process and it will not happen in a day. The more you practice, the better you will get at it. So, don't leave hope and love yourself a bit more every day.

Conclusion

Let's hope it was informative and able to provide you with all of the tools you need to achieve your goals whatever they may be. The lessons in this guide are tried and true and have been practiced by hundreds of Empaths over the years. I have helped my own Empath abilities develop and become more impactful in my life as a result and am happy to be sharing these tools and techniques with you.

The step is to take the knowledge you have learned in this and put it into practice. It might not get better overnight and you may feel some things grow out of you that you weren't expecting, but that is the best part. As you embrace your gift and face the challenge of making your life fit you and your Empath skills better, you will begin to notice such a difference in your energy, your relationships, your career, and your life.

You don't have to study these techniques every day or use them in every situation but I guarantee that as you do utilize these concepts and create more space for yourself and your own feelings, it will change your life and you will see your potential in a new way.

Continue to blossom and grow with your gifts by honoring what you need to do to take care of your own energy first. Make it an important part of your life experience and enjoy what being an Empath has to offer you in more ways than one. Explore the possibilities of what you can do when you are living well with your gift.

There will always be ups and downs in life and the decision to become better acquainted with your abilities will help you navigate those times more fluidly and effectively. You can always use these tools to help you support your path and your energy so that it doesn't get out of hand ever again.

Take time for yourself and follow your heart. The gift of being an Empath will always guide you in the right direction. Let it show you the way by following your instincts, intuition, and understanding of the world with your heightened senses. Being an Empath is only difficult if you allow it to be. Take control of your gifts and let the world see how wonderful you truly are.

PART II

COGNITIVE BEHAVIORAL THERAPY

Introduction PART II – COGNITIVE BEHAVIORAL THERAPY

Cognitive behavioral therapy works by transforming your thinking patterns in the hopes of improving your mood and your overall life. While CBT is based on theory, its real-life applications have indicated a high rate of success. This is why CBT is a very popular therapeutic approach taken by many counselors and psychologists with patients.

The theory behind CBT is that your thoughts greatly influence your emotions. What you think has a dramatic impact on your feelings. Even a single thought can create a violent burst of emotion within you. Now since humans are believed to think at least seventy thousand thoughts a day, that means that you feel at least seventy thousand bursts of emotion your day.

Negative thoughts are believed to lead to negative emotions, such as sadness and anger. If you frequently think negative thoughts, you are feeling nearly constant bursts of negative emotion throughout the day. If you feel more negative emotion than positive emotion, then your mood is going to be lower overall.

CBT believes that repeatedly subjecting yourself to bad feelings from negative thoughts leads to your emotional suffering. When you exist in a state of constant emotional suffering, your life can become rife with problems. You can also develop mental illnesses such as depression, anger, and anxiety because your constant low mood influences the chemicals in your brain. Life is much harder for people with mental illness because mental illness leads to poor judgment and physical symptoms such as lack of energy.

You may not be able to live a fulfilling life if your low mood and negative thoughts are constantly zapping your will to live and your ability to function.

You don't have to suffer from your thoughts. It may not feel like it but your thinking is totally at your disposal. You have control over your thoughts. If they run wild, this is simply because you have not developed the strength you need to control your thoughts.

This is how CBT can help you. This therapy approach trains you how to take control of your thoughts. With this control, you can make your thoughts more positive and reject the negative thoughts that bring you down.

You can begin to heal your emotional wounds and recover from your mental problems if you are more positive. Imagine how good you might feel if you experience seventy thousand bursts of positive emotion rather than negative emotion throughout the day. Imagine how great life will be.

CBT is goal-oriented. It guides you to make firm resolutions to change your life. You are encouraged to find problems in your life and then find solutions rather than sitting around feeling miserable. CBT thus gives you the power to change your mind and solve your problems just by adjusting your thinking.

Instead of thinking about how awful you feel about a break-up or problems at work, you can learn to think instead of how to make your relationship or work better. Overcoming and removing problems from your life will also make your thinking more positive because you have fewer stressful burdens weighing on your mind.

Randomized empirical studies have proven that CBT works. Various studies have been conducted on patients receiving CBT and patients not receiving CBT to see the difference that the patients experienced with their mental health. The results were then combined and analyzed to yield the conclusion that in simple English says: CBT works.

Patients who received CBT had faster results in recovering from their mental illnesses than patients who did not. CBT can change people's thinking and treat their mental disorders.

Five years ago, a psychoanalyst named Dr. David M Allen attacked CBT as a "simplistic approach that only treats simple problems." Sadly, Dr. Allen underestimated CBT. Studies have proved that CBT works, even if it is simplistic. Perhaps a simplistic approach is the best approach to the complex issue of mental illness.

CBT also deals with very serious issues. The emotional havoc that thoughts wreak on you have serious consequences, such as mental illness, and CBT addresses these problems. Dismissing CBT as a silly new fad is missing out on a great method of healing.

After reading all of this theory behind CBT, you may be skeptical. CBT sounds so amazing that it must be very hard work. How can you possibly do all that by yourself?

Cognitive behavioral therapy can be helpful for a wide range of mental disorders, including anxiety, depression, some phobias, and coping with severe illness or death. Many people suffer from one or more of these things at some points in their lives, and CBT is a useful approach to addressing them, either alone or with a therapist.

CBT majors on the problem at hand with the aim of achieving the goal of making the life of a person more convenient and better. The aim of CBT is to ensure that people can keep their emotions and behaviors in check at all times.

The CBT session is not meant to last forever. As a matter of fact, it is always timed in such a way that the one who attends the therapy session knows so well about when the entire program would end. The way that the CBT session is wired is in such a way that it is goals oriented, and the goals therein are such that the patient feels better at the end of the entire session with the caregiver.

Chapter 54. What Is Cognitive Behavioral Therapy

This is one of the questions that so many people ask, whether they have a specific problem or not. Well, Cognitive Behavioral Therapy (CBT) can be defined as an effective technique that combines talk therapy with behavioral therapy. In other words, it is a type of psychotherapy that involves patients reframing their negative thought patterns into positive thought patterns.

When you transform your thoughts, you will ultimately realize positive outcomes in your actions and behaviors whenever you are experiencing challenging situations. This technique is very useful if you are struggling with such conditions as depression, anxiety, and eating disorders, among other problems.

The good thing with this technique is that when you are in the middle of therapy, you have the opportunity to work hand in hand with your therapist so that you can identify the source of your negative thoughts. This is the best way in which you can transform these negative thoughts into positive ones, and hence, ultimately grow a positive mindset.

One thing that you have to understand with CBT is that the main goal is for you to replace those negative thoughts and behaviors with productive ones. Ask yourself 'Are these thoughts bringing out the best in me? Are my actions causing me more harm than good?' When you try to evaluate the impact that these feelings have on you and the people around you, you will be able to use CBT to equip yourself to overcome difficult moments.

In other words, you will use the technique to recognize how your thoughts influence your emotions. You will simply establish a rather personalized mechanism that will help you cope with the real-world-situation.

How does CBT work?

Well, so many people think that this technique is difficult, but trust me, it is one of the simplest ways in which you can overcome your problem. It works by helping you make sense of overwhelming issues by simply breaking them down into five major parts, namely:

- Situations
- Thoughts
- Emotions
- Feelings
- Actions

These five parts form the major concepts that underlie CBT. They are interconnected with each other and hence affect one another. For instance, when you face a particular situation, you begin to fuel thoughts about it, and this affects the way you feel; emotionally and physically. These feelings begin to take control of your physical body and hence influence how you act in response to the situation.

So many people wonder how this technique is different from other psychotherapies. Well, CBT is more pragmatic in the sense that it helps people identify the problems that they have and then helps them address them. It is also structured in that, instead of you talking about your life openly, you work with your therapist to discuss specific problems and then set goals for you to achieve while at it.

Additionally, CBT, unlike other psychotherapies, is focused mainly on the current problem. In other words, rather than trying to address issues that happened in the past, it aims at your thought process and your actions in response to them. In this case, the therapist will not tell you what to do, but they will work with you to identify solutions to your problems.

Using CBT to stop negative thought cycles

Did you know that there are helpful and unhelpful ways of reacting to a situation? Did you also know that your thoughts affect how you react to a situation?

Let us consider an example: if your marriage ends in divorce, the chances of you thinking you are the one to blame are high. You may even begin to think that you are not capable of a meaningful relationship. These thoughts might get the best of you and make you feel hopeless, depressed, lonely, and fed up. You then stop going out and hence, shutter your chances of meeting new people. You simply get trapped in a negative cycle where you feel bad for and about yourself.

Instead of accepting these thoughts, you should see your situation like any other marriage that has ended. Take that moment to reflect on what happened and learn from your mistakes and that of your partner. This way, you will not only come to terms with what has happened but also feel optimistic about the future. It is this kind of optimism that will fuel the social cues that will help you interact more with new people and better yourself.

Maybe your situation is not about divorce. It could be that you lost your job, closed your business or are facing some other problem. What you have to remember is that if you allow negative thoughts to cloud your mind, you will get trapped in negative feelings, sensations, and actions. This negative cycle will fuel new situations that will make you feel worse than you already do.

With CBT, you can stop these negative thoughts by simply breaking down that situation that is making you feel bad, scared or even anxious. In other words, it makes the whole situation manageable. It helps you transform each of these parts from negative patterns to positive ones, hence improve how you feel. It will help you transition from working with a therapist to working on your own in addressing problems you face every day with a high degree of success.

Exposure therapy

This is one form of CBT that is particularly aimed at helping people with the obsessive-compulsive disorder to deal with their issues. In this case, you have to bear in mind that talking about your problem is not very helpful. What is important is for you to learn to face your fears in a rather structured and methodical way through exposure.

You have to start with the things that bring you anxiety, but choose one that you can handle most easily. You then stay in this situation for an hour or two or until the time when you feel your fears and anxiety subsiding for a long while.

Most therapists insist on you repeating these exercises of exposure for at least three times each day. What is interesting is that, when you start facing your fears often, that anxiety begins to decline rather than increase, and will not last for very long.

You will then begin to gradually move to a more difficult situation. Then continue with the process until you have tackled all the things and situations that cause you panic and anxiety.

CBT Session

You can take part in a one-on-one session with your therapist or in a group of people dealing with the same issues as you are. If you choose to have a session with your therapist alone, you will have at least 5-20 sessions per week or fortnight. Every session will last from half-an-hour to one hour.

If you go through exposure therapy, one thing that you have to understand is that the sessions might be longer. The main aim of this is to ensure that you deal with anxiety hands-on so that it reduces by the end of every session. This may be in the clinic, outdoors, especially if you have specific fears, or in your home, especially if you have agoraphobia or OCD that involves certain items in your home.

What is important is for you to ensure that you are working with a professional who is trained in CBT. This can be a mental health nurse, psychiatrist or a psychologist.

Your first session

Before you can get all warmed up, the first thing is to determine whether CBT is the right mode of treatment for you. This upfront check ensures that you are comfortable during the process. In this case, your therapist will ask you a series of simple questions concerning your life and background.

In cases where you are struggling with anxiety or depression, it is important that you openly let your therapist know whether your issue interferes with your family, work and/or social life. You should also let them know about the events that you think are related to the problem, whether you have had treatment before and the objectives that you would like to achieve with the therapy.

If the CBT sessions are appropriate for you, it is important that you learn from your therapist what to expect during treatment. However, if CBT is evaluated to be inappropriate for your situation, or you do not feel comfortable with the process, you should work with your therapist to determine alternative treatments.

Further CBT sessions

Once you are through with the first session, start working with your therapist to break down your problem into various parts. To help you through this phase, your therapist will ask to keep a diary and notes on your behavioral patterns and thoughts, as well as their assessment of your progress.

During this time, you will both analyze what your thoughts, feelings and actions are like so that you can determine whether they are realistic and helpful when faced with a situation. The main aim of this analysis is to enable you to accurately determine what effects they have on you and each other. Then your therapist will help you work out ways in which you can change these thoughts and behaviors to improve your situation.

Once you know what you can change, you will have to practice the tips daily. Some of these include questioning thoughts that are upsetting and then replacing them with helpful ones; and recognizing when you are about to respond in a manner likely to make the situation worse rather than better.

To help with this exercise, it may be important to do homework sessions to help improve the process. Otherwise, during each session, it is important that you discuss with your therapist ways in which you have been able to practice these tips and come up with suggestions to help you further.

Remember that confronting your fears and anxieties can be tough, but your therapist will not ask you to do anything that you do not want to do. In other words, they will work at your pace so that you are comfortable with and during the sessions and the progress you are making. Once you are through with your sessions, the good thing is that you can keep applying principles that you learned to your daily life, hence lowering the chances of your symptoms recurring.

Types of Cognitive Behavior Therapy

As mentioned, it is evident that CBT utilizes some different approaches in addressing specific problems affecting people. Some of the types of CBT include:

Rational emotive behavior therapy (REBT)

This type of CBT is mainly focused on identifying any irrational beliefs that the patient might have and then trying to alter them. The process is characterized by first identifying the underlying source of the irrational beliefs, then actively challenging them and eventually learning ways to recognize and change these thoughts.

Cognitive therapy

This is a form of CBT that is mainly concerned with the identification of any distorted thought patterns, behaviors, and emotional responses; and then changing them.

Multimodal therapy

This is also a form of CBT that emphasizes that treatment of any psychological issue involves addressing seven distinct modalities that are interconnected with each other. These modalities include: affect, behavior, imagery, sensation, interpersonal factors, cognition, and biological aspects.

Dialectical Behavior Therapy (DBT)

This is also a variant of CBT that mainly pays attention to thought processes and behaviors of an individual by integrating such strategies as emotional intelligence and mindfulness in addressing them.

One thing fueling your anxiety and depression

Anxiety and depression can be incredibly debilitating. It can suck the fun out of everything, leaving you an empty shell worried sick the entire night and day. You are left sweating, having stomach cramps and experiencing a recurring negative cycle of more and more anxiety each time.

But the real question here is 'what is that one thing that fuels your anxiety and depression?' Well, it's negative thoughts! Everything is a result of your thoughts. Your perception of every situation has an impact on how hard and frequent your vibrations are.

The main issue with depression is the fact that your reality becomes distorted. The things that you used to find enjoyable are all of a sudden less fun. In other words, you simply have a hard time seeing the positive aspects of your life. Your mind latches on to and cycles through negative thoughts repeatedly until you are convinced that the worst is true!

You simply feel a strong voice telling you that you cannot make it; it is your fault and so on. What is disturbing is the fact that it is very hard to challenge these beliefs. This is not just because your thoughts tell you that they are true, but also because you might already be deep in the situation making it seem true.

One thing that you have to tell yourself is: perception does not equal reality!

The first thing that you have to do is to set aside anxiety for a moment. Realize that even people who are successful and do not suffer anxiety often experience a disconnect between reality and their perception.

One of the biggest tricks that the brain plays on you is convincing you that everyone around you is successful and talented but you.

It is this trick that takes away your motivation and passion that is fundamental in fighting off all distortions. Note that people who do not suffer from anxiety often feel as though they are fake, but they keep reminding themselves that this is all in the head and all others around them feel the same. However, since you are suffering from anxiety and depression, doing the same can be challenging.

Ten years ago, I was depressed, and every time my circumstances changed, and I had evidence for the contrary, I found myself holding on to the worst-case scenario of myself. Indeed, that was what the brain wanted me to believe. The truth is, it did not matter how much validation I got or whom it was coming from. It is a hard fact to bear in mind.

The point is, your thoughts are playing a trick on you, only that you are falling for it. Therefore, rather than allowing your thoughts to steer your life to a dark pit of fear and frustration, take a moment to tell yourself that even though you think something about yourself, that does not mean that it is true.

Chapter 55. What Are Automatic Thoughts

Once you have identified your underlying core beliefs, you are ready to start identifying whether they are negative automatic thoughts or cognitive distortions. While these two concepts are similar, there are small nuances that differ the two that you should be sure to brush up on prior to completing this step. This step will have you analyze your core beliefs, one by one, checking them past the provided lists and criteria to decide if they fall into negative automatic thoughts or cognitive distortions. If they fall into either, you know they are thoughts that are not beneficial to you or productive in any way, shape, or form. This is critical, as it will provide you with concrete reasons to define your thoughts and provide you a reason to change them. If you can actively identify which of your thoughts are unhealthy or unproductive, you will better be able to identify which ones require you to change them in order to fix your mindset. Remember, these negative and distorted thoughts influence your feelings and behaviors, and cause your feelings and behaviors to become just as negative and hurtful as these thoughts, so changing them will always be in your best interest. The first step to changing them is by identifying them.

Common Negative Automatic Thoughts

Negative automatic thoughts, as defined, are automatic thoughts that occur unconsciously and are oftentimes ignored, but accepted as fact. They color your perceptions of yourself and the way you interact with the world. When trying to identify whether thoughts are negative, you may struggle with thoughts that do not outwardly appear negative. Or, you may think that some of your negative thoughts are not necessarily harmful. After all, negativity is a natural part of being human. We all have negative thoughts from time to time. When trying to identify whether your thoughts are negative, you should consider whether or not that thought is beneficial to you in any way.

For example, imagine that you have a core belief that any effort you put forth in order to control your anxiety is useless. Stop and consider whether that thought is beneficial in any way. Does it help you to hold that thought? Does that thought make you feel better or worse about your situation? If you do not think it is beneficial to you, regardless of whether it is true or not, or whether you believe it or not, it may be a negative thought that requires restructuring for you to get out of the rut of negativity. Remember, those negative thoughts will sour your mood and make you behave in more negative ways.

Common Cognitive Distortions

Cognitive distortions are more than just negative thoughts, though they are most often negative. They are usually false. Something about them just does not make sense. Much like how you can have fallacies in logic that automatically disqualify the argument, you have cognitive distortions that will invalidate your core beliefs and thoughts. Take your time to analyze and really absorb the most common kinds of cognitive distortions. When you have an idea of what to expect, you can more accurately identify when they are occurring, which will help you to recognize that the thoughts you are having are distorted, and therefore, should not be trusted.

Blame

Oftentimes, we find ways to use blame to either cause or avoid guilt. When you are using blame, you often think in terms of should or should not, or must or must not. The problem with these conditional words; however, is that when they fail, they result in feeling guilt or a sense of not being good enough. This can quickly become catastrophic as you blame yourself for failing, and that guilt you feel only further solidifies your blame, while negatively influencing your feelings and behaviors, which will likely result in more of the same failures, over and over again. For example, say that you suffer from social anxiety.

You promise your friend that you absolutely will go with her to the party this weekend. When the weekend comes, your anxiety starts building up because you know you should go to the party because you promised. However, as this anxiety builds up, you eventually cave and decide not to go, leaving you with all of the guilt associated with letting your friend down. That guilt may make you feel as though you are a bad friend, which only further exacerbates your social anxiety. Instead of motivating yourself with your conditional expectation and obligation, you have demotivated yourself and made the problem worse.

Catastrophizing

This distortion always involves immediately jumping to the worst-case scenario and assuming that it will occur. No matter how unrealistic that worst case scenario is, you automatically assume that will happen. For example, if your friend went on a trip, but never texted you upon landing safely at the airport at the scheduled time, you immediately assume something bad happened on the plane, imagining it crashing on the runway or disappearing over the ocean as opposed to the more logical assumption of her phone dying during the trip. You spend the following several hours scouring the internet for any sources that mention your friend's plane crash, and when that turns up nothing, you assume that your friend got kidnapped, held up by immigration, or even hit by a car in the airport parking lot. All of those scenarios seem more realistic to you than the simple assumption that your friend's phone died. To an outsider, this is clearly illogical, but to you at the moment, you cannot help but assume the worst.

Emotional reasoning

In contrast to rational thinking is emotional thinking. This form of thinking appeals to your emotions, allowing them to rule over your judgment. There is a reason that emotional reasoning is a sort of oxymoron: The two are incompatible. When you allow your emotions to rule over your rational part of your brain, you will not be able to make truly rational decisions. Instead, you will rely on our emotions as justification for whatever distortion you hold. Remember that emotions are fickle and constantly changing: This means that your emotional reasoning will be changing every time your mood changes. For example, consider the idea that you feel anxious about going up in front of your coworkers to lead an important meeting about a project that your department completed. You know that you feel anxious, and that anxiety precedes bad things happening. With that emotional feeling, you decide that you will fail your presentation because you feel anxious. There is nothing indicating that you will fail aside from that anxiety you feel, and unfortunately, that anxiety makes you more likely to fail. This creates a sort of self-defeating prophecy in which you let your negative emotions guide you, only to confirm their validity because of those negative emotions. Remind yourself that just because you may feel anxious today does not mean that something back will happen. You may feel differently tomorrow, so do not allow your feelings today to dissuade you from trying your best. Do not dwell on those negative feelings as they will most likely pass.

Focusing on the negative

This is exactly what it sounds like: When your thought is taking the distortion of focusing on the negative, you ignore all of the positive in favor of letting the negative define your experience or perception. No matter how little the negative might happen compared to the positive, you will look to the negative to pass judgment. For example, if you occasionally argue with your spouse, as spouses do, you may get so caught up in the occasional arguments that you allow them to color your perception of the entire relationship. While you may have had an argument that made you feel as though you and your spouse are incompatible because you fight, you do not recognize that after the argument, your spouse asked to play your favorite game with you, or got your favorite take out for dinner in a sort of peace offering. All of the ways you and your spouse are compatible seem irrelevant in comparison to your occasional arguments, and you let that negativity overshadow the vast amount of positive interactions and feelings in the relationship. Because you dwell on the negativity, you see every individual argument as more and more evidence that your relationship will fail. When you think it will fail, you obviously would not be putting in the effort your relationship needs, and if your spouse ever decides that your negativity has gone on too far and does leave you, you will point to every trivial argument as justification that you were never compatible, to begin with instead of recognizing that your own negativity drove your spouse to end the marriage.

Focusing on regret

When you focus on the past and all the things you could have done differently, you keep yourself in a mindset of regret. Instead of seeing things in the past that did not go according to plan as learning experiences that can teach you what not to do following time, you dwell on what you did wrong. You constantly think of ways you could have fixed the problem at that moment instead of ways that you could learn from your mistake and do better in the future. This does two things: It leaves you feeling intense guilt and regret, and also keeps your mindset in the past, which is not productive in fixing your thoughts or behaviors.

To further illustrate this concept, consider a situation in which you got into a car accident. The other driver was drunk and crashed into the passenger side of your car. No one was seriously injured, but you were out of work for a week for car repairs and to allow your minor injuries and aches and pains to heal. You need your car for daily tasks at work, but it was so damaged that it was totaled, and even with insurance, you did not receive enough money to cover the costs of getting a new car that you could use for your job. Because you had no car for an extended period of time, you missed more work, and ultimately, you had to use the insurance payout just to cover your bills, and you lost your job.

Now, this is an extremely unlucky occurrence, but it was not your fault. You were following all of the rules of the road, but the other person was drunk and hit you. Rather than recognizing that you had no fault, you instead focused on all the ways things could have been different. You wonder if you should have left work on time instead of ten minutes late to avoid the encounter, or that you should have seen the car veering into your lane when you were driving and reacted quicker. You should have had better savings stash, so being out of work temporarily would not have cost you your job due to finances. Rather than looking at how you could learn, or in this case, recognizing that this was not your fault in any way, shape, or form, you focus on regret and continue to demean and belittle yourself over something that you cannot change. It is a waste of your energy to focus on the past when it will not fix your current situation.

Labeling

This simple distortion focuses on name-calling. However, just because it is simple does not mean it is harmless. Name-calling will not fix your problems, nor is it a healthy way to cope with stress or unforeseen circumstances. Oftentimes, core beliefs rooted in labeling are calling yourself things, such as saying, "I am unlovable," or "I am stupid and worthless." These labels do nothing more than label you and do not help you in any way. You get so caught up in your own beliefs and negative labels that you find yourself unable to prove them wrong. For example, if you believe that you are unlovable, you will likely act with low self-esteem, which may push away anyone who does love you or wants to be with you. The fact that you pushed them away with your lack of self-confidence only further iterates to yourself that you are unlovable when in reality, the problem was that you were so demanding and needy that the other person felt overwhelmed and unable to keep up. In this case, your label of being unlovable crippled you, ruining potential relationships that would have proven that label wrong.

Mind reading

Oftentimes, we assume we know exactly what someone else is thinking. You may feel like you know just by looking at the other person. Usually, whatever thought you are assuming is true is negative in some way, shape, or form, and is most frequently related to you somehow. For example, you may assume that your best friend really only pities you and hangs out with you as a sort of good gesture and out of the kindness of his heart, rather than recognizing that your friend likely sees the best in you and therefore wants to be around you to enjoy your personality. You assume this is true just because you think it is, and act in that fashion. So, if you feel like your friend does not truly see you as a best friend the way he says he does, you will constantly be leery when he offers you something or asks to hang out, thinking there has to be an ulterior motive in there somewhere because no one would ever want to willingly hang out with someone like you. Remember, you are not a mind reader, so you have no way of identifying these thoughts as true, so you should not dwell on them. Take people's word at face value because they are the only ones privy to their thoughts, no matter how sure you may be of them.

Predicting the future

With this cognitive distortion, you predict that bad things will happen. Similar to catastrophizing and focusing on the negative, you assume that the bad thing will happen, and because of that, you may find yourself avoiding attempting things you should out of fear of failing. You do not want to fail, so you instead opt not to attempt it at all, feeling like the only way to win is to not engage. For example, if you feel as though you will fail at a job interview, you may decide not to go at all to save yourself the embarrassment. This is somewhat ironic, however, as by refusing to at least try to complete whatever you fear you will fail at, you have failed by omission. Because you did not try at all, you upped your chances of failing to achieve your goal to 100%.

Taking it personally

When you make things personal, you assume that everything negative around you has to do with you somehow. If your spouse is stressed out or quieter than usual, you assume he or she is upset with you. If your boss was short with you at the coffee stand, it is because you are failing at your job and will be fired soon. If your friend does not message you back immediately, you wonder if you upset them. Instead of recognizing that you likely had nothing to do with any of their negative moods, you have inserted yourself as the cause. This can happen with total strangers as well: If the cashier is short with you, you may assume that you said something offensive as opposed to considering that he might have some familial problems at home, or be worrying about finals following week. Remind yourself that you are not responsible for everyone else's feelings, and no matter how sure you are that you are the root of everyone else's problems, remind yourself that the world does not revolve around you and you should not put such a heavy burden on your shoulders. Your spouse may have had an argument with a coworker. Your boss could have received bad news about a family member's health. Your friend's phone's battery could be dead. None of those is your fault.

Thinking in black and white

When you think of black and white, you refuse to acknowledge that there is a grey area in all things. You see things as exactly right or exactly wrong with no middle ground. This is a problem, however, as everything in the world has nuances and shades of grey, and forcing yourself to think in extremes only serves to set yourself up for failure. When you think in extremes, you may feel as though you are a failure if you fail even once with a wide range of successes. After all, one failure means you are not perfect 100% of the time, and that lack of perfection is enough to deem you as a failure if you define things as true or false or black and white. Oftentimes, these distortions will involve using words such as always, never, all, none, or other absolutes. To illustrate this example, imagine that you have a core belief of, "I always fail when I attempt to alleviate my anxiety."

Every time you have an anxiety attack, you use it as proof that you are a failure, no matter how much you may have reduced the frequency of your anxiety attacks.

Chapter 56. The Behavior Side Of CBT

According to the definition of cognitive-behavioral therapy that is mostly used, it is a form of psychotherapy. In today's world, it has become one of the most common approaches that are being used to treat problems like depression, anxiety, and even substance abuse. In short, with cognitive behavioral therapy which is also known as CBT, you will be working on your thoughts and beliefs.

Thus, CBT will guide you on how you should perceive the different events taking place around you and how you should react to them. In simpler terms, you will be working towards changing your reaction towards certain problems. When you change the way you feel about something, you will automatically find better ways to deal with them. The approach used in CBT is not like any other psychotherapy. Besides, CBT has a definite structure which is followed.

Traditional therapies often have the tendency of digging into your past forcing you to relive all the bad memories. But with CBT, it is not your past that you will be digging into. Instead, you will be working on how you can make your present better. You can also say that CBT is the perfect mélange of behavioral therapy and cognitive therapy.

Thus, the working principle of CBT is based on the fact that human interpretation of a situation plays a great role in their reactions. For example, if something happens in your life and you see only the negative things in it, you will start developing negative feelings. So, CBT helps you to change your views and perceptions in a way that you will feel confident and happy.

So, here are the benefits that you will get if you turn to cognitive behavioral therapy in your time of need.

Benefit 1 – Enhances Self-Esteem and Confidence

In most cases, people suffer from various types of psychological problems just because they suffer from low self-esteem. But with CBT, the patient works towards building a solution that will help him/her overcome the problems of low self-esteem and increase their level of confidence in the process. Suffering from low-esteem does not necessarily be related to any type of psychological disorder. You might simply be feeling negative about your life and CBT can still be helpful in enhancing your confidence and belief in your own abilities. Once you start with CBT, you will start developing positive thoughts and expectations that will remove all negativity from your life.

An excessive amount of self-criticism is also sometimes the underlying cause of low self-esteem and with CBT, you will learn how to deal with all of this. Thus, you will feel motivated to try newer things in life and not succumb to the thoughts of depression and anxiety. CBT will help you learn about numerous stress-reducing techniques. With time, you will be able to build healthy relationships with people around you. You will find positive answers to the questions you have in mind and amidst all of this, you learn how to fight against the problems that you are facing.

Benefit 2 – Builds Positive Thoughts

Are you having a lot of negative thoughts lately? With CBT, you will learn to develop a healthier way of thinking – one that doesn't involve any negativity. CBT involves inculcating different techniques in the patient that will help him/her to engage in positive thinking naturally. When negative thought patterns start emerging in an adult, they usually take control of your life and change you as a person. But with CBT, you will get to know how you can identify those negative and irrational thoughts right in the beginning and thus, stop them from spreading.

A major part of building positive thoughts is done through cognitive restructuring which has been explained in detail in a of this. You will also be working on your assertiveness skill so that you can give proper responses to any level of criticism that is put in front of you. You will also get in-depth mindfulness training where you will learn how you can control how you feel.

Benefit 3 – Helps with Anger Management

Cognitive-behavioral therapy or CBT has proven to be quite effective in terms of anger management in the past years. Anger is something that has to be managed before it takes on a bad shape. When left unmanaged, anger starts bottling up and one day, it might just explode causing adverse series of reactions. This hamper both the social and work relationships of the person concerned. The development of resentment and anger can be a result of ineffective stress management as well.

So, are you dealing with anger issues that are hampering with your everyday life? Then CBT can definitely be one of the most effective ways to manage your anger. There can be different types of approaches in this treatment and what works for a person generally depends on the root cause of their anger. But it is often noticed that people who are having anger management issues do not really know why they are behaving in that manner. They cannot really explain what happens to them when they have an angry outburst. But when you go to a therapist, he/she will help you with personal awareness and gradually develop control over your anger issues.

Benefit 4 – Improves Your Coping Skills

PTSD or post-traumatic stress disorder is a problem that has become quite common in teens. Trauma and excessive grief have long been known for causing several disorders. In both situations, people are unable to open up and this ultimately causes their emotions to bottle up. But with CBT, you will learn how you can express your feelings and eventually, you will feel better. You will learn how to cope with your situation instead of shoving it aside.

Many people also turn to alcohol when they fail to cope with their problems. But with the implementation of CBT strategies, the patient will learn how not to rely on alcohol as it is a maladaptive coping strategy and instead try other positive methods. The therapist will help you to identify the situations which can trigger you and then you will learn how to address the issues in a step-by-step manner.

Benefit 5 – Reduces Substance Abuse and Any Kind of Addictive Behavior

People often become victims of addiction due to several instances. Drug dependencies often can be treated effectively with a properly strategized CBT. The therapy can also be used in cases where people are addicted to gambling or cigarettes. As you already know, CBT helps people understand why they feel things in a certain way and how that has impacted their actions. When addicts start realizing the reasons behind their substance abuse, it helps them overcome their problems. Thus, with a proper CBT, a person will be able to dismiss all those misleading thoughts they used to have which eventually leads to substance abuse.

CBT will also help the patient in identifying the exact reason behind succumbing to substance abuse so that they also pinpoint their triggers. After that, the therapist will teach them how they can keep themselves away from any such situation which can act as the trigger. Finally, they will also learn about techniques to use in order to keep thoughts of substance abuse at bay.

Benefit 6 – Improves Communication Skills

SEBD or social, emotional, and behavioral difficulties are often seen in children and the absence of proper power of communication is one of the major reasons why children face SEBD. The worst part is that children who do have these problems are not identified when they should have been and thus, they go unnoticed until they enter school. When they enter school, they start developing a different type of problem known as ADHD or attention deficit hyperactivity disorder. CBT has recently been recognized as a very useful form of treatment in such cases. There are several communication enhancement techniques that are used during the treatment procedure.

Apart from the above-mentioned scenario, the effective strategies used in CBT can also help adults who face difficulties in reaching out about their problems. When people are suffering from conditions like addiction, depression, or anxiety, they often fail to maintain their relationships with the close ones in their family or friend circle. They, sometimes, even feel shame about communicating what they are feeling inside. But with CBT, these patients are able to overcome all these barriers and communicate openly.

Benefit 7 – Prevents Relapse

According to research and proven examples, CBT is highly effective in preventing the occurrence of relapse situations. The biggest contributors to any relapse situation are social pressure, interpersonal conflict, and the development of a negative state of mind. But with the coping strategies that fall under CBT, the patient learns how they can forego their addictive behaviors and start developing healthy patterns instead. Integration of validation, acceptance, and mindfulness is initiated by CBT. All of this encourages the patient to walk on the path of recovery.

CBT strategies that are based on mindfulness help the patients identify their thought patterns and recognize whether they are negative or positive. Negativity is one of the biggest potential causes of relapse and it needs to be completely eliminated in order to get the best results. With a properly framed approach, achieving the desired results of relapse prevention is not tough.

Benefit 8 – Helps in Treatment of Eating Disorders

When it comes to bulimia nervosa, CBT is considered to be one of the effective modes of treatment. It also works well for people facing binge eating disorders. The main problem underlying almost all types of eating disorders is the fact that people tend to become over-concerned about their weight. The reason behind the manifestation of this over-concern varies from person to person but this incident often leads to the development of abnormally strict dieting, loss in weight, displaying binge-eating tendency or even compensatory behaviors like performing excessive exercises or self-induced vomiting.

But CBT in these cases is structured in a way that the patient is introduced to sessions of psychoeducation where they learn about the various medical consequences of their eating disorder. A normal eating pattern with healthy meal-charts is prescribed to the patient in order to replace their abnormal diet charts. CBT also helps in the development of strategies that will prevent any further compensatory behaviors in the patient. Once all of this is established, the patient is also introduced to those foods which they fear the most so that a normal lifestyle can be reinstated. Apart from this, relapse prevention strategies are also designed.

In the initial days, when CBT was introduced to the masses, the therapy dealt with simple cases of depression and anxiety only. But with time, CBT can be used to treat some of the most complex problems and various types of mental disorders. Moreover, CBT is not specifically meant for people having a mental illness. The best part about CBT is that it can be applied to a variety of problems that are not even related to mental disorders. One of the very common aspects of Cognitive Behavioral Therapy is the need to complete homework assignments that are specially designed for each patient. The main reason behind this is the collaborative and interactive nature of CBT.

One of the biggest advantages that you can enjoy with CBT is that the therapy is not limited to the time you are with your therapist. The formal sessions will end after a certain period of time but the therapy can continue. The patients can keep on practicing the different techniques they have learned. This, in turn, can give them prolong benefits. The main role of the therapist in CBT is to promote positivity and encourage the patient while the patient's role is to be as expressive and open as possible.

The following step in the process of CBT is identifying which of the core beliefs you have identified are negative. When you run into negative thought patterns, you know that they ought to be challenged in order to ensure that they are corrected. After all, most of these negative thought patterns are formed from cognitive distortions, which are distorted, false thoughts that should not be fostered at all.

Defining Negative Thoughts

Negative thoughts are any problematic thought patterns that you may develop. Some are cognitive distortions, meaning they are false by nature, while others are simply thoughts that are so focused on the negative, they cause you issues. For example, if you think that you are a horrible person after dropping a plate on the floor and shattering it, you may have a problem with negative thoughts and cognitive distortions. These distortions should not be entertained and instead need to be banished and ignored, and yet people everywhere foster them.

By and large, these negative thoughts can corrupt your core beliefs, turning them into false; negative beliefs about yourself that then become problematic in general. When this happens, you frequently are stuck on those negative thoughts, so caught up in them that you cannot move past them. You instead fixate upon them and let them corrupt your image of yourself or those around you. This struggle can lead to all sorts of anxiety problems in the future.

Problems with Negative Thoughts

When you let negative thoughts rule you, you essentially allow yourself to root your mind in negativity. You are accepting the fact that your negative thought patterns run your life once you become aware of them and do nothing to change them. They can ruin relationships, destroy self-esteem, cause myriads of mental health issues, and yet, some people prefer to hide their heads in the sand and pretend there is nothing wrong despite the clear issues ahead of them.

This is problematic—people are then so stuck in these negative thoughts that they cannot control the negative feelings or behaviors that follow as a result.

Remember, negative thoughts deserve to be challenged. You do not have to live a life rooted in negativity in which you are stuck living out the same negative cycles over and over again. You deserve to challenge those negative thoughts and develop happier, healthier mindsets that can benefit you greatly, ensuring more success and happiness in your relationships in the future.

Chapter 57. Identifying Negative Thought Patterns

The following step in the process of CBT is identifying which of the core beliefs you have identified are negative. When you run into negative thought patterns, you know that they ought to be challenged in order to ensure that they are corrected. After all, most of these negative thought patterns are formed from cognitive distortions, which are distorted, false thoughts that should not be fostered at all.

Defining Negative Thoughts

Negative thoughts are any problematic thought patterns that you may develop. Some are cognitive distortions, meaning they are false by nature, while others are simply thoughts that are so focused on the negative, they cause you issues. For example, if you think that you are a horrible person after dropping a plate on the floor and shattering it, you may have a problem with negative thoughts and cognitive distortions. These distortions should not be entertained and instead need to be banished and ignored, and yet people everywhere foster them.

By and large, these negative thoughts can corrupt your core beliefs, turning them into false; negative beliefs about yourself that then become problematic in general. When this happens, you frequently are stuck on those negative thoughts, so caught up in them that you cannot move past them. You instead fixate upon them and let them corrupt your image of yourself or those around you. This struggle can lead to all sorts of anxiety problems in the future.

Problems With Negative Thoughts

When you let negative thoughts rule you, you essentially allow yourself to root your mind in negativity. You are accepting the fact that your negative thought patterns run your life once you become aware of them and do nothing to change them. They can ruin relationships, destroy self-esteem, cause myriads of mental health issues, and yet, some people prefer to hide their heads in the sand and pretend there is nothing wrong despite the clear issues ahead of them. This is problematic—people are then so stuck in these negative thoughts that they cannot control the negative feelings or behaviors that follow as a result.

Remember, negative thoughts deserve to be challenged. You do not have to live a life rooted in negativity in which you are stuck living out the same negative cycles over and over again. You deserve to challenge those negative thoughts and develop happier, healthier mindsets that can benefit you greatly, ensuring more success and happiness in your relationships in the future.

Most Common Negative Thought Patterns

When you are engaging in negative thought patterns, you are likely unaware of it. However, there are 15 common negative thought patterns known as cognitive distortions that people regularly find themselves caught up in. Take the time to study these 15 distortions and identify whether you yourself suffer from them. If you do, you know that challenging them is within your future.

•Filtering: When you filter, you see things as entirely negative. You ignore the existence of the positive entirely, only allowing negative occurrences to define the way you see the world. For example, you decide that because you dropped a bottle of milk and shattered it once, you are a horrible, wasteful person, despite the fact that you rarely actually waste milk.

•Polarized thinking: When you engage in polarized thinking, everything is black and white with no in-between. Things are good or bad, right or wrong, perfect or failed. For example, you decide that you are largely undeserving of friendship simply because you accidentally betrayed your friend once and therefore, are not worthy of being a good friend.

•Overgeneralizing: When you overgeneralize, you assume that people and experiences are all the same based on a small sample size. For example, you may have gotten sick once at an ethnic restaurant, and after that, you assume that all restaurants of that ethnicity are to be avoided.

•Jumping to conclusions: when you jump to a conclusion, you essentially state that you know exactly what will happen following without actually knowing or having any evidence to prove it. For example, you assume that your best friend will drop you without warning because you have a gut feeling it will happen.

•Worst-case scenario thinking: When you engage in worst-case scenario thinking, you essentially assume that the worst possible result has occurred before having any evidence that supports it. For example, when your friend does not answer the phone, she must have been kidnapped and murdered because she always answers the phone, but did not that time.

•Personalizing: When you personalize, you assume that you are the cause of all misfortune around you, at least in part. If someone is having a bad day, it must be your fault. If someone is angry, they must be angry with you. If there is a car accident, you must have done something to cause it.

•Control fallacy: When you have a control fallacy, either you blame yourself wholeheartedly for everything around you or you reject the fault of anything that happens around you. For example, you decide that it is your fault that your neighbor's house was robbed instead of yours because you left a light on.

•Fairness fallacy: When you act under a fairness fallacy, you assume that everything has to be fair and pursue utter fairness despite the fact that life is not, in fact, fair, and you may not be deserving of it. For example, you assume that if someone else got a job with the same degree and credentials you have, you should be able to get the same job and pay rate, with no regard to differences in personality.

•Blame: When you fall for the blame fallacy, you point at other people as the cause of problems rather than acknowledging that you could have some fault in the matter.

You essentially refuse any accountability. For example, you may tell someone that you had no fault in the matter of a car accident because the sun shone in your eyes and you could not possibly see the other car because of it.

•Should have: You focus so much on whether something should or should not be, rather than seeing the world for the way it is. For example, you fixate on the fact that you should have gotten the job you interviewed for, so you refuse to try for other jobs, assuming that you will, in fact, be called back for that job.

•Emotional reasoning: When you engage in this, you assume that anything you feel must be true simply because you feel that it is true despite the fact that it is not the case. You may feel like you failed and therefore deem yourself a failure

•Change fallacy: Within this fallacy, you assume that other people will change for you to meet what you want or need, and when they do not, you get flustered or struggle to function.

Chapter 58. Setting Goals

How To Set Goals

Goals are very important to an individual. They keep you motivated and focused. Going about life without goals is shooting aimlessly, and you will not achieve anything meaningful, you will be discouraged and frustrated. To set goals, you must write them down with the expected date to achieve them. They act as a constant reminder and help to keep you in check.

Goals are essential because they give you a target or a purpose. Goals are also important because they enable you to measure your progress. When you set a big goal, you set up other smaller goals that guide you to achieving the big goal. This enables you to measure your progress and help you celebrate small successes. For instance, if you want to save $1 million so that you can start a business, you set other smaller goals. How much you must save each month in order to achieve your target of $1 million in 2 years or more. When you set goals, you avoid distractions and stay locked into your course in order to achieve it.

Another importance of goals is that it helps you overcome procrastination. Setting goals makes you accountable. They help you avoid waiting indefinitely to achieve something. They act as constant reminders of what you need to achieve and by when. This enables you to use your time well and avoid postponing doing things. Goals are also motivational. They set a base for your drive and give you a solid endpoint.

You cannot go about life without direction. If you have no purpose in life, then you have no reason for living. Every successful person sets out with a goal in mind that they want to achieve. For instance, if you also desire to be a millionaire, then you must also have a goal.

What is your Vision?

Having a vision is one of the most important things if you want to be successful. It is your most important dream or mental picture. It doesn't have to be one; it can be a set of dreams and goals that are long-term. It defines your desired state in the future; it communicates what you desire to achieve over time. On a personal level, a vision can be termed as your WHY, while at an organizational level, it should define its purpose for existence.

Purpose of a vision

A vision is what describes what you are doing because people want to know. However, every person or organization should have a vision. There are two main reasons why you should have a vision, these are;

•First, a vision acts to inspire and give you energy. It helps guide you and give purpose to all your efforts. When you come into terms with your WHY, you get connected with your core values. It opens up your strongest motivations making a connection between your daily work and strongest values hence making you unstoppable.

•A vision helps give you direction in a world full of choices. It allows you to focus on what needs to be done and what should not be done for purposes of your achievements in the future. When you become clear about your vision and goals, it becomes easier to say yes or no with valid reasons and no fear of rejection.

How to identify and develop your vision

When you are looking to identify your vision, it is best to do this in a quiet place where you find inspiration and no distractions. When building your vision, your main question is usually WHY. What are your dreams, how do you visualize your future? Once you identify your WHY, then it becomes easy to identify your WHAT and HOW. Focus on your biggest and long-term mental picture now.

When coming up with your vision, consider the following:

•Unique – ensure that your vision is unique and fits into your values and passion. This means imagining yourself maybe three years from now in the role. How do you see yourself, and do you like your role?

•Simple – a vision must be simple, clear, and easy to understand. You are likely going to need other people to help you actualize it like employees; they need to be able to understand your vision in order to work towards its actualization.

•Focused – a good vision is not broad. It is narrow and precise.

•Bold – a vision needs to be brave and big. It must test your abilities and skills

•Beneficial –a good vision has a purpose, and it is intended to benefit you as well as others.

•Aligned – your vision should be aligned to your objectives and ways of achieving it. For purposes of authenticity, ensure that there are no contradictions with your objectives.

•Inspiring – write down your vision in a manner that is inspiring. Your vision must be inspiring not only to you but to your team as well.

•Engaging – a vision should be engaging; it must arouse your curiosity and that of your team.

Overall, to be successful, you must have a vision and work towards that vision as it acts as a road map to your destination.

Making and Achieving Goals

If you want to accomplish anything in life, setting goals is one of the most important things to do. People that do not set goals tend to have no direction and believe that life just happens to them, and that luck is what determines what they have or do not have in life. The setting goals is the difference between having control over your life and letting life have control over you. When you take charge of your life, it means you enjoy it at the same time being aware of where it is headed, and you put work towards it until you arrive at your destination.

How to set and achieve your goals

1.Let your goals align with your purpose

Sometimes you may find that you have set goals, and you are not motivated to achieve them, yet the goals look very good and relevant. The problem is not lack of motivation but that your goals lack alignment. There are two ways to set goals. The traditional and superficial way is where you set goals based on what you think you should do or accomplish. These goals can be achievable, and they do work, but they are the kind of goals that you will likely drop because they are not in harmony with your higher self or purpose. If you get to achieve them, you may not have the feeling or experience you expected because the goal was not aligned to your purpose.

When setting goals, focus on your deepest desires, passions or dreams, and your calling. Do not allow anything to dissuade you by telling you that it is unachievable. Purpose of setting goals that are aligned with your purpose and soul.

2.Let your goals be visible

Knowing what you want or how you want it is not enough. It is important to write down your plan for what you want to achieve and how you plan to achieve it. You should also make a point of looking at your goal often so that you never get distracted from them. When you write them down, keep them somewhere that you can easily see them daily and stay focused.

3.Get a partner for accountability

Goals are supposed to be achieved, especially when connected to your purpose in life. When you set goals, share them with someone so that they help you stay on course and avoid distractions.

4.Identify a goal that is worth your life

This simply means ensuring that the goals you set are so important. In the event that you find challenges or obstacles, you must still stay motivated and find the strength to keep moving on. When a goal is not important, it is easy to give up on it when you face challenges.

5.Prepare for obstacles

You already know that your journey is not smooth and that you will face opposition and obstacles. You must be mentally prepared for any roadblocks you may come across. If you do not anticipate these roadblocks beforehand and prepare for them when they happen, they can discourage you, and you give up. As you set your goals, think of all the possible roadblocks and prepare for them.

Stop Procrastination

Procrastination is when a person tries all they can to avoid doing unpleasant tasks. Many people like procrastinating. You have a task that you must accomplish, but you do not want to because it is not pleasant to do it. There are various reasons why people procrastinate. These may include:

•They find the task to be unpleasant, and they prefer to be doing something else instead. For instance, not many people want to change their behavior. They would rather stay with what is familiar rather than come up with ways to eliminate or change the habit.

•Sometimes a person does not know how to carry out the task, and as such, prefers to avoid it altogether. For instance, a person may know that something is not right with the way they react to situations and behave. However, they avoid making changes in their behavior because they don't know how to do it or to ask for help.

•Most perfectionists have a habit of procrastinating. They do this either because they feel they have nothing to change concerning behavioral change, or they feel they do not have the time to change perfectly.

Changing behavior is not a pleasant task. However, it must be done, and avoiding procrastination is a sure way to achieving your goal. Once you have identified behaviors and thoughts you want to change, you must avoid procrastination. There are various strategies to help you avoid procrastination. These include:

•A reward system – encourage yourself to do it first then have a way to reward yourself once you have done it. Try and face the unpleasant task of dealing with your negative thoughts or analyzing your negative behaviors in the morning when you are fresh.

•Do it often – if you find yourself struggling to analyze things in your past that may be contributing to your current behavior, you can break them into small tasks. Practice evaluating yourself every day for a few minutes to establish the unpleasant things. When you do it more often, you start getting used and realize it is not so bad after all.

•Note it down – have a diary or a day-to-day to-do list. When you have things written down, it is hard to ignore them. For instance, if in your to-do list, you have indicated meditating for 20 minutes each morning, you will find it difficult to skip to the following task without completing the first one.

•Have an accountability partner – some people struggle with motivating themselves. For instance, if you have decided to get rid of physical clutter that could be causing you anxiety and stress, you may find it hard to part with some items. Get someone that you will be accountable to and will help you through the journey of getting rid of the clutter.

•Ask yourself the benefits of putting it off against doing it – asking this kind of question will help in persuading you to do the unpleasant thing of transforming your thinking pattern.

•Imagine how good it will feel to accomplish your goals – the feeling of accomplishment is great. You want to transform your life for the better, but you keep putting it off. You know how you are living now is not what you desire. Imagine the feeling of being able to accomplish the change and let it motivate you.

•Stop arguing with your mind. Just get up and do it. Once you have started, it gets easier than when you have not started.

•Imagine the pain of not accomplishing it – fear can also motivate you. Imagine losing your friends or your job due to your behavior. Think of what you stand to lose and stop procrastinating today.

Breaking Bad Habits

We all have habits that we need to get rid of. Unfortunately, habits are not easy to break. Whether it is procrastinating, or changing from bad behavior, it requires discipline. Below are various strategies that one can use in order to successfully break from a bad habit.

•For every time you repeat the bad habit, find yourself. Money is a good motivator, and no one wants to part with it. You can decide the money you raise every time you repeat the bad habit will go towards a charity.

•Identify what triggers the bad habit. Knowing this is the first step towards working at breaking it.

•Make slow changes. Most people fail when they try making drastic changes at once. Take time to form new habits as you systematically break the old habits

•Think of the old habit and the new habit you want to replace with. See the best way to break it and how to start practicing the new habit.

•Constantly remind yourself of the benefits of breaking the bad habits and gaining good habits

•Change your surroundings. If your environment is the cause of your bad habits, consider changing it to avoid the triggers.

•Train yourself out of bad habits. You can do this by recording each time you behave wrongly and remind yourself to stop. This will make you stay conscious of your behavior.

•If you relapse on your bad habit, don't be too hard on yourself; instead, read the reasons why and see how you can do better.

•Think differently regarding your bad habits. Note down facts that are against your bad habits and work towards changing them.

Where to start

So you are at the deciding point if you want to be a change or not. If your answer is No, then there is no point going further, but if it is yes, then there is a journey after. When you decide that it is a Yes, you must change your mind-set to start thinking like a changed person and acting like one too.

Make an intentional decision to activate the better person within you and analyze all the ideas or critically think of other ideas. Once you identify what you want to do, it is time to come up with your vision and set out goals that are in line with your vision and your purpose. Follow all the tips in this so far and prepare for the journey ahead.

People without a vision and goals in life have no direction. They go through life aimlessly and often get frustrated.

When things do not seem to work, they develop anxiety and depression. They view the world as being unfair, develop anger issues, and often have negative thought patterns.

Breaking bad habits and forming achievable goals is a way of treating anxiety and depression through Cognitive Behavioral therapy.

Chapter 59. Overcoming Negativity And Negative Thoughts

Negative thoughts are a big cause of failure in life. Very many people allow negativity to grow up in their lives and allow negative thoughts to occupy large aspects of their daily routine. Once negativity infiltrates your mind, you are unable to take positive steps. You may stay at the same level for years just because you are afraid of time. Negative thoughts will limit your choices and actions in life. If you allow your mind to operate in negativity, you will feel limited in trying to achieve all the goals of your life.

If you want to succeed in life, you must be in a position to fight all negative thoughts. Fighting negativity starts by discovering the source of negativity in your life. You must first determine the reason why you have negative thoughts and start working on changing all the negative perspectives. If you realize that you are a negative person, you have to try and work on changing your negative perspective of life. However, you first need to find the root cause of your negativity so that you can work on it from the start.

The origin of negativity

Trying to find the source of your negativity will not only help you overcome your limitations but will also propel you to achieving your goals. The root of negativity can be any life circumstance that made you feel as if you are unworthy or unable to achieve your dreams. As we go through life, we have to encounter circumstances or people who try to show us that we are not worthy or that we may never achieve our goals. If you want to overcome all the negativity in life, you need to observe your past life experiences and try to find out any specific life-changing event that might have caused you to change your mind. Some of the activities that cause people to develop negative thoughts include:

Negative friends: Negative friends are individuals who are constantly talking about negativity. The content you allow into your mind determines the person you become. If you keep negative friends, you are likely going to have a negative perspective on life. Negative friends are individuals who do not believe in their dreams. There are many people who do not have a positive view of life. Allowing such people in your life only means that you also allow their negative thoughts and ideas into your life. One of the main reasons why people grow negative thoughts is allowing individuals who think negatively become close friends. If you are a friend with a person who does not believe in the possibility of success in any business, they will poison your mind against a business. Any time you try starting a business, they will fill you with negative ideas about making losses and eventually take away your zeal towards the venture.

For you to see success in life, you have to get rid of some people. You have to take all the negative people out of your life and focus on cresting positivity around yourself. Examine all your friends and close family members to see if there is any person who is negative. After keen observation, get rid of all the negative voices around your life. Sometimes, you have to cut some connections for you to advance to the following levels in life. Do not allow any person with negative ideas to be a part of your life.

Rejection: The other cause of negative thoughts is rejection. If you have been rejected by someone you loved or your family, you may end up allowing negative thoughts into your mind. You may end up thinking that you are worthless and that the world does not need you. Such thoughts of negativity will make you stop trying to follow your dreams. It is important for you to understand that although some people may reject you or your ideas, you are still a talented individual. If someone rejects your ideas or your vision, you need to work hard and prove them wrong.

Do not allow the words of people who doubt your ability to infiltrate your mind. Work hard and try to prove those who doubt your abilities wrong. Show them that you are dedicated to your goals and that you are willing to achieve your goals.

Failure: Failure is another cause of negativity. Failure causes a person to think that they are not worthy or that they may never achieve their dreams. When you experience failure in life, you start doubting your ability or your capacity to achieve certain goals in life. When you allow failure to infiltrate your mind, you will not try achieving anything else in life. Every time you fail at something, you need to wake up, dust yourself, and start all over again. Do not allow one instance of failure to put you on the ground. If you do fail for a minute, you should stand up and start working towards your dream again. You must stop all the negative thoughts that are associated with your past failures and start pushing your life forward towards achieving your dreams once more. Every time you fail, do not stop or try to feel sorry for yourself. Stopping even for a minute, only hinders your objectives. Failing in one objective only teaches you a new way to approach your issues. After taking the lessons, you need to try and achieve the same or something different.

Abuse: Abusive relationships are a big cause of negativity among many people. When a person suffers abuse, they end up associating everybody with the same abuse. People who have been in abusive relationships have to train themselves to get over the pain of the abuse. If you suffered abuse and chose to hold the issue in your heart, you may never be in a position to live a happy life again. Negative thoughts will infiltrate your mind, and you may end up associating any person who wants a relationship with you to negativity. You may end up thinking that every person who comes to your life is abusive or that they have evil intentions. Such negative thoughts may hinder you from getting into relationships. Most people who have suffered abuse are afraid of loving or trusting people again. They stay outside the borders of relationships and are often resistant if they are asked to get into a relationship. Such negative thoughts may hinder growth in all areas of life. Life is about interacting with people. If you do not trust the people around you, it is very hard for you to socialize or to make development in life.

Betrayal: Betrayal from friends and family members can also lead to negativity. Betrayal is a case where you get heartbroken by someone you trusted so much. Betrayal often leads to heartbreaks and loss of trust. A person who has been betrayed is unable to trust or even love. Such people look at every person with suspicious eyes and tend to think that every person is out to hurt them. It is important to ensure that you deal with all the painful instances in your life that may cause you to have negative thoughts. If you have suffered betrayal, you may try associating every person in your life with negativity. You look at people as if their only intention is to hurt your life, or they want to break your heart again. Locking yours hear and refusing to give love a chance only limits your life. For you to enjoy love and success in life, you have to open your heart up and accept all the good gestures that the people around you are trying to show.

Consequences of intrusive thoughts

Intrusive thoughts are the random ideas that pop up in your mind. In most cases, random ideas are ideas that build negativity. For instance, you might just be enjoying your meal during lunch, suddenly an idea that someone might be standing behind you pops up. Such thoughts may cause you to lack peace. It is such thoughts that cause people to have panic attacks. Intrusive thoughts are very dangerous and must be avoided at all costs. When intrusive thoughts go through our minds, they arouse our emotions and lead to a continuous flow of negative thoughts. These thoughts may light up a wildfire of negative thoughts that may lead to devastating consequences. Some of the consequences of intrusive thoughts include:

They are emotional triggers: Intrusive thoughts will instantly paint a picture of a negative situation. Some of the thoughts are reminders of past traumatic situations. If any intrusive thought comes to your mind and reminds you of a moment that was horrific in your life, you may end up suffering emotional pain caused by the same instance.

Emotional wounds take long to heal. Any trigger that gives a person the memories of the situation can lead to emotional pain.

When a person is reminded of a past emotional situation, they may experience a surge of the emotions reoccurring as if the instance just occurred again. Since the intrusive thoughts may trigger painful emotional memories, it is important for you to protect yourself from such thoughts. As soon as you feel that an intrusive idea of memories wants to pop up in your mind, choose an activity that will distract your mind. You must work hard to stop any thoughts that might take you through a negative emotional moment.

They develop negative thoughts: Intrusive thoughts do not just pop up and disappear in an instant. Once you allow the intrusive thoughts to have room in your mind, they dominate. The thoughts start spreading, and negative ideas grow. For instance, if a thought pops up in your mind making you feel that someone is standing behind you, it is easy for you to start thinking about that person having a weapon. In most cases, intrusive thoughts grow from one to another. If you choose to pay attention to your thoughts, you may find yourself thinking negatively about other things in your life. Intrusive thoughts cause a person to grow negative in all aspects of life. The negativity quickly spreads and takes over your life.

They lead to fear, worry, and anxiety: Fear worry and anxiety are all aspects of intrusive thoughts. When you allow negative thoughts to penetrate your mind, you start imagining that something negative is about to happen. If you allow such thoughts, you will start thinking about something negative happening to you. We have mentioned that people who suffer from anxiety and depression perceive negativity in the world. Such individuals are always afraid that the people around them may be harmful. Some are usually afraid of their incapacities, while others are generally afraid of the world. In all these cases, it is vital for every person to stand against negative thoughts.

If you are thinking negatively about yourself, you need to encourage yourself and boost your self-esteem. You should not be afraid of showing your talents and abilities to the world just because some people may laugh at you. Even if a person laughs at your talent, there is another person who will appreciate it. If you are afraid that the people around you may be dangerous, you need to give them a chance and try to see the beauty in every person. Intrusive thoughts will make you feel that all the people around you are harmful or that they intend to harm your life. The only way to get rid of such thoughts is by allowing yourself to see the beauty in the people around you. Allow yourself to love and to be loved, and eventually, you will see the beauty in the world.

They affect moods and emotions: Intrusive thoughts can instantly mess up your moods and emotions. You have probably seen a person who was happy suddenly turning gloomy. In some instances, a person can completely change their mood without reason. You have also probably witnessed a person smiling or laughing out loudly out of the blues. All these instances are caused by intrusive thoughts. If you allow intrusive thoughts to penetrate your mind, you may find yourself experiencing mood changes. A person may change from happy to sad just by remembering something sad.

Although intrusive thoughts try to access our minds and to remind us of past experiences, you should never allow such thoughts to influence your actions. You should not give intrusive thoughts so much power to the extent that they control your mood in the day. Even if you are reminded of an emotional moment, you have to fight such emotions.

Generally, intrusive thoughts target our emotions. If the thought targets your emotions, you should also try to control your emotions. The coordination between your mind and your thoughts should allow you to overcome all the fears in your life. You should control your emotions if you want to overcome negative thoughts. You must ensure that you break all the negative fears in your life and deal with the emotional situations brought about by intrusive thoughts on the spot.

The types of emotions you experience play an important role in your overall outlook on life. You must condition your mind to have positivity. You must learn to train your mind in such a way that you may experience more positive emotions. Positive emotions include joy, happiness, amusement, love, hope, pride, etc. All these emotions contribute to your growth as a person. They help you push your life forward in a positive direction, and they take away all the negativity in your life. When you condition your mind to experience positive emotions, you stop focusing on the negative ones. In life, there are individuals who are generally happy and joyful. Such individuals experience joy, happiness, and love more than others. At the same time, there are those who are generally sad. Such individuals experience bitterness, hatred, and other negative emotions. Your happiness and progress in life depend on the type of emotions that you allow yourself to experience. If you allow yourself to experience positive emotions, you will live a positive life. If you condition your mind to experience negative emotions, you may experience negativity in all areas of life. But how exactly do you condition your mind to experience positive emotions?

Focus on positive things

You are the product of the things you think about. As mentioned, the mind is structured in such a way that a person becomes what they believe. If you think about something long enough, you start believing it. Whatever you focus your thoughts on becomes part of you. If you focus your thoughts on the negative side of life, you start believing in it, and it becomes part of your emotions. However, if you focus your thoughts on the positive side of life, positivity becomes part of your belief, and it starts manifesting in your life. If you want to show positivity, you need to start thinking about the benefits of everything you do. Anything that troubles your mind must be looked at positively. When you are in the deepest of all troubles, you should ask yourself whether there is anything positive about the situation. Always try to pick the positives out of every condition. When things aren't working for you, think about the positive side of life. Before you start a project, either a business or a family project, first count the positives. This is not to mean that there will be no negatives in life, but you should choose to ignore them and choose positivity. To live a positive life, your main objective should always be to attain happiness.

Attract positive friends

What you hear also has a way of influencing your life. If you spend a lot of time listening to negative people, the negative ideas start building up in your mind. If you spend time with people who always view negativity in every situation, you also become negative. If you want to have positive emotions, attract positive people. Stay close to people who believe in love, joy, and happiness. It is believed that positive emotions, such as joy and happiness, are infectious. If you stay close to a jovial person, you will find yourself being happy and showing happiness. It is important to understand how the people who are close to you impact your life.

If you get to the office and realize that your colleague is moody or sad, the chances are that you will have a rough day at work. The same case applies to every aspect of your life. In every aspect of life, try staying together with people who exude confidence. Stay with people who feel confident, loving, and warm if you want to start showing these, traits too.

Plan a positive routine

The actions you take on a daily basis also play a major role in your emotions. If you spend the day taking care of things that make you feel good about yourself, you are likely to exude positivity and show positive emotions. For instance, reading a may make you feel intelligent and lead to confidence in everything you do.

Other activities that may bring out the positive side of your life include physical activities such as running, dancing to music, and lifting weights. Workout activities enhance the flow of blood in the body, keeping you light and energetic. Physical activities make you feel fit and beautiful. Loving your self-image and your body makes you experience positive emotions such as love and happiness. When creating your daily routine, incorporate activities that attract positive emotions. Think of anything that makes you feel confident, beautiful, and intelligent. Avoid activities that make you dull and gloomy such as oversleeping or overeating. Think about activities that are entertaining while at the same time, educational and impactful to your overall health.

Chapter 60. Identifying Assumptions And Core Beliefs

One of the first steps you engage in when you begin the process of CBT is learning how to identify core beliefs and values. When you are able to do that, you are able to begin the process of identifying problematic thoughts. When you want to identify a core value, you are essentially signing yourself up to delve deep into your mind, diving into your unconscious thoughts and feelings in hopes of gaining insight into your situation. These beliefs and values are largely unnoticed in your day-to-day life unless you actively know how to look for them and decide to do so, so most people struggle to even acknowledge them. When you learn to do so, however, you unlock an important skill necessary to understand yourself.

When you learn to identify your core beliefs, you begin to understand your own motivators, learning about the things that make you behave the way you do. This is crucial to this process, which is all about recognizing the cycle between thoughts, feelings, and behaviors. You are essentially learning to identify the thoughts within that cycle so you can learn how to best cope with them.

What Are The Core Beliefs And Values?

Core beliefs are automatic thoughts that you have that you believe wholeheartedly are true about yourself. They compose the way you think of yourself, influencing everything from how you behave to what you think you deserve in relationships.

They determine whether you put up with abuse or assume that you deserve to be abandoned or rejected. They determine how likely you are to anything, and they occur without you being aware of them.

Your core beliefs exist deep in your unconscious, swaying your behavior without requiring you to use up any important cognitive resources considering things. They decide many of your emotional, instinctive behaviors, and you always default to them. You will always take your core beliefs as factual unless you are given a good enough reason to reject them. Even then, rejecting them can be a long, arduous struggle on its own simply because you do not want to admit that you do not know your own behaviors and personality type. In correcting your core beliefs, you are essentially declaring that you do not know how to judge yourself and that you do not have a good understanding of who you are as a person.

How Do Core Beliefs Impact Behavior?

Core beliefs have a major impact on behavior. They are determining factors for much of your own behavioral patterns. When you act upon your core beliefs, you are essentially behaving in ways that you accept to be true inherently. For example, if you have a core belief that says that your family and friends all reject you in the end because you are unworthy of love or affection, you will always approach relationships feeling guarded and tense. You will constantly assume the worst in those around you, which can have a hugely negative impact on your relationships, pushing people away, and of course, as soon as someone chooses to leave the relationship after being treated accordingly, you automatically assume it is to justify your core belief. This can go even further, with you even contorting what has happened around you into delusional interpretations of what has happened. If your friend legitimately is held up at work, for example, and has to cancel your girls' night out, you may immediately convince yourself that it is, in fact, proof that your friend does not like you. You assume that your friend is intentionally trying to lie to you and instead of behaving in an understanding manner, you get standoffish and offended before getting upset simply because you assume it was intentionally done to bother you.

Identifying Core Beliefs With CBT

Identifying core beliefs is a relatively simple concept to understand, though the process can cause distress. It is common for people to feel upset or distressed as they parse through their thoughts and feelings simply because they are uncovering some of these distortions that imply that they believe they are not good enough. They are essentially admitting that even they, themselves, believe they are unworthy of care and attention, and in doing so, they have to admit that the one person that should like them, themselves, have low opinions.

When you want to identify a core belief, what you are going to do is approach the situation first with identifying the thought behind an emotion, and then attempt to analyze it until you arrive at a statement about yourself. For example, you may feel anxious about your social interactions, believing that they are largely unhappy because no one legitimately likes you.

You may point to a recent time in which you felt intense sadness and anxiety. That intense feeling is there to tell you that something was wrong there and you need to pay attention to it to get to the root of the situation. Identify that situation and ask yourself what happened at that moment. You may notice that it coincided with your friend having to skip out on girls' night because she was too busy at work and was forced into mandatory overtime. You felt sad, followed by anxious, followed by angry.

Now that you have that feeling identified, you should take the moment to understand what those feelings implied about you. You may spend some time reflecting on the situation before finally settling on the fact that feeling upset meant that you felt insecure. That is a good observation, but it is not the end of the thought chain. You must then consider what that means to you. You may ask why you feel so insecure and consider why. The answer may be something along the lines of feeling as though you are unimportant or unwanted in your friends' groups. Again, consider why that matter—you may decide that you feel like people only like you out of pity. One last time, identify why that is relevant to you and what that says about you, and you reach the core belief: You feel unworthy and undeserving of love.

With that core belief identified, you are then ready to move on to other steps in the CBT process. There are, of course, several ways that you could go through this process to identify any core beliefs you hold. For example, you could use journaling to go through that process or decide that you would rather do self-reflection, simply letting your thoughts run loose and dictate where they go on their own.

Journaling

Some people prefer to resort to journaling to understand their thought processes. This is actually quite smart—it enables you to have a relatively easy to follow written record of the thoughts you are tracking, and in developing them, you will be able to understand how you think. This can be essential, especially if you are trying to understand behavioral or thought patterns that you may hold.

When you want to engage in journaling, one of the most important points is ensuring that you have a quiet time in which you can stop and consider what is happening without stress or interruption. You want to be able to entirely focus on your train of thought as you go through this process. Try setting aside the same time every day for a chance to reflect.

Once you sit down to journal, stop and consider any trains of thought you may have at that particular moment. You want to know exactly what is on your mind and acknowledge it. Then, follow that one train of thought, identifying what it means to you, how it is relevant, and searching for the core belief at the heart of it. As you do this, over time, you will begin to uncover more and more core beliefs about yourself. While this does not necessarily have any structure, it helps to keep each journal entry limited somewhat to a similar theme so you can analyze it to understand how it relates.

Your thought process likely looks something like this in written form:

Notice how the chain is a repeated attempt to identify the meaning of the realization all the way down until you arrive at the core belief or thought behind the process. This is important—you are essentially spiraling down the rabbit hole of your thoughts and implications until you reach the truth that you hold.

Self-Reflection

Self-reflection, again, follows a similar pattern. When you are self-reflecting, however, you are going to follow the trains of thought within yourself.

You are not focusing so much on writing down what has occurred so much as pursuing your natural trains of thought. You simply allow your thoughts to go without stopping them, waiting to see where they end up eventually.

This is for those who struggle to journal or write about emotions, or perhaps people who cannot write at that moment, such as if they are driving but would like to get to the core beliefs located at the heart of some pretty negative emotional reactions.

The important part is not so much to get everything written down, but rather to ensure you understand yourself. You need to recognize how you truly feel about yourself, and when you learn to recognize that, you can then begin to cope with it or change it to something effective that you would rather see yourself as. Either way, you develop a useful skill as a result of identifying the core belief.

Remember, no matter the method you choose to identify your core beliefs, you are likely to feel some pretty strong emotions. This is okay and even expected in many situations, and despite the emotions, you feel, you need to recognize that you are worth going through the process. It is worth challenging these beliefs despite the fact that doing so can and likely will bring about pain as well. When you are challenging these beliefs, you are essentially challenging yourself as a person, despite the fact that your perception of you may very well be too negative to actually be healthy or maintained, or even accurate to begin with. It is okay to get upset, and it is even okay to cry—understand that the pain says it is working. All healing processes involve pain, but that is okay—the pain says your body and mind are processing the issues you are facing, and in processing them, you are able to better cope in the future.

Chapter 61. Mindfulness

What Is Mindfulness?

If you pay attention to what your mind is doing, you'll notice two strong tendencies:

1The mind focuses on things other than what is happening right now. Most of the time we're thinking about events that have already happened or that might happen in the future. Thus our well-being is often affected by things that have little to do with the moment in which we find ourselves.

2The mind continually evaluates our reality as good or bad. It does so based on whether things are working out the way we want them to. We try to cling to circumstances we like and push away those we dislike.

These tendencies are part of what it means to be human. They can also cause us problems and needless suffering. Focusing on the future can lead to worry and anxiety, most often about things that will never happen. Ruminating on events from the past can lead to distress and regret about things that are no longer in our control.

In the process, we miss the once-in-a-lifetime experience that each moment offers. We don't really take in the people around us, the natural beauty of our surroundings, or the sights, sounds, and other sensations that are here right now.

Our constant and automatic effort to judge things as either for us or against us also creates unnecessary pain. We often end up resisting things we don't like, even when such resistance is futile.

A perfect example is raging against the weather—no amount of cursing the rain will make it stop, and we'll only frustrate ourselves in the process.

The practice of mindfulness offers an antidote to both of these habits.

PRESENCE

Mindfulness is as simple as bringing our awareness to the present. That's it. If you're walking the dog, pay attention to that experience. If you're having lunch, focus on having lunch. If you're arguing with your partner or embracing afterward, be fully in that experience.

Sometimes when we learn what mindfulness is we say, "I already know that I'm walking the dog. I know I'm having lunch. How is that supposed to be helpful?" But mindfulness is more than knowing that we're doing something. It's about going deeper, intentionally cultivating a connection with our experience. We don't just walk the dog—we notice the color of the sky, the feel of the ground under our feet, the sounds our dog makes, the periodic pulls on the leash. It's opening our awareness to elements of our experience that we normally miss.

At the same time, a mindful approach doesn't require that we do anything in addition to what we're engaging in. If we're running, we're running. If we're driving, we're driving. People sometimes protest that being mindful in certain situations would be distracting, even dangerous. In fact, the opposite is true—we're safer and less distracted when our attention is fixed on what we're doing.

Simply being present in our lives accomplishes two things at once. First, it allows us to get more out of what's happening, so we don't sleepwalk through our lives. We can discover the richness in our reality, even in the most mundane activities. Second, when we're present, we're not ruminating about the past or fearing the future, which is a big part of why mindfulness practice reduces anxiety and depression.

So much of our unhappiness arises from things that have nothing to do with what's real in this moment. For example, I was walking home from the train one evening and started thinking about my children's health. Before I knew it, I was imagining a tragic scenario in which one of them was gravely sick, and I began to feel anxious and downcast as though it were already happening. When I caught myself and came back to the present, I noticed what was real: the lengthening light, the birds flying, the green grass, and blue sky. My kids were healthy as far as I knew. I didn't have to live in my tragic fantasy. It was hard not to smile with that realization as I headed home to see them.

"The way to experience nowness is to realize that this very moment, this very point in your life, is always the occasion." —Chögyam Trungpa, Shambhala: The Sacred Path of the Warrior

ACCEPTANCE

The second core feature of mindful awareness is acceptance, which means opening to our experience as it unfolds.

After a couple miserable nights, Matt realized he needed a new perspective on his daughter's bedtime. The following night he decided to try a different approach—what if he let the night play out however it was going to? It's not like his resistance made things better: it was making him frustrated toward his baby every night. He resolved to do his best to help her fall asleep, and to release his fierce attachment to controlling exactly when that happened.

The first time his daughter began to cry, Matt took a calming breath before going in to her room. Instead of telling himself, "I hate this," or, "This is ridiculous," he thought, "This is what's happening right now." Then he took stock of what that statement actually meant: He was standing by the crib of his baby girl, whom he loved more than words. He was patting her tiny back, which was the size of his hand. He could hear her breathing begin to slow. He realized how in that moment he had no real complaint about anything. He wasn't cold, hungry, thirsty, or in danger. His daughter was healthy. She just wasn't asleep yet. Maybe things were exactly as they ought to be.

Matt's example reveals important corollaries of mindful acceptance. First, it doesn't mean we stop having preferences for how things go. Of course, Matt still wanted his baby to fall asleep quickly and easily, and wanted to have more of the evening to himself to unwind.

Accepting meant holding those preferences more lightly, and not assuming his daughter was doing something wrong by not being asleep when he wanted her to be.

Accordingly, Matt didn't throw in the towel and stop following the bedtime routine he and his wife had agreed on to transition their baby to falling asleep on her own in her crib. He stuck to his plan, offering predictability and consistency while recognizing that he couldn't control his daughter's sleep.

When we stop fighting against the way things are, we relieve an enormous portion of our stress. In my career I had a very difficult supervisor, and I often found myself tied up in my thoughts as I tried to make sense of how unreasonable she was. Finally, I reached a point of accepting that she could just be difficult, period. My acceptance didn't change her behavior, but it did free me from acting as if she were doing something surprising. She was simply being true to form.

A crucial part of acceptance is that it lets us respond appropriately to the facts in front of us. My acceptance of my boss's temperament made it clear to me that I needed to find work elsewhere, which underscores the distinction between acceptance and apathy.

Benefits of Mindfulness

Training in mindfulness helps with a wide range of conditions. A partial list includes anxiety, attention deficit/hyperactivity disorder (ADHD), chronic pain, depression, eating disorders, excessive anger, insomnia, obsessive-compulsive disorder (OCD), relationship difficulties, smoking cessation, and stress. Many treatment programs have been developed that integrate mindfulness practices into CBT. One of the first was mindfulness-based cognitive therapy (MBCT) for depression, developed by psychologists Zindel Segal, John Teasdale, and Mark Williams. These developers reasoned that the tools of mindfulness were well suited to remedy some of the factors that contribute to depression. For example, practicing paying attention to one's internal experience could strengthen one's ability to detect early warning signs of depression, like unrealistic negative automatic thoughts.

MBCT includes elements of traditional CBT for depression and integrates training in mindfulness to protect against relapse. Much of the training focuses on using mindful awareness to notice problematic thoughts. It also emphasizes learning a different relationship with our thoughts. We can learn to recognize them as simply thoughts rather than something we need to react to.

Multiple studies have shown that MBCT achieves this aim. For example, a study by Teasdale, Segal, Williams, and their colleagues found that among individuals with recurrent depression, MBCT reduced the risk for relapse by nearly half versus the comparison group that received treatments other than MBCT (e.g., antidepressant medication, other types of psychotherapy).

Acceptance and Commitment Therapy (ACT), developed by Steven Hayes, has also received strong research support for treating several conditions like depression, anxiety, and chronic pain. As the name suggests, it emphasizes acceptance of our experience in the service of committing to action that supports our values. Closely related to ACT is Acceptance-Based Behavioral Therapy, designed by Susan Orsillo and Lizabeth Roemer to treat generalized anxiety disorder. And the best-tested treatment for borderline personality disorder—a debilitating and difficult-to-treat condition—includes a strong mindfulness component to address the difficulty handling the strong emotion that is part of this diagnosis. Mindfulness clearly has beneficial effects on many psychological issues. How does this approach lead to improvements?

Mindfulness Myths

Many people have objections to the idea of mindfulness when they first learn about it, and these objections can prevent a person from engaging in the practice. Most of these objections seem to come from misunderstandings about what it means to be mindful. Common myths include:

Mindfulness is a religious or cultish practice. Because mindfulness is an integral part of some religious traditions, we might assume it's an inherently religious activity. However, being in our lives and actually doing what we're doing doesn't belong to any particular religious or spiritual approach, and can be practiced without adherence to any religious tradition (including mystical or New Age spirituality). Still, mindfulness is not contradictory to religion. Whatever our beliefs and values, we can embrace them more completely through a mindful approach.

Mindfulness is unscientific. People sometimes object to the concept of mindfulness because they "prefer to live in the realm of fact and science." If you need solid evidence for the benefits of mindfulness, you're in luck—a large and growing number of rigorous studies have found that mindfulness helps with a wide range of conditions like anxiety and depression. It has even been found to change the brain. Mindfulness practice is supported by solid science.

Mindfulness means spending a lot of time in our heads. Language is an imperfect tool, and it's easy to misunderstand what "mindfulness" refers to. Rather than dwelling in our minds, mindfulness is about connecting with our basic experiences and letting go of the stories we wrap them in. To be mindful is to be aware and in a state of openness to what we discover.

Mindfulness means giving up any efforts to affect our world for the better. The word acceptance can mean we're not going to try to change something, like when we say, "I've accepted that I'm not going to play professional sports." In the context of mindfulness, acceptance means we don't deny that reality is reality. We're willing to see a situation the way it is. This kind of acceptance can actually be the catalyst for change, as when we accept that there is crushing poverty in our community and decide to take action to ameliorate it.

Mindfulness is weakness. If we assume mindfulness means never taking a stand, it would follow that mindfulness is a sort of milquetoast practice—especially if we equate fighting and resistance with strength. But on the contrary, letting go is difficult. It takes hard work and determination to let go of our habits of perseverating on the past and fearing the future. Mindfulness helps us direct our strength in ways that serve us.

Mindfulness means never having goals. If we're focused on the present and practicing acceptance, how can we set goals or plan for the future? It might seem paradoxical, but planning for the future and setting goals are completely compatible with mindfulness practice. As noted, accepting reality can give rise to efforts to change a situation. For example, I might accept that my house is too hot and decide to buy an air conditioner. And we can practice presence even while setting goals or making plans, being immersed in the reality of those forward-looking activities.

Mindfulness equals meditation. The word mindfulness often conjures up images of someone sitting cross-legged and meditating, which makes sense as meditation is a very common mindfulness practice. But meditation is not the only way to practice being mindful. An infinite number of activities offer opportunities to develop openness to our experience, from relaxing with friends to running an ultra-marathon. The advantage of formal practice like meditation is that it offers a concentrated dose of training the mind to focus on the now. We can then bring that training into any moment of our lives. Indeed, I've found that practicing meditation leads to more experiences of spontaneous mindful presence in our day-to-day activities.

MINDFULNESS-BASED STRESS REDUCTION (MBSR)

You don't have to be dealing with a psychological disorder to benefit from training in mindfulness. Most of us would be well served by tools to deal with the ordinary stresses of being alive. Jon Kabat-Zinn developed a well-known eight-week program called MBSR, which thousands of people have completed. It includes:

•Education about the principles of mindfulness

•Training in meditation

•Mindful awareness of the body

•Gentle yoga
•Mindfulness in activities
The MBSR program is a reliable way to reduce anxiety and increase one's ability to manage stress. If you're interested in learning more, Dr. Kabat-Zinn details the program in his Full Catastrophe Living. You can also check online for MBSR or mindfulness-based courses near you.
MINDFUL WALKING
If you're ready to put mindfulness into action, an easy way to get started is to go for a mindful walk. In this exercise you'll practice bringing to your experience greater attention and curiosity than usual. You might choose to notice:
•The solidness of the ground beneath your feet
•The movements and muscle contractions required to balance and walk: the swing of your arms, the push-off of each foot, the contractions in your leg muscles and lower back, etc.
•Sounds you're creating, like your breath and your footfalls
•Surrounding sounds, like birds, cars, and the wind through the trees
•The sights around you, including things you might have passed countless times but never really noticed
•Smells in the air
•The sensation of air on your skin and the warmth of the sun
•The quality of the light—its angle, intensity, the colors it creates
•The particularities of the sky above you
This approach can be applied to any experience you choose, from the most mundane to the most sublime.

Chapter 62. Building Self-Esteem

In the world that we live in, it is easy to get lost in the hustle and bustle of the fast-paced happenings around us. So much so that, one finds themselves unable to take time and sit down and reflect on how they are going through life. Am I living indeed? Or am I just drifting like a paper boat in the river? What drives me? And what gives me my self-confidence? What kind of person am I, and how do I interact with the world outside?

Well, in all honesty, sitting down and reflecting can be, well, tiresome for some, and uncomfortable and exhausting for others, especially with so many exciting things going on around us. The little screen beckons on your palm. On the other end, your job calls, to your other side, the family wants a piece of you. Ahead of you, your friends want to know what your plans for Friday are. Then, they want to know your plans for Monday and Tuesday and the rest of the year. Behind you, well, many other things going on but we are not in a horror movie so we won't focus on what's behind you. That's for you to find it out. Sorry.

So, now that I have your attention, what exactly do we consider our self-esteem? What comes to mind when we talk of self-esteem? Is it your job that gives you so much joy? Your family and friends? Your downtime?

Well, we have come to think of self-esteem and self-confidence as two of the same, and we use them interchangeably most of the time. But down to the finer details, these two are different. You could, for example, be someone who has very high self-esteem but then, suffer frequently from bouts of low self-confidence. Yes, you look at this text funny, but it's possible and accurate.

Self-esteem refers to how you view yourself generally. This view is often shaped by what we have experienced and how we then were able to react to our experiences. People who have gone through trauma or abuse, for example, may have low self-esteem. This issue is because the experiences subjected them to negative experiences that stressed them to the point that they lost hope in their existence. Your self-esteem means being comfortable in your entire humanity, down to those bits of yourself that perhaps are embarrassing or shameful. It is about knowing how you feel, act, think, behave, and how that shapes your existence in the world today.

Self-confidence, on the other hand, is your ability to trust in yourself and rise to new challenges. Often, one builds their confidence through their achievements and skills. Unlike self-esteem, which touches based on one's entire person (the physical, emotional, mental, and spiritual) and therefore once built can be hard to shake, self-confidence may vary from one situation to another. Since it we link it to abilities and one that people tie to high visibility, it can, therefore, change with regards to the situation. So, for example, I may be a person with very high self-esteem, but I am not good at solving complex mathematical problems, then I will experience low self-confidence in situations that would need me to focus on mathematical problems.

The above passage then brings us then to introverts and how self-esteem and self-confidence will come out different in a brooder.

Many people conflate introversion with shyness, which may not be necessarily true. Shyness is a state of being that we link to social anxiety and the inability of a shy person to create contact with other people. One can be shy either from nature or nurture. On most occasions, self-esteem and self-confidence could be low in a shy person. Shyness always means that the shy person is willing to go out and make friends, but their low view of themselves (low self-esteem) and their abilities (self-confidence) hold them back.

However, an introvert is someone who often loves to spend time on their own because that is where they get their energy. The introverts are happier, more at ease when they are alone. While introversion and shyness may overlap, they do not always occur at the same time all the time. An introvert maybe someone who is adept at making friends, and they may be socially well-adjusted and confident, with high self-esteem, but because their brain is wired in such a way that they function better and are happier and more productive when in their own company, they often tend to spend a significant chunk of their time alone, preferably indoors. An introvert will usually avoid the spotlight.

So, since the introverts love spending time on their own, surely there are downsides to that. Yes, indeed, there are weaknesses in being introverted.

Weaknesses of Being an Introvert

You Get Overlooked

As we said early in the chapter, as an introvert, you tend to get lost in your world, even when with others. So, this can lead to you being overlooked and ignored in a group setting.

You Appear Snobbish

Because of an introvert's desire to avoid being the center of attention, you will then avoid making overtures to other people. You will avoid making small talks for fear of the awkwardness that comes with it, and you will turn down invitations to parties and events. These situations then mean that people will label you as a snob to may who do not understand you. Thus, people will avoid you because of this.

Lack of a Wide Network

To grow in many things, one needs a network, and to build a network, you will need to go out there and meet people. But this is not easy for an introvert. They want their space for themselves and may find networking stressful and thus avoid it entirely doesn't mean that they are incapable of networking. They do not want the stress that comes from being around many people at once, trying to build rapport. An introvert will want to be social at their convenience, which, unfortunately, is not how the world works.

Workplace Struggles

Because of their dislike of shallow socialization, many introverts will often struggle with workplace interactions, which calls for frequent interactions between colleagues but does not allow for the formation of deep, meaningful bonds between co-workers. As such, because of their distaste for pointless interactions, they will often avoid the situations that need them to be or do that, thus, will not create the impression that they value teamwork, even when the reality is quite different. As we said, the workplace and school are built for extroverts, so, the introverts will often not get their end of the bargain met.

Bad First Impression

Let's be honest p- we often make judgments about other people based on our first interaction with them. As such, the first impression matters a lot and often goes a long way to shape how you interact further with the new stranger.

For an introvert, though, their dislike for the spot often means that they will appear aloof when meeting new people. Because they are so protective of their personal space, they will appear unfriendly and rude. This situation could be damaging to an introvert's limited but highly valuable social life.

But there are strengths to this too.

Strengths of Being an Introvert

Focused

Because of their desire to avoid too much clutter, introverts will often tend to be more focused and may become more productive at work or in school.

They Think A Lot

The word introvert comes from introspecting. An introvert, therefore, will more likely be a person who is often deeply engaged in their thought process. Because they spend a lot of time on their own, they develop an inner voice that allows them to build their self-awareness, which makes them likely to become better problem solvers.

Many critical thinkers have been described as introverts, among them Albert Einstein, Charles Darwin, and Sir Isaac Newton. Albert Einstein has often been quoted saying that the monotony that came with being on your own is what stimulates creativity, which then would explain why many of the most prominent thinkers are introverts.

Great Listeners

Introverts tend to be great listeners. Because they think a lot to themselves, they become more aware of how their actions affect the world around them. This ability then makes them more willing to listen to others and thus, make great friends.

The fact that they talk less also makes them unlikely to interfere when the other person tells.

Planners

An introvert will often do the most to avoid being in the spotlight, whether for wrong reasons or the right reasons. If their boss calls them to, say, make a presentation, an introvert will take their time to make the preparations necessary to carry through the situation. This ability to make a point of making sufficient preparation means that they will often avoid being caught flat-footed and they will ensure that they say the right things when the time comes. This preparation allows them to become great orators.

They Tend to Be Creative

While this is not true for all creatives and all introverts, being introverts makes it more likely that one can develop their creativity. In solitude, an introvert may find that they spend more time in their thoughts, which allows for ideas to form and evolve. Among the many introverted creatives are; the father of modern horror H. P Lovecraft, Harry Porter Creator J.K Rowling, Dr. Seuss among others.

Creativity tends to need time for creative person to be on their own so that it can develop. In a rush to do one thing or another, the creative mind, which is spontaneous, will be stifled under the stress of plans and schedules and will often be buried deep when one is continuously in motions. Therefore, the ability for the creative to find peace and calm, even when they are in the presence of noise and distraction is a testament to how may introvert can dominate the creative field. Plus, because many creative projects often mean working alone most of the time, at least, this is heaven to the introvert who prefers solitude. And if you are an introvert and can make a career out of your solitude fortress, then why not?

Quiet, So Less problematic - Most of The Time

Now this is not to say that extroverts are problematic, though to be honest, aren't they?

However, as we have said, introverts do not thrive when under too much attention, or when put under the spotlight. This revelation means that their being quiet is often a way of drawing attention away from themselves, which makes them then a darling in situations that requires repose and calmness.

Unlike the extrovert who is more outgoing and gets energized when around others, an introvert will often want to maintain their peace and will thus, be unlikely to cause problems. They will not court unnecessary controversy or perform things they do not feel comfortable doing. This situation then means that having them around, say as friends and family at a time when you want someone to be around to keep you company is glorious.

They Are Less Reckless

This advantage is because introverts are naturally inclined to be deliberative and thoughtful. Because an introvert spends more time observing, thinking, and reflecting, they often gain a deeper understanding of whatever they want to do. This understanding then allows them to gauge what the risks and paybacks for a particular course of action are worth it. This ties in to their need to plan to the last detail.

As such, they may then make better leaders since they will often try to find the best course of action which they wouldn't want to regret. As such, they avoid making hasty choices

Tend to Cultivate Better Relationships

This point is again, not to say that extroverts don't form great relationships. However, some of the predisposing traits of introversion make them more likely to want to create a strong personal bond, over them becoming popular among a large group of people.

Again, we can tie this to many of their other traits. Because of their tendency to think a lot, and more deeply, they will extend their trust to very few people, with the intent of forming deep, meaningful relationships with them. As a result, because of their ability to listen better and take their time to think through things, they often gain the complete trust of the people that they allow into their world, which allows for more vulnerable, cherished interactions with their friends.

Chapter 63. Meditation

People who practice meditation are happier, healthier and in some cases prosperous than the people who do not. Practicing mindfulness and meditation has stunning benefits to anybody who takes their time to put these skills into test.

If in any case, you have already tried mindfulness, meditation, as well as other positive psychological interventions, you might have been for the idea that these exercises "were not for you..." after trying them out a couple of times. However, similar to any other skill, mindfulness requires practice. Do it over and over again! In some cases, the only hindrance to achieving our goals is a little bit of direction.

Mindfulness Activities For Groups And Group Therapy

Group therapy that involves mindfulness has shown a series of reassuring results. Its effectiveness can be compared to Cognitive Behavioral Therapy (CBT) that is unarguably predominant in the world of clinical psychology.

There is also proof that carrying out group mindful meditation therapy has the same flattering results as individual cognitive-behavioral therapy (CBT). In a world with very few clinical psychologists in comparison to their need for them, as well as in a period when individual therapy time is expensive and limited, the proven effectiveness of group-based therapy is exceptional news.

You might not really feel like visiting a therapist and that is okay because there are mindfulness- focused groups that deepen and share meditation practice. Here, we will be focusing on four crucial practical exercises from such groups.

Fleming And Kocovski's Treatment Plan

Fleming band Kocovski came up with this program in 2007 as a form of group mindfulness-based treatment. It primarily aims at alleviating social anxiety. It is a good illustration of how mindfulness exercises can be integrated into a group setting because of its numerous benefits.

The treatment program entails a group of roughly 8 members who meet for 2 hours weekly for a period of 12 weeks. The first part of each session is dedicated to a brief mindful exercises followed by a discussion. The treatment program's mindfulness exercise can be broken down as follows:

Session 1: Raisin Technique

The raisin technique is unarguably the best preliminary exercise for amateurs to commence exercising mindfulness. With a variety of foods, anybody can carry out this technique. However, the exercise would be more effective if the food has a peculiar smell, taste or texture. The coordinator in this exercise gives the participants raisins and instructs them to pretend that they have never ever seen a raisin. The coordinator then brings to their attention the following things:

□ How the raisin feels
□ How it looks
□ It's smell
□ How the participant's skin reacts to the manipulation
□ How it tastes

Directing the entire focus on raisin is aims at pulling the mind of the participant to the contemporary, to whatever has been placed before them. We may have encountered raisins almost every day but we have never taken time to really notice them

"By directing their focus on the raisin, they are holding in their hand and making an effort to notice all the details about it, the improbability of them expending time, energy and attention on ruminating or worrying about other areas of their lives."

When you systematically follow these directions and observe, it is very easy to concentrate your focus on what is before you. It is normal for your mind to wander off sometimes. All you have to do is guide it back into the exercise.

Session 2: The Body Scan

This exercises very little in terms of tools and props and it is also advantageous to beginners because it is easily accessible. For effective, somebody has to follow the following guide by the founder and expert of mindfulness-based stress reduction.

1: Here, the participants have to lie on their backs with their feet slightly falling apart and their palms facing up.

2: Here, the coordinator instructs the participants to try and stay calm during this exercise, and can only move when it is extremely mandatory to change their position.

3: The coordinator then starts guides the body scan. This begins by participants concentrating on their breathtaking note of the rhythm and the feeling of breathing in and out.

The coordinator cautions the participants against trying to alter their breathing but instead concentrate on the rhythm and feeling of breathing bin and out.

4: The coordinator shifts focus to the body: how the cloth feels like on the skin, the temperature of the body and the surroundings as well as the texture of the surface on which the body is lying.

5: The coordinator directs awareness to the sore, tingling, or feeling remarkably light or heavy, he/she instructs the participant to take note of any part of their body that does not feel anything or the parts that are highly responsive.

A normal body scan is supposed to run through all parts of the body, keenly taking note of how each area feels. Usually, the scan moves in a systematic manner through the body. For example, beginning from the feet and moving upwards to the toes, lower limbs, knees, laps, pelvic area, abdomen, chest area, upper back, lower back, the arms, neck, the head as well as the face.

After the scan is done to completion, the participants can come back into the real world by opening their eyes slowly then proceeding to a snug sitting posture.

Session 3: Mindfulness In Seeing

To some people, lacking the visual spur can result into a suffocating feeling. Ultimately, naturally experiencing a healthy imagination is not something that everybody goes through. The process of mindful seeing may be instrumental to anybody who relates to this.

It is an easy exercise that requires a window that has some sort of panorama.

The coordinator instructs the participants as follows:

1: Locate a window that has beautiful things to be seen.

2: Take a look at everything that is visible. Do not engage in any form of categorization and labeling of what you see outside the window. For instance, instead of seeing things in terms of 'stop sign' or 'bird' try to concentrate on aspects like colors, textures or patterns.

3: Take note of the movement of leave or grass in the breeze. Take note of the numerous shapes available in this miniature part of the world that you have your eyes focused on. Try to view things from the point of view of somebody who is not familiar with sights.

4: You are only allowed to observe without making any form of criticism. Stay aware but avoid being distracted.

5: In case your mind drifts away, take note of something like a color that will help revert your focus to the seeing.

Session 4: Mindfulness In Listening

This exercise is a product of the positive psychology toolkit and it presents mindfulness in listening as group therapy.

Mindfulness in listening is a very crucial mastery and can be significant to the mindfulness exercise of groups. Generally, people flourish they feel fully "seen" and "heard" and the exercise of mindful listening offers a break from directing our focus at the self or our own response.

Alternatively, mindful listening can develop an inner calmness where both individuals feel fee of judgments, preconceptions, and the listener's attention is not 'stolen' by inner chatter while grasping positive communication capabilities that are valuable.

This technique involves:

1: Instruct participants to think about something that is stressing them and something that they look forward to.

2: When everybody is done, every person shares his/her problem with the group in turns.

3: Instruct every person to direct their consciousness into what talking makes them feel, what they think about sharing with other people something that is stressful or something positive that they are looking forward to.

4: The coordinator instructs participants to observe their feelings, thoughts, as well as body reaction during listening and talking.

Mindfulness Techniques For Depression And Anger

Depression

Mindfulness is important in the treatment of depression because it reduces symptoms as well as the risk of debilitating deterioration. One study that involved eleven individuals undergoing depression came to the conclusion that there are three important aspects that make mindfulness efficacious in the treatment of depression.

I. Mindfulness assists patients in learning how to be present at the moment. This enables the patients to take some time and get hold of feelings and thoughts and as a result, choose a response that is not guided by their current emotions.

II. Mindfulness explains to patients that it is okay to give "NO" as an answer to others. This gives them a balance in their lives and also improve their confidence.

III. Mindfulness enables patients to be present with others. This means that they become more aware of their relationship and are capable of acknowledging their communication shortcomings and therefore more efficiently relate with others

IV. We have already taken a look at practices that focus on muscle relaxation and breathing. For example, the body scan and the three-minute breathing space. The Eye of the Hurricane also seeks to take a peek into your inner peace as a way of handling depression. The Eye of the Hurricane is divided into two parts. The first part introduces the Eye of the Hurricane metaphor.

When you find a place with tranquility and calmness, assume a tall but relaxed sitting posture. Inhale and exhale deeply three times, ensuring that you take it slow as you begin to feel an awareness of your body as well as any other physical feelings that may be present.

The second part is a reflection. What was the feeling like from an observatory point of view? Did you experience any other feelings during meditation?

Anger

Meditation exercises can also eject acute or chronic anger. Anger being one of the strongest emotions, it can be a little bit hard to view objectively and defuse. Mindfulness can help in creating a space between an immediate impulsive response and stimulus.

The technique below can be helpful to anyone experiencing anger:

I.To begin with, sit comfortably, close your eyes and take note of the places where your body is touching. It could be the floor, chair or mat.

II. Inhale deeply a few times to appoint that your lungs are completely filled then exhale quickly.

III. Tried to a recent time that you experienced anger. A mild type of anger is advisable in this case. Give yourself some time to experience that anger like you did the first time.

IV. Let go of any feelings that this memory brings up. For instance, guilt or sadness.

V. Direct your attention to how you are feeling the anger in your body. Along with take note of parts of the body that are reacting to anger with sensations like cold or warmth, the impact of these reactions and whether they depict any changes when you move your body or observe them

VI. Let go of the anger and slowly revert your attention to your breath and stay in this state for a while until your feelings have settled down or subsided.

VII. Take some time to do a reflection of the experience. Take note of the sensations that this process brought to your body. Try to find out if they underwent many changes throughout the process. Also, find out whether you applied anger or compassion and if so, how did you do it? Try and find out what happened to the angry feeling when you showed it empathy.

This technique can be done over and over again as many times as it is needed. It is recommended that you start off with milder anger experiences as you build-up to the most memorable and intense episodes.

Putting this technique into practice can be important in helping you defuse chronic anger in a manner that is counterintuitive: by accepting your anger issues and mindfully feeling it, you can take control of the situation and empathetically address it.

Breathing Exercises

Breathing exercises are an excellent, fast and easy solution for anxiety and stress relief. Proper execution of breathing techniques works on anxiety issues at a psychological level by naturally slowing the heart rate. The effects of anxiety are almost instantaneous. Considering the fact that relaxed breathing is a psychological plan, this approach is almost universally efficacious for getting relief from anxiety. It is almost impossible to go wrong with it.

Before you get started, keep the following tips in mind:

- □ Do not force it. This can intensify the stress.
- □ Think of a suitable place to do your breathing exercise This might be your bed, your bedroom floor or on a comfortable chair.

- □ Put on comfortable outfits.

Super Simple Meditation Breathing.

Breathing exercises do not have to be complicated. Super simple meditation breathing is a simple breathing exercise that is arguably the most successful anxiety relief technique. The main trick behind it is to breathe slowly. You need to completely ignore how you breath in and focus on how you breathe out. The length of your breath will increase naturally when you breath out for a longer time. That is why there is no need to consciously focus on how you breathe in.

When you are breathing out, try and make it slow, gentle and steady. Some people liken this process of blowing a balloon, slow, steady and with a very little amount of force. Breath out entirely until the last drop of breath is let out.

As you breathe slowly, also try to take note of places in your body that may be holding tension. Usually, these places may include your shoulders, lips, and jaws. Every time you breathe out, try to let out the tension as well, and let relaxation to come in.

Deep Breathing or Slow Breathing?

People usually think that it is advisable to use deep breathing techniques for anxiety relief. However, putting your focus on a slow kind of breathing is much easier. Breathing slowly is less likely to generate deep breathing anxiety that comes about when people take a deep breath.

Breathing slowly is one of the best breathing exercises for panic attacks because it helps you in slowing down your heart rate and consequently naturally causing a calming effect on all the body systems involved in your body's flight/fight/freeze response. This is because the slow breathing exercise above is simple, it is not easy to fail to remember the instructions when you are battling panic attacks.

A Slightly More Involved Breathing Exercise

If you would like to get to know a myriad of meditation breathing exercises, you have to consider attempting alternate nostril breathing. This is equally an easy, natural breathing exercise for managing stress and anxiety. This technique can be performed by closing one nostril by gently placing your finger on it. Breath out then breath in through the open nostril. After every complete breath cycle, change the nostril that is being covered.

Breath Focus.

While you engage in deep breathing, create a picture in your mind and a phrase or word that will boost your relaxation. You can do this as follows:

Close your eyes, breath in a few deep breaths. As you breathe in, imagine that the air has a sense of tranquility and calm. Make an attempt to feel this way throughout your body. Breath out, and as you do so, imagine that the air going out is taking away the tension and stress. This time around as you breathe in again, say to yourself in silence, " I breathe in calm and peace." When breathing out, say to yourself, " I am breathing out tension and stress. "Repeat this procedure for 10-20 minutes.

Equal Time for Breathing in and Out

This technique involves matching the duration of your breath-in with how long you take to breathe out. As you keep doing this over and over you will notice that you are capable of breathing in and out at a time.

This technique can be practically executed as follows:

Ensure that you are comfortable sitting on the floor or a chair, breath in and as you do so, count to five, breath out and count to five as well. Repeat the same process a couple of times.

Progressive Muscle Relaxation

This exercise involves you breathing and simultaneously tensing a muscle group and consequently releasing the muscle group when you breathe out. Progressive muscle relaxation can be very instrumental in case you want to have a sense of physical and mental relaxation.

Chapter 64. Retraining The Mind

CBT teaches the importance of paying attention to behaviors and increasing the frequency of positive activities through Behavioral Activation. You have learned about the key elements of experience: thoughts, emotions, behaviors, and bodily sensations. You have learned the common Thinking Traps. You have started to learn how the Thought Record is used in CBT to connect automatic thoughts and feelings to particular situations that are arising in day-to-day life, and how CBT defines a number of Thinking Traps that people commonly fall into. The fact that you have learned all this is already an accomplishment.

It is possible, however, to go a step further in your understanding of CBT. What you will now learn is how CBT teaches people actively to dispute automatic thoughts that involve Thinking Traps. But before we get into the details, it will help if you have some background on the cognitive model on which CBT is based. That way, you'll be in a better position to understand what it is a CBT client is trying to do when they are disputing their thoughts. Let's take a quick tour of the cognitive model.

The Cognitive Revolution

It wasn't too long ago that the computer was first invented. It was even more recently that computers became part of our everyday lives. Many of us can remember when the first personal computers first came on the market in the 1980s and 1990s. Since their invention, computers have changed many aspects of life and they have affected the way we think about ourselves.

One very big area of change occurred in psychology. Psychologists began to replace ways of understanding the mind and brain with a computer-based understanding. They started to think of the mind as functioning as a computer. Most importantly, just as computers function to process information, so can the human mind. And just as computers can malfunction in processing information, so can the human mind. To better understand this idea, imagine a user who is using a computer to perform a basic arithmetic operation, like adding 2 + 2. The user inputs “2+2” into the computer, and it processes the input to yield an answer: “4.”

Now imagine this same user who is faced with a broken, malfunctioning computer. She inputs “2+2” into the computer, but when it processes the input it outputs something false: “5”

Just as a computer can fail to process information properly, the human mind can also fail properly to process the information it is presented with. The development in psychology of thinking of the mind as a computer is known as the “cognitive revolution.” This psychological revolution has allowed for new approaches to treating mental distress like depression and anxiety. Cognitive-behavioral therapy emerged out of this revolutionary new approach. CBT starts from the idea that common mental health disorders can be understood as the mind failing properly to process the information it is taking in.

The Cognitive Model of Anxiety and Depression

According to the cognitive model, anxiety and mood disorders are caused when the mind makes errors in processing information in the environment, resulting in higher levels of distress than is appropriate. Anxious and depressive states are sometimes normal - they become problems when they are triggered because our automatic thoughts are falsely causing these states to arise.

But it is not useful to you to become anxious in situations in which there is no likely threat. It is the mind that, like a computer, processes information about which situations are threatening to you, and which are not. In anxiety disorders, this information-processing function of your mind malfunctions. It is exaggerating the threat level that you face. For example, if you see a leashed miniature poodle at the other end of the park, and you feel a lot of anxiety, then there is likely a problem with the way that your mind is processing information.

In cases of anxiety disorders, the mind is operating like a smoke detector that is giving "false alarms."

Although it can seem odd to think of it this way, the ability to depressive responses can also sometimes be useful to us. Evolutionary psychologists have suggested that certain depressive responses can be normal reactions if we have invested our energy in a person or project, and then face a loss. A period of low mood and detachment may actually help us to help the person to withdraw our investment in what we have lost so that they may go on to re-invest in new things and move on with our lives.

You may be familiar with this idea if you have ever been through the "grieving process" that often happens after a major transition or loss. But experiencing a depressive state is only useful to you if it is happening as part of a constructive process such as working through a loss. It is not useful to you if you are becoming very depressed and there is no such process unfolding. According to the cognitive model, in depressive disorders, the mind is malfunctioning in the way it is processing information, making situations seem far more negative than they actually are. The minds of people who are depressed are known to produce a stream of negative thoughts that do not provide a full and balanced picture of the situations they are in. These include negative thoughts about themselves, others, the world, and the future. For example, if someone who is depressed fails an exam, their thoughts may interpret the situation through an extremely negative lens as being one of hopelessness. By contrast, the thoughts of someone who is not depressed would provide a more balanced view of the situation.

Questioning Automatic Thoughts

Just as a malfunctioning computer can be reprogrammed, so can a human mind that is malfunctioning to create excessive anxiety or depression. To reprogram the mind, a person will need to deliberately attend to the way it is automatically interpreting situations in his or her life. That way, they can start a process of learning that results in forming new habits of thought - habits that are not as biased towards negative or catastrophic interpretations.

There are two key ways to start to correct the automatic thoughts that distort the situation:

- By asking questions that dispute or challenge distorted automatic thoughts
- By carrying out "behavioral experiments" in which the person deliberately enters situations that will provide direct evidence against distorted automatic thoughts

According to CBT, there are some key questions that people can ask about their automatic thoughts in order to reprogram negative or catastrophic biases in their thinking.

- What is the evidence in favor of, and against, my interpretation of the situation?
- What is another way to view the situation?
- Have I overlooked any important information about the situation?
- Is the way I'm thinking helpful to me?
- How might someone else (who is not already depressed or anxious) view the situation?

In a CBT program, the therapist asks the client questions like these to help them to challenge their automatic thoughts. This type of questioning is known as "Socratic" questioning, after the Ancient Greek philosopher Socrates. Socrates would ask people challenging questions in the course of philosophical discussions that would lead them fundamentally to rethink some of their basic beliefs. When someone is continuing with CBT on their own after they have finished working with a therapist, they are encouraged to continue to ask themselves challenging questions such as these. In this way, one goal of a CBT program is to eventually help people to become their own therapists.

Let's illustrate this process by considering how Sam begins to ask herself questions that challenge some of the automatic thoughts connected with her anxiety and depression.

Recall that, last week, when Sam woke up one morning and checked her email, she discovered an email from her manager. Right away, she started to panic and feel bad. Her automatic thought was "I must be in trouble." When she found the courage to read the email, it turned out that her manager was asking about her return-to-work plan. Sam identified her Thinking Trap as Fortune Telling since she was anticipating a bad event (getting in trouble) but did not have direct evidence that this was going to happen.

We have already seen how Sam completed the first four columns of her Thought Record. Now we can focus on the last two columns. In these columns, she will dispute the automatic thought, "I must be in trouble," in order to arrive at a more balanced thought.

5. Disputation - Evidence for and against

For: My manager has been critical in the past

Against: She has Not criticized me in all of our interactions, and I know that I have not done anything wrong

6. New balanced, realistic thought

"Although there is a chance that my manager will be upset with me, there is no good reason for her to be upset with me now"

Notice the question Sam asks herself in disputing her automatic thought about being in trouble. She asks the first question listed above: What is the evidence in favor of and against my interpretation of the situation? Many people find it helpful to start with this question.

But the choice of which question or questions to ask is a matter of preference. Sam might have chosen instead to focus on the question "How might someone else (who is not already depressed or anxious) view the situation?" In that case, she might have brought to mind a friend or family member who is doing well emotionally, and who would have brushed off the email from the manager without taking seriously the possibility that they were in trouble.

To further illustrate the disputation of thoughts, let's consider a second example.

Sam was planning to go to the gym to work out after lunch, since she has found that this has been helping her to feel better. But while she was eating lunch, she started thinking about work and had the thought, "I will never be any good at my job." This made her feel depressed, and caused her to lose the motivation to go to the gym. That day, she realized that this thought had derailed her plans to take care of herself. She completed an entry in her Thought Record.

This is what Sam's entry in her Thought Record looks like:

1. Activating Event

Wednesday PM: Eating lunch, started to think about work

2. Belief / Thought

"I will never be any good at my job"

3. Consequences - Emotions, behaviors, bodily sensations

Sadness, low energy, lying down on the couch (instead of going to the gym)

4. Thinking Trap

All-or-nothing thinking

5. Disputation - Evidence for and against

For: my new manager has criticized me for mistakes I've made at my job

Against: I have produced a lot of good work and my other colleagues come to me when they have questions

6. New balanced, realistic thought

"Although I have not been perfect at my job, there are many things I do well and many people do believe that I'm good at my job"

In this Thought Record entry, Sam decided to focus on the Thinking Trap of All-or-Nothing thinking. There might be other Thinking Traps, too (such as Fortune Telling or Mental Filter). But it is often helpful to focus on the one that stands out most prominently in the situation. In this case, Sam was struck by the way her automatic thoughts had made it seem to her that she was either all-good or all-bad at her job. In fact, the reality lies somewhere in-between.

Chapter 65. Proven, Powerful, And Practical Strategies For Overcoming Obstacles

If you are struggling with anxiety, just like other mental health conditions, you will experience good times and bad times. The good times are simply when your symptoms are under control, and you feel strong. On the other hand, when you are in bad times, you experience challenging setbacks, and your symptoms are worse.

These setbacks are often referred to as 'relapses.' In most cases, if they are very serious, this can lead to hospitalization. The truth is, relapses happen even though one may already be under medication.

Therefore, it is important that you develop skills that will help you cope so that you can deal with these challenges more subtly and effectively possible. In most cases, certain triggers such as situations or behaviors can cause a relapse. Knowing your trigger(s) helps you develop strategies to help you deal with them and lower your risk of a relapse.

Some of the proven ways that have been shown to help in overcoming obstacles to avoid a relapse contributing to poor mental health include:

Practice as much as you can

The best way in which one can prevent the occurrence of relapse is to keep practicing CBT skills as much as they can. This is because, when you practice regularly, you ensure that you stay in shape and hence when a situation arises, you are capable of facing it hands-on.

You can fit in practice by simply making a schedule for the skills you would like to work on each week.

Some of the techniques that you can practice regularly may include exposure, relaxation, calm breathing and others. You can get friends and family to support you in maintaining your schedule.

Know what your red flags are

If you know what triggers your fears and anxiety, there is a better chance that you can spot them from afar. In other words, when you are more vulnerable to experiencing a trigger, you become self-aware, and this makes it less likely to occur.

The best thing in such a case is for you to make a list of all the warning signs that tell you that you are likely to be having an anxiety attack. Some of these might include feeling sweaty, feeling anxious, having too many responsibilities at work or home, engaging in an argument or going through major life changes.

When you are aware of the red flags, you can make a plan of action. This will ensure that you have the situation under control. In other words, reliance on a plan is your coping mechanism. Your plan may include taking a break from work, practicing relaxation and CBT skills.

Coming up with new challenges

You have to understand that, just like everyone else in the Universe, you are not perfect. You are simply a work in progress. In other words, each day is a new opportunity to improve something in your life so that you can make it more fulfilling and enjoyable.

To prevent future relapses, it is important that you keep working on new challenges and situations that make you fearful in your life. The best approach is for you to make a list of all situations that you find scary and work on each one at a time.

This way, there is less chance that you will slide back to old habits. The brain will shift focus from older habits to establishing new ones and learning how to cope with new dangers, fears, and worries.

Learn a lesson or two from your relapses

It is normal to have a relapse occasionally! Every day, we face new situations, some of which are not stressful while others are stressful. If you are struggling with anxiety issues, coping with such events can make you more vulnerable to relapse.

However, the good news is that you can learn from the relapses that you have had in the past. Use your past experiences to find out what the situation was that caused you to relapse.

The best way to get clarity on this is by asking yourself these questions:

 Did you have angry and anxious thought patterns?

 Was the level of your anxiety high?

 What did you do?

 Was there something that you did each time differently?

 Were you aware that the situation would be difficult or was it a surprise?

Knowing how and why your relapse was difficult can be useful in helping you prepare for the following one. Ensure that you have plans that will help you cope effectively in the future.

Know your facts

Did you know that what you say to yourself after having a relapse has a great impact on how you react, respond or behave? When you have had a relapse, it is important that you focus on what is helpful to you. Rather than thinking that you are a failure, think of the lessons that you can learn to make it better the following time.

This is because, when you see yourself as a failure, you will feel as though you have undone all the good work. This simply strips you of your self-confidence, driving you into giving up, hence making you relapse.

However, with some of these facts, you can ensure that everything is under control. These facts include knowing that it is impossible to go back to the starting point. In other words, accepting that you cannot unlearn all the skills and techniques that CBT has taught you. Realize that, if you went back to the starting point, there is an increased chance that you will go into relapse and not know how to handle the situation. However, once you have started CBT, you are certain that if relapse occurred in the future, you are fully equipped to handle it.

If you encounter another relapse, you have the potential to get back on track. The truth is, you might have taken weeks or even months to practice CBT techniques that help you reduce anxiety symptoms, but it will not take you an eternity to find out how to get back on track before you encounter another episode. Understand that when you keep practicing your CBT skills, you stand a better chance of mastering your anxiety each time.

Just think of it as riding a bike. It takes time to learn, but once you know how, you are good to go, and that skill sticks with you forever. If you stop riding for a while, you get rusty, but it will not be long before you get back on track.

Be kind to yourself

It is important that you bear in mind that relapses are normal. So many people beat themselves up or demean themselves because they just had an episode. You have to understand that by blaming yourself, you are just making it even worse than it already is. Realize that just like anybody else, you are not perfect and that mistakes are bound to happen from time to time.

Ask yourself, if it were someone else having a relapse, would you speak to them the same way you are doing to yourself? Probably not! Trust me when I tell you that it can be helpful to have a relapse. I know this might sound crazy but hear me out; having a relapse gives you an opportunity to learn that relapses are not only normal but they also help a lot in overcoming triggers the following time they occur. This is mainly because you will have learned skills that help you tackle the situation and move forward with your life.

Celebrate your wins

Overcoming situations that challenge your fears, anxiety, and worry is commendable. It is very important that you take the time to appreciate yourself for the progress and hard work you are doing. When you treat yourself after every win, however small it may seem to you, you become motivated to tackle even bigger situations.

The reward can be something like treating yourself to a nice meal, buying that beautiful jewelry you have meant to, going out with your family or friends, or just enjoying pampering yourself. The truth is, managing anxiety is hard work and the progress you make is because of the effort that you put in. Think about, isn't that worth a reward?

That said, for you to overcome your anxiety and fear, it is important that you plan well for a relapse. It is important that you do the planning ahead of time so that you can have all the support and help you might need.

When you plan, you ease your worries about what might happen if you were to have an episode. This is mainly because you know that you have a plan in place in case you need it.

Plans may be formal agreements between you and your therapist. They can also be informal understandings between you and your friends, family or other people within your support network. Whatever form you choose, remember that the most important thing for you is to outline clearly what might happen, the warning signs and what each person's responsibility will be.

Others need to know the signs that indicate a relapse is about to happen. It is important that the plan also identifies the point at which outside help is needed. Is it soon after the red flags begin to show or is it the time when you can no longer manage the symptoms of your anxiety by yourself?

The plan should also entail directives about where to go for help in case you are alone or with unfamiliar people. In other words, who are your first points of contact if an emergency happened? Also, include the treatment you would prefer to have administered within such a situation.

Your action plan can also include all the practical steps that your support network agreed to take. For instance, your loved ones may be required to contact your employer so that everything is kept in order: from the rent to bill payments and other formal financial tasks, especially if you need to spend more time in the hospital.

What if you have children and this happens? Well, children need care, so a guardian's access to finances is important. It is best to seek a lawyer's advice so that you know what options you have. The good news is that there are many legal procedures and tools at your disposal that will facilitate planning for your children's care. When you work with a legal professional, you will get the best advice on what choices suit your situation.

Emotional Self-awareness

You may be thinking 'What does this have to do with my anxiety issues?' Well, trust me, it has everything to do with resolving anxiety! Emotional awareness is all about being able to recognize and understand your emotions and how they affect or influence your behavior.

We have already seen how anxiety issues or occurrence of a situation that triggers your anxiety issues and fear can trigger a relapse and the various ways in which you can avoid that from happening. However, during the process, there are so many emotional changes that take place, and if you are going to respond well to situations, you have to be aware of your emotions.

The good thing is that you know how you feel and the reasons why you feel that way. This simply means that you can see how your emotions can be helpful or hurtful to what you do. In such a situation, there is also a chance that you are aware of how people view you. But there is a huge difference between emotional intelligence and cognitive self-awareness, which mainly pays attention to your thoughts and ideas instead of your feelings.

Emotional intelligence is one of the core competencies that help you manage your emotions, relationships, and awareness of others. following, we will discuss the various steps that you can follow to help you develop awareness of your feelings and how they are interconnected with your thoughts.

Step 1: Choose a triggering situation

By now, you already know the things that trigger anger, anxiety and upsetting feelings for you. Try to put them down on paper and select one that is least challenging to you just for starters. The reason why we begin with the least challenging is so that you can practice your skills successfully one at a time until you can face your worst fears.

This may take days to weeks, hence the need for patience. Try to stretch yourself out of your comfort zone while still ensuring that you do not get overwhelmed in the process. However, if you feel that this process is emotionally overwhelming, it is important that you seek help from someone that can work with you □ like a therapist, friend or family member.

Step 2: Center yourself in the present while taking in slow and deep breaths

Once you know what trigger you would like to work on, it is important that you pause for a moment and close your eyes. Take in slow and deep breaths for about 5-10 minutes. Breath from your belly and allow your whole body to come to the point of relaxation.

Focus your mind on your breath with your eyes closed. In your mind, scan your body from head to toe allowing every tension to be released. Let loose every tightness in your body so that you relax.

Now, start imagining yourself at a safe place. Try to remind yourself that you are not the emotions or the thoughts but just an observer and a person that can choose the thoughts and emotions that appeal to you. How does that make you feel? Do you feel that you are in charge of your body, responses, thoughts, and feelings? Imagine not having anyone around you making you feel what you do not want to without your permission. You are simply the observer of your emotional feelings.

Now, start shifting your mind into creating a mental note to yourself. In this note, tell yourself that the emotions you are experiencing are old energy pockets, wounds that come from your past experiences, and your childhood. Tell yourself that this is okay because, during that time, you had no cognitive ability to know or even see yourself from different points of view. Now, you have become an intelligent adult who is well able to take charge of all processes and changes taking place in your life.

Repeat it over and over until your brain gets a positive attitude towards your inner and outer person.

If you need to stop this exercise in the middle of it at any time, you can do so if necessary, otherwise, ensure that you can do it to the end without any interruptions.

Step 3: Identify and feel your emotions

While feeling centered in your breathing, start to bring that trigger into your mind. You can do this by simply trying to recall the latest/most recent occurrence. Avoid making any judgments and pause for a moment to get in touch with your feelings and sensations. Take note of any emotions and feelings you had inside.

Now, try to take deep and slow breaths while still feeling what you felt when you had the occurrence. Begin to ask yourself what you are feeling at that moment. Do you feel anger? Do you feel scared? Are you anxious? Start looking for the emotions that run beneath it. Anger is but a secondary emotion that comes on as a means of trying to protect yourself from feeling vulnerable.

Is there something that underlies that anger? Is it hurt, shame, fear or something else? What emotional feelings do you have? Write them down on a plain sheet of paper or in a journal.

Step 4: Feel and take note of the location of sensations in your body

At this point, it is critical that you take a moment, pause and feel each emotion run through your body. Take note of the sensations that you feel at different parts of your body. For each of the emotions that is triggered, record the sensation that you feel and what part of the body you feel it in. You can do this by ensuring that you maintain the picture of your triggering event in your mind.

Ensure that while you're at it, you take in deep breaths and place your hand(s) on the place where you feel the sensation. As you do this, begin to let go of any impulse that pulls you towards judging, stopping, repressing or fixing your emotions and sensations.

Keep probing your emotions and taking note of the emotional feelings until they lessen in intensity.

If you feel that anger is primary, keep asking yourself whether there is something other than anger that you are feeling. Give a description of your sensations and the body parts where you feel them. Record them and keep repeating this until you have exhausted all the primary emotions.

Chapter 66. The Key To Feeling Good

Being happy is so important, yet it's often overlooked. If you don't feel good, you won't feel as motivated to accomplish your goals. It will be harder to be driven and get to where you need to be, as you simply won't feel up to anything. Taking care of yourself is crucial. When you feel good, you may form better relationships with others and have people that can support you and have a good time with you. You can get more done, as you will actually want to improve yourself and succeed. You will be more confident in yourself because you'll be treating yourself the way that you should be and recognizing your worth instead of feeling sorry for yourself. It will be easier to succeed, achieve your goals, and have access to more opportunities. When you are able to adjust your life so that you feel good, you can make drastic changes for the better. You may first focus on your mental health, which will allow you to better handle all of your emotions. You may then work on your outlook on life. When you have a more positive outlook, you will feel more confident in yourself and your decisions. Caring for your physical health can make you feel good, both physically and mentally. You'll take care of your body while also improving the way that you see yourself. Finally, you may work on having more positive relationships with others, as that can help you to surround yourself with the right people.

Improving Your Mental Health

Your mental health is so important, yet most people seem to forget that it even exists. You can go to the gym and eat as healthily as you'd like, yet that won't help you if your mental health is suffering. You must take some time to care for your mental health, as you can't be happy otherwise. There are a few ways that you can make an effort to improve your mental health, and you may incorporate some great habits into your life to better your mental health.

One way to improve your mental health is to practice self-care. Every day, take some time to care for yourself. You may do this a few ways, such as reading a or relaxing. Find out what works best for you to help you calm down. It's important to make the effort to fully devote some time to yourself. It may even be as simple as lighting a candle and breathing. There are many ways that you can practice self-care, and it's important to find out what works best for you. Maybe you can even practice a new self-care activity every day! You may plan ahead for the upcoming month and pick simple ways for you to practice self-care. Perhaps you can do it for under thirty minutes every weekday and an hour or more on weekends. You may even choose one self-care item for each day of the week. Regardless, it's important to choose an activity that you genuinely enjoy and really go out of your way to take care of yourself. There are so many ways to practice self-care!

Another way to improve your mental health is by treating yourself well. Learn how to master self-compassion and self-esteem. Practice being more understanding with yourself and forgive yourself for making mistakes. Also, remember that you deserve happiness and success. Respect yourself and your decisions, and don't be so hard on yourself.

You may also work on improving your self-confidence. One great way to do this is by building your confidence. Set goals and accomplish them, even if they're small. Successes, no matter how small they are, will help you recognize that you are capable of success.

Practicing mindfulness is a great way to improve your mental health. When you are faced with a difficult situation, learn how to live in the moment. Focus on the present instead of worrying about what will happen in the future or what did happen in the past. If you live your life with regrets, you will never be able to move forward. Wasting your time on worrying will not help solve any of your problems. Instead, take time to appreciate the present for what it is.

Therapy can be a wonderful solution for bettering your mental health. If you have tried to help improve your mental health by yourself but haven't had luck, it may be time for you to seek help from someone else through therapy. Cognitive-behavioral therapy can be a great way to find solutions to your problems. Therapy can be especially helpful if you haven't had luck improving your mental health by yourself or if you feel like you have nobody to talk to. Therapy can give you an outside perspective on you.

Having a Positive Outlook

Having a positive outlook on life can really help you to be more positive and have an overall greater appreciation for life. You will be able to find joy in life instead of focusing on any negativity. When you can improve your mindset, your whole world will change. Your perspective can turn a bad situation into a good one. Learning to appreciate life can help you to be happier with how everything is going. A negative outlook on life can prevent you from making the most out of your life, and it can cause those around you to be unhappy as well. There are a few simple tips that you can use to change your perspective and have a more positive outlook.

You may start journaling. This can help you to feel like you're in more control of your life, and you may take it any direction that you'd like to. Perhaps you wish to write down what you're grateful for and the good aspects of life. You may also want to write down how you feel so that you can cope with it in a healthier way. Journaling is also great for writing down your goals and your progress toward accomplishing those goals.

Another way to have a more positive outlook is by focusing on the good. For every negative thing that you notice, you must also come up with two positive aspects of it. For instance, you may be stuck in traffic and get upset about being late. However, this can give you some time to call a friend that you haven't gotten the chance to talk to in a while and help you to take time to yourself.

There are always positive aspects of every situation. It might just take a bit of effort to find them.

Similarly, you must view challenging situations and mistakes as beneficial to you. If you can learn to view life in the way that everything happens for a reason, you will be much better off. Instead of thinking that your life is ruined because you didn't get the job, know that there is a better job waiting out there for you that will be an even better fit for you. If you can't get past challenges, you'll never grow. You can't let mistakes or failures bring you down, as they are inevitable and will always be a part of your life.

It's important to change your mindset when it comes to change. Without change, you can't grow or improve. Although you may enjoy the risk-free aspect of comfort, it will not get you anywhere. Go for your goals! Chase your dreams! If you don't make the effort to take some risks, you won't get any further in life. Change can be frightening, but it's also very important. You'll never know if you like something until you try it, and it's okay to change your mind. Change is a blessing, not a curse. You must learn how to appreciate change instead of fearing it.

Improving Your Physical Health

Your physical health is also important for your happiness. When your body is healthy, and you take care of it, you will be able to function the best. Taking care of your body can help you to have more energy and feel better overall. It can also help you to do more instead of being held back by your health. Taking care of your body will also help you to feel better about yourself. You will be able to realize that you are capable of taking care of yourself and doing what's best for yourself. You may feel more confident in your body and your ability to accomplish your goals.

First, you must get a proper amount of sleep. This is necessary for allowing you to function at your best and have a proper amount of energy. The amount of sleep that you need will depend on your age and personal preferences.

However, it is very helpful to have a sleeping schedule. Going to bed and waking up at the same time every day can help your body to get used to sleeping for the proper amount. You may form routines to perform before going to bed and after waking up to really maximize this effect.

Eating properly is essential for taking care of your mental health. It is important to allow yourself to occasionally eat unhealthy foods, but you should eat an overall healthy diet. Portions are also very important, as eating the proper amount can help you to maintain an ideal weight. Eating at the same time each day can also improve your metabolic health. Determine when you would like to eat and how often you would like to eat. Making these simple changes can really help you to improve the way you eat.

When you scar physically, almost immediately, the healing process is activated. You may still feel the pain over a few hours, days or weeks depending on the extent of the injury. But it does not negate the fact that healing is happening somewhere underneath it all. However, there are certain things that could slow down or completely halt the healing process. If the wound is not cleaned and treated properly, it could become infected and worsen the state of the wound. In some instances, you would need to cover the wound to protect it from outside elements that might contaminate the wound and trigger an infection. For injuries that are very complicated, you may have to seek out professional medical options to facilitate healing. All of these processes apply with psychological injuries, too.

When you suffer psychological trauma, the shockwave of pain and other elemental emotions such as fear, anger and sadness alert you to this. These primary emotions could be experienced for hours, days or weeks and like the physical injuries we discussed, the timespan would depend on the extent of the trauma. Plenty of us have a tendency to get frustrated at this point and who can blame you? Emotions like these force you to relive the moments leading up to and during the trauma and each replay is worse than the actual event that occurred.

If you are in this phase, it is time to cut back on any activity or thought process that you engage in that feeds the habit of blocking out your feeling. Think of it as cleaning the wound so to speak. When you want to clean and disinfect a physical injury, the chances are it will hurt. But if you skip that process because you want to avoid the hurt, you leave an open door for infections and we all know how that would end.

Staying hydrated is also important for your health. You must get a proper amount of water each day to be at your best. One way to motivate yourself to do so is by getting a water bottle that looks nice. This can encourage you to drink from it more. You may even label the side with the hours of the day as a way to set hydration goals for yourself. Cutting out beverages besides water can really help you, especially since most other drinks contain excessive amounts of sugar. Caffeine and alcohol consumption should also be limited to obtain the best health possible.

Exercising is very important to keep your body healthy. You must choose activities that you enjoy. For some, this may very well be going to the gym. Others don't thrive in that environment and prefer to exercise by themselves. This may be running, swimming, walking, or biking. You may even try at-home workouts. Taking classes or lessons can be a great way to learn how to exercise a certain way. You may also involve yourself in sports or clubs. This is a great way to get out and workout, and you'll be able to meet others with similar interests.

Cultivating Positive Relationships

To improve your relationships with others, it's very important to surround yourself with the right people. Make sure that you are spending your time with people who motivate, inspire, and encourage you to live your best life possible. It is okay to say no to people, and you must learn to value yourself. Holding on to grudges will not get you anywhere, and it's important to eliminate the conflict that you have. You may also spend more time caring for others. When you put in the effort, others will start doing the same. Work on building positive relationships with those around you.

Feeling good can help you to live your best life. You're at your best when you are happy. It is possible to achieve happiness. You may do this by improving your mental health, which can allow you to think more clearly about the positivity in your life. Similarly, you may have a more positive outlook on life. Improving your physical health can make you feel better, both physically and mentally. You may also work on improving your relationships with others so that you can surround yourself with the right people that can support you and encourage you to be your best.

Conclusion

Depending on how quickly you have read through this book, you may still be experiencing fairly intense symptoms of your emotional struggles despite having read everything within this book. It is important that you do not simply toss it aside and forget about it as you continue to face your daily struggles. Simply educating yourself on what needs to be done will not support you in healing. You will actually need to do the healing work. By remaining devoted and showing up for yourself every single day, you give yourself the attention that you need to truly embrace your healing journey with CBT.

It is important that you truly understand that self-healing does not mean isolating yourself from others. Isolating yourself is a common desire when you are experiencing something like anxiety or depression. However, doing so can impede your healing. Even on days where you do not feel like it, show up for yourself and attempt to make contact with at least one person per day who does not live with you. Doing so will support you in feeling a deeper sense of connection with those around you and will help you feel more attuned with the outside world.

You also need to make sure that you consistently practice your new mindfulness and CBT practices. Even though individuals who recover from psychological disorders using CBT are far less likely to relapse than those who are solely being treated with medicine, you will always be vulnerable to experiencing a relapse in your symptoms. Continuous self-monitoring and keeping yourself well-educated and equipped with the knowledge that you need to combat potential relapses will support you in overcoming them before they become problematic. Even if they do become problematic again, it is no reason to be ashamed.

If you know of someone else who may benefit from CBT, you may also consider letting them know about this book. The more that we can spread the message of healing and empower others to discover how they can heal themselves, the fewer people need to suffer from symptoms of anxiety and depression.

PART III

DIALECTICAL BEHAVIOR THERAPY

Introduction PART III – DIALECTICAL BEHAVIOR THERAPY

Dialectical Behavior Therapy is a proof-based cognitive-behavioral treatment created by Dr. Marsha Linehan. DBT has been proved to be robust for people battling with directing feelings and tolerating distress. The objective of DBT is to enable patients to find out how to deal with their painful emotions by allowing them to experience, perceive, and accept them. As you learn to acknowledge and manage your feelings, you can supplant maladaptive methods for dealing with stress with healthy/versatile adapting skill. To enable you to accomplish this, DBT advisors use an equalization of acceptance and change strategies.

Dialectical Behavior Therapy or DBT was initially created by Marsha Linehan in the late 1980s as an approach to treat and help deal with the symptoms of Borderline Personality Disorder.

The Dialectical part, or the "D" in DBT, is a Buddhist idea of contradicting powers. For instance, somebody who was sexually abused by a parent may feel both loves and loathe for that parent simultaneously. That is a hard division to experience, and the moving part instructs us to sit tranquility with those warring powers within our brains.

The Behavior Therapy ("BT") alludes to the use of standards of Cognitive Behavioral Therapy, or CBT, for example, the possibility that we as a whole have thoughts that cause us to have feelings, which at that point cause us to follow up on those emotions. Take, for example, when somebody cuts you off in traffic, and you think, "That individual place me in risk (and different interjections)!" That idea causes you to be furious and frightened, which at that point causes you to blare your horn or demonstrate that driver one of your fingers.

There are four components of full DBT: skill training group, singular treatment, DBT telephone instructing, and consultation group.

DBT abilities preparing group is focused on improving clients' capacities by showing them behavioral skills. The group is run like a class where the group head teaches the skills and assigns schoolwork for clients to work on utilizing the skills in their regular day to day existences. Groups meet on week by week basis for around 2.5 hours, and it takes 24 weeks to get past the full skill educational program, which is regularly rehashed to make a 1-year program. Briefer timetables that show just a subset of the skills have also been produced for specific populaces and settings.

DBT singular therapy is focused on improving clients inspiration and helping clients to apply the skills to specific challenges and occasions in their lives. In the standard DBT example, singular therapy happens once per week for around an hour and runs simultaneously with skill groups.

DBT telephone instructing is focused on giving clients in-the-minute training on how to use skill to successfully adapt to stressful situations that emerge in their regular day to day existences. Clients can call their specialist between sessions to get training at the occasions when they need assistance the most.

DBT therapist meeting group is expected to be therapy for the therapists and to help DBT suppliers in their work with people who frequently have a serious, intricate, difficult-to-treat issue. The counsel group is intended to enable specialists to remain persuaded and skilled so they can give the ideal treatment. Groups typically meet weekly and are made out of individual therapists and group pioneers who offer obligation regarding every customer's consideration.

There are many things you can do on your own when it comes to practicing dialectical behavior therapy strategies. Many people who are not struggling with any mental health issue disorder decide to embrace those DBT strategies and techniques to boost their mental health, to bring more joy and happiness into their lives and to simply feel better.

This is where dialectical behavior therapy steps in with its highly valuable skills and strategies that everyone can benefit from. In fact, those dialectical behavior therapy strategies which patients learn during their treatments are very valuable to everyone.

There are three major skills which patients learn during their dialectical behavior therapy sessions, you can embrace as well.

Today, DBT is used for treating patients struggling with many different mental health disorders while its valuable strategies can be of great importance to all people. DBT teaches valuable behavioral skills including interpersonal effectiveness, emotion regulation, distress tolerance and mindfulness which can be beneficial to everyone.

No matter if you have a mental health disorder or not, you can take these valuable lessons, incorporate them into your life and enjoy benefits which they bring.

As you embrace these valuable lessons, you get to enjoy a much healthier and happier lifestyle with almost no negative emotions to distract you.

As you learn how to properly manage your emotions, you get to take control over your life fully, you get to build more meaningful relationships, be more present in all social environments and simply enjoy the life as you should.

As patients learn at their DBT sessions, the first thing you need to embrace is mindfulness. This means you must live your life more in the current moment instead of thinking about those past things and instead of anticipating what may happen in the future.

You should not let yourself to be hijacked by the future or by the past. As you practice mindfulness, you will be more aware of your surroundings, of people around you. You will also be more aware of your reactions, actions, feelings, and thought.

Practicing mindfulness also means that you gain control over your emotions, so you can check in, pause as well as analyze and identify all your emotions, so you can easily make those healthy decisions.

Chapter 67. What is Borderline Personality Disorder (BPD)?

A personality disorder refers to a pattern of feelings and behaviors that causes a person to have a lot of problems in his/her own life. Although these behaviors and feelings cause this person to go through serious problems in their lives, they still see their behavior and reactions to everyday life situations as justified and appropriate.

Borderline personality disorder is a personality disorder is also characterized by a painful mix of emotional confusion, self-distractive impulsivity, self-image, and unstable relationships. People with BPD usually have extreme emotional reactions and impulsive behaviors. They are extremely sensitive and small things can trigger intense emotional reactions. Once upset, he or she will have trouble calming down. This emotional volatility and the inability to calm down are what lead to relationship problems and even reckless behavior. People with borderline personality disorder sometimes may act in inappropriate/dangerous ways that make them feel ashamed or guilty afterward. This is a painful cycle.

Recognizing Borderline Personality Disorder

If you identify with the following statements, then there are high possibilities that you are suffering from borderline personality disorder.

□ Sometimes I feel "empty"

□ I can't define my emotions. There are times that experience extreme anxiety, anger and sadness. My emotions generally shift very quickly.

□ I am always afraid of losing the people I care about. I am also afraid to be abandoned by the people who care about me.

□ There are times that I do things that I know are dangerous or rather unhealthy like unhealthy eating, binge drinking, unsafe sex, reckless driving, or using drugs

□ There are times that when pressured, I attempt to hurt myself by engaging in self-harming behaviors like cutting myself or threatening to commit suicide.

□ In my romantic relationships, I always feel insecure. This makes me try to keep my partner close and in doing this, I sometimes make impulsive gestures.

A Short Story of Borderline Personality Disorder

Mercy Anne found herself in love again. Her relationship with Francisco started when they met at an exchange program organized by her company. Francisco, an immigrant from Spain, happened to get a good job opportunity, which made him relocate. Yet he was not that fluent in English. He would occasionally add some Spanish words in his conversations. As Mercy recalls, their first conversation was, "Hello, Como estás? Goodbye." It was even more interesting that they happened to be living in the same housing development. They also took the same subway ride back home from work. With time, as they got to know more about each other, their bond even grew stronger.

Mercy had two sons and one daughter, each with two different men. Unfortunately, both men were abusive to Mercy even though she tried desperately to leave them. Yet her profound fear of abandonment made things complicated for her. Having tried her best to resolve her situation so she could move away from these men, she went from one psychiatric care facility to another with no success. Eventually, Mercy began doing things to harm herself. She attempted suicide, began cutting herself, binge drank, and even at times refused to eat for several days.

Mercy had been a bright girl who did excellently well in her studies. She passed her high school exams with excellent grades and attempting to a meaningful profession, Mercy enrolled in college to study computer science.

Mercy's mother had not been in her life since the age of six. After graduating from high-school, Mercy happily reunited with her mother, only to lose her mother in a car accident right after graduating from college. Mercy had been in the crash with her mother. The experience of her mother dying in her arms is one that affected Mercy deeply.

Mercy met Erick while still grieving her mother. She saw Erick as the person who would make her forget her past. She immersed herself in Erick's world. Erick's interests soon became her own. This was a pattern of behavior for Mercy when falling in love with someone. In fact, as a teen, there was a time that she followed her first boyfriend from Texas to Florida. Her second boyfriend loved baseball; something that caused Mercy become an instant expert baseball analysis of players and statistics.

After meeting Francisco, Mercy started learning Spanish. She got so interested in Spanish she would occasionally buy a Spanish newspaper. She soon enjoyed watching Spanish Telenovela with Francisco's sisters and would spend her weekends with Francisco's family. "When I loved, I loved with all my heart and I would depend on the person I was with," Mercy says. "I would take my time to learn about what the person likes and dislikes were, so the person I was with could never any reason to leave me."

Mercy decided to quit her job so she could stay at home to help her daughter manage her son's diabetic condition.

Mercy even attempted to take her own life by injecting herself with 60 units of insulin meant for her son. This was a very lethal dose. "I wanted to die and go rest with mom," she says. However, she only fainted and hours, she was shocked to herself still alive. She found herself shaky and very hungry.

Francisco showed up ten days. And confessed that he had a wife back in Cortes de la Frontera, Spain. Mercy told Francisco that the emotional blow made her attempt killing herself.

This meant that the stakes in this new relationship were very high. From that moment, Francisco became worried and even expressed that he was not sure whether he wanted to continue with the relationship. "If Mercy tried to kill herself because of me, I think she will also it easy to kill me!" Francisco confided

Francisco already knew much about Mercy's past. Now, Mercy had to tell these other Francisco that she had a borderline personality disorder. Francisco, however, did not understand this disorder. So Mercy tried to videos on the internet in Spanish that explained what people with this disorder go through. In the video, Francisco learned that people with borderline personality disorder are characterized by difficult to control emotions, feelings of anger, have self-hatred, and feel very insecure. They try as much as possible to avoid being abandoned, they are characterized by self-harming behaviors like cutting or even attempting suicide, they have extreme mood swings and they always feel empty. This information opened Francisco's eyes. He was able to recognize the symptoms in Mercy. "So this is you!" he said. "Oh my God!"

When a person with BPD falls in love, they fall deeply and hard. They idealize their partners and friends forming obsessive relationships. Therefore, when their loved one or their close people disappoint them, they suffer to an extreme. They are terrorized by abandonment and this drives them to be anxious, paranoid or enraged. The love drama by people with borderline personality disorder has always been fodder for the entertainment industry. An example of such movie is the Fatal Attraction which dwells on Glenn's murderous jilted lover. Another love drama about borderline personality disorder is the musical comedy series called Crazy Ex-Girlfriend which has a character who is obsessed with heroin who tries to kill herself.

Borderline Personality disorder does not have a boundary. Anyone can have this disorder. Comedian Pete Davidson got engaged to pop star Ariana Grande just after one month of dating. The comedian was open about his borderline personality disorder diagnosis. Many people criticized their engagement pinning on the widespread belief that people with BPD should never be in relationships.

In most cases, people with BPD crave to win over the bonds of affection of their family, close friends, and lovers. However, it is always a challenge for them to sustain intimacy because this disorder embodies a most poignant paradox: People with this disorder yearn for closeness but due to their overriding insecurity, they end up driving away those people who are most dear to them.

Discussion: Hungers Most Human

A person with BPD never feels satisfied. They pursue their own feelings fully in their relationships yet they do not fill their partner's feelings. Yet the vulnerability and volatility of borderlines nearly reflect a universal human hunger.

Humans are amazing yet sometimes difficult to deal with. There are times that each of us shuts down our willingness to help or understand others as part of our human self-protection mechanism. There are times that we want to be fed and nurtured, so we can continue to nurture and feed others. And we are all wired to react strongly whenever the prospect of rejection looms.

The fear of abandonment for someone with BPD is terrifically scary. It gives them a constant sense of insecurity, especially in relationships. So for someone with BPD, it is natural that when people close to us, like friends or work colleagues try to avoid them it is taken very personally. The person with BPD may grapple with a paranoia as to whether or not they are being cast aside. They are also very afraid of dissolution of our serious relationships. This typically causes them to have a series of trying emotions, and even at times, a diminished sense of self.

Our darkest and most difficult parts of our lives are reflected in the experiences that people with BPD have. Borderlines typically reject any sense of "attachment injury". As rational beings, we all have attachment injuries. People with BPD tend to seek an ideal of perfect love and when they fall in love, they tend to pursue love zealously. However, the moment the people they love disappoint them even a little bit, they suffer. They will do all sorts of crazy things like stop eating or view their partner as an enemy even when the relationship is strong, or even attempt to harm themselves. Any slight disappointment like failing to answer a phone call or failing to reply to a text message makes them angry and is interpreted as rejection.

The key feature of borderline personality disorder is "rejection sensitivity". In most cases, people with BPD tend to forge emotional bonds with anyone close to them. There are also times that they over the trust. Because they are scared of rejection, they will try to throw caution to the wind when they enter a new relationship. When their partners or friends let them down they feel betrayed. More often, people with BPD feel trapped in their relationships because they are afraid that they will feel worse if alone. They may also feel compelled to deny inadequacies and flaws in their partners or friends just to keep them in their lives.

An Unquiet Amygdala

The extreme way with which borderlines experience the world can be attributed to a glitch in their brain dynamics. The prefrontal cortex, which is centered in the amygdala, is the part of the forebrain responsible for decision making and self-control. This part also governs the limbic system. The limbic system is an evolutionary ancient set of brain regions responsible for the generation of primal emotions like fear. Therefore, people with borderline personality disorder seem to have little input from the prefrontal cortex to the amygdala.

Experts explain that brain scans of people with borderline personality disorder show that they have an overactive amygdala. In other words, there is always an increase in amygdala activity showing reactions that are more elevated during stressful experiences. Researchers believe that the high levels of amygdala activity also motivate borderlines to misinterpret some social cues. Borderlines are likely to misinterpret neutral facial expressions. For instance, they may misinterpret that someone is angry with them and will exclude themselves from further discourse with this person. One way of understanding this issue is by looking at the subjective experience of closeness in personal space, and how borderlines behave around people close to them.

Researchers explain that the amygdala is very important when it comes to regulating interpersonal distance. The activity of the amygdala increases when someone gets close to the borderlines. It is suspected that amygdala activity is likely to be the factor that makes it difficult for borderlines to regulate personal closeness.

In research conducted by Yale University to test the interpersonal distance in people with BPD, 30 women with BPD and 23 healthy women were tested by walking slowly towards them. They were then asked to indicate when they began to feel uncomfortable. It was found that those with BPD halted at a greater distance when compared with the ones with healthy controls. In most instances, people with this condition need more space around them in order to feel safe.

This is due to their brain signals "telling" them that the people they interact with could be harmful to them in some way. Research has found that borderlines are highly attentive to "social cues" – that is – how they feel they are being treated or must behave or react, in any given circumstance. It is this noticing and reacting negatively to social cues that cause relational problems, especially since someone with BPD can adapt more slowly when circumstances shift. The slightest sour expression will make them feel afraid or angry. People with BPD have it in mind that trying to change their minds is ineffective, especially when things get unpredictable. Therefore, they keep using the same old paradigm and set of emotions especially when things don't work well for them.

Chapter 68. Understanding Borderline Personality Disorder

While seeking appropriate psychotherapy treatments is essential for those with BPD, your psychologist can't be there every hour of the day! It's likely that they will be able to advise you on local support groups or helplines where you can get additional support. In addition, simple coping skills can help to reduce the effects of BPD on a day-to-day basis. In this chapter we'll look at some simple steps and skills to help manage the condition – and particularly your emotions.

The symptoms of BPD include mood swings, self-harming, suicidal behaviors, intense emotions, emotional sensitivity and impulsive behavior. All of these symptoms have one common root – known as emotional dis-regulation. This is the ability to manage or rather not manage our emotions. As the those with BPD suffer from such strong emotions, they can be inclined to avoid them, resulting in self-harm, substance abuse or inability to deal with situations. Coping skills are designed to help limit the effects of emotional dis-regulation making managing day-to-day life much easier.

Why Learn Coping Skills?

Learning coping skills is all about replacing negative, dangerous or unhelpful ways of coping with strong emotions. BPD is characterized by strong emotion and many would argue that having strong feelings is not, in itself, a negative trait. The ways in which BPD sufferers tend to manage those emotions is where the problem is more often found. By learning new coping skills, you may be able to avoid damaging habits and ways of dealing with your emotions.

The benefits of learning new coping skills include;

Reducing the intensity of the emotions you feel.

Lessening the risk of using self-harm behaviors.

Avoiding engaging in behavior which can damage relationships.
Increase your abilities at operating under stress.
Build, or re-build, your own confidence in your abilities to deal with difficult situations.

Basic Coping Skills.

There are hundreds, possibly thousands, of different types of skills that will help you to achieve this result. However, some basic techniques include;

Support techniques; this includes ing a friend or relative to whom you can talk through issues. Support groups may also help and pair you up with someone who you can contact when the need arises.

Behavioral Activation; this is a technique designed to move the focus away from stressful or distressing thoughts for a few minutes.

Relaxation techniques. Again, there are hundreds of these and using them to simply re-focus and calm yourself is very effective.

Grounding. These exercises are designed to help you to learn to live in the moment, banishing fears, worries or distressing thoughts.

Mindfulness Meditation. This is commonly used in many illnesses which effect the emotions and is a simple technique to learn, with strong similitudes to grounding techniques.

Problem solving skills. Simple as this may seem it's an important tool for those with BPD to learn or re-learn. When faced with a problem it can become "too big" for those with BPD as a result of their emotional response. Learning new techniques to deal with problems can have a profound impact.

Some of the above skills will require input from others – ing the right support group or individual for example. However, others are relatively straightforward to implement for yourself and we'll take a closer look at them in the few.

Mindfulness Meditation Skills.

Practiced as part of the Buddhist tradition for many centuries, mindfulness is now gaining increasing recognition from the medical establishment. In the UK it is prescribed as part of a treatment for those suffering from a range of emotional conditions including depression, chronic pain and anxiety disorder (to name but a few). For those with BPD it has significant advantages.

What is Mindfulness Meditation?

With many different descriptions, including that as a relaxation technique, a stress management technique or a spiritual path, perhaps the most relevant to BPD is using a particular technique to pay attention purely to the present moment without taking a judgmental approach. The last part is perhaps the most important. Mindfulness meditation techniques are varied but the aim of the technique is to experience the moment clearly, calmly and without judging yourself or others.

By clearing the mind and quietly focusing your thoughts you can achieve a calmer emotional state, thereby dealing more easily with difficult emotions or situations. Mindfulness encourages us to look, observe and experience the outer world and our own inner world. This can be the harder part of the meditation to master for those with BPD.

Basic Mindfulness Techniques.

Sit in a quiet place and take a simple object, a piece of fruit is recommended as it presents a number of sensory prompts. Examine the fruit carefully, the feel, the texture, the smell. Inhale the scent deeply, consider the shape of the object. As you do so clear your mind of other thoughts, breathing slowly and gently. After only a few seconds thoughts will begin to intrude on your meditation. They may be positive or they may be negative; either way take a mental note of them and then dismiss them. This is the crucial part of mindfulness for those with BPD. Practice this daily – at the start and end of the day are great times. Also as you develop the skill, you can use focusing in the moment at anytime, anywhere. Simply try to quiet your brain and focus on your own breathing.

Benefits of Mindfulness.

Not only can mindfulness help you to learn to banish difficult emotions, without suppressing them, it can help you to cope in difficult emotional situations. In personal relationships those with BPD often that they react quickly, without thinking through their actions. By using mindfulness techniques, you can learn to slow that process, perhaps learning to step back, explain you cannot deal with the issue here and now as it is affecting you too strongly. This gives you the opportunity to take time and chose your behavior (and reaction) with more care.

Mindfulness techniques can be applied to all areas of your life – from driving to doing the housework. Allowing yourself to experience the moment only, and to avoid becoming overly negative, is a very positive way in which to learn how to cope with stress and strong emotion. It's important to note that you should allow negative thoughts to rise to the surface of your mind but simply accept them and move on to the thought and the sensation of the moment. While learning the technique some people the example given above useful but you can focus your awareness on something as simple as breathing or as complex as a piece of music.

Self-Care Techniques.

Feelings of low self-esteem, shame, loneliness and emptiness can all be profoundly affected by poor self-care. It can be a "Catch 22" situation, with poor self-care compounding these emotions and these in turn lead to more negative behaviors. Self-care includes getting enough exercise, having good sleep habits, ensuring you eat a nutritious diet, not drinking or smoking to excess (or at all), taking any medication that you have been prescribed and managing stress well in your life. Good self-care is important for everyone but has particular importance for those with BPD. Most people will admit that when they are tired, they may experience emotions more intensely and for those with BPD this is an important factor to consider. Reducing the impact of your emotions, or the strength of them, is a helpful way in which you can learn to manage them. Here are some quick tips for learning some useful self-care techniques.

Sleep Hygiene

Reduce or avoid alcohol, caffeine and nicotine before bedtime (preferably three hours before).

Don't eat a large meal just before bedtime but consider a light snack as being either too hungry or too full can interfere with sleep.

Create a bedtime ritual and keep to it. Our brains like to respond to habits!

Use Mindfulness or another relaxation technique to help you to drift off to sleep.

Only use your bed for sleeping. Don't read, watch TV, surf the net or eat in bed. Your brain associates these activities with wakefulness. Sex is the only exception in this case!

Avoid day time napping, however tired you feel. This is important if you've had a bad night's sleep. By napping you'll continue the cycle.

Get help. Speak to your main clinician or psychiatrist if your sleep problem is chronic, as medication may be the underlying cause.

Chapter 69. Symptoms of Borderline Personality Disorder

The primary signs that a person may be suffering from borderline personality disorder is an evident pattern of unstable personal relationships, negative self-image, and being too emotional. People with BPD are also usually very impulsive and may resort to self-destructive behavior such as suicide attempts and risky sexual behavior. Symptoms of BPD are consistent and observed in a wide range of social as well as personal situations. Eventually, if left untreated, these can lead to added stress and inability to function properly in social and work situations. The patterns are also noticeable because they are stable and tend to be long in duration.

1. Emotional Instability: BPD is also referred to as Emotionally Unstable Disorder because it is the prevalent characteristic in most cases. This is characterized as impulsivity, a rapid shift in emotions, chaotic relationships, and hostility. It is also common for people with BPD to jump from one emotional crisis to another.

While most people tend to experience impulsivity and rapid mood shifts during adolescence, those with borderline personality disorder exhibit it in life although it will last for a longer period of time. Adults who have BPD tend to suffer from extreme mood swings and anger. It is also normal for people to experience occasional mood shifts and emotional changes but for those who have BPD, these episodes are much more intense that it will impact their work, social, and personal lives.

Those with borderline personality disorder also have other problems with emotions. They tend to feel more negative emotions than other people. They also feel more "empty" and in fact may even describe the feeling as though they have nothing inside.

People with borderline personality disorder also feel emotions more intensely than others. It is not uncommon to meet people with BPD who live generally joyful and happy lives, but when they encounter negative emotions they instantly feel overwhelmed. Examples of these are instead of feeling sadness, they feel grief; instead of feeling embarrassed they feel humiliation and shame; instead of being annoyed they experience rage; and instead of feeling nervous they panic. For this reason, people with BPD are extremely sensitive to feelings associated with failure, isolation, and rejection.

Since they are not able to cope with these intense emotions they may result to self-harm. People with BPD are aware of the fact that they are having difficulties dealing with negative emotions and because they are unable to an outlet to cope they try to shut off these emotions completely.

Mood swings are part of the emotional instability experienced by individuals who have borderline personality disorder. These mood swings can happen often, in fact someone with BPD may go through many episodes in the course of a day. On the other hand, a mentally healthy person will experience mood swings just twice in a week. The mood swings brought about by borderline personality disorder are consistent over time.

There are also distinguishing features of mood swings caused by BPD. The primary difference is that BPD mood swings are caused by triggers, usually when the trigger is related to perceived rejection by another person. However, if a person is suffering from mood swings alone it is not enough to diagnose them of borderline personality disorder since it is just one of the many symptoms.

2. Impulsive behavior: Impulsive behavior is common in people with borderline personality disorder. It refers to acting quickly on something without contemplating the consequences of one's actions. Acting on impulse is usually a response to an event that causes extreme emotions that are usually negative, but for those with borderline personality disorder they act impulsively as a way to deal

with their emotions. It provides them with immediate relief from pain.

Common characteristics include alcohol or substance abuse, risky sexual behavior include participation in unprotected sex with multiple partners, reckless driving, irresponsible spending, and eating disorders. They also tend to change jobs and leave relationships more often. While it is normal for people to participate in these impulsive activities occasionally, for those with BPD it lasts for a longer period of time because they see these activities as an attempt to restore some normalcy in their lives and respond to extreme emotion. Impulsive behavior is one of the most troubling aspects of borderline personality disorder because it can lead to severe health problems, relationship issues, financial woes, and even legal issues down the line. People with borderline personality disorder also experience feelings of shame and guilt after giving into their impulsive behavior.

It is a dangerous cycle that involves feeling extreme emotions, resorting to impulsive behavior

as way of relieving their pain, then immediately feeling shameful and guilty about their behavior, resulting in emotional pain. This all leads to more extreme emotional pain to which a person with BPD will resort to new impulsive behavior in order to cope with their new pain. Over time, impulsive behavior will become an automatic way of dealing with emotional pain. This cycle explains why many people with borderline personality disorder tend to become addicted to different things that give them temporary relief from their emotions. For the same reason it is also why addiction and impulsivity in borderline personality disorder overlaps.

The common characteristics of people suffering from addiction and borderline personality disorder include:

□ Impulsive and harmful behavior

□ Severe mood swings ranging from depression and feelings of joy

□ Manipulative actions

□ A lack of concern for one's health and safety

- Pursuing dangerous activity despite the high risks involved
- A pattern of instability in finances, relationships, and jobs

The relationship between borderline personality disorder and addiction can be rather volatile. Drug and substance abuse will further aggravate the other dangerous symptoms of BPD particularly depression and anger. In some cases, this leads to more profound feelings of emotional emptiness.

Dialectical Behavior Therapy (DBT) is the best course of treatment in addressing this co-occurring disorder. It teaches skills such as mood awareness, meditation exercises, and training in social skills where the end goal is to reduce one's impulsivity. One of the key features of DBT that is useful in treating impulsivity is mindfulness which helps people become more aware of the consequences of the actions they are about to engage in. With the practice of mindfulness, impulsive people take the time to make better informed and healthy decisions as well as have better responses even in the light of extreme emotions and stress.

Some medications may also help reduce the symptoms of impulsivity in a person. However, the drugs are only effective when they are used together with psychotherapy. It should be noted that medication should not be the first course of treatment for impulsivity although it is useful for BPD and other co-occurring disorders. Antidepressants such as selective serotonin reuptake inhibitors are effective in treating impulsive behavior that occurs with borderline personality disorder. Other medicines such as

Effexor and Serzone have been shown to reduce symptoms of impulsivity.

3. Unstable Relationships: People suffering from BPD are not capable of having stable personal relationships. They cannot be alone for long periods of time because they also tend to suffer from abandonment anxiety. People with borderline personality disorder will try to hide their manipulative characteristics and dependency on their partners.

The inability to have lasting, stable relationships is also connected to impulsive behavior stemming from borderline personality behavior. Promiscuity and substance abuse creates conflict with romantic partners, resulting in separation, divorce, and even domestic violence. People who suffer from BPD have difficulty trusting other people. They feel irritable and angry, exhibiting temper tantrums even toward people that they care for. Because people with borderline personality disorder have a distorted view of what is socially acceptable, they experience difficulty in trusting people and cooperating with others. If they experience challenges within their relationships, they don't respond in a manner that would help to repair it unlike others. Doing this severely limits their capacity to be fully cooperative in romantic relationships as well as friendships.

The main reason why people with borderline personality disorder it difficult to focus on the emotions of other people is because they themselves are too overwhelmed with their own feelings. They that their emotional pain is a major obstacle. Individuals with borderline personality disorder also tend to feel that regardless of what their partner does, their emotional needs are never met. In spite of this, they don't have the ability to assert what they need in a healthy, productive manner. This results in frustrations because at the end of the day they don't get what they want and they feel angry.

People with BPD lack the skills to manage their anger and end up lashing out at their partners. Many cases of sexual and physical aggression towards partners are associated to borderline personality disorder.

Additionally, individuals with BPD view relationships as black or white. For them, people are either all good or all bad, there is no middle ground. In relationships, this kind of mentality devalues one's partners. But since they have extreme fears of abandonment, they may also resort to manipulation to prevent their partners from leaving them.

In particular, men who have borderline personality disorder can be emotionally explosive. Men with BPD are usually jealous, depressive, and angry most of the time. They may resort to physical aggression once they feel that their female partners are placing a distance between them, whether socially or emotionally.

This kind of behavior is also observed in lesbian relationships wherein one partner is suffering from borderline personality disorder. These situations found one partner resorting to violence when they felt that their partner was becoming physically or emotionally distant in the relationship. Studies have also shown that women with BPD are at higher risk of using aggression in relationships than those without BPD.

Couples wherein one partner suffers from borderline personality disorder usually have to turn to counseling as a form of therapy. It is necessary for each person in the relationship to see a therapist separately from the other so that they can each work on their own issues followed by addressing the relationship as a whole. There are therapists specializing in borderline personality disorder who can help couples manage their relationships better and move forward despite BPD.

4. Identity disturbance: People with BPD don't have a stable secure personality or sense of self. They are more sensitive to their environment and the people that they spend time with. As a result they will end up adopting habits, values, and even mimicking the attitudes of the people they spend time with the most.

Identity disturbance is also characterized by sudden but intense changes in a person's image. The instability in one's identity can also result to dramatic changes in career, values, life goals, types of friends, sexual identity, and even opinions.

5. Paranoia: In some cases, people with borderline personality disorder also suffer from paranoia. They are overtly suspicious of other people's behaviors and intentions, sometimes feeling like everyone is out to get them. These episodes of paranoia may come

and go, and are usually short lived. At most, it can last for a few days and often occur in periods of distress or trauma. People with paranoia tend to think that the world is out to get them, and have fears that include people spying on them or that friends are talking behind their back.

Paranoid thinking can be mild and short lived, although there are people that experience severe paranoia that lasts for months. Individuals that suffer from delusional disorder or psychotic disorders have chronic, severe paranoia which is completely unrelated from anything going on in reality.

6. Fears of Abandonment: Unlike separation anxiety, people with BPD experience abandonment fears wherein they perceive separation or a change in routine in their near future. This will cause them to react by extreme changes in behavior, self-image, thought, and mannerisms. If the thought of abandonment traumatizes them, they may resort to self-harm and even attempt suicide as a means of coping.

Most people with BPD who suffer from abandonment issues don't realize it but their behavior tells it all. There are certain characteristics of people with BPD that are related to their fear of abandonment. These include:

□ Staying in an unhealthy relationship because they cannot overcome their fear of being alone. Oftentimes people with BPD have extreme fears of abandonment that even if they are in a dysfunctional relationship that does not benefit them in any way whatsoever, they refuse to get out of it as they have formed a dependency on their partner. As a result both partners end up staying in a relationship that is full of conflict and drama.

□ Fear of abandonment may also be manifested through depression because the sadness is turned inwards.

□ People who have abandonment issues may show rage to people that they love. While it sounds like the complete opposite behavior you would expect from someone who does not want to be left by a loved one, people with BPD feel vulnerable and helpless and may end up lashing at their partner to regain a sense of control.

□ It is common for partners to experience being harassed by their partners who have BPD. It may be in the form of being bombarded by phone calls, texts, and emails because a person with BPD constantly needs reassurance that they will not be abandoned. Furthermore, fear of abandonment causes people to solitude or isolation completely unbearable and constantly trying to be in contact with their partner.

The cause of abandonment issues in people with borderline personality disorder varies. For some, it may be traumatic childhood issues that stemmed from neglect or abuse by a caregiver. Children who have been adopted, experienced the separation of their parents, or had a loved one die are also more prone to abandonment issues on.

7. Anger: Most people with borderline personality disorder feel angry all the time. They may or may not express it, but the feelings of anger or rage are there. Their anger may be caused by a variety of factors but primarily it is a result of feeling neglected, ignored, or uncared for especially by people they are close to. People with BPD may also feel shameful or guilty if they express their anger.

8. Dissociation: Defined as a form of attachment that leaves a person feeling unreal and numb, dissociation usually occurs on its own. Everyone can experience dissociation at some point in their lives, where they feel like they just went on automatic pilot in a particular situation. Because borderline personality disorder is considered a dissociative disorder, it gives the feeling that one is merely going through the motions of life without actually having any control. People who experience dissociation end up doing things without feeling emotions or connecting to the situation or people at all. In conditions of extreme dissociation, people can sometimes experience a complete block in memory. They are unable to recall situations

where they encountered trauma, abuse, and major stress as a survival mechanism.

For some people, the intensity of BPD symptoms doesn't last and in fact may decrease over time. This may be attributed to age, although there is no explanation yet on why some symptoms remain and others decline. There are some theories that attempt to explain this:

 Treatment and knowledge of borderline personality disorder can greatly reduce the symptoms' intensity through the years.

This is an obvious reason, as people who receive treatment and learn how to improve their lifestyles eventually reduce the problems they encountered before which was a result of BPD behavior.

 Burn out may also occur as BPD symptoms lessen with age. It is also a fact that individuals with borderline personality disorder just engage in less impulsive activities.

 People with BPD may also reduce interpersonal relationships altogether after many years of conflict and drama. Simply put, they avoid forming relationships to avoid problems.

Despite the observable decline of BPD symptoms in people as they age, there is no substitute for treatment. It is not a reason for people to avoid seeking help, thinking that things will improve in time. BPD people already put their lives in enough risk with impulsive behavior and miss out living their lives to their full potential.

9. Self-harm: Self-harm is a common symptom in people with borderline personality disorder. However, it is not to be confused with suicide because the two are completely different. Individuals resort to self-harm as a method of numbing emotional pain or as a way of punishing themselves. People also engage in self-harm as a way of reducing suicidal thoughts. In some cases, people with BPD fear that if they stop giving in to the urges to harm themselves they may actually become suicidal.

10. Suicide: Almost 80% of people with BPD have attempted suicide at least once in their lifetime. Unfortunately, around 10% of these people will actually succeed at their suicide attempt.

This is why it is necessary for those with a higher suicidal risk to be treated with inpatient methods and be confined in hospitals where they will be detached from anything that they can use to harm themselves.

Chapter 70. Dealing With BPD

Take Care of Yourself First

When a spouse, family member, or close friend suffers from BPD; there are times that you will get embroiled in your persistent efforts to please him/her. After a while, it dawns on you that you have invested a lot of your time and energy on this individual and are forgetting to take care of your emotional and personal needs. You have to realize that neglecting your own needs can be a gateway to depression, physical illness, and burnout. You cannot be of assistance to somebody or enjoy a satisfying and sustainable relationship with them when you have been knocked down by stress.

Imagine yourself ing a way to reduce your stress by stepping away from the stress. You can continue to care for yourself by following these few simple rules of self-care.

Do not give in to the temptation of isolating yourself: In as much as dealing with a family member or friend suffering from BPD may take a toll on you, it is not advisable to completely cut links with other friends and family that have always been a part of your life. During this moment of despair, hopelessness, and pain, you will definitely need a shoulder to cry on. You will certainly need people who are ready to listen to you, people who make you feel that you are loved and are available to help you whenever you get knocked down.

You are allowed and encouraged to build a life for yourself. You should take up the initiative to build a life separate from the one you have with the individual suffering from BPD. Avoid feeling guilty because you think that this is a selfish move. It is not selfish to set aside some time away from all the drama, to have fun, and relax. As a matter of fact, whenever you go back to the person with BPD after quality alone time, both of you stand a chance to benefit from how you have been relieved of stress.

You can opt to enroll in a support group for individuals who have friends and family members suffering from BPD: Interacting with people who have first-hand experience of what you are going through can be extremely life-changing. If it happens that there is no support group in your area, you should consider selecting a genuine and convenient online BPD support group.

Do not forget to take care of your physical health: Exercising, eating healthy food, and getting enough quality rest can go a long way in helping you deal with the frustration that comes with the drama from a loved one suffering from BPD. Try as much as possible to dodge this pitfall. When your health is in perfect shape and you are well-rested, you will be in a better position to handle stressful situations and control your behavior and emotions.

Teach yourself how to manage stress: Being anxious and upset as a result of a strained relationship with the individual suffering from BPD will only worsen the situation. It will increase their anger and agitation. Learning how to manage and relieve stress and staying relaxed and calm when the pressure hits the roof is very important to you as well as the person with BPD.

Communicate with the Person Suffering from BPD

Communication is a crucial part of any type of relationship. Nonetheless, communicating with an individual suffering from BPD can be extremely difficult. People who are closely related to an adult with the BPD condition usually compare talking to the person with getting into an argument with a child.

Usually, people with BPD it difficult to make sense of body language or comprehending the nonverbal part of a conversation. It is common for them to do things that are unfair, irrational, and cruel. The fear of being abandoned can trigger them to overreact to virtually anything, and their aggressive behavior can cause rage, impulsive fits, violence or verbal abuse.

The reason why they act this way is because BPD alters the way they hear and interpret things. The sentences and words that they hear appear, inside out, backward, sideways and completely different from their intended context.

Taking the initiative to listen to your loved one and taking into consideration his or her emotions is one of the most recommended ways of helping an individual with BPD to calm down. When you acknowledge how a person with BPD interprets your messages and make adjustments on how to handle communication with them, you will be halfway into the process of subsidizing their rages and attacks and building a closer and healthier relationship.

Communication Tips

It is critical to determine when it is safe to initiate a conversation. It is obviously not advisable to start a conversation if the person is threatening you, or when he or she is verbally abusive or in a rage. Calmly reschedule the conversation by using phrases such as, "Let us talk some other time when we are both relaxed and calm. I am willing to give you my undivided attention but it is not easy for me to do so at the moment."

When they calm down:

1.Listen keenly and be supportive. Try to avoid being distracted by things like your cellphone, computer, or TV. You should strive not to interrupt them or change the purpose of the conversation to a platform for you to express your concerns. Withhold any blame that you have against them, avoid judging them and show that you are interested in whatever they are talking about by nodding your head to show approval or giving short verbal feedbacks like, " go on" or "I understand." You do not have to necessarily be in agreement with what the person is saying to create the impression that you are listening to them and being supportive.

2.Direct your focus on the emotions they depict and not the words they say. People suffering from BPD communicate more using their emotions than their words. These people need acknowledgment and validation of the pain they are battling with. Therefore, take note of the emotions the individual with BPD is trying to put across without showing signs of being bogged down as you attempt to make sense of the words they are using.

3.Strive to make your loved feel like they are being listened to. Do not try to show them that they are wrong, do not try to come out victorious in the altercation or discredit their feelings, even if the things they are saying are not rational.

4.Try as much as possible to remain calm when individual with BDP is being over reactive. Try to avoid making it look like you are being defensive in the wake of criticisms and accusations, regardless of how irrational and unfair they seem. Stepping up to defend yourself will only make them angrier. You can opt to walk away if you feel that you need some time alone to cool down.

5.Try to distract the person with BPD when emotions surface. Anything that catches the attention of your loved one can work. However, the distraction will be more effective if the activity brings calm, such as taking a dog for a walk or doing simple chores in the house.

6.Try to avoid talking about the disorder. Talk about other topics of interest instead. In as much as the disorder has taken a toll on you and your loved one, you should come to the realization that the disorder does not define both of you entirely. Therefore, take the initiative to explore and discuss other topics of interest. Talking about less serious things can be helpful in reducing the animosity between the two of you. It may even be an avenue for your loved one to develop interests in new things or take up old hobbies.

Set Healthy Boundaries with Loved Ones Suffering from BPD

The most efficient way to help somebody with borderline personality disorder to control his or her behavior is by setting and enforcing healthy boundaries or limits. Setting boundaries helps this person realize that they need to improve how they handle the needs of the environment they are living in, where the legal system, workplaces, and schools, for instance, all come up with and enforce strict rules on what acceptable and unacceptable behavior is.

Coming up with boundaries can be instrumental in mitigating the instability and chaos of your situation at that moment and can also give you a number of new choices on how to handle negative behavior. If both parties respect the set boundaries, you will be in a position to trust each other. This is a major step in the right direction since trust is a fundamental factor in any relationship.

Before you come up with and enforce boundaries, ensure that you talk to your loved ones about it. Ensure that you bring up this discussion at a moment when both of you are calm and not embroiled into the heat of an altercation. Make the decision on what type of behavior you will put up with and what you will not advocate for.

Make it clear to them that you expect them to respect those boundaries. For instance, you can tell them that if they cannot talk to you without abusing you or screaming at you, you will walk out.1

It is important to note that setting boundaries is not a miraculous fix for a strained relationship. As a matter of fact, things might kick off by getting worse than they were before they get better. The individual with BPD is afraid of rejection and expresses sensitivity to any perceived insult. This insinuates that if you had never taken the initiative to set boundaries in your relationship forward on, your loved one may react negatively when you start enforcing these boundaries. If you show signs of defeat or surrender in the wake of your loved one's abuse or rage, you will be strengthening their bad behavior and the cycle will keep on repeating itself. Remaining firm and not backing down on your decisions can be a source of empowerment for you. For your loved one it may eventually transform how they relate to you and others.

Dos and Don’ts of healthy boundaries

Let us take a look at some of the DOs and DONTs of setting up healthy boundaries:

DOs

1.Calmly give reassurance to the individual with BPD when you set those boundaries. Use reassuring words like “I love you and I really want us to have a healthy relationship, but I cannot handle the stress I go through because of your behavior. I really need you to make this adjustment for me."

2.Ensure that everybody in the relationship with the person with BPD agrees with the boundaries and how to execute the consequences if they are not respected.

3.It is important to treat setting limits as a process instead of an event that is carried out instantaneously. Rather than bombarding the person with BPD with a chain of limits all at once, try to introduce them slowly, probably one or two at a time.

DON’Ts

1.Avoid giving ultimatums and making threats and promises that you cannot follow up on. It is the nature of human beings to test the limits that have been put in place. Similarly, your loved one will also test the boundaries you set. If you slacken and do not put into action the consequences, they will come to the conclusion that your boundaries are meaningless and the bad behavior will re-occur. Giving ultimatums should be a last option. However, you should be ready to follow through.

2.Do not put up with abusive behavior. Nobody should ever have to tolerate physical violence or verbal abuse. In as much as the person, you care about is behaving in a certain way because he has BPD does not make the impact of the behavior any less damaging or real to you as well as other members of the family.

3.Do not encourage negative behavior from the person with BPD by shielding them from the repercussions of their actions. If the person you care about will not be respectful of your boundaries and continues to instill fear and anxiety in you, then you might be forced to leave. It does not mean that you do not care about them, still, you should always prioritize taking care of yourself.

Supporting the BPD Treatment for the People You Care About

It is important to make it clear that borderline personality disorder is treatable. Nonetheless, it common for individuals with the condition to avoid going for treatment or denying the fact that they have a problem. If the person you care about exhibits some of these characteristics, you can still support them, communicate with them more effectively, and set boundaries as you continue to encourage them to seek help from a professional.

Although options for medication are available, the guidance and advice of a trained therapist can be a major step toward the recovery of your loved one.

Borderline personality disorder therapies like schema-focused therapy as well as dialectic behavior therapy can be very helpful in helping your loved one to work on their trust and relationship issues. Try out a number of new or more effective coping techniques, in helping them learn how to handle their emotional eruptions or how to calm themselves down in a healthy manner.

How to Support Treatment

1.If the person you care about does not accept that they have borderline personality disorder, you might want to take into consideration other approaches like couple's therapy for instance, where attention is directed on the relationship and how to improve communication, instead of dwelling on your partner's disorder. Taking this approach might make your partner agree to going for BPD treatment in the long run.

2.Talk to your loved one and advise them to look for and try out better ways of dealing with stressful situations and emotions. For example, the use of relaxation techniques such as deep breathing, meditation, and yoga or mindfulness can relieve stress fast and easily.

You can choose to join your loved one in any of these therapies. This may be instrumental in strengthening your bond and might also inspire them to seek other treatment avenues.

3.If the person with BPD develops the ability to handle distress, hero she can teach themselves how to press the 'calm down' button when they feel the urge to behave irrationally.

Do Not Ignore Threats of Self-Harm or Suicide

Threats of suicide or self-harm are very common among people with BPD. Sadly, most of people see these threats as attention-seeking strategies, especially if the person they care about has failed to follow through.

It is important to make it clear that actual self-harm and suicide are a common occurrence among people suffering from BPD. Roughly 10% of people diagnosed with BPD commit suicide, while 80% of individuals who plot to commit suicide show their intentions to other people. Some even express their thoughts and plans openly.

If somebody you care about threatens to commit suicide or cause harm to themselves, do not ignore or argue with them. Avoid accusing them of manipulativeness or attention-seeking. Instead, acknowledge that they are going through a tough time and genuinely show your concern. Talk to them or keep them company until you hand them over to a professional. In as much as it is never your fault if someone you care about makes an attempt to commit suicide or self-harm, it is critically important to make sure that you keep them from danger.

Take up the Initiative to Learn about the Disorder

BPD can be a very confusing diagnosis. This explains why there are numerous misconceptions about individuals with BPD. Learning about the disorder, its signs, symptoms, and prognostication can help you get a clearer understanding of what the person you care about is going through.

With the emergence of new technology, there are numerous sources of information from reliable sources on the internet. In addition, also get in touch with a professional who specializes in mental health, for a much more detailed and practical one-on-one conversation. Comprehending borderline personality disorder can help you sail through the confusion and genuinely understand the problem your loved one is going through. You will be better equipped to give them the necessary support all through their healing process.

Understand That It Is Not Their Fault

BPD is well-known for exerting too much stress on relationships. It can be an enormous challenge-even an impossibility for somebody with BPD to manage their condition in a manner that does not affect the people around him or her. Whenever these symptoms erupt and a person with BPD starts to act abusively or violently, put it in mind that they literally do not have control of the situation.

This condition is always identified by an inability for one to regulate, or control their behaviors, thoughts, and emotions. The same way you would not blame a person who has cancer symptoms, do not blame somebody who has a mental disorder that has active symptoms.

Chapter 71. Borderline Personality Disorder Guidelines

Are you practicing self-care? If you answered no, you are not alone, because those with borderline personality disorder often have difficulties taking good care of themselves. However, if you have BPD you need to make self-care a priority, because many symptoms become worse when you aren't taking good care of yourself and other symptoms can be reduced when you do take good care of you. You're important and you need to make sure that you make yourself important!

Defining Self-Care

Engaging in activities that promotes good mental and physical health and help relax you are the basics of self-care. Self-care activities include establishing good sleep habits, getting regular exercise, eating a nutritious diet, managing your stress, taking medications as prescribed, and attending sessions that are part of your treatment.

Self-Care is Important When You Have BPD

For the most part, those who take good care of themselves, generally have fewer physical and mental health ailments, so you can see why self-care is important to all, whether you have BPD or not. If you have BPD, self-care is even more important. That's because many borderline personality disorder symptoms are much worse if you don't participate in self-care.

For example, when you are overtired you tend to have much stronger emotional reactions or when you are stressed you are more likely to participate in impulsive behaviors. Self-care can help to reduce your impulsive behavior, mood changes, irritability and other BPD symptoms.

Making Good Sleep Hygiene a Priority

Sleep is one of the most important things you can do for yourself and yet far too many people overlook it. When you don't get enough sleep or your sleep is interrupted, your BPD symptoms can become much worse, so it's important to work at getting a good night's sleep. Let's look at what you can do.

Avoid caffeine, nicotine and alcohol - If you have trouble sleeping, you should avoid caffeine, nicotine and alcohol several hours before your bedtime.

Don't eat a large meal before bedtime - Avoid eating foods that could upset your stomach, heavy meals or large meals for at least four hours before bedtime.

Have a light snack – If you are hungry before bed make sure to eat something light, because while a heavy meal interferes with your sleep an empty stomach also does.

Create a pre-bed ritual – Establish a routine that you carry out every night before you go to bed. This should relax you and prepare your body for sleep. It might be reading quietly, listening to meditation music or having a warm bath. It's not what you do that's important, but that you do it every night at the same time.

Your bedroom should be comfortable – The environment of your bedroom should be designed for you to sleep. Things like reduced noise, lights off and a comfortable temperature are all ways to create a comfortable sleep environment.

Have a regular sleep schedule – Every day you should get up at the same time and every night you should try to go to bed at around the same time.

Use relaxation techniques – Before you go to bed, practice relaxation technique that works for you. This can include imagery, deep breathing or progressive muscle relaxation.

If you can't sleep, get out of bed - Go to bed when you are sleepy. However, if you aren't able to fall asleep you need to get out of bed. Return to your bed only when you feel sleepy.

Your bed is only for sleeping – It's not for watching television or eating or playing on your tablet. Other than sleep, sex is the only thing that should happen in your bed. By doing this you train your body that when you go to bed it's time to sleep.

No naps – Don't take a nap during the day, even if you are really tired because you will disrupt your night's sleep.

Exercise during the day – Exercise before bed should be limited because it can actually energize you and make it hard to sleep.

Talk to your doctor – If you have tried everything and sleep still eludes you, then it's time to talk to your doctor, who may be able to prescribe a sleeping pill to help you or have other techniques that might work.

Get Physical

The connection between our minds and our bodies is significant. This is why many scientists are now studying the impact of exercise on mental health, and why they are ing that exercise can have a dramatic impact on mental health.

The problem is when you are suffering from borderline personality disorder you are less likely to think about your physical health. The sedentary lifestyle is likely to result in you having additional health concerns.

There's very few illnesses that physical activity doesn't help with. Whether you walk, run, dance or go to the gym, it doesn't matter. It's not what you do that's important but that you do something. Physical activity helps a number of ways. The most obvious is that it distracts you from your current emotions.

There are all kinds of exercise regime. You can make it as simple or as complicated as you want to. Choose something you like to do, because then you are much more likely to follow through. Make your exercise part of your daily routine. Before long you'll be looking forward to it and enjoying the benefits.

Ensure You Are Eating a Healthy Diet

If you have BPD, your feet are very important. Eating a well-balanced, nutritious meal regularly is key and you also need to avoid. Improper eating can have a major impact on your BPD symptoms and mood. Let's look at how to improve your diet.

Eat plenty of fresh fruits and vegetables

Avoid fast food, junk food and processed food

Avoid sugar

Choose lean cuts of meat

Eat plenty of fish

Reduce your salt intake

Eat regularly – do not let yourself become extremely hungry

Drink plenty of water every day

Healthy eating really isn't that difficult. It's more about making it a habit. It's so easy to grab something quick like a burger from fast food. Then we get into that habit and we spend less time creating healthy meals, which can also be put together quickly with a little practice. You'll feel much better once you are eating healthy.

Take Your Medications As Prescribed

You might not think of your medication as part of your self-care, but it actually is a very important part of your self-care. It's easy to forget to take your medication, but it is so important to take it as prescribed. By making it part of your daily routine you are more likely to remember. You might even consider scheduling a reminder into your smart phone to remind you when it's time to take your medication.

Learn To Manage Your Stress

One of the most important ways you can care for yourself is to learn how you can effectively manage your stress. Not all stress is bad. Studies have shown we are at our peak mental health when we have a small amount of stress in our lives, but not too much, stress. It is when your stress starts to overwhelm that it can be a problem and you can develop techniques to help you manage that stress. There are many ways to reduce stress. Here are just a few examples.

Play Music – Music can help to relax and de-stress you. It can create feelings of happiness and joy. It can help to reduce anxiety and it can lift you up. Best of all, it's easy to music. Just turn on your radio or television. If you have a smart phone apps like Songza have tons of free music you can listen to.

Talk to Someone – Having someone you trust is a big help during those times when you are struggling with stress. Call someone you are close to or call a crisis line.

Quiet Time – If you are stressed make some quiet time for you. That can be a walk, a quiet relaxing bath, some time with your favorite author or anything that you enjoy. The key is that everyone must respect that this your time to unwind and you must be left alone.

Meditation - Taking some quiet time in peaceful surroundings can be very helpful when you are stressed. a quiet spot where you can meditate without interruption.

Grounding Exercises - Sights, smells and sensations can help you focus on the moment. For example, take a deep breath, and start to mentally list the things you see around you; listen to the sounds around you and how they change; snap a rubber band against your wrist.

Breathing Exercises - Sit somewhere that's quiet and focus your attention to your breathing. Breathe deeply, evenly and slowly letting your stomach rise and fall with each breath.

Chapter 72. Communicating With BPD

Most of the time, we flippantly speak of the essence of communication as if it is an easy and simple task. Communication is not easy in normal circumstances, and that is why we are always insisting on improving it in our marriages, our workplace, in just about every interaction that we have. Imagine how much more difficult communication is with a person who has a borderline personality disorder. To a person with BPD normal communication seems impossible. They often feel that family and friends don't understand them no matter how hard they try to make themselves understood...

On the other hand, you as the guardian of your loved one might also it hard to understand what they are trying to express. In such situations, it becomes very frustrating for both parties. You may end up arguing over something or become defensive. To avoid such miscommunications, it is important for your loved ones to have trust, understand your experiences and feelings and have common terminologies when communicating.

There is no magic for creating easy communication between you and your loved one suffering from BPD. Despite that, we can all overcome the difficulties if we are willing to adopt a patient approach. Understanding where the source and origin of the difficulties come from, it might help us to pave the way for compassion on all sides.

So, why is it so hard to communicate with people with BPD?

Quality changes in BPD sufferers

A person who is suffering from BPD experiences changes in their qualities. One day they will have different beliefs and devotions, and in the next one, they will shift in the opposite direction. They lack consistency in their sense of self, making it difficult to communicate with them. These "quality shifts" make them disagree on things they had believed a while ago, making them refute agreements they had made forward or change their minds quickly.

It Affects People from Their Childhood

BPD affects people when they are still young before their brain is fully formed. It colors their view of the world at a young age. BPD gives them symptoms like black and white thinking and emotional sensitivity. It becomes difficult to be reasonable, and that is why most people with the disorder are labeled as stubborn.

BPD Sufferer's Experience Overwhelming Emotions

Have you ever experienced uncontrollable anger where you end up yelling at the other party or cursing at them? For people with BPD, the anger experience is more overwhelming than for normal people. They experience a magnitude of emotions that cripples their ability to express themselves and speak calmly. They, therefore, express their feelings with the intensity in which they are feeling them.

BPD Sufferers Experience Contradicting Emotions

This personality disorder makes our loved one's experience contradictory emotions simultaneously. They may want to be around you while at the same time, they are pushing you away. It makes them hurt themselves to relive emotional pains. It puts them in emotional states that are difficult for them to talk about.

They Lack the Medical Understanding to Compare Their Experiences

Most people with BPD are not aware of their illness. Some who are aware have no idea how to ease the symptoms with treatment or therapy. It makes them believe what their illness tells them; that they are useless, hopeless, and will always live in pain. These are just some examples of what the disease makes them believe. Not having a medical background to help them know that they are just symptoms of a treatable disorder, makes it tough to reason with them that their future has hope.

Tips for Communicating with Someone with BPD

Our loved ones suffering from BPD disorder are important in our lives, and we cannot live without them. How can we make communication with our loved ones simpler?

1.Be realistic

It is important to note that you can never eliminate your loved ones BPD, no matter how much you make communication easier for them. All you can do is communicate in a way that is shows respect for you and your loved one.

2.Leave

If your loved one makes physical threats or verbal abuse, you should not tolerate it. Leave if necessary, and come back when they are calm.

3.Simplify your communication

When communicating with a person with BPD keep in mind that emotions are likely to be strong and you cannot reason with them while they are on a "high level", especially on sensitive issues. Use simple language and try not to give them reason to misinterpret your messages.

4.Separate their behavior from them

Most actions from a BPD might irritate you and, in such situations, assure them that you might dislike their behavior, but that does not mean that you dislike them. Make this a habit and assure them of your love often.

5.Learn to address facts after feelings

In normal circumstances, we address facts before feelings. We usually weigh the facts and their pros and cons before we can react. People with BPD reverse this process and often have feelings before looking at the facts. By doing so, they may end up changing the facts to match their feelings.

6.Keep calm and focus on your message

During conversations with people with BPD, they might use threats that are attacks to try and change the subject. In such cases, stay calm and stick with your point of view. If it gets bad, there is no shame in leaving and explaining to them that you will be back when they are calm. When you get back to the discussion, you should stick with your point of view and support it.

7.Ask questions

Turn the tables and let your loved ones feel in control by making suggestions. Let them give you alternative solutions by asking questions such as, "

"You have pushed me to the end, and I have no idea what to do, what do you think we should do?" Allowing them this input can lessen the tension in your discourse with them.

8.Good timing

It is important to know their vulnerable times and normal times. Avoid conversations when you loved in is in a vulnerable state as your communication will be difficult. Having conversations when they are vulnerable will make them feel rejected and abandoned.

9.Remind your loved one that you care

It might sound obvious, but this is magic for someone with BPD. Most of the time a person with BPD has a hard time believing that people care about them, especially when they don't see or talk with you in a while. They believe that the lack of communication from the people they love means that they don't care. Keep communicating and assuring them that you care and you always will. For example: If you go for a long time without communicating and then you communicate to ask for a favor, it may make them think that you are only contacting them because you need their help. Send messages, tweets or any communication that works for them to remind them you care about them.

10.Ask them how they are faring

Most people with this disorder bottle up shame and fear about themselves. They do this because they fear rejection, and it is not easy to lay open their vulnerabilities. By asking them how they are faring, it reminds them that they are important and that you care. If you notice your loved one looking depressed or see a post on social media indicating that they are sad, ask them how they are faring. It might look simple to you, but it is very effective for people with BPD.

11.Cushion difficult information with empathy and support

When delivering a difficult message to your loved one, you should look for ways to curb their fears to enable them to take the information. Begin with reminding them that you care and acknowledge their feelings before hitting them with the hard truth. You can implement SET communication skills. The SET method lets you address their assertions, feelings, and demands honestly and at the same time maintain boundaries.

 -Support- This is the initial statement that shows that you support your loved one. You should always start that statement with 'I' to show your concern and wish to help. Your statement should establish a foundation for communication. This support statement is supposed to reassure your loved one that your relationship is great and that their needs are still important despite the difficulty at hand.

 -Empathy- By displaying empathy, you show your loved one that you understand their feelings. It should not be confused with sympathy or pity. Empathy is being aware of their feelings and validating them. Let your loved one know that you understand their uncomfortable feelings and reassure them that it is okay to have them.

 -Truth- Truth, in this case, is the sincere assessment of the situation at hand and your loved one's role in solving the problem. It focuses on the objective matter and not on the experience of either of you. With truth, you can respond to your loved one's demands and at the same time place responsibility where it belongs.

Using the above method does not mean that you agree with your loved one's behavior or demands. You are only validating and recognizing their feelings. SET does not mean that you are setting the person with BPD off the hook but rather ensuring they have been heard.

12.Avoid describing their behavior with judgmental words

I am not trying to tell you that we don't have people with BPD who are abusive. No, they can be abusive, but most of them are not. They have unkind behaviors and actions. When dealing with a person with BPD, the language you use can make a great difference in how they perceive you and their reactions towards your feedback. Never characterize them or their behaviors with judgmental words.

13. Be sensitive to their triggers

this might be a little difficult as everyone has different triggers. You can commit yourself to learn and observe what triggers your loved one. Most of the people with BPD are sensitive to abandonment and rejection. Situations and conversations that can make your loved one feel like they are being rejected or abandoned should be handled with care. True, we cannot avoid such situations in life, but before presenting them, it is good to reassure them that you still love and care for them and you are not abandoning them.

14.Time out

Give your loved ones a break and don't be too hard on them. Remember all they do is unacceptable in society. They spend a lot of money and time to unlearn themselves, and after all that sacrifice, we still require them to change to meet society's expectations. Always aim to understand them and never be judgmental.

15. Validate

We all need validation in our lives, and people living with this disorder need it more- they have received a lot of the opposite the whole of their lives. It does not mean that we agree with them, their behavior, and actions. Let them know you understand how they are feeling and that it is okay to feel that way.

16. Practice delay, distract, depersonalize, and detach

during intense discussions, delay them to give them time to digest what you are saying. Be calm to affirm them but not confirming their claims.

 Distract – Distract them from the topic at hand and request to do something else with them like going for a walk.
 Depersonalize - During conversations; keep reminding yourself of the effects of harsh criticism on your loved one. Also, don't take their criticism personally.
 Detach - Make it a point not to get involved in the emotional whirlwind.

Chapter 73. What is Dialectical Behavior Therapy

BPD or borderline personality disorder is a serious psychological condition that makes it difficult for a person to feel comfortable in themselves. It is characterized by unstable moods and emotions, behavior as well as relationships which makes it hard for people to control their impulses and emotions. BPD is one of the several personality disorders recognized by the American Psychiatric Association (APA).

Understanding BPD

BPD commonly begins in adolescence or early adulthood, and it can continue for a long period of time, often causing serious issues when relating to the people around them. If left untreated, BPD can cause a great deal of distress. People with BPD have high levels of anger, often taking offense at things people say or do. They also have high levels of distress and struggle with beliefs and painful thoughts about themselves, as well as the people, come to know. BPD has a serious impact on almost every aspect of the person's life, from family, relationships, siblings, social as well as work life. Some people with BPD also resorts to harming themselves.

Symptoms usually begin during their teen years or as a young adult, some improve as they get older, but most don't without the right treatment. It is important for you to realize that BPD is a condition of the mind and the brain, and if someone has BPD, it is not their fault as they did not cause it.

Why is it called 'Borderline'?

The word borderline is added to this order simply due to historical reasons. Before medical science and therapy science began to develop, BPD was categorized as a 'neuroses' and 'psychoses' by psychiatrists. When it was first being researched and written about, BPD did not fall into any of the above-mentioned categories, so psychiatrists decided to put it in its own category, on an imaginary line between 'psychoses' and 'neuroses.'

When is BPD Diagnosed?

Doctors or psychiatrists look for five major symptoms or criteria that you have the experience to evaluate and assess if you have BPD. Apart from these five factors, they also investigate the time period of these symptoms - if they have lasted for a considerable amount of time:

You worry about people abandoning you

You have intense emotions that last anywhere between a few hours to a few days, and it can also change quickly

You do not have a strong sense of who you are, and it also changes depending on who you are with

You also it difficult to make and keep stable relationships

You act impulsively and do things that harm yourself

You feel emptiness

You often self-harm

You also have suicidal feelings

You have intense feelings of anger, and you it difficult to control

You may also experience dissociation as well as paranoia

Getting a diagnosis for a mental disorder can answer many of the questions running through your mind and bring you calmness as it can help formulate proper treatment and speed up you or your loved one's recovery process. The issue with BPD is that it is difficult to diagnose. Many of the symptoms associated with BPD, such as impulsivity and self-image, are common in other disorders as well.

For children, it can also be difficult to diagnose BPD as their brain and mind are still in early development and is constantly changing.

A study found in Psychiatric Times reported that among the adolescents that showed symptoms of BPD between the ages of 15 to 18, only 40 percent of them met the specific criteria two years. Research on BPD is still not substantial enough, which makes treatment even more difficult. However, if your child is under the age of 18, and you believe that they may have BPD with symptoms that have maintained over at least 1 year, then they may be diagnosed with this disorder.

Signs & Symptoms of BPD

Many mental health care professionals in the past often it difficult to treat borderline personality disorder, concluding that there is little help available. However, it's 2019, and mental health science and therapy have come a long way.

As many experts can tell you know, BPD is treatable, so if you have it, or your adolescent child has it, take a deep breath and know that you will get better. You will know what is going on with your mind and brain, and you will be alright. The best part is long term projection for BPD is much better than the ones with bipolar disorders as well as depression.

For this to happen, diagnosis and treatment are crucial treating BPD requires a specialized approach.

When you start to heal, it is about breaking those feelings, thoughts, and behaviors that are detrimental to a dysfunctional, simultaneously freeing you. It is not easy to change lifelong habits, but when you choose to change through practicing reflecting, mindfulness and emplacing the desire to change, you will better. It may seem unnatural and uncomfortable at first, but with time, you will form better, healthier and less destructive habits that enable you to stay in control and have a better emotional balance.

Recognizing borderline personality disorder

One way or step towards getting a diagnosis is to do a little self-exploration. Ask yourself if you feel any of these feelings or emotions:

I feel' empty' sometimes.

My feelings are shifting very rapidly, and I am sometimes extremely sad, frustrated, and nervous.

The people I care about, I'm just afraid they'll give me up or leave me.

Most of my romantic relations would be characterized as deep yet volatile.

I don't always understand why I think of people differently all the time

Why do I always do things that are unhealthy for me?

Why am I always hurting myself?

If I am insecure in a relationship, I tend to lash out to the other person or act out impulsively

What causes BPD?

Just like other mental disorders, borderline personality disorder causes are not fully understood. There are also environmental factors to consider, such as a history of trauma, neglect, or abuse. The borderline disorder may also be linked to:

Genetics. Research done on twins and families show that personality disorders among family members may be hereditary or strongly linked to other mental health disorders.

Brain abnormalities. Certain research shows improvements in emotion regulation, impulsiveness, and violence in specific areas of the brain. However, other brain chemicals such as serotonin that helps to control or regulate moods may not be functioning the right way.

Risk factors

Certain factors that are related to PBD can also increase the risk of developing PBD. These risk factors include:

Hereditary predisposition. You may be at higher risk when the same or related condition happens to a close relative— your mother, uncle, brother, or sister.

Stressful childhood. Sexual or physical abuse during childhood or even neglect are also high factors that cause PBD. An adult could have been separated from a parent when they were young, or their parents/caregivers could have been substance-abusers or even had mental issues of their own to deal with. It could also be volatile and violent environments that the adult grew up in that included unstable and unsafe relationships.

Complications

Most aspects of your life can be affected by borderline personality disorder. Intimate relationships, employment, education, social activities, and self-image can be negatively affected, resulting in:

- Always changing jobs
- Getting Fired
- Not completing their education
- Having constant legal problems
- Relationships are filled with stress and conflict
- Always self-harming
- Frequent hospitalization
- Tendency to be involved in abusive relationships
- Suicide attempts
- STDs, motor vehicle accidents
- Unplanned pregnancies
- Physical fights because of risky behavior

You may also have other mental health problems, such as:

- Bipolar disorder
- Depression
- Alcohol or other substance misuses
- Eating disorders, Anxiety disorders
- Post-traumatic stress disorder (PTSD)
- Attention-deficit/hyperactivity disorder (ADHD)

- Other personality disorders

BPD Signs & Symptoms

- Abandonment- The prospect of being left alone or abandoned terrifies these individuals. Something as simple as a loved one going away on a weekend may cause them to have intense fear. Their response would be frenzied attempts to keep them close by begging, clinging, starting a fight, or even stalking to prevent them from leaving. This behavior always has the opposite effect, which is driving loved ones away.
- Unstable relationships. Relationships of individuals with BPD are often extreme and short. Falling in love is hard and quick, but they also get disappointed quickly. There is no middle ground in the relationship- it is either perfect or horrible. Their friends, lovers, family members often bear the brunt of this emotional whiplash because of the rapid swings from devaluation to idealization, hate to anger, happiness to sadness.
- Vague or fluctuating self-image- When a person has BPD, their sense of self is usually unstable. They may feel good about themselves at one point, but there are times when they hate themselves. They also do not have a clear idea of what they want in their life or who they are. Because of this, they often change jobs frequently, have various partners, change religion, and have various values and goals, even sexual identity.
- Exhibit impetuous, self-damaging behaviors. There is often this need for sensation seeking, which involves extremely injurious behaviors, especially when they are upset or sad. This could be anything from binge eating to shoplifting, reckless driving, risky sex, or even substance abuse. These actions may help them feel momentarily better but usually ends up hurting them and the people around them.
- Harming themselves. Dangerous behavior or attempting suicide and intentionally harming themselves are common tendencies in people with BPD. When it comes to suicide, it often revolves around

making threats of killing themselves, suicidal suggestions or talk, and also attempting to kill themselves. Self-harm involves all other attempts without suicidal intent to hurt yourself. Cutting and burning are common forms of self-harm.

- Extreme emotional swings. BPD also involves unstable moods and emotions where one minute you feel happy, and the next, you are sad. These things that are no big deal for other people are an emotional tailspin for you. When a person with BPD experiences these mood swings, it is usually very intense, but they also pass quickly, lasting for a few minutes or even a few hours, unlike the emotional swings of depression or bipolar disorder.
- Lingering feelings of emptiness. Feelings of hollowness, like a hole or gap, is what they feel often, and it also feels like nothingness or feeling like you are nobody and nothing. This feeling eats the individual inside, making them feel even more isolated, and this hole is usually filled with binge eating, alcohol, sex or substances.
- Explosive anger. You may be struggling with intense anger and a short temperature if you have BPD. You may also have trouble controlling yourself and begin to do things like yell, be consumed by rate and start throwing things, or bashing your fists into the wall. It is crucial to realize and be aware that this anger isn't always outwardly targeted. You may be angry at yourself for most of the time.
- Feeling suspicious or out of touch with reality. BPD people also deal with suspicion or suspicious thinking about the intentions of others. You can even lose touch with reality when you are under stress — an experience referred to as dissociation. These individuals may feel spaced out, foggy like having an out of body experience.

Common co-occurring disorders

There are always co-occurring disorders or issues that are diagnosed alongside BPD. These are:

- anxiety disorders
- depression or bipolar disorder
- substance misuse

- eating disorders

A successful BPD intervention would also mean the diminishing of all these other co-occurring disorders. But it is always not the case. For example, you may be successfully treated for your depression symptoms and still struggle with BPD.

DBT for Borderline Personality Disorder

DBT was primarily intended for people with borderline personality disorder (BPD), and it has been adapted over the years to address other conditions patients have exhibited, such as eating disorders, self-destructive behaviors as well as substance abuse. DBT is also administered for patients with post-traumatic stress disorder.

You'd be glad to know that the American Psychiatric Association has given its endorsement for BPD as an effective treatment for borderline personality disorder. This endorsement classifies the following benefits of DBT:

- Lower and less frequent acts tendencies of suicide
- Hospitalizations periods are shorter less frequently
- Reduced anger
- Less probability of dropping out of treatment
- enhanced social performance

DBT's primary objective is to help anyone going through this therapy to manage their difficult emotions. When you go through a DBT therapy, you explore these emotions by allowing yourself to experience it, recognize it, and accept it. As you journey into accepting and regulating these emotions, you open the prospect of changing any harmful and dangerous behaviors. Therapists using the DPT method use a combination of hospitalization periods that are shorter less frequently of change and acceptance techniques.

The therapist's aim is to form a healthy balance between change and acceptance:

- Acceptance- is all about accepting you just as you are
- Change- is about making positive changes in your life

Acceptance Techniques

Through acceptance techniques, the focus here is to understand yourself as a person and making sense of why you the things you do, such as binge drinking, self-harming, and drug abuse. The therapist might point out to you that these negative behaviors are just a result of being the only way you know how to deal with the intensive feelings you have. So, while it may make sense to you, it is damaging in the long-term, and it is alarming for other people.

Change Techniques

Change techniques are used by DBT therapists to encourage a change in behavior patterns that are destructive and instead focus all that attention towards learning healthier ways of coping and dealing with stress and distress. Therapists will help in replacing these behaviors and to help you move forward in your life using better coping mechanisms. For instance, one of the things you will be learning is to challenge your unhealthy thoughts and develop a different point of view of looking at things. In DBT Therapy, you must go all in, take a leap of faith knowing that you are in good hands, and be open and willing to have your behaviors and thoughts challenged. It is hard work on both sides- you and the therapist, but it is worth the effort and life starts to get better after this

Benefits of DBT for Borderline Personality Disorder

Dialectical Behavior Theory has been used over the past 30 years, and based on the extensive research on this theory, DBT is a treatment recognized as the treatment with the strongest demonstration of effectiveness when it comes to BPD. It also has the highest research support by Division 12 of the American Psychological Association for Borderline Personality Disorder.

The benefits of DBT include:

- Lowering behaviors of suicide and self-harm.
- Reduced suicidal ideation and depression for adolescents with BPD characteristics.
- Beneficial in keeping people at risk from achieving full diagnostic criteria for BPD.

- Help people with BPD develop more active emotion-regulating techniques to create more controlled feelings, attitudes, and thoughts.

According to Linehan & Dimeff (2001), DBT serves as comprehensive treatment using these five functions:

- Strives to improve behavioral efficiency.
- Enhances the incentive to change by working to change contingencies of resistance and strengthening.
- Ensures patients that new capabilities are common in the natural environment.
- Framework the therapeutic process so that the patient and the therapist are properly supported.
- Improves the therapist's ability to provide motivation for effective patient treatment.

The Theory Behind Mindfulness

In this, you will plenty of references to mindfulness. There are plenty of questions as to why to use mindfulness in Borderline Personality Disorder. The bigger question is 'Why not?'. Mindfulness, in its very core, is just training the mind to pay attention to life in a particular way, and that way is by being present in the moment, experiencing the here and the now.

Where BPD is concerned, if you act mindlessly, you can also act mindfully. Anything that you do mindlessly can also be done mindfully. Simple right?

Most of our behavior is very routine based that a large percentage of our lives just go by with us doing things by the roster. Including mindfulness as part of this routine, means that we put a pause to fully experience even the most mundane of things such as driving to work or blowing the candles off.

We need to approach mindfulness with an 'I know absolutely nothing' attitude or a beginner's mindset, which would help us all bring sense to the newness of every moment in life and childlike wonder.

Chapter 74. How To Help Yourself if You Have BPD

If you have borderline personality disorder, it is necessary to take that first step to seek medical care even though it may be difficult in the beginning. It is important to realize that you can get better with treatment despite the fact that being diagnosed with BPD may be overwhelming and frustrating in the beginning.

Living with borderline personality disorder does not have to be stressful. To make it manageable, it is necessary to commit to the treatment prescribed after your doctor has diagnosed you with borderline personality disorder. Therapy can provide you with valuable life lessons which will teach you how to cope with mood swings and control emotions that otherwise would be difficult to manage.

Everyone's experience with borderline personality disorder may vary and because of this medication may or may not be prescribed in conjunction with therapy. If your doctor prescribes medication it will be used to mitigate the most harmful effects of BPD such as anxiety and depression. Medications combined with therapy can help you more effectively deal with the ups and downs of life that arise from the symptoms of borderline personality disorder. As a result, you will be able to have clear thinking space and maximize the therapy provided for you.

Commitment to therapy can't be emphasized enough: this can make or break the healing process. It is the most important thing that you can do to manage living with borderline personality disorder. The illness can cause people to experience extreme emotions and even resort to self-destructive behavior as a means of coping and masking emotions. Committing to therapy will help you learn how to cope in a healthy manner. Otherwise, you may continue living in a world where you constantly succumb to emotional triggers and struggle with your own personal relationships. It will be a constant cycle of challenges and pain.

On top of treatment and medication, one major aspect that will truly help you in your journey towards healing is the moral support from your loved ones. Family, friends, relatives, coworkers, and significant others can all provide you with the strength that you need to manage borderline personality disorder. Just like getting over any serious mental or physical illness, the recovery period could be a lengthy and challenging process but the support of loved ones can make it much easier.

If you begin treatment for borderline personality disorder, honest conversations about the process with those close to you can help relieve anxiety and stress. Don't be afraid to ask them to support you in your process. Borderline personality disorder can place a strain on relationships with people in your life, but asking them to understand and get involved can help them identify what they can also do to help you. Communication is a two-way process, and initiating a dialogue on changes you can make with someone important in your life will lift a great load off your shoulders.

If your family prefers not to get involved in helping you with your treatment, this is not a sign for you to give up. You can still move forward with the many support groups found in your local mental health center or community. You may be able to form a valuable network of people who are going through the same experience and can provide you with the support that you need.

As long as you go through the diagnosis, treatment, medication, and support, there is no reason that you can't enjoy a normal life again. You are on your way to living in a world where you can enjoy healthy, stable relationships.

In addition, there are also other things you can do that will contribute to improving your situation:

 Discuss various treatment options with your doctor and ask all the questions you have in mind. Once you are given treatment, be as disciplined as possible and stick to the treatment schedules.
 Make an effort to stick to a healthy lifestyle with proper nutrition, exercise, and sleep.
 To help reduce the stress or anxieties of treatment, talk to friends or engage in constructive activities such as hobbies or exercise.
 Set goals for each day and break down large tasks into smaller, manageable ones. You will feel better about being able to accomplish something each day.
 Identify the situations, places, or people that make you feel better about yourself. Spend more time doing things that make you happy provided that these are not dangerous or will make the situation worse such as engaging in drugs or drinking alcohol.
 Keep yourself informed with all that you can out regarding borderline personality disorder. Being in the dark about BPD may make you uneasy and trigger anxiety.
If you don't know where to begin asking for help, talk to a doctor. You can also talk to other people who can offer help, which include:
 Outpatient clinics
 Employee assistance programs at your office
 Local psychiatric societies
 Hospital psychiatric departments
 Community mental health centers
 Private clinics
Resisting the Urge to Cut
The urge to harm oneself is a symptom of borderline personality disorder that should be managed properly. This can be carried out in different ways such as burning, pulling hair out, and banging your head. If you are diagnosed with BPD you may already be familiar with self-harm but there are ways you can overcome it although it may feel like a major challenge in the beginning.

1. Make yourself aware of situations or circumstances that provoke you to cut. For people with BPD, cutting is an impulsive act and provides a temporary solution for overwhelming emotions. Talking to your therapist can help you identify these triggers and how to deal with them in a healthy manner.
2. Have a list of things that soothe and relax you. Each time you feel an urge to cut, do one of the activities that let you feel good. Cutting often results in feelings of guilt and shame afterward, but engaging in activities that make you feel good will result in a more permanent high. These activities may include taking a warm bath, reading a, listening to music, or exercising.
3. Keep in mind that the urge to cut is merely a feeling that will pass. While the trigger provokes a sense of darkness, try to simply wait out the moment until it has passed completely.
4. Understand that recovery will take time, so be patient with yourself. Your goals should be realistic because behaviors will not change overnight. Your negative emotions do not define you, it is a matter of being committed to the positive change and a better life that awaits.

Self-Soothing

If you live with borderline personality disorder, you are most likely feeling distressed most of the time. You may have a skewed perception of the way other people react and behave. You are prone to living in fear of abandonment from those that close to you, and constantly experience self-loathing.

Because of these extreme emotions it has become especially important for people with borderline personality disorder to resort to self-soothing. Learning how to self-soothe will prevent you from attempting to control others as a method of coping.

Self-soothing refers to the ability to consciously calm yourself down when you are overwhelmed with your emotions. People are capable of self-soothing even when they aren't conscious about it, but for those who have BPD it may take time and effort to learn this skill.

When you practice self-soothing you will know that the negative emotional state you are currently experiencing is only temporary.

You can resort to self-soothing by doing simple things such as taking a long walk, enjoying a warm bath, watching a movie or listening to music as a form of escapism, or talk to a friend that you trust. Even though these activities seem so simple, they are effective in helping you return to a more stable mindset. Additionally, these methods of self-soothing are perfectly natural and healthy ways of coping with the emotional intensity that BPD brings about.

Self-soothing provides an outlet for people with BPD to deal with emotions positively. Without it, people end up resorting to unhealthy activities such as substance abuse, alcoholism, isolation, depression, rage, and self-harm. In order to release pent-up negative emotions, they resort to destructive behavior that harms them and those that love them because they don't think about the consequences of their actions. As a result the emotional pain is intensified rather than resolved.

The practice of self-soothing techniques can aid in the successful recovery from borderline personality disorder. The goal of treatment is to teach people with BPD that the emotional intensity they are feeling are temporary and that it is possible to redirect their energies into something more productive.

People who suffer from BPD are vulnerable to feeling empty and lack a strong sense of self. When you engage in therapy and activities that make you feel good, such as with self-soothing techniques, these negative feelings can be addressed properly. Once you accept that you deserve all the love and care instead of succumbing to anxiety and depression, you can begin to take better care of yourself. When learning self-soothing techniques, it is important that you are patient with yourself. Over time, these activities can turn into healthy habits if you are dedicated. The end goal of self-soothing techniques is achieving control over intense emotional states and eventually recovering successfully from borderline personality disorder.

It is important for people who are diagnosed with borderline personality disorder to keep in mind that therapy is a process. Patience, hard work, and commitment are all necessary in order for therapy to work. Each time you are faced with a new skill, it is important that you approach this with an open mind. You may that you'll be able to learn a new skill which will serve you the most good along the way especially when dealing with triggers and emotional responses.

During therapy, it is also normal for people with BPD to fall and sometimes get off track. As long as you get back on the path and stay on course despite the challenges you encounter along the way. If you yourself feeling lost or lacking motivation, the best thing that you can do is talk to your therapist right away.

It is also important to change the way you view yourself, especially during treatment and recovery. Be kind, compassionate, and forgiving to yourself most of all. Accept the situation for all it's worth and take it as a learning curve. Remember that the skills you can learn from therapy will also serve a purpose in life. You are not the one to blame for the problems you encounter but improving the situation lies in your own hands.

Part of the recovery process is transitioning back to your normal life once you have completed treatment. Your treatment center should be able to provide you with a helpful exit strategy to help you transition back into your home with as little problems as possible.

The world may seem different once you're in the recovery phase, as compared to how it seemed when you first started. However, keep in mind that this change in perception is positive. As you ease your way back into the world, group therapy may continue to be helpful because it helps you discover that you are not alone in your struggles. During recovery you are also encouraged to seek out support from social circles that are outside the treatment facility, such as reconnecting with old friends or forming new friendships out of healthy activities. Recovery will be made much smoother with the support of friends who share the same passions and interests as you do.

If you want to get back to work after recovery, your treatment center may be able to provide vocational support. Be open if you aren't sure where to start as they have the expertise to identify your strengths and build a career based on it. Ask for help from the treatment center, or from close friends and family on how to write a resume and cover letter that you can send out to job applications. The job search may bring about anxiety but you can overcome it by participating in individual and group therapy sessions. Similarly, if you want to go back to school you may also discuss this option with your treatment center.

Staying active will bring about tremendous benefits whether or not you have BPD. It is especially beneficial during the recovery stage as it helps maintain a healthy relationship with your body. Get involved in yoga, running, sports, and other forms of physical activity that you enjoy. It will not only keep you fit but also give you a sense of accomplishment and control over your body and mind. Physical activity is also an excellent outlet in case you encounter stressful situations.

Chapter 75. Distress Tolerance

Sooner or in our lives, we all need to adapt to misery and torment. It is possible that it tends to be physical, like a honey bee sting or a messed up arm, or it very well may be emotional, like trouble or outrage. In the two cases, the torment is regularly unavoidable and capricious. You can't generally foresee when the honey bee will sting you or when something will make you pitiful. Usually, all the better you can do is to use the adapting abilities that you have and trust that they work.

But for specific individuals, emotional and physical agony feels more exceptional and happens more frequently than it accomplishes for other people. Their pain goes ahead more rapidly and feels like a colossal bore. Regularly, these situations feel like they'll never end, and the people experiencing them don't have a clue how to adapt to the seriousness of their torment. For the motivations behind this , we'll call this issue "overpowering feeling". (But recall, passionate and physical torture frequently happen together.)

Individuals battling with overwhelming feelings regularly manage their agony in exceptionally unhealthy, ineffective ways because they don't have the foggiest idea what else to do. This is understandable. When an individual is in emotional torment, it's difficult to be reasonable and to think about a decent arrangement. By the by, numerous individuals of the adapting methodologies used by people with overpowering feelings serve to worsen their issues.

Here's a list of some basic adapting systems used by individuals managing this issue. Check the ones that you use to adapt to your distressing situations:

□ You spend a lot of energy considering past torments, mistakes, and problems.

□ You get restless stressing over plausible future pains, missteps, and issues.

□ You seclude yourself from other individuals to abstain from upsetting states.

□ You make yourself sensation numb with alcohol or medications.

□ You take your sentiments out on other people by getting too much furious at them or attempting to control them.

□ You participate in dangerous behaviors, for example, trimming, hitting, picking at, or consuming yourself or hauling out your very own hair.

□ You take part in unsafe sexual activities, for example, having intercourse with outsiders or having successive unprotected sex.

□ You abstain from managing the causes of your issues, for example, an oppressive or useless relationship.

□ You use food to rebuff or control yourself by overeating, not eating at all, or by hurling what you do eat.

□ You try suicide or take part in high-risk exercises, like careless driving or taking risks measures of alcohol and medications.

□ You maintain a strategic distance from pleasant exercises, for example, get-togethers and use, possibly because you don't imagine that you have the right to feel much improved.

□ You give up to your agony and leave yourself to carrying on with a hopeless and unfulfilling life.

All of these procedures are ways to much more profound passionate torment because even the strategies that offer brief help will cause you all the more enduring on. Use the Cost of Self-Destructive Surviving Approaches worksheet to perceive how. Note the techniques that you use as well as their costs, and then incorporate any extra charges that you can consider. Toward the finish of the worksheet, don't hesitate to include any of your procedures that are excluded as well as their expenses.

The primary trouble resilience abilities you'll learn in this part will enable you to occupy yourself from the situations that are causing you passionate agony. Diversion abilities are significant because (1) they can incidentally prevent you from considering your pain and, accordingly, (2) they allow you to locate a proper adapting reaction. Diversion can enable you to relinquish the torment by helping you consider something different. Diversion also gets you time so your emotions can settle down before you make a move to manage an upsetting situation.

However, don't confuse diversion with evasion. When you keep away from an upsetting situation, you decide not to manage it. But when you occupy yourself from a troubling situation, despite everything you expect to achieve it on, when your emotions have quieted down to a reasonable level.

The second group of trouble resilience abilities you'll learn in this are a self-mitigating skills (Johnson, 1985; Linehan, 1993b). It's regularly necessary to alleviate yourself before you face the cause of your trouble because your feelings may be too "hot." Many people with overpowering feelings alarm when looked with a contention, dismissal, disappointment, or other difficult occasions. Before you can address these issues with your new feeling guideline skill or your new relational viability abilities, it's frequently essential to relieving yourself to recover your quality. In situations like these, trouble resilience skill is like refilling the gas in your vehicle so you can continue onward. Self-mitigating is intended to present to you some measure of harmony and lessening from your pain with the goal that you can make sense of what you will do straightaway.

The self-mitigating skill also fills another need. They'll enable you to find out how to treat yourself compassionately. Numerous individuals with overpowering feelings have been abused or dismissed as youngsters. Thus, they were shown more how to hurt than to support themselves. The second reason for oneself relieving skill, therefore, is to show you how to treat yourself compassionate and affectionately.

Radical Acceptance

Increasing your capacity to undergo misery begins with an adjustment in your mentality. You're going to need something many refer to as radical acceptance. This is another method for taking a look at your life. In the following, you'll be given some essential inquiries to enable you to look at your experiences using radical acceptance. But for the present, it will be adequate to cover this idea quickly.

Regularly, when an individual is in torment, his or her first response is to blow up or vexed or to blame somebody for causing the torture in any case. But shockingly, regardless of who you fault for your misery, your torment still exists, and you keep on torment. Now and again, the angrier you get, the more awful your suffering will feel.

Blowing up or resentful about a situation also prevents you from seeing what is occurring. Have you at any idea got the articulation "being blinded by anger"? This regularly happens to people with overpowering feelings. Reprimanding yourself all the time or being excessively judgmental of a situation is like wearing dark sunglasses inside. By doing this, you're feeling the loss of the subtleties and not considering each to be as it is. By blowing up and feeling that a situation ought to never have occurred, you're overlooking the main issue that it did happen and that you need to manage it.

Being excessively basic about a situation keeps you from ing a way to change that situation. You can't change the past. And if you invest your energy battling the past—impractically feeling that your displeasure will change the result of an occasion that has just occurred—you'll become deadened and defenseless. At that point, nothing will improve.

In this way, to survey—being excessively judgmental of a situation or too condemning of yourself frequently prompts more torment, missed subtleties, and loss of motion. Blowing up, upset, or doesn't improve a situation. So, what else would you be able to do?

The other choice, which radical acceptance recommends, is to recognize your current situation, whatever it is, without making a decision about the occasions or scrutinizing yourself. Instead, attempt to perceive that your current situation exists because of a long chain of events that started far in the past. For instance,

Some time prior, you (or another person) thought you needed assistance for the passionate torment you were experiencing. Along these lines, a couple of days after the fact, you went to the shop and purchased this. At that point today you pondered perusing this part, and eventually, you plunked down, opened the, and started reading. Presently, you are up to the words you see here. Precluding this chain from claiming occasions does nothing to change what has just occurred. Attempting to battle this minute or state that it shouldn't be only prompted all the more languishing over you. Radical acceptance means taking a look at yourself and the situation and considering it to be it is.

Remember that extreme acceptance does not imply that you overlook or concur with awful

Behavior in others. But it means that you quit attempting to change what's occurred by blowing up and accusing the situation. For instance, if you're in a damaging relationship and you need to get out, at that point get out. Try not to waste your time and keep on enduring by accusing yourself or the other individual. That won't support you. Refocus your consideration on what you can do now. This will allow you to think all the more plainly and make sense of a superior method to adapt to your misery.

Divert Yourself From Self-Destructive Behaviors

One of the most significant motivations behind dialectical behavior therapy is to enable you to quit taking part in pointless practices, for example, cutting, scratching, and damaging yourself.

Nobody can prevent the sum from claiming torment you are in when you take part in one of these behaviors. A few people with overpowering feelings state that self-damage briefly mitigates them of a portion of the torment they're feeling. This may be valid, but it's also apparent that these activities can cause genuine perpetual harm and even passing if taken to an unusual.

Consider all the agony you've just experienced in your life. Consider all the people who have harmed you physically, sexually, emotionally, and verbally. Does it bode well to keep hurting yourself considerably more in the present? Doesn't it bode well to begin recuperating yourself and your injuries? If you want to recover from the agony you've expertly experienced, halting these pointless behaviors is the initial step you should take. This can be difficult to do. You may be dependent on the surge of ordinary painkillers called endorphins that are released when you hurt yourself. Nonetheless, these kinds of pointless activities are exceptionally risks and positively merit your earnest attempts to control them.

Occupy yourself by leaving

Once in awhile, the best thing that you can do is go. If you're in a tough situation with somebody and you perceive that your feelings will overpower you and conceivably exacerbate stuff than it is as of now, at that point frequently, it's ideal to leave. Keep in mind; if you're as of soon overpowered by your emotions, it will be more emotionally for you to think about health goals to your concern. Perhaps it's ideal for putting some separation among you and the situation to allow yourself to quiet your emotions and consider what to do straightaway. Leave if that is all the better you can do. It will be superior to adding fuel to the passionate flame.

Here's a case of leaving to divert yourself. Anna was in an enormous retail establishment shop-ping for a blouse. She wanted one of the representatives to help her locate her size, but the store agent was occupied with different clients. Anna held up as long as she could and continued attempting to stand out enough to be noticed, but nothing worked. Anna perceived that she was blowing up all around rapidly. Was prepared to tear the blouse into equal parts. Didn't have even an inkling what else to do. In the past, she would have remained in the store and gotten angrier, but this time, she made sure to leave. She left the store, did some shopping elsewhere, and came back to get the blouse, when the store was less packed and when she was feeling more responsible for her behaviors.

Make Your Distraction Plan

Presently identify those diversion skills that you're willing to use whenever you're in a situation that is causing you torment and distress. These picked abilities will make up your diversion plan. Keep in mind; these are the preliminary steps you will use in your arrangement to occupy, unwind, and adapt. Compose your picked diversion strategies underneath. When you're set, re-record them on a 3 x 5-inch notecard or a sticky note to bear with you in your wallet or tote. At that point, whenever you're in a troubling situation, you can dismantle out the card to help yourself to remember your diversion plan.

Chapter 76. DBT Mindfulness Skills

Choosing a definition for mindfulness can be simple and daunting at the same time, so I have decided to settle for what it is simply about and discuss the reasons why the concept of mindfulness might seem complex. Mindfulness involves making a choice, a choice to focus and be attentive to the present, without judgment. This allows us to attain a massive awareness of our thoughts, emotions, sensations, behaviors and ultimately, our relationships and environment. The improved self-awareness and self-knowledge helps to make better informed and effective decisions in our lives (both short-term and long term). This ultimately leads to an improved and more satisfying life experience.

The idea behind mindfulness is "making the choice" and this indicates "control," control of our thoughts, emotions, influences and life experience. Mindfulness implies that we control all of these factors instead of having them control us.

It would be wrong to insinuate that it is a day's task, neither can anyone call it a week's or a month's task. All anyone can say is that mindfulness is a skill that you must train yourself to attain.

It involves learning how to gather, unify, conduct and direct your focus and attention. When done properly, mindfulness allows us to connect with our environment and the universe in general.

In a way, it is the direct opposite of our default human mode. A normal human being is influenced by feeling, disconnected and lonely, and judgmental. Mindfulness rectifies that. When we practice mindfulness, our feelings and thoughts are no longer hastily and inadequately processed in a procedure that reduces them to categories and labels, thus reducing our experience and understanding. The skills and techniques of mindfulness allow us to pay closer attention, better connect the dots and see the bigger picture.

So you can see that mindfulness is much simpler than it seems. The idea is very simple but it requires patience, diligence, perseverance, discipline and commitment, among other attributes. It is not hard but it requires consistent effort. This is why may people start to waver and get the wrong opinion about mindfulness.
As one of the first main skills in DBT and the first one we are going to completely analyze in this, mindfulness in DBT is about getting to the Wise Mind. The Wise Mind is a mode that allows us to use our mind and hearts to create and maintain a balanced and centered life. The skills of mindfulness allow us to connect with ourselves and the universe. It also allows us to dwell in the present, or visit the past or consider the future without passing judgments.
In very simple words, mindfulness is a way for us to match the brake and slowdown in our ridiculously fast paced world. It is a great way to enjoyment and at least peace and contentment in our daily activities.
Why people have problems with mindfulness
It is difficult to sell the idea and practice mindfulness to many people, it is also not easier for some people to effectively practice mindfulness. These problems are due to misconceptions about mindfulness. While this is about the myths on mindfulness is written to help therapists and other health professionals understand their clients and their (the client's) opinion of mindfulness, it would be wrong not to mention that some professionals don't also share these myths about mindfulness. So we must address the most common of these myths before we move forward or else we won't be able to fully and openly discuss and understand mindfulness. Here are some of the most common myths about mindfulness:
Mindfulness is a religious (especially Buddhist) activity
Pop culture is most people's first and maybe only introduction to mindfulness.
In pop culture, mindfulness techniques are mostly performed by philosophers and religious people or people trying to appropriate or

to use a less harsh term, integrate religious techniques into their lives. This image of mindfulness in pop culture has created a lopsided and incorrect idea of mindfulness. Mindfulness is not owned by religion or a school of thought. It is a general human activity, belonging to all man and therefore it cannot be appropriated. Sure the techniques vary mostly depending on religions, and practicing a technique that is associated with a particular religion or philosophy can make it seem like you are practicing the religion or appropriating the technique, but you are ignoring the big picture, which is mindfulness itself, a practice that belongs to all human beings. The techniques you choose really doesn't matter as long as you effectively attain mindfulness, and you don't have to actively practice the principles of any religion before you can enjoy the benefits of mindfulness.

Mindfulness is a trend

There is no denying that humanity has an insane tendency to create and follow trends. From fashion trends, to food/diet trends, and exercising trends or lifestyle trends, we flock to join the bandwagon. One simple explanation is that we are social animals and doing what other people are doing gives us a sense of community and security. The thing with trends is that they usually come out of nowhere but mindfulness has been around for almost as long as man himself.

You can even say that we have unknowingly practiced mindfulness since the first moment we attained consciousness. Some trends have also been around for a long time before they became trends, so this argument may not cut it, so I want you to remember that just because something is a trend doesn't mean it is not good. Mindfulness requires a lot of effort and I believe nobody will put in that much effort if it is without benefits.

Mindfulness is time consuming

Yes, mindfulness is a daily activity and it takes some people over forty minutes or even hours, every day to practice it. This doesn't mean that it will or should take that much time out of your day. Experts advocate minimum time period to practice mindfulness every day but it is not an ironclad principle or law that you must abide by. Practicing mindfulness for even just a few minutes every day is enough to benefit to benefit from it.

Mindfulness makes you perfect and/or resolves your problems

Many people expect people that practice mindfulness to be perfect and of one mind but this is incorrect because mindfulness is not about perfection. It is about living in the moment and sometimes living in the moment may involve multitasking.

Another common misconception is that mindfulness is an escape or even a solution to your problems.

This opinion is delusional because mindfulness won't solve the problem or make it disappear, what it does is to allow you to focus on something else. Mindfulness allows you to direct your focus away from the problem and focus it unto something else, probably on a task that is more productive than worrying.

Mindfulness is all about relaxation and peace; you know all that Namaste shebang

Relaxation and inner peace are the two most common benefits of mindfulness, we all love and want both of them but they are not the only benefits of mindfulness. Mindfulness practices such as meditation is a way to exercise the brain. The impact of mindfulness to the brain is very similar to the impact of physical exercises to the body. It also improves our ability to process information and manage pain, manage our behavior and improve our relationships with other people and our environment.

There is only one way or one place to practice mindfulness

Most people have this image of people practicing mindfulness in specific locations. The locations are mostly quiet, secluded and private.

All these are good because mindfulness involves channeling you attention and the aforementioned common attributes of these locations allows a person to limit and shut out external influences and disturbances, but you have neglected to account that or are unaware that the people you pictured practicing mindfulness in these locations are mostly practicing meditation. Meditation may be the most common type of mindfulness, in fact it is probably the first thing that comes to your mind when talking about mindfulness but mindfulness is much more than meditation. Even meditation has different types, so you don't need to be in a quiet, secluded or private location before you can practice mindfulness.

Whenever or wherever you yourself, whatever you are doing, you can practice mindfulness if it the activity and location allows you to completely connect to and inhabit that moment. This means that whether you are working or performing a hobby, playing a sport, gardening, cooking, playing a musical instrument or any other activity that you are involved in, you can practice mindfulness.

Not everybody can practice mindfulness

Mindfulness is about feelings, emotions, thoughts and focus so people generally assume that some people cannot practice mindfulness because they will be hindered by a certain attribute of deficiency that they have.

This includes children, people with problems (financial, relationship etc.), people who have issues intrusive and racing thoughts or with general problems retaining attention, and people with cognitive disabilities. On the contrary, mindfulness actually helps them. Also, believing that these people can't practice mindfulness is actually having a narrow opinion of mindfulness. Remember that mindfulness is more than just meditation, it also involves visualization and contemplation. Above all, mind can be practiced in different activities and in different locations. Therefore all you have to do is the activity that allows the client to practice mindfulness.

States of Mind

Mindfulness in itself is a means to an end in DBT. The aim is getting to the Wise Mind Mode. You need to understand the state of the mind before we can proceed. There are three primary states of the mind. On one end we have the Reasonable Mind, on the other end we have the Emotional Mind and in-between them at the mind point is the Wise Mind. The Wise Mind is the dialectical balance of the Reasonable Mind and the Emotional Mind.

The Reasonable Mind controls reason, while the Emotional Mind controls emotion. Some may even say that the Reasonable Mind is the head and therefore the brain while the Emotional mind is the heart. Both are on each end of the spectrum as I stated forward and there is continuum maintained between them. Neither is explicitly good or bad but it is not great if the scales is tip to one side of the continuum (too much of either) although the gravity of the problem depends on how extremely the scale is tipped.

Some situations require emotions in order for us to process them properly while some require reasoning. That is why we must strive to stay as close to Wise Mind (in the balance) as much as possible.

The Wise Mind is essentially the balance between the two extreme states of mind. It acknowledges the emotions and uses the ability to reason logically. In using both the emotion and reason, it ends up getting the most out of both. We can feel and analyze without being consumed by emotions and feelings. This makes Wise Wind an important aim in DBT.

The journey to Wise Mind

We have been talking about the skills and techniques of mindfulness, now is the time to further discus these skills and how they can help us attain the Wise Mind. Understanding the What and the How skills will make it easier to reach the Wise Mind.

In the What skills, we have three basic What skills that we must perform before we can get to the Wise Mind, namely Observe, Describe and participate. We also have three basic how skills, meaning how we perform the What skills. These how skills are Nonjudgmentally, effectively and One-Mindfully.

All six skills (three What and three How) work together and one is not more important than the others. We must first understand each of these skills individually before apply them together and that is what we shall do next.

The What skills

Observe

This seems pretty simply until you consider that the human mind is not set to merely observe at the default mode. Our mind immediately starts analyzing and judging a situation after observing it. The Observe skill requires that we only witness the experience, no need to analyze it.

We are to use our senses to collect details, our sight, ears, skin, taste buds and nose. We are to note our thoughts, emotions and reaction to the experience.

Describe

At this stage we write down our observations about the experience. Language and words is the key because we are going to write it with detailed descriptions that make it easy for anybody to understand. This way, we will be able to better understand it because it is easier to understand language than it is to understand thoughts.

It is not yet time for us to analyze them. At this stage all we need to understand is that these feelings are mere feelings, thoughts are mere thoughts, urges are mere urges and sensations are mere sensations. They are mere products of the mind and they don't fully represent who you are.

Participate

The first two skills are supposed to increase our awareness. It is now time to use the knowledge we have gathered to make informed choices.

We are going to use the information to decide if we want to further experience the situation or if we want to stay away from it. The decision should be based on if the experience benefits us or if it's problematic to us.

The point of Participate is to direct our attention and focus to whatever choice we make. Observe and describe encourages passivity, but this time around we are to engage with the experience.

The How skills

Nonjudgmentally

Imagine yourself as a reporter who is there to collect the facts without passing judgment or skewering the truth. This skill requires that we respect ourselves and that includes not using abusive or exaggerated words to make ourselves look better or worse than we actually are.

We have to remember that we are trying not to be judgmental. Good or bad are mostly relative, so what we think of something may actually be wrong. That is not to say that we won't ourselves slipping and passing judgment. We just have let go of these judgment after we notice them.

This is not to say that judgments are bad. They are can help us to categorize, label, understand and analyze our experiences. That is the good part of judgments but we have to watch out for judgments that prevent us from functioning properly.

One-mindfully

This is an important part of mindfulness. Focusing our attention requires cutting out external and internal distractions. External distractions may seem easy to eliminate and I am sure you have some pointers on how to cut them out, so let's talk about internal distractions.

What we have to do focus on one task at a time and let go of distractions as soon as we notice them. We can't judge ourselves or our distractions, we should accept them. Attention will waver less as we get better at mindfulness.

For a better understanding, let's talk about some of the issues that can complicate our goal of achieving one-mindedness.

Partial attention and multitasking

Instinctively and subconsciously, most people attend to different stimuli at the same time throughout our day. Whenever we do this consciously, it becomes what we call multitasking. We make phone calls while driving, we eat while watching television and we are involved in other activities while having a conversation, more examples of this abound. The problem is that we are not paying full attention to a specific task because our attention is divided between tasks. It results in a state of continual partial attention which is technically known as "monkey mind" or "unquiet mind."

Our society sees multitasking as an advantage and it is but in some situations, it makes people into robots. Increasing ability to multitask means that you have learned the behavior and it has become automated into your brain. What happens if we overlearned a behavior? At best the behavior becomes a part of our subconscious and at worst, we become robots. This is problematic if the task requires conscious action. We end up increasing the probability of making mistakes.

Overall, multitasking decrease productivity. If you want to confirm these try comparing the energy, efficiency and time it takes to complete two tasks, separately and simultaneously. Let's say the tasks are saying the alphabets from A to Z and counting 1 to 26. First recite the alphabets and then recite from 1 to 26, then calculate the time, effort and efficiency of both tasks, combined.

Take another example of any electronic gadget, for example your phone or PC. You will notice that even though your gadget was designed for multitasking, at a certain stage, the number of tasks it is performing begins to affect the speed and functionality of your device.

Chapter 77. How to control your emotions

When normal people are born, they usually have almost no emotional intensity, but then their emotion regulation rises up a bit when they are bullied at school. When they experience a breakup at secondary school, their emotion regulation rises up even further. In life, they get a sack letter from their workplace, and then their emotional intensity goes up a little bit.

When they get a divorce, it goes up a bit further. Their emotional intensity continues to rise until the moment that it reaches a breaking point. The breaking point is the point where people attempt to kill themselves, participate in self-harm, or take harmful drugs.

However, for people suffering BDP, they're born with a lot of emotional intensity. They go through life the same way that a normal person would go through, but at each stage of their life, their emotional intensity increases and refuses to come back down like it would for a normal person. That's why they reach the breaking point forward in your life and begin to have all strong impulsive emotions to commit suicide.

So that is why you need to learn how to regulate and manage your emotions instead of allowing your emotions to manage you. What you'll is that you'll have intense emotions that change frequently. Your emotions are what drive your behaviors. It's your emotions that make you do the things that you do.

Sometimes, your behavior comes as a result of trying to get some validation from your emotions or trying to block your emotions or run away from them because they're so painful. So in the DBT technique, you'll learn the skills to successfully manage your emotions and how to become less vulnerable to negative emotions. You'll also learn what emotions are and why you have them. Not only that, you'll learn the techniques for increasing positive experiences and emotions because your life right now is filled up with too many negative emotions. You'll learn how to decrease your emotional suffering. You're not going to invalidate your emotions because your emotions are very real and you have to believe and accept them. You are not going to learn to avoid them or dismiss them. Emotions are okay, even negative ones. The problem is that they cause a lot of disturbance and negativity in our lives. That's why you must learn to manage them. This emotion regulation is not here to dismiss or invalidate your feeling even though other people are currently invalidating your feelings and telling you to get over it. They are telling you that just to cheer you up and make you feel like you don't have it that bad, but deep within you, you know that your feelings are very real to you, and they're there for a reason, even the bad negative feelings. So here you'll learn to look at those feelings and accept them the way they are. Your behaviors are driven by your emotions. You're either behaving in a certain way to get your emotions validated so that people know how you're feeling or you're overdrinking to hide your emotions.

Using Opposite Actions

One of the emotional regulation skills that are very effective for DBT is 'the opposite action'. Opposite action is basically what it says. It means doing the opposite action of exactly what you're feeling or acting opposite to the way that you want to act. You can use the opposite action when you're experiencing emotions that don't fit the facts. That's not to say that your emotions aren't valid enough. Of course, they're valid, but they might not be at the intensity level that makes sense for that situation. You can also use the opposite action when you're having urges and want to act on those urges. Acting on those urges is not going to be effective. If you're feeling really angry, you might want to punch someone in the face or start a fight. The opposite of that will be not to fight but to walk away from the situation. Now, doing the opposite action doesn't mean that you're suppressing or invalidating your emotions. You're still going to feel the emotions, but now, you're going to be doing the opposite action of what you're supposed to do. Then overtime, doing the opposite action of your emotions will help to change those emotions. It'll give you a better outcome because if you punch someone in the face, the outcome will never be as good as if you had just walked away and calmed down. The opposite action walks for different kinds of emotions. If you have terrible anxiety, that's making you so scared of leaving the house, then the opposite action of that will be to face your fears and just go out. It may not be easy to do, but it'll keep getting easier once you've done and achieved it the first time. It'll keep getting easier and easier to the point where you can go out without that fear of anxiety.

If you're depressed, the normal thing for you will be to refuse to get out of bed, avoid seeing anyone, or refuse to do anything. Because, when you're depressed, you'll feel so tired and drained to the point where you just want to lie down and be left alone. So the opposite action will be to go for a run, go to the gym, or have a nice energetic workout. Of course, it won't be easy to do the first time you try to go for a run, because, when you're in a depressed state, the last thing that you'll want to do will be to go for a run, go to the gym or do something energetic. However, if you manage to do it, you'll out that you don't feel depressed anymore. You'll feel good because the exercise will boost the dopamine, and serotonin in the brain (The feel-good chemicals). Even if you can't go for a run, just get up and go for a walk. Do anything to get out.

If you're feeling sad, the normal thing to do will be to cry your eyes out, but then the opposite of crying will be to do something that makes you laugh. Although there are certain times, where it's good to let yourself cry out loud so that you can feel better, when you yourself crying constantly, you need to do the opposite action of crying, which is to laugh. By doing the opposite of the negative emotions, you're still acting on the emotions, but you're doing so in a different way, and the outcome won't be negative, It'll be positive.

The 3 Steps for Taking Opposite Actions

The first step of the opposite action is to Identify the emotions. For instance, let's say that you're experiencing anxiety before writing a test. The first step is to check the facts about the anxiety that you're feeling. You can tell yourself that you've studied already even though you know that you could have studied more. You tell yourself that you've been doing okay in other tests, and It's not a midterm exam, not a unit test. After checking the facts, you'll notice that you're not supposed to be feeling as anxious as to how you're feeling.

The second step is to identify your urges. In the case of the anxiety, your urges might be to skip school, fake a sickness, call ahead of time to inform your professor that you're not taking the test. However, if you closely look at all these urges, you'll see that none of them are going to be effective in dealing with the situation. Even though they take you out of the test, they just push the test to a much longer date, which will likely increase your anxiety even more. So you have to understand that that action urges are not going to be effective.

The third step to using the opposite action is to Ask your wise mind –which we talked about before as the combination of your emotions and logic. In the case of the test, the opposite action will be to go and take the test. So you use your wise mind and ask yourself, "what is the most effective thing for me to do at this moment." After asking yourself this question, you'll notice that the opposite thing for you to do at that moment might be to go to school, talk to your professor about it, talk to your guidance counselor about it, and do anything that'll be effective in taking down your anxiety in the long term. So once you've identified the opposite actions, and you've findd out which one you're going to take, proceed and do that damn thing. Go to school and take that test. Do the opposite action of the thing that you want to do now. To make your brain to know if taking the test if the right action to do now, Just go take the damn test. Then after taking the test, you can now tell your teacher about your anxiety on the test, and that you'll like to know what you can do about the next test, so as not to feel really anxious again. You could ask your professor to cover things for you in those that you're not really comfortable about. So go the extra mile about your anxiety, so that next time your anxiety levels will come down and everything will start to click in your head. If you try the opposite action the first time, and it didn't work, you can simply go back to your wise mind to see what you can do next and then just repeat acting opposite until it clicks, and you the opposite action that makes sense to you.

You also want to use the opposite Action when the intensity of the emotion you're exhibiting does not fit the facts of the situation or when you're exhibiting an emotion to a situation for a longer period than you're supposed to.

When using the opposite action, you need to identify the emotions that you intend changing. And then check to see if the emotions that you're exhibiting fit the facts of the situation or not. If the emotion does not fit the facts of the emotion that you're trying to change, then you should try to identify the action urges. For instance, If getting angry does not fit the facts, then you want to identify the action urges which might be to scream, yell, throw things, or raise your voice. So when you feel that emotion, identify the behaviors that you want to do. Next, you want to act the opposite of each emotion. So you want to repeat the opposite action event continually until the tendency for you to follow through with your action urges goes down, and your emotional sensitivity goes down. So continue to practice the opposite action as long it takes to lower your emotional response. Over the long hall, just keep practicing it repeatedly, until eventually condition yourself to act more effectively. So let's go over the opposite action that you'll use for the different emotions. Let's go over some emotions and the opposite action that you can use for that situation, let's start with fear.

Fear: When fear does not fit the facts of the situation, then the opposite action is to do what you're scared of doing over and over again. If you're afraid of going to your exposure group, then the best way to act opposite to that will be to go to your group over and over again. Another way to deal with the fear emotion is to approach people, activities, tasks, and events that you're scared of and also practice to gain a sense of control and confidence over your fears. The most important point to note while doing the opposite action of fear is to keep your sight and hearing really focused on the event. Be aware that you're still physically and mentally safe, even though you're afraid of exhibiting fear right now. So while doing the fear-based opposite action, try to change your posture and let your tone of voice remain confidence. Do pace breathing and try to breathe more slowly and deeply into your diaphragm.

Anger: when your anger does not fit the fact of the actions, the opposite action is to avoid the person that you're angry with rather than throwing an attack on that person. Now gently avoiding is different from fully avoiding, because if you're feeling like yelling or shouting at the person, then you want to avoid the person until you calm down. Do some little paced breathing, and when you become a little bit calmer, you can come back to the person. You can also decide to take some time out to breathe, deeply and slowly. People with BPD tend to react strongly whenever they're angry. So you need to take a moment to breathe in slowly until you get calm, then you can come back and start trying to communicate again.

Another thing you can do when you're angry is to do something really nice to the person rather than pouring insults on that person. For instance, when you call a customer hotline number, you might have the urge to get utterly disgruntled. So instead of been mean and rude to the customer hotline, think of the fact that if you want someone to help you, you have to be his or her friend rather than their enemy. So you should try to be a little bit nice to them instead of reacting to your urge to get upset and yell. Instead of yelling, you can say something like, "I know this isn't your fault that my acct is this way, but I don't know if you can help me.. ". When doing the opposite action for your anger, try to understand and empathize with the other person. Also, try to see the situation from the other person's point of view. For instance, in the case of the calling customer care that we talked about forward, the person on the phone may be really putting off and not paying attention to what you're saying because they lost someone and still had to come to work. So trying to see this from this other person's perspective can help you to take the opposite action. Always imagine possible reasons for why they're behaving the way they're behaving. In the customer care example, for instance, it may also be the person on the first day at work, and he might not be used to talking to customers on the phone; that's why he's really nervous. They might be many reasons for someone to act the way they're acting. Another way to act opposite to anger is to use the anger energy to do a workout. You can also pour cold water on your body to help change your body temperature both physically and figuratively in your mind, where you're really hot and angry.

Disgust: when disgust does not fit the fact, the opposite action will be to eat, drink, or move closer to the thing that you're feeling disgusted about. This is particularly helpful if you're dealing with people from other cultures and races. Approach them, try to be near them and walk in their own shoes so that you can get to know them as just humans. Also, try to distract yourself from any disgusting image or thought in your mind. If something is really grossing you out, then think about something else.

Envy: when envy does not fit the fact, the opposite action will be to stop yourself from destroying what the other person has accomplished. For instance, if you're in a competition that you got first runner-up, instead of trying to ruin the experience for the other person by talking behind their back, do the opposite action of the envious urges. So if your urge was to bring the person down, or say negative things about them, then you should congratulate that person for doing a really great job. Also, be grateful for the things that you've accomplished. Be grateful for being the first runner-up out of the many people that participated in the competition. Try to look at the things that you do have and be thankful for them and avoid discounting some blessings. Don't discount some blessings because you have the urge to be envious. Avoid exaggerating your deprivations. Also, don't be too harsh on yourself or make comments like, "I am such a loser, I never win anything." Stop exaggerating other people's net worth or value by saying things like, "They have everything, while I don't" the fact that someone is Rich doesn't necessarily mean that another aspect of their life is also balanced, so check the facts. Instead of exaggerating the other person's Blessings or discounting it, check the facts to see why the other person has what you don't have. Maybe the person worked a little harder than you to become rich, or maybe the person entered the competition a little bit forward and had more time to prepare.

Chapter 78. How to recover from Emotional trauma

Emotional trauma can be as weakening as physical trauma. Emotional trauma is a physical trauma's automatic side effect. Although without physical trauma one can have emotional trauma, we are physically affected by emotional trauma. We are well aware of the debilitating effects of trauma. Therefore it is vital to recover from any trauma if an individual wants to live a life as healthy as possible.

Safety is the most important ingredient in recovery from any trauma. Secure people are a must in safe places. The safest people are those trained in listening, being non-judgmental, and being empathic. My experience is that most of these people are counselors and mental / emotional therapists. Continuous research supports discussing a trauma experience with another person as the most effective way to recover from trauma. Telling the story as many times as needed to remove the burden of total responsibility from one's self, trying to make sense of the trauma, and integrating the experience into one's self-understanding. This can also involve processing the traumatic experience, including the somatic and visual levels, at different levels. It is challenging to a therapist / counselor with whom one feels safe. Many have been written about ing a good therapist and what a good therapy is. A good therapist is not going to pathologize the client, but will perceive a client as being greater than their problems. A good therapist therefore recognizes that when an individual expresses anger, he / she needs to handle his / her problems and learn how to safely cope with and express that anger. A good therapist is not going to call a person an "angry person." Good therapists also know how to empower their clients, and as they become healthier they have experienced many people changing and growing. A good therapist is self-conscious, sensitive, empathetic, creative, and confident about the abilities of her clients. There is a spirit of collaboration in good therapy, and the therapist-client relationship is vital. Good therapy is both expressive and cognitive, using techniques of emotion and cognition that allow a person to heal holistically and deeply. A good therapist can also refer a client to another therapist if they think it's best for the client.

A powerful method of healing traumatic experiences is group work. A client can discover in a group setting that many people have similar problems. Another advantage is listening to various techniques that have helped different people. For this type of healing, while support groups are excellent, therapy groups can be better. A support group is made up of like-minded people and often has no trained leader. A therapy group also consists of people with similar problems, but the group process will be facilitated by a trained therapist. Education is an important component of trauma recovery. Therapists have been trauma educated and will often use research-based approaches, such as dialectical behavioral therapy, to facilitate group work.

Sometimes an individual works on a trauma that they are aware of and s memories of other traumas underneath. In an attempt to resolve early childhood trauma, our unresolved, implicit memories often result in our re-creating similar situations. Our implicit memory is hard-wired to create a "prophecy that fulfills itself." They will also work on forward traumas as an individual is working on a current trauma.

For individuals, it is important to investigate the type of therapy they wish to use. The use of expressive therapies is supported by recent research. Expressive therapies involve recognizing and validating trauma-related emotions. Emotions involve multiple processes that are vital to the mind. Cognitions and emotions work together. You can't separate them. Emotions connect people to each other. Unfortunately, during the first three years of their lives, many people have not been given a healthy attachment experience, which often results in those people being unable to be aware of their feelings. Being aware of our feelings is vital, they give us important information on an ongoing basis. Trauma can lead to people trying to anesthetize their feelings. These efforts sometimes take the form of an addiction. Other times a person simply becomes convinced that he has no feelings or that he is "not emotional." For these people, as well as for those who are more aware of their feelings, expressive therapies can be very helpful.

It is often best to combine cognitive and expressive therapies. Expressive therapy can relatively easily evoke emotions. Then, cognitive therapy can be used to teach emotional coping skills. Behaviors are the result of feelings and thoughts. Behaviors will improve as the emotional and cognitive health of the individual is improving. A distinctive feature of good therapy is when the therapist can meet a customer "where they are." The highly intellectualized client would be an example of this. A good therapist would start with a lot of cognitive and educational work while introducing emotional and expressive work gradually.

It is hard work to do good therapy. It involves choosing to use on a daily basis what they have learned from their therapy. Or you don't. It can be messy to have good therapy. It involves feeling that we may not want to feel emotions. And it's just one way to go through it. Without it, we can't work through trauma. Unresolved feelings have a negative impact on us. Because I worked with many people who had the courage to work through their trauma, I developed a deep and high regard for people's resilience and strength. Most people are surprised by their own ability to recover completely from trauma and create the life they want to lead. That's why I've got endless hope now.

Significant New Ways to Prevent Suicide: Dialectical Behavior Therapy as an Emerging Best Practice

With more than one million suicide attempts in the United States annually, it is important to recognize suicide as a public health issue. You need to be comfortable talking about the problem and knowing the emerging best practices to prevent suicide from happening to someone you care about. In 1986, when my father died of a self-inflicted gunshot wound while at the hospital awaiting the birth of my triplets, I became comfortable talking about suicide. My hope is that this will help you avoid the death of someone you care about.

Best Practices in Risk Assessment and Treatment of Suicidal Individuals

Thomas Ellis, a national leader in suicidal treatment, notes the emergence of best practices in risk assessment and suicidal treatment. Dr. Ellis describes different skills for care providers to save lives as part of a task force. As professionals learn best practices, I feel it is imperative that friends, family members, and non-professionals also understand the latest emerging best practices. These are: assessing the situation without fear; focusing on warning signs before risk factors; recognizing the importance of the state of mind of a person; jointly identifying a safety plan; forgetting "No-Suicide Contracts," recommending suicide-focused therapy; and knowing that hospitalization may not prevent suicide. Let's look further at these emerging best practices: evaluate the situation without fear. Talk to your friends or family without denying your suicide feelings. Even though they're afraid to "go there" with suicidal people, cultivate empathy and be on their side, so they're not feeling alone. Ask them to tell you more about it when they talk about suicide. Work together to ensure they are safe until they can get some help.

Focus on signs of warning against risk factors. Ask the individuals what warning signs they may see in themselves (i.e. severe panic / anxiety attacks, insomnia, or agitation). Focus on what you can do to distract yourself. Suggestions include calling a friend; going to a hospital or going to the emergency room. Remember the mnemonic "IS PATH WARM" created by the American Association of Suicidology that focuses on warning signs: idea / threatened or communicated; substance abuse; intentional; anxiety, trapped, hopelessness, withdrawal, anger, recklessness, and changes in mood.

State of mind. Since cognitive vulnerabilities can cause suicide, focus on those thoughts that make them vulnerable, such as rigidity, problem-solving inability, hopelessness, irrational beliefs, and perfectionism. Discuss the vulnerabilities of traits such as self-hate and low tolerance of Stress.

Develop a safety plan jointly. Together, develop strategies as to what to do and who to call in a crisis. Work on problem-solving strategies to save their own lives from simple scenarios. Ask them how to help alleviate their suffering. Building an alliance and recognizing suicide is a response to coping. The problem is that they need to feel better to avoid dying.

Forget "No-Suicide Contracts." These contracts do not work and give professionals and family members a false sense of security. Although one study found that 57 percent of psychiatrists use contracts for no-suicide and a Canadian study found that 83 percent of psychiatrists use them, there is no empirical evidence that contracts for No-Suicide actually work.

Focused therapy on suicide. Make sure to focus on suicide-focused therapy rather than conventional therapy by the professionals helping your friends or loved ones. Treatment should focus first on suicide, recognizing that processes of thought contribute to the risk of suicide. Professionals should focus on "suicide" rather than "symptoms." Professionals should use the best current suicide prevention interventions, including: Dialectical Behavioral Therapy (DBT); Rudd and Joiner's CBT; Beck's Cognitive Suicidal Therapy; Mentalization-based Therapy; and Collaborative Suicidal Assessment and Management (CAMS).

It is not possible for hospitalization to prevent suicide. Hundreds of suicides happen in hospitals every year. While many people believe that hospitalization is going to prevent suicide, this is not always the case. While some people benefit from regulating their drugs, there is no scientific evidence to confirm that hospitalization saves lives.

Let suicidal people know when it comes to their thoughts that they have to level with you. If they tell you they want to kill themselves, tell them that it's okay to have suicidal thoughts and they're not alone. Recognize that their thoughts about dying are a manifestation of their suffering when they tell you they want to die. Don't overreact and tell them not to think their way of thinking. Don't tell them all the reasons why they should live because their thoughts are invalidated.

Think about what you've learned in the past about suicide, what's no longer meaningful at the moment, and what emerging best practices will prevent future suicide of people you care about.

Understanding Self Injury is key to helping Self Injurers

Kristy slammed on the table over and over her cell phone until the frame broke apart. Why couldn't she understand her boyfriend? He didn't care if she had a fight last night with her best friend or had a D on her final math examination. She started to ruminate over the years on all the negative details. Why should she care for anybody? She never had anything to do with anybody before, so this proves she doesn't matter now! Kristy fell to the floor and started to rock her anger at her building back and forth. Her eyes were swelling with tears as her fists were tightly squeezed. She felt her mind boiling in rage to the point that she didn't feel it existed anymore. She was so in her pain that around her she didn't have the awareness of reality. She thought of the random temper bursts of her dad, the constant demeaning remarks of her mom, the perfect all-star football scholarship of her brother, and academic achievements. She felt nothing at all. Kristy grabbed a safety pin in a daze and began carving on her arm ' Help Me.' The deeper she carved, the more she felt like hurting someone else.

Self-injuries are in emotional agony. SI never learned to express their feelings, or somebody stifled them if they tried to keep them to themselves. As a result, it is impossible for SI to a way or know how to release emotions pent up. SI may also feel out of control, scared of' losing it' and never again being the same. It's like an earthquake building, where tensions need to be released so that the earth doesn't collapse or erupt in epic proportions altogether. By default or feeling overwhelmed by emotions, as a way to manage their feelings, they learned to harm themselves. Sometimes, after self-injury, physiological endorphins act in the brain where they get a feeling of calm. Some people feel nothing (numb) as they enter an' unconscious' state of surreal moments. They know they're physically there, but at the moment they're not mentally connected to reality. This is also referred to as dissociation. Usually SI does not feel any physical pain as long as the emotional pain subsides in the act of self-injury. However, people who suffer self-injury do not necessarily seek added attention, at the same time it is a cry for help. Often self-injury coincides with feelings of guilt or shame where the SI is again afraid of being judged or criticized for choosing to cope.

Kristy's arms were full of etched words and diagrams in designs with tiny bubbling blood dots. She returned to reality and smeared the blood around her, now able to breathe, she got up and wiped her face out of tears. Her scars were important for Kristy. It told her that she was alive and that she only endured something unique for her. Unfortunately, it is unique to about 1 percent of the population, according to statistics.

So where are we going to start when we try to help SI? The need to change the patterns of coping when dealing with intense emotions is one of the major goals of self-injury. Part of this starts with SI learning to verbally choose words instead of physically acting on one self. An SI must feel validated in who it is and what it feels like. Many times IS feeling lonely and disconnected from others, including friends and family. Research shows that many IS have low self-esteem and do not feel worthy of attention and love from others. Maybe starting with a secure and available attachment such as a specific family member, understanding friend, or engaging in sports, music, dance, group, weekend outing, etc. will provide a bond that eventually becomes a sense of belonging.

Many IS indicate that their self-injury is impulsive and not one of a lot of "thought." The feelings are so extreme that they hurt even before they realize it. Before they act, it is hard to tell an SI to stop and think. The act is nearly automatic. However, it is still a choice, and in Stressed situations, relearning behaviors come with it. Wendy Lader, M.Ed., Ph.D. And Karen Conterio, CEO of Self Abuse Finally Ends (SAFE) Alternatives program has developed a behavioral log to counteract these impulsive instincts and become aware of what happens emotionally before self-injury occurs. It's a time, place, feelings, situation, etc. account. This allows the SI to put what is happening in perspective and to keep SI before injury in reality.

Dr. Marcia Linehan (1993a) developed a Borderline Personality Disorder (BPD) integrative approach called Dialectical Behavior Therapy (DBT). Since empirical studies show a high correlation between BPD and self-injury, dialectical behavioral therapy can also be effective with self-injuries. Dialectical therapy of behavior combines techniques of cognitive and behavioral therapy. It involves a team approach with the therapist and client to work on problem solving, training skills, and cognitive modification where the client s some form of balance in dealing with impulsive behaviors and thoughts.

A lot of research still needs to be done to better understand self-injury and its people. We have to look at biological, social and environmental aspects of how SI starts or why it goes on. You can give your understanding and patience at this time as a loved one. It's difficult for everyone to deal with self-injury, it takes time and patience, but there's hope.

Chapter 79. ACT Therapy

The practice of mindfulness has been around for centuries. With OCD, mindfulness can teach you how to be present with disturbing thoughts without giving them any significance. It's easy to fall into the OCD trap of trying to find out reasons why the thoughts shouldn't bother you. Usually, when you think you've found the answer, the OCD pops up and forces you to reconsider your rationale. Consider what your OCD might say if it could talk. Perhaps something like, "Yeah, but have you thought of this?"

Take, for example, a person who has the type of obsessive thoughts mentioned forward, pertaining to shouting "I have a gun" at an airport. A mindfulness exercise associated with this could simply be noticing the thoughts, then focusing instead on their breathing. Learning mindfulness techniques can help you develop the capacity to stay in the moment, observe whatever you're experiencing, and accept your thoughts without placing any judgments on yourself for having them. You can learn to disengage from trying to find out your thoughts. Sounds terrific, doesn't it? It's also very hard work. It takes practice and patience, but the outcomes are worthwhile.

Acceptance and commitment therapy (ACT) offers additional help for people working to develop the skill to accept the obsessive thoughts without trying to change them. This protocol calls for people to understand that their thoughts are considered neither good nor bad. The idea is to take your thoughts at face value, then take some actions toward building a life that is consistent with your own set of values. In essence, we can have obsessions while also engaging in life in meaningful ways.

A primary goal of exposure-based therapy for OCD is to reduce anxiety while disengaging from compulsions. ACT also works toward that goal, though with differing techniques. It encourages people to accept their obsessions as random thoughts and to ways to continue to live life even though the distress may still be present. The uncomfortable thoughts, images, or urges all may be there, but you can still work, go to school, have relationships, and do whatever else is important to you.

What do you think? Are these new concepts to you? Have you seen them before? As you write your thoughts below, please include how you feel about engaging in these techniques and any trepidations you may have about doing so.

Maintaining Mindfulness

forward in my career, I taught a stress management class for the Palo Alto Medical Foundation. The people who attended had a variety of health conditions, such as chronic pain, high blood pressure, irritable bowel syndrome, insomnia, depression and anxiety, and numerous other medical and psychological issues. Before I received training to facilitate the workshop, I had little experience with mindfulness and frankly relied on the more traditional forms of therapy to treat anxiety disorders. While I became skilled in the various techniques associated with CBT, I paid little attention to the potential benefits of mindfulness. I now see the tremendous relief it can bring people who have various psychiatric illnesses, including OCD. I wouldn't say that I completely discounted mindfulness, but I didn't see the point of using it when so much research supported other evidence-based treatment. I now believe that mindfulness for OCD can be very beneficial when used together with CBT.

Furthermore, he cited several other articles indicating that mindfulness has been shown to be beneficial for those suffering from various medical conditions, such as type 1 diabetes, chronic pain, lower back pain, hypertension, myocardial ischemia, irritable bowel syndrome, insomnia, and HIV. Additionally, mindfulness is known to help lessen mood-related problems, such as depression, and to ease stress and anxiety. On the whole, people who consistently practice mindfulness can achieve a greater overall sense of emotional wellbeing and learn to better cope with acute and chronic medical and emotional problems. Seems like a good idea to me.

The key is to try to accept that the obsessions are simply thoughts. The emphasis is on observing them and staying focused on whatever mindfulness exercises you may use. As people learn to do this effectively, they begin recognizing that their obsessive thoughts have no real power and are of no real significance. In fact, all they really mean is that you have OCD. I've seen mindfulness be especially helpful in people whose obsessive thoughts continue to resurface and their ERP exercises can't provide relief. Similarly, I have found that people who have sensorimotor OCD, with the emphasis on automatic bodily functions, such as breathing, blinking, and swallowing, benefit from mindfulness strategies. The practice teaches them how to disengage from the frustrations associated with paying so much attention to these sensations

Many clients have told me that they've tried mindfulness and that it didn't work for them, only to learn that they either weren't really engaging in mindfulness or didn't put enough time into truly getting good at it. While I realize it's not for everyone, what do you think? Do you see some benefit in it for yourself? If yes, take a moment to write your thoughts down here, and if not, also write those thoughts down as well.

Exposure and Response Prevention

When it comes to OCD, I use behavior therapy much more than I do cognitive therapy. I often say, "The proof is in the doing." Many if not most people who have OCD have fairly good insight about what they're going through. They generally know that what they're thinking and what they're doing as a result doesn't actually make much sense, but they're unable to control it. For example, I have yet to meet someone with harm obsessions who has told me that they want to harm anyone. It's usually the exact opposite. Even though they've experienced thousands of harm-related thoughts without ever acting on them, knowing that truth doesn't stop their obsession. A main component of cognitive therapy is to look at evidence that supports a person's negative thoughts, then to examine evidence that suggests that these thoughts may not be true, all in an attempt to promote more rational thinking.

I remember once meeting with a patient who had a terrible fear of hitting someone with his car, which is often referred to as "hit-and-run" OCD. One day I asked him how many times he had been in his car over the past week, and he said 10. I asked him how many times he hit someone, and he told me zero times. We then made similar estimates for a month and a year. By the time we got to 10 years, he estimated that he had driven about 5,000 times and never hit a person. At this point I usually ask the big question: "What does that tell you?" My hope is that that someone will see there isn't much evidence to support their fear and stop worrying so much about it. What do I hear is "well, I guess it's more likely to happen now," or "it just hasn't happened yet."

As I said forward, the proof to treating the disorder is in the doing. A person with "hit-and-run" OCD is likely going to have to get in the car and drive in areas that trigger the obsession, and only then will they begin to believe that the odds of nothing bad happening are truly on their side. Over the years, I've learned that I'm not likely to talk someone out of their obsessive fears. They're going to have to prove it to themselves, and that typically means doing the exposure therapy. When I teach on OCD, I always do some exposure exercises in class. I it's the best way to learn how to actually do ERP. So, let's try an ERP exercise. Take a moment to touch the bottom of your shoe, provided that you haven't just stepped in something someone without OCD might consider worrisome. Please don't feel pressured to do this if you're not feeling ready.

Be careful not to just touch your shoe with your fingertip or cup your hand around the sole so you don't actually touch the bottom. In order for this to be effective, you have to touch it. Thoroughly. No shortcuts.

How do you feel now? I would expect that there would be some discomfort, even for someone without contamination fears. It bothers me, too. It's gross. But is it dangerous? I don't think so, unless you've stepped in toxic chemicals. Now, with that same hand, rub the bottom of your shoe again, and this time place your hand on your face and rub your face with that same hand. Still pretty disgusting, right? It is for me, too.

OK, the first step is done. You've done the exposure part, now comes the response prevention: no handwashing, no using hand sanitizer, and no rubbing your hands on some other object in an attempt to decontaminate. Now touch other objects at home with those hands, including furniture, clothes, plates, cups, and even other family members. Get everything good and dirty. How much anxiety are you experiencing now? Wait a little while, then assess your level of anxiety again. How about in 10 minutes? How about after 30 minutes? One hour? Have you noticed that time is on your side? It has to—no one stays anxious forever.

Exposure Therapy Cycle (ERP)

find 2.1The ERP cycle still begins with a trigger, but now we need to prevent the compulsion from happening. For the ERP process to work, it must cause some anxiety. If the compulsion is resisted long enough, the urge to act on it will subside.

MANAGING DISCOMFORT

Managing the discomfort caused by ERP is an interesting and somewhat controversial topic. Done properly, this therapy and the subsequent work toward eliminating compulsive actions will cause anxious feelings for a while. It makes sense. Removing the compulsions takes away the very action that's used to manage the discomfort. This usually leaves a very important question: How does someone deal with all of these uncomfortable feelings that this process brings?

It depends on whom you ask. Many OCD experts view relaxation exercises and meditation as means to avoid anxiety. If the goal is to learn that the anxiety can't hurt you, then these relaxation techniques are viewed as counterproductive. On the other hand, some experts see the goal of OCD treatment as learning how to manage anxiety. So why not use these exercises to get to that point?

Frankly, I'm a fan of what works for each individual I treat. I do use some relaxation techniques, such as deep breathing and progressive muscle relaxation if the anxiety caused by ERP feels unmanageable. I do prefer to let my patient sit with their anxiety, as I believe those feelings will lessen as the compulsions aren't acted upon. If the anxiety doesn't subside, it may mean that we've selected an ERP exercise the person isn't ready for yet. If that's the case, we need to do a different exposure that doesn't provoke as much anxiety, then revisit the other exercise when the person is ready.

Conclusion

This was written to provide you with more clarity about various psychological and behavioral health disorders and how you can overcome them. Although it is recommended that you work with a Mental Health Professional as you move through your own journey, the strategies that are provided in this can help you whether or not you decide to work with a Psychiatrist or Therapist. The strategies are powerful and effective and many people who have used them properly have reported seeing significant changes in their lives very quickly.

I must caution you that as you begin to implement these strategies and become more masterful with them, it is likely that you will start to feel better very quickly. Some people express a desire to remove themselves from their psychotropic medication because they are no longer experiencing intense symptoms. Changing your medication regimen is a very important decision and it should be a process that you and your doctor work on together. You do not want to sabotage your success or your health by discontinuing your medication abruptly without consulting your Physician.

As this has explored, CBT is a very effective therapy for people who are struggling in many ways. It emerged as an alternative to the traditional talk therapies and has since been scientifically proven to be very effective in treating people who are emotionally struggling. The early pioneers of this therapy recognized the connection between thoughts, emotions, and behavior and that link is emphasized throughout this text. The fundamental premise of CBT, as is described in this, is that you can make significant changes in the way that you feel and behave by making some adjustments to how you think. Take a moment to thoroughly consider what Thinking Errors you tend to adhere to so that you can create healthier alternative thoughts.

The CBT homework assignments and practical strategies that are described in this are provided so that you can take the theoretical information in this and make practical use out of it. The more you practice the techniques, the more masterful you will ultimately become as you take control over the emotions and behaviors that have been plaguing you for days, weeks, months, or even years.

For those of you who tend to experience emotions stronger and identify yourself as emotionally vulnerable, particularly if you experience symptoms of Borderline Personality Disorder, I encourage you to really dig deep into the DBT section of this. Although I do encourage you to work with a Therapist, the techniques that are described are some of the very same techniques that are provided in the individual and group sessions of DBT during treatment. Having additional support to help you as you move forward is ideal however this can give you the boost that you need to make the first step toward effective treatment.

You've learned a lot in this book. If you also want to understand Narcissistic Abuse Syndrome and how to heal from a codependent relationship, then don't miss my second book *"Empath: How to Understand Narcissistic Abuse Syndrome and Heal from a Codependent Relationship with Your Parents or Ex-partner. No More Narcissists, Codependency, Emotional Abuse. It's Time to Be Happy"*

CPSIA information can be obtained
at www.ICGtesting.com
Printed in the USA
LVHW101530101120
671304LV00010B/317